FROMMER'S
COMPREHENSIVE TRAVEL GUIDE
PUERTO VALLARTA, MANZANILLO & GUADALAJARA '92-'93

by Marita Adair
Assisted by Reed Glenn
and Melanie Young

PRENTICE HALL TRAVEL

NEW YORK • LONDON • TORONTO • SYDNEY • TOKYO • SINGAPORE

FROMMER BOOKS
Published by Prentice Hall General Reference
A division of Simon & Schuster Inc.
15 Columbus Circle
New York, NY 10023

Copyright © 1992 by Simon & Schuster Inc.

All rights reserved including the right of reproduction in whole or in part in any form.

PRENTICE HALL and colophon are registered trademarks of Simon & Schuster Inc.

ISBN 0-13-334855-5
ISSN 1060-3727

Manufactured in the United States of America

FROMMER'S PUERTO VALLARTA, MANZANILLO & GUADALAJARA '92-'93

Editor-in-Chief: Marilyn Wood
Senior Editors: Judith de Rubini, Alice Fellows
Editors: Paige Hughes, Sara Hinsey Raveret, Lisa Renaud, Theodore Stavrou
Assistant Editors: Peter Katucki, Lisa Legarde
Managing Editor: Leanne Coupe

CONTENTS

1 GETTING TO KNOW MEXICO'S PACIFIC COAST   1

1. Geography, Ecology, History & Politics   4
2. Mexico's Famous People   11
3. Art, Architecture & Literature   16
4. Religion, Myth & Folklore   19
5. Cultural & Social Life   21
6. Performing Arts   21
7. Sports & Recreation   22
8. Food & Drink   23
9. Recommended Books, Films & Recordings   25

SPECIAL FEATURES
- What's Special About Mexico's Pacific Coast   2
- Dateline   5

2 PLANNING A TRIP TO THE REGION   29

1. Information, Entry Requirements & Money   29
2. When to Go—Climate, Holidays & Events   36
3. Health & Insurance   40
4. What to Pack   43
5. Tips for the Disabled, Seniors, Singles, Families & Students   44
6. Alternative/Adventure Travel   47
7. Shopping   48
8. Getting There & Departing   50
9. Getting Around   54

SPECIAL FEATURES
- What Things Cost in Puerto Vallarta   33
- What Things Cost in Manzanillo   33
- What Things Cost in Guadalajara   34
- Calendar of Events   37
- Fast Facts: Mexico   62

3 GETTING TO KNOW PUERTO VALLARTA   71

1. Orientation   71
2. Getting Around   76

SPECIAL FEATURES
- Did You Know . . . ?   72
- Fast Facts: Puerto Vallarta   77

4 WHERE TO STAY & DINE IN PUERTO VALLARTA 78

1. Where to Stay 78
2. Where to Dine 92

SPECIAL FEATURES
- *Frommer's Smart Traveler: Hotels 79*
- *Frommer's Smart Traveler: Restaurants 93*

5 WHAT TO SEE & DO IN PUERTO VALLARTA 101

1. Organized Tours 102
2. Sports & Recreation 102
3. Shopping 107
4. Evening Entertainment 108
5. Easy Excursions 111

SPECIAL FEATURES
- *Suggested Itineraries 101*
- *Frommer's Favorite Puerto Vallarta Experiences 106*

6 GETTING TO KNOW MANZANILLO 118

1. Orientation 118
2. Getting Around 123

SPECIAL FEATURES
- *Did You Know . . . ? 119*
- *Fast Facts: Manzanillo 123*

7 WHERE TO STAY & DINE IN MANZANILLO 124

1. Where to Stay 124
2. Where to Dine 130

8 WHAT TO SEE & DO IN MANZANILLO 137

1. Organized Tours 138
2. Sports & Recreation 139
3. Shopping 139
4. Evening Entertainment 140
5. Easy Excursions 140

SPECIAL FEATURES
- *Suggested Itineraries 137*
- *Frommer's Favorite Manzanillo Experiences 138*

9 GETTING TO KNOW GUADALAJARA 155

1. Orientation 155
2. Getting Around 160

SPECIAL FEATURES
- *Did You Know . . . ? 160*
- *Fast Facts: Guadalajara 162*

10 WHERE TO STAY & DINE IN GUADALAJARA 165

1. Where to Stay 165
2. Where to Dine 174

SPECIAL FEATURES
- *Frommer's Smart Traveler: Hotels 166*
- *Frommer's Smart Traveler: Restaurants 173*

11 WHAT TO SEE & DO IN GUADALAJARA 181

1. The Major Attractions 182
2. More Attractions 185
3. Organized Tours 188
4. Special Events 188
5. Sports & Recreation 190
6. Shopping 191
7. Evening Entertainment 192
8. Easy Excursions 195

SPECIAL FEATURES
- *Suggested Itineraries 181*
- *Walking Tour—Major Attractions 182*
- *Frommer's Favorite Guadalajara Experiences 187*

APPENDIX 224

A. Vocabulary 224
B. Menu Savvy 226
C. Conversion Tables 233

INDEX 235

General Information 235
Sights & Attractions 237
Accommodations 238
Restaurants 240

LIST OF MAPS

Mexico's Mid-Pacific Coast   3

PUERTO VALLARTA

Puerto Vallarta
   Orientation   74–75
Puerto Vallarta Area
   Accommodations &
   Dining   80–81
Downtown Puerto Vallarta Area
   Accommodations &
   Dining   95
Puerto Vallarta Attractions   105

MANZANILLO

Manzanillo Area
   Orientation   120–121
Manzanillo Area Accommodations
   & Dining   126–127
Downtown Manzanillo
   Accommodations &
   Dining   133
Barra de Navidad Bay
   Area   141

GUADALAJARA

Guadalajara & Environs   159
Greater Guadalajara
   Accommodations &
   Dining   171
Downtown Guadalajara
   Accommodations &
   Dining   175
Walking Tour—The Top
   Attractions   183
Greater Guadalajara
   Attractions   189
Lake Chapala   203
Chapala Village   205
Ajijic   211

INVITATION TO THE READERS

In researching this book, our author has come across many wonderful establishments, the best of which we have included here. We are sure that many of you will also come across appealing hotels, inns, restaurants, guest houses, shops, and attractions. Please don't keep them to yourself. Share your experiences, especially if you want to comment on places that have been included in this edition that have changed for the worse. You can address your letters to:

Marita Adair
Puerto Vallarta, Manzanillo, and Guadalajara '92–'93
Prentice Hall Travel
15 Columbus Circle
New York, NY 10023

A DISCLAIMER

Readers are advised that prices fluctuate in the course of time and travel information changes under the impact of the varied and volatile factors that affect the travel industry. Neither the author nor the publisher can be held responsible for the experiences of readers while traveling. Readers are invited to write to the publisher with ideas, comments, and suggestions for future editions.

A WORD ABOUT PRICES

In this book, I've listed only dollar prices, which are a more reliable guide than peso prices. In this age of inflation, prices may change by the time you reach Mexico. Mexico's inflation has been running nearly 20% to 30% a year.

Mexico has a Value Added Tax of 10% (*Impuesto de Valor Agregado,* or "IVA," pronounced "ee-bah") on almost everything, including hotel rooms, restaurant meals, bus tickets, and souvenirs. In 1985 the Mexican government passed a law requiring that this tax be included, or "hidden" in the price of goods and service, not added at the time of sale. Thus, prices quoted to you should be *IVA incluido,* "tax included." All prices given in this book already include the tax.

Important note: In Mexico, the dollar sign is used to denote pesos, and a Mexican sign reading $5,000 means 5,000 pesos, not 5,000 dollars. To eliminate confusion, the dollar sign in this book is used only to indicate U.S. dollars.

As of this writing, the rate of exchange in Mexico is about 3,000 pesos for U.S. $1. This will certainly change by the time you visit Mexico, but any commercial bank will be glad to provide you with the current rate.

CHAPTER 1

GETTING TO KNOW MEXICO'S PACIFIC COAST

- **WHAT'S SPECIAL ABOUT MEXICO'S PACIFIC COAST**
1. **GEOGRAPHY, ECOLOGY, HISTORY & POLITICS**
- **DATELINE**
2. **MEXICO'S FAMOUS PEOPLE**
3. **ART, ARCHITECTURE & LITERATURE**
4. **RELIGION, MYTH & FOLKLORE**
5. **CULTURAL & SOCIAL LIFE**
6. **PERFORMING ARTS**
7. **SPORTS & RECREATION**
8. **FOOD & DRINK**
9. **RECOMMENDED BOOKS, FILMS & RECORDINGS**

Everyone north of the Río Grande has at least some idea (usually an old-fashioned one) about what Mexico is like, but only those who go there can know the real Mexico, for the country is undergoing fast-paced and far-reaching change, as are most countries touched by modern technology. Being so close to the United States and Canada, Mexico is so forcefully affected by what goes on in its neighboring countries to the north that the Old Mexico of cowboy songs and movies has long ago been replaced by a land full of familiar signs of 20th-century life. But this does not mean that a trip to Mexico will reveal people, sights, and sounds just like home, for Mexico is very much its own country, the result of a particular blending of the land itself and of ancient Indian, colonial, European, and modern industrial influences. These elements are the basis of a unique culture and tradition.

This book encompasses a triangle of cities—two resorts, Puerto Vallarta and Manzanillo, and inland through the mountains, sophisticated Guadalajara. These cities are found in two neighboring states, Jalisco (Hah-*leez*-coh), Mexico's sixth-largest state, and Colima (Coh-*lee*-mah), the second-largest state, both on Mexico's Pacific Coast. San Blas, suggested as a side trip from Puerto Vallarta, is in the state of Nayarit.

Puerto Vallarta, Jalisco, a leading Pacific Coast resort city, has a picturesque cobblestoned town center flanked by high- and low-rise resort hotels leading in and out of town. Manzanillo, Colima, 175 miles south of Puerto Vallarta, is built around a major port and a string of beaches and bays. Between them lie some of the Pacific Coast's most beautiful mountains and undeveloped coastal landscape, with beautiful beaches at Tenacatita, Careyes, and Tecuan, as well as isolated beaches all along the coast. Thick mountain vegetation and plantations of banana, mango, lime, and

WHAT'S SPECIAL ABOUT MEXICO'S PACIFIC COAST

Birding
- San Blas's famous mangrove trips and its 300 bird species.
- Colima's rich bird life, especially around Laguna Cuyutlán, Manzanillo's lagoon, and near the volcanoes east of Colima City.

Beaches
- Some of the country's best beaches, stretching from San Blas to Manzanillo, many of them unspoiled.

Fishing
- The abundance of marlin and sailfish.

Food & Drink
- Ceviche, birria, red pozole of Jalisco, and Colima's white version, Jalisco-style menudo, caldo michi, and tortas ahogadas from the Lake Chapala region, and frijoles boda (married beans), a Colima specialty. The town of Tequila, the heart of the tequila-producing region near Guadalajara.

Museums
- Colima's Museum of Western Cultures, with its pre-Hispanic artifacts including clay dancing dogs.
- Colima's Museum of Popular Culture Pomar, showing regional clothing from throughout Mexico.

Nightlife
- Puerto Vallarta's diverse nightlife.

Shopping
- Guadalajara, for huaraches and silver; Tonalá and Tlaquepaque, for fine decorative objects, equipale furniture, blown glass and pottery; Colima, for pre-Hispanic reproductions; and Puerto Vallarta, for contemporary art.

Weird Phenomena
- A magnetic field near Comala that causes vehicles to move without motors turned on.

---

coconut hide remote vacation spots. This stretch of coast is slated for development before the end of this decade, so get there soon to see it in all its natural grandeur.

Inland 260 miles east of Puerto Vallarta and 167 miles northeast of Manzanillo is Guadalajara, Jalisco, capital of the state, and Mexico's second-largest city. The delightful metropolis provides an alternate to resort vacationing with its colonial-era center, museums, and nearby artisan villages of Tlaquepaque and Tonalá. And 34 miles south of Guadalajara is Lake Chapala, with its springlike climate and lakeside and mountain resort villages, all showing another completely different and very relaxed face of Jalisco. Surrounding Jalisco and Colima are other culturally interesting states, Nayarit, Zacatecas, Aguascalientes, Guanajauto, and Michoacán, all with influences on Jalisco and Colima where their borders touch.

Thirty years ago reaching Puerto Vallarta meant a 2-day bus trip from Guadalajara, a journey over an unpaved mountain road from Manzanillo, or a flight to Puerto Vallarta's new airport from Tepic or Guadalajara—all cities more developed and well known than Puerto Vallarta. What a difference three decades makes! Within the last 5 years Puerto Vallarta has doubled the number of luxury hotel rooms, making it rival

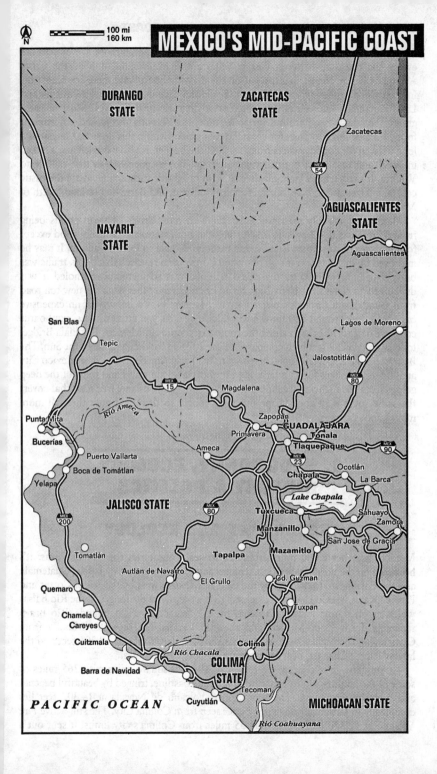

Acapulco for accommodations; there are plans to expand even more. Developers are eyeing the coastline between Puerto Vallarta and Manzanillo (dubbed the Costa Alegre, or happy coast); an airport is on the drawing board, and there are blueprints for expansion at the resorts of Tenacatita—Hotel Tecuan, Hotel Costa Careyes, and Las Alamandas—as well as a new resort at Chamela near Careyes. Most of these grand plans have been around for some time, but recently the Jalisco government formed a task force to push for coastal development within this decade. Manzanillo, long a haven for condo owners from north of the border, is also experiencing a boom in hotel and restaurant construction, although not as energetic as that of Puerto Vallarta. It's still a more tranquil alternative to beachside vacationing, as are the rustic coastal villages of San Blas, north of Puerto Vallarta, and Barra de Navidad, north of Manzanillo.

Distances are easily manageable by car with most drives between points being from 45 minutes to 6 hours. Roads throughout both states are generally good except for Highway 15 west from Guadalajara through Tequila to Puerto Vallarta. It may be improved by the time you travel, but when I drove it to research this book, traffic was bumper-to-bumper because the paved roadbed was so incredibly-potholed it was difficult to go faster than 10 to 20 miles an hour. On the other hand the new toll road from Guadalajara through Colima City to Manzanillo is a dream—if an expensive one. Tolls cost around $20 for the whole distance. As you cross bridges, signboards compare heights of bridges along the route to pyramids in Mexico. The Piala Bridge, for example, is 292 feet high compared to the 207 feet for the Pyramid of the Sun. The Beltrán bridge is 459 feet high compared to the Latin American Tower in Mexico City at 590 feet. It makes for an interesting bit of trivia as you travel and some of the deep gorges from the highway are incredibly beautiful. The two-lane, free road that covers the same route is in good shape but takes longer to drive and goes through more mountainous curves.

1. GEOGRAPHY, ECOLOGY, HISTORY & POLITICS

GEOGRAPHY AND ECOLOGY

Mexico stretches 2,000 miles from sea to sea. Four times the size of Texas, it's bordered on the north by the United States and to the southeast by Belize, Guatemala and the Caribbean, to the east by the Gulf of Mexico, west by the Sea of Cortez and Pacific Ocean. Mexico lacks an extensive river system, but the longest is the Río Balsas which empties near Lázaro Cárdenas on the Pacific. The Río Grande/Río Bravo separates Texas from Mexico and the Río Usumacinta separates Mexico from Guatemala. The highest volcanic peak is the Pico de Orizaba at 18,201 feet and the largest lake is Chapala, near Guadalajara, at 666 square miles.

Colima and Jalisco occupy a region of 103,229 square miles with 265 miles of some of the country's most beautiful mountain coastline, fringed by beautiful beaches and rocky outcroppings. The snowcapped Volcano de Nevada at 14,302 feet lies completely in Jalisco although it is better seen from Colima City. The still-active Fire Volcano at 12,870 feet looms only 35 miles from Colima's city limits. It sent out a stream of lava as late as 1991 after years of nothing but willowy plumes of smoke. In Jalisco the mountains reach to the sea, but for the most part, the mountainous part of Colima is set back a bit from the coast.

Among the wildlife of the untouched coastline of both Colima and Jalisco are jaguars, alligators, and ocelots. Of 70 species of mammals, the most numerous are bats, including the vampire bat. Hundreds of bird species have been counted between Cuixmala and Teopa, near Careyes.

At least four of Mexico's nine species of marine turtles nest on the beaches of Colima and Jalisco. Just before nesting time, fishermen report seeing the turtles mating offshore. Most turtles will return to the same beach to lay eggs year after year, and as often as three times in a season. They only nest on dark beaches; lights of any kind repel them. It takes an hour or more for the turtle to dig the nest in the sand with her back flippers. Of the more than 100 eggs in each nest (*nido*) only 5% of those that hatch will live to return. Programs to save the turtles involve taking the eggs from the original nest to a fenced-off, protected area (maya) and placing them in a nest of identical depth and size. The hatchlings, which appear about 45 days later, wait until all their nestmates are ready before they scurry by the hundreds to the ocean. Crabs, birds, and other ocean denizens as well as humans endanger the turtles' precarious existence. A recent Mexican law carrying serious penalties for destroying turtles or their eggs has had some effect; the belief persists, however, that turtle eggs are an aphrodisiac, and turtles are still killed for their shells and meat. The Biological Station at Chamela, near Careyes, has ongoing studies of the region and produces numerous publications describing their work.

HISTORY OF MEXICO

The earliest "Mexicans" were Stone Age men and women, descendants of the race that had crossed the Bering Strait and reached North America before 10,000 B.C. These were Homo sapiens who hunted mastodons and bison, and gathered other food as they could. Later (Archaic period, 5200–1500 B.C.), signs of agriculture and domestication appeared: Baskets were woven; corn, beans, squash, and tomatoes were grown; turkeys and dogs were kept for food. By 2400 B.C. the art of pot making had been discovered (use of pottery was a significant advance). "Artists" made clay figurines for use as votive offerings or household gods. Actually, "goddesses" is a better term, for all of the figurines found so far have been female, and supposedly symbolize Mother Earth or fertility.

THE PRECLASSIC PERIOD

It was in the Preclassic period (1500 B.C.–A.D. 300) that the area known by archeologists as Mesoamerica (from the northern Mexico Valley to Costa Rica) began to show signs of a farming culture. Farming was either by the "slash-and-burn" method—cutting grass and trees, then setting fire to the area to clear it for planting—or by construction of

DATELINE

- **1500–300 B.C.** Preclassic period: Olmec culture spreads over Gulf Coast, southern Mexico, Central America, and lower Mexican Pacific coast. La Venta Olmec cultural zenith in 600.
- **500 B.C.** Zapotecs lay out great mountaintop plaza of Monte Alban.
- **100 B.C.** Olmec culture disintegrates.
- **A.D. 100** Building begins on Sun and Moon pyramids at Teoti-

(continues)

DATELINE

huacán which eventually becomes largest city in the world. Palenque dynasty emerges in Yucatán.

- **300–900** Classic period: Xochicalco established in 300. Maya civilization develops in Yucatán and Chiapas.
- **650–800** El Tajín reaches cultural zenith on coast of Veracruz.
- **650** Teotihuacán burns and is deserted by A.D. 700.
- **750** Zapotecs conquer Valley of Oaxaca. Casas Grandes culture begins on northern desert.
- **800** Bonampak battle/victory mural painted.
- **900–1154** Chichimecas descend on the territories of today's Jalisco and Colima.
- **900–1500** Postclassic period: Toltec culture emerges at Tula and spreads to Chichén Itzá by 978.
- **1156 or 1168** After a fire, the Toltecs abandon Tula.
- **1230** El Tajín abandoned by this year.

(continues)

terraces and irrigation ducts, this latter method being the one used principally in the highlands around what is now Mexico City, where the first large towns developed. At some time during this period, religion became an institution as certain men took the role of shaman, or guardian of magical and religious secrets. They were the predecessors of the folk healers and native priests still found in modern Mexico.

The most highly developed culture of this Preclassic period was that of the Olmecs, flourishing from 1500 to 100 B.C. They lived in what are today the states of Veracruz and Tabasco, where they used river rafts to transport the colossal multiton blocks of basalt, used to carve roundish heads. These sculptures still present problems to archeologists: What do they signify? The heads seem infantile in their roundness, but all have the peculiar "jaguar mouth" with a high-arched upper lip, the identifying mark of the Olmecs. The Olmecs were the first in Mexico to use a calendar and to develop writing, both of which were later perfected by the Maya.

The link between the Olmecs and the Maya has not been clearly established, but Izapa (400 B.C.–A.D. 400), a ceremonial site in the Chiapan cacao-growing region near the Pacific coast, appears to be one of several transitional sites between the two cultures. When it was discovered, the monuments and stelae were in place, not having undergone destruction as have so many sites.

THE CLASSIC PERIOD

Most artistic and cultural achievement came during the Classic period (A.D. 300–900), when life centered in cities. Class distinctions arose as the military and religious aristocracy took control; a class of merchants and artisans grew, with the independent farmer falling under a landlord's control. The cultural centers of the Classic period were Yucatán and Guatemala (also home of the Maya), the Mexican Highlands at Teotihuacán, the Zapotec cities of Monte Alban and Mitla (near Oaxaca), and the cities of El Tajín and Zempoala on the Gulf coast.

THE POSTCLASSIC PERIOD

In the Postclassic period (A.D. 900–1500), warlike cultures developed impressive societies of their own, although they never surpassed the Classic peoples. All paintings and hieroglyphs of this period show war, migration, and disruption. Somehow the glue of society became unstuck; people wandered from their homes, and the religious hierarchy lost influence. During these years Colima and Jalisco were inhabited by Otomis, Toltecs, and Tarascans and later by nomadic Chichimecas, who left abundant pottery and underground tombs, but few buildings. Finally, in the 1300s, the warlike Aztecs settled in the Mexico Valley on Lake Texcoco (site of Mexico City), with the island city of Tenochtitlán as their capital. Legend has it that as the wandering Aztecs were passing the lake they saw a sign predicted by their prophets: an eagle perched on a cactus plant with a snake in its mouth. They built their city there and it eventually became a huge (pop. 300,000) and impressive capital. The Aztec empire more or less loosely united territories of great size. The high lords of the capital became fabulously rich in gold, stores of food, cotton, and perfumes; skilled artisans were prosperous; events of state were elaborately ceremonial. Victorious Aztecs returning from battle sacrificed thousands of captives on the altars atop the pyramids, cutting their chests open with stone knives and ripping out their still living hearts to offer to the gods.

QUETZALCOATL

The legend of Quetzalcoatl, a holy man who appeared during the time of troubles at the end of the Classic period, is one of the most important tales in Mexican history and folklore, and contributed to the overthrow of the Aztec empire by the Spaniards. Quetzalcoatl means "feathered serpent." Learned beyond his years, he became the high priest and leader of the Toltecs at Tula, and put an end to human sacrifice. His influence completely changed the Toltecs from a group of warriors to peaceful and productive farmers, artisans, and craftspeople. But his success upset the old priests who wanted human sacrifice, and they called upon their ancient god of darkness, Texcatlipoca, to degrade Quetzalcoatl in the eyes of the people. One night the priests conspired to dress Quetzalcoatl in ridiculous garb, get him drunk, and tempt him to break his vow of chastity. The next morning shame of this night of debauchery drove him out of his own land and into the wilderness, where he lived for 20 years. He emerged in Coatzacoalcos, in the Isthmus of Tehuantepec, bade his few followers farewell, and sailed away, having promised to return in a future age. But artistic influences noted at Chichén Itzá in the Yucatán suggest that in fact he landed there and began his "ministry" again with much success among the Maya, who called him Kukulkán. He died there, but the legend of his return in a future age remained.

DATELINE

- **1290** Zapotecs decline and Mixtecs emerge at Monte Alban and Mitla becomes refuge of Zapotecs by this year.
- **1325–45** Aztec capital Tenochtitlán founded. Aztecs dominate Mexico until 1521 when they are defeated by Spaniards.
- **1519–21** Conquest of Mexico: Cortés and troops arrive near present-day Veracruz and conquest of Mexico is complete when Cortés defeats Aztecs at Tlaltelolco near Tenochtitlán in 1521.
- **1521–24** Hernán Cortés organizes Spanish empire in Mexico and begins building Mexico City on top of ruins of Tenochtitlán.
- **1523** City of Colima founded.
- **1524** First Franciscan friars arrive from Spain.
- **1531** Tepic founded. Nuño de Guzmán begins the conquest of western Mexico, terrorizing and killing inhabitants of Jalisco.

(continues)

DATELINE

Colima, Michoacán, and Nayarit.
- **1524–35** Cortés removed from leadership. Spanish king sends officials, judges, and finally an audiencia to govern.
- **1535** Cortés visits Manzanillo for the first time.
- **1535–1821** Viceregal Period: Mexico governed by viceroys appointed by king of Spain; landed aristocracy emerges.
- **1537** Mexico's first printing press is installed in Mexico City.
- **1538** Nuño de Guzmán imprisoned for his reign of destruction across western Mexico.
- **1542** Guadalajara founded for the final time.
- **1562** Friar Diego de Landa destroys 5,000 Mayan religious stone figures and burns 27 hieroglyphic-painted manuscripts at Maní, Yucatán.
- **1571** The Inquisition is established in Mexico.

(continues)

SPANISH CONQUISTADORES

When Hernán Cortés and his men landed in 1519 the Aztec empire was ruled by Moctezuma (often misspelled Montezuma) in great splendor. The emperor was uncertain of his course; if the strangers were Quetzalcoatl and his followers returning at last, no resistance must be offered; on the other hand, if they were not, they might be a threat to his empire. Moctezuma tried to bribe them with gold to go away, but this only whetted their appetites. Despite the fact that Moctezuma and his ministers received the conquistadores with full pomp and glory when they reached Mexico City, Cortés eventually took Moctezuma captive.

Though the Spaniards were no match for the hundreds of thousands of Aztecs, they skillfully kept things under their control until a revolt threatened Cortés's entire enterprise. He retreated to the countryside, made alliances with non-Aztec tribes, and finally marched on the empire when it was governed by the last Aztec emperor, Cuauhtémoc. Though Cuauhtémoc defended his people valiantly for almost 3 months, he was finally captured, tortured, and ultimately executed.

The Spanish conquest had started out as an adventure, unauthorized by the Spanish Crown or its governor in Cuba. Soon Christianity was being spread through "New Spain." Guatemala and Honduras were explored and conquered, and by 1540 the territory of New Spain included Spanish possessions from Vancouver to Panama. During that time the cruel Spaniard Nuño de Guzmán was president of the governing audiencia. Before he could be deposed, he led an army of conquest to western Mexico, killing, terrorizing, and exploiting native inhabitants of the present states of Michoacán, Jalisco, Colima, and Nayarit. In the two centuries that followed, Franciscan and Augustinian friars converted great numbers of Indians to Christianity, and the Spanish lords built up huge feudal estates on which the native farmers were little more than serfs. The silver and gold that Cortés had sought made Spain the richest country in Europe.

INDEPENDENCE

Mexico finally gained its independence from Spain in 1821 after a decade of upheaval. The independence movement began in 1810 when a priest, Father Miguel Hidalgo, gave the cry for independence from his pulpit in the town of Dolores, Guanajuato. The revolt soon became a revolution, and Hidalgo, Ignacio Allende, and another priest, José María Morelos, gathered an "army" of citizens and threatened Mexico City. Ultimately Hidalgo was executed, but he is honored as "the Father of Mexican Independence." Morelos kept the revolt alive until 1815, when he was executed.

When independence finally came, Agustín de Iturbide was ready to take over. Iturbide founded a short-lived "empire" with himself as emperor in 1822. The next year it fell and was followed by the proclamation of a republic with Gen. Guadalupe Victoria as first president. A succession of presidents and military dictators followed Guadalupe Victoria until one of the most bizarre and extraordinary episodes in modern times: the French intervention. In the 1860s, Mexican factions offered the Habsburg Archduke Maximilian the crown of Mexico, and with the support of the ambitious French emperor, Napoléon III, the young Austrian actually came to Mexico and "ruled" for 3 years (1864–67), while the country was in a state of civil war. This European interference in New World affairs was unwelcomed by the United States, and the French emperor finally withdrew his troops, leaving misguided Maximilian to be captured and executed by firing squad in Querétaro. His adversary and successor was Benito Juárez, a Zapotec lawyer and one of the most heroic figures in Mexican history. After victory over Maximilian, Juárez did his best to unify and strengthen his country before dying of a heart attack in 1872. His effect on Mexico's future was profound, however, and his plans and visions bore fruit for decades. From 1877 to 1911, a period now called the Porfiriato, the prime role in Mexico was played by Porfirio Díaz, a Juárez general. Recognized as a modernizer, he was a terror to his enemies and to challengers of his absolute power. He was forced to abdicate in 1911 by Francisco Madero and public opinion.

After the fall of the Porfirist dictatorship several factions split the country, including those led by "Pancho Villa" (whose real name was Doroteo Arango), Alvaro Obregón, Venustiano Carranza, Francisco Madero, Lázaro Cárdenas, and Emiliano Zapata. The decade that followed is referred to as the Mexican Revolution. Drastic reforms occurred in this period, and the surge of vitality and progress from this exciting if turbulent time has inspired Mexicans to the present. Succeeding presidents have invoked the spirit of the revolution, which is still studied and discussed.

THE 20TH CENTURY

After the turmoil of the revolution, Mexico sought stability in the form of the Partido Revolucionario Institucional (el PRI), the country's dominant political party. With the aim

DATELINE

- **1703** Population of Guadalajara is 6,000.
- **1742–48** Construction on the Seminario Conciliar de San José is finished; today it's the Regional Museum of Guadalajara.
- **1767** Jesuits expelled from New Spain.
- **1794** Guadalajara's first printing press starts operation.
- **1803** Guadalajara's population is almost 40,000.
- **1804** In Guadalajara, construction begins on Hospicio Cabañas designed by Manuel Tolsá.
- **1810** Independence War begins. Father Miguel Hidalgo starts movement for Mexico's independence from Spain and leads a large group of insurgents to Guadalajara.
- **1818** Earthquake destroys the towers of Guadalajara's cathedral.
- **1821** Independence from Spain achieved.
- **1822** First Empire: Agustín de

(continues)

DATELINE

Iturbide, independence leader, orchestrates his ascendancy to throne as emperor of Mexico. Guadalajara's population 70,000.

- **1823** Jalisco becomes a free state.
- **1833** Cholera epidemic kills thousands in Guadlajara.
- **1838** After 34 years of construction the Hospicio Cabañas is finally finished in Guadalajara.
- **1824** Iturbide is expelled, returns, and is executed by firing squad.
- **1824** Priciliano Sanchez is elected first governor of Jalisco. Federal Republic period begins: Guadalupe Victoria is elected first president of Mexico.
- **1828** Slavery abolished.
- **1835** Texas declares independence from Mexico.
- **1836** Santa Anna defeats Texans at Battle of the Alamo, at San Antonio. Texas, but is

(continues)

of "institutionalizing the revolution," el PRI (ell-pree) literally engulfed Mexican society, leaving little room for vigorous, independent opposition. For over half a century the monolithic party has had control of the government, labor unions, trade organizations, and other centers of power in Mexican society.

The most outstanding Mexican president of the century was Gen. Lázaro Cárdenas (1934–40). An effective leader, Cárdenas broke up vast tracts of agricultural land and distributed parcels to small cooperative farms called *ejidos*, reorganized the labor unions along democratic lines, and provided funding for village schools. His most famous action was the expropriation of Mexico's oil industry from U.S. and European interests, which became Petroleros Mexicanos (Pemex), the government petroleum monopoly.

The PRI has selected Mexico's president (and, in fact, virtually everyone else on the government payroll) from its own ranks since Cárdenas, the national election being only a confirmation of the choice. Among these men have been Avila Camacho, who continued many of Cárdenas's policies; Miguel Alemán, who expanded national industrial and infrastructural development; Adolfo López Mateos, who expanded the highway system and increased hydroelectric power sources; and Gustavo Díaz Ordaz, who provided credit and technical help to the agricultural sector.

In 1970 Luis Echeverría came to power, followed in 1976 by José López Portillo. During their presidencies there emerged a studied coolness in relations with the United States and an activist role in international affairs. This period also saw an increase in charges of large-scale corruption in the upper echelons of Mexican society. The corruption, though endemic to the system, was encouraged by the river of money from the rise in oil prices. When oil income skyrocketed, Mexican borrowing and spending did likewise. The reduction of oil prices in the 1980s left Mexico with an enormous foreign bank debt and serious infrastructure deficiencies.

MEXICO TODAY

Without king oil, Mexico must rebuild agriculture and industry, cut expenditures, tame corruption, and keep creditors at bay. President Miguel de la Madrid Hurtado, who assumed the presidency in 1982, struggled with these problems, and made important progress. The present president, Carlos Salinas de Gortari, has managed to slow inflation from 200% annually to between 20% and 30%. But the economy, and society, are still under tremendous economic pressure, and charges of government corruption still abound although less so than in the past.

Mexico's current economic difficulties have led to a newly vigorous and open political life with opposition parties gaining strength. The traditionally victorious PRI party won the hotly contested presidential election in 1988, but its candidate, Carlos Salinas de Gortari, only managed to claim a historically low 50.36% of the vote amid claims of fraud by his chief rival, Cuauhtémoc Cárdenas of the newly formed National Democratic Front (FDN). Ironically, Cárdenas is the son of Mexico's beloved president who founded the PRI. However, opposition parties managed to win a few Senate seats for the first time since the PRI came to power, and recent local elections produced strong opposition candidates. Whether Sr. Salinas de Gortari's promised reforms for greater democracy will be lasting is debatable, but Mexico remains the most stable country in Latin America.

MEXICAN FACTS & FIGURES

The Republic of Mexico is headed today by an elected president and has a bicameral legislature. It is divided into 31 states, plus the Federal District (Mexico City). Economically, Mexico is not by any means a poor country. Only about a sixth of the economy is in agriculture. Mining is still fairly important. Mining for iron ore around Manzanillo is one of the city's major forms of income. Gold and silver and many other important minerals are still mined in the rest of Mexico, but the big industry today is oil. Mexico is also well industrialized, manufacturing textiles, food products, and everything from tape cassettes to automobiles.

In short, Mexico is well into the 20th century, with all the benefits and problems of contemporary life, and although vast sums are spent on education and public welfare, a high birthrate, high unemployment, and unequal distribution of wealth show that much remains to be done.

2. MEXICO'S FAMOUS PEOPLE

Raul Anguiano Valdez (1915–   ) Born in Guadalajara, at 21 Anguiano had his first exhibition at the Palacio de Bellas Artes in Mexico City. One of his most famous paintings, *The Thorn*, depicts a young Indian removing a thorn from her foot with a knife. It hangs in the National Museum of Art in Mexico City. His teaching

DATELINE

later defeated and captured at the Battle of San Jacinto outside Houston, Texas.
- **1838** France invades Mexico at Veracruz.
- **1845** U.S. annexes Texas.
- **1846–48** War with U.S.; for a payment of $15 million Mexico relinquishes half of its national territory to the U.S. in treaty of Guadalupe Hidalgo.
- **1855** Santos Degollado is named governor of Guadalajara. Reform years begin. Country wages 3-year war on itself, pitting cities against villages and rich against poor. Benito Juárez becomes president, in fact and in exile.
- **1862** England, Spain, and France send troops to demand debt payment and all except France withdraw.
- **1864–67** Second Empire: French Emperor Napoléon III sends the Hapsburg Ferdinand Maximilian Joseph, 32, and his wife, Marie Char-

(continues)

12 • GETTING TO KNOW MEXICO'S PACIFIC COAST

DATELINE

lotte Amélie Léopoldine, 24, to be emperor and empress of Mexico.
- **1866** Guadalajara is seized by troops loyal to Juárez.
- **1867** Juárez orders execution of Maximilian at Querétaro and resumes presidency in Mexico City until his death in 1872.
- **1872–84** Post-Reform period: Only four presidents hold office but country is nearly bankrupt.
- **1876–1911** Porfiriato: With one 4-year exception, Porfirio Díaz is president/dictator of Mexico for 35 years, leading country in tremendous modernization at the expense of human rights.
- **1880** Mule-drawn trolleys serve as public transportation in Guadalajara.
- **1884** Electric lights go on in Guadalajara for the first time.
- **1887** Gen. Ramón Corona is elected governor of Jalisco in 1887.

(continues)

career took him to the Escuela Nacional de Pintura y Escultura in Mexico City in 1935 when he was only 20, where he remained until 1967. Simultaneously he became a professor at the Universidad Nacional Autónoma de Mexico in Mexico City in 1959, and guest professor at Trinity University in San Antonio, Texas, in 1966. One-man shows organized for him took him to Guadalajara, the Carnegie Cultural Arts Center in Oxnard, California, and the San Diego Museum of Man.

Luis Barragán (1902–89) One of Mexico's most influential architects, he was from a wealthy Guadalajara family but spent his youth in the forested mountains of Jalisco, near Mazamitla. Though a skilled landscape architect he was known primarily as an architect/designer of homes and for his use of bold Mexican colors and incorporation of hacienda styles into modern buildings. Unschooled in either architecture or landscape gardening he nevertheless succeeded in becoming prominent in both and his techniques and designs influence Mexican architecture today. He won the coveted Pritzker Award for architecture in 1980.

Hernán Cortés (1485–1547) Brash, bold, greedy, and a brilliant military leader, 34-year-old Hernán Cortés conquered Mexico in the name of Spain without the knowledge of that country's king. He sank his ships to prevent desertion and with only 550 men and 16 horses, he conquered a nation of 30,000 and a territory larger than his native country. He became governor and captain general of New Spain immediately after the conquest and later he was given title of Marqués of the Valley of Oaxaca and substantial landholdings. He began silver mining in Taxco and introduced sugarcane cultivation around Cuernavaca. But by 1528 he was removed from governorship and the king sent other Spaniards to take charge. Cortés died in Spain while seeking proper recognition and a more significant title from the Spanish court, which shunned him. Mexicans regard him as the destroyer of a nation and no monuments honor him. He is buried in a vault in the Church of the Hospital of Jésus Nazareño, Mexico City.

Porfirio Díaz (1830–1915) Born in Oaxaca and schooled in law, at age 32 he distinguished himself at the famous Puebla battle and within 14 years became president of Mexico. He remained as dictator for the next 34 years, with one 4-year interruption. His contributions were enormous: He moved the country from turmoil and bankruptcy into peace and stability through improvements in communication, railroads, agriculture, manufacturing, mining, port enlargement, oil exploration, and foreign investment. He built lavish public buildings, and sent promising art students to Europe on full scholarship. His love for all things French was legendary. He achieved these successes by disregarding the law and at the expense of the poor, Indians, and intellectuals who opposed his methods, all of which brought about his downfall in 1911 and the Mexican Revolution which lasted until 1917. He died in exile in Paris and is buried in the Père Lachaise Cemetery there.

Miguel Hidalgo y Costilla (1753–1811) In 1792, the man later to be known as the Father of Mexican Independence, was the parish priest in Colima. By 1810, however, he was a small-town priest in the town of Dolores, Guanajuato. At the time he was better known for his anticelibacy beliefs, and disbelief in papal supremacy. As priest he taught parishioners to grow mulberry trees for silkworms (for making silk) and grapes (for winemaking, prohibited by the crown), and to make ceramics; the latter two still thrive in the region. He was among several in his area who secretly conspired to free Mexico from Spanish domination. On the morning of September 16, 1810, a messenger from Josefa Ortiz de Dominguez brought Hidalgo word that the conspiracy was uncovered. He quickly decided to publicly call for independence (known today as the *grito* or "cry") from his parish church after which he galloped from village to village spreading the news, and gathering troops. His small home, today a museum, is on Morelos Street, corner of Hidalgo in Dolores Hidalgo, Guanajuato, and he is buried in the Independence Monument, Mexico City.

Agustín de Iturbide (1783–1824) In an elaborate ceremony that took months to plan, he was crowned emperor of Mexico and created an elaborate imperial monarchy with titles and right of succession by his children. But he reigned only briefly from 1822 to 1824, when General Santa Anna led a successful rebellion to dethrone him. He returned surreptitiously from exile but was captured and shot by a firing squad in Padilla, Tamaulipas. For years regarded as a usurper and self-interested politican, in a rare move public sentiment recognized his role in gaining Mexico's independence from Spain and his remains were interred more fittingly in the Mexico City Cathedral.

María Izquierdo (1906–55) Born in San Juan de los Lagos, Jalisco, Izquierdo's career was a brief but important one. Contemporary with Frida Kahlo (Diego Rivera's wife), her work, like Kahlo's, had a skilled but primitive edge to it. Her first art lessons began at age 6 and by 21 she spent a year in school at the Academia de San Carlos in Mexico City. The following year her first one-woman show appeared at the Galería de Arte Moderno and she began work with Rufino Tamayo, another of

DATELINE

- **1888** The Mexico City–to–Guadalajara railroad is inaugurated.
- **1907** Electric trolleys are installed in Guadalajara.
- **1909** Francisco Madero's political tour of Mexico includes Manzanillo and Guadalajara as he becomes a more visible anti-Díaz leader. The Guadalajara-to-Manzanillo railroad is inaugurated.
- **1911–17** Mexican Revolution: Díaz resigns and many factions jockey for power. Period of great violence, national upheaval, and tremendous loss of life. Starvation reaches epidemic proportions, dramatically affecting Guadalajara.
- **1913** President Madero assassinated.
- **1914–1916** Two U.S. invasions of Mexico.
- **1917–40** Reconstruction: Mexican constitution signed. Reforms initiated, labor unions

(continues)

DATELINE

strengthened, and Mexico expels U.S. oil companies and nationalizes all natural resources and railroads. Presidents Obregón and Carranza assassinated as are Pancho Villa and Emiliano Zapata.

- **1926–29** The Cristero Rebellion in response to President Calles's action limiting the Catholic church; violence between church and government is particularly strong in Jalisco, Colima, and Michoacán.
- **1940–present** Mexico enters period of political stability and economic progress though with continued problems of corruption, inflation, national health, and unresolved land and agricultural issues.
- **1955** Women given full voting rights.
- **1982** Nationalization of banks.
- **1988** Mexico enters the General Agreement on Trade and Tariffs (GATT).

(continues)

Mexico's renowned artists. In 1930 a one-woman show was mounted for her at the New York Art Center and in 1933 in Paris at the Galerie René Highe. Her subjects were those of everyday Mexican life. Intellectuals from around the world honored her talent and beauty with poetry and praise during her lifetime. Much of her work is in private collections, but good examples are at the Museum of Modern Art in Mexico City.

Benito Juárez (1806–72) A full-blooded Zapotec, he was orphaned at the age of 3. He became governor of Oaxaca in 1847 after which he was exiled to New Orleans by grudge-holding President Santa Anna because Juárez refused to grant him asylum in Oaxaca years before. On becoming president of Mexico first in 1858, his terms were interrupted once during the Reform Wars and again during the French intervention. Juárez cast the deciding vote favoring the execution of Maximilian. He died from a heart attack before completing his fourth term. Devoid of personal excesses, Juárez had a clear vision for Mexico, that included honest leadership, separation of church and state, imposition of civilian rule, reduction of the military, and education reform. He is buried in the San Fernando Cemetery, Mexico City.

Miguel de la Madrid Hurtado (1934–   ) President of Mexico from 1982 to 1988, he was born in Colima. He received a degree in law in 1957 from the Universidad Nacional Autónima de Mexico, and in 1965 a master's degree in public administration from Harvard University. He was an able administrator and good president, who unfortunately inherited scandalous excesses of two presidents immediately before him, a bankrupt country with 200% inflation, and a mess from his immediate predecessor, José López Portillo, who, among other ill-advised acts, nationalized the banks overnight just before turning over the government to de la Madrid. Among de la Madrid's credits he began returning to the private sector many government holdings, steered Mexico toward world competition through membership in GATT (General Agreement on Trade and Tariffs), and managed to continue Mexico's payment on its enormous debt at great sacrifice by the Mexican people and economy. His presidency set the stage for the present one in which Mexico heads even faster into world trade, lower inflation, and greater stability.

Alfonso Michel (1897–1957) Born in Colima, capital of Colima state, Michel's career took him all over the world in search of study, but it wasn't until 1942 that he began to be noticed. Using his mastery of impressionism, he directed his themes to Mexican subjects and shared a studio with Roberto Montenegro from 1935 to 1940.

MEXICO'S FAMOUS PEOPLE • 15

Roberto Montenegro (1887–1968) Another of Mexico's child prodigies, Montenegro, born in Guadalajara, began studying painting in 1903. The following year he went to Mexico City to study at the Escuela Nacional de Arte where he began acquaintances with some of Mexico's famous artists, Diego Rivera among them. On scholarship and working, he traveled, studied, and exhibited in Europe for almost 15 years, becoming one of Mexico's most skilled artists. When he returned to Mexico, he began an intense discovery of Mexican folk art and his paintings, besides featuring peasant folk, usually include folk art from everyday life. In 1934 he was appointed director of the Museo de Artes Populares de Bellas Artes, and for 5 years shared a studio in Guadalajara with fellow painter, Alfonso Michel.

DATELINE
• **1991** Mexico, Canada, and the United States begin free-trade agreement negotiations.

Gerardo Murillo [Dr. Atl] (1875–1964) Possessing enormous energy as well as political and artistic passion, Gerardo Murillo (who, for a political statement, changed his name to Dr. Atl, a Náhuatl word meaning water) was a painter, writer, and not-too-successful politician who was driven by art and political causes and attracted by the outdoors, mountain climbing, and science. Born in Guadalajara, he is best known for his vast landscapes, usually including volcanoes, in which he produced an aerial feeling of the Mexican landscape. His influence on Mexican art and artists was enormous. Among his students, when he was director of the San Carlos Academy, were José Clemente Orozco and David Siquieros. One of his books, *Las Artes Populares en Mexico* (Popular Arts in Mexico), produced as a catalog for the first exhibition of Mexican folk art, upheld the common artisans of Mexico and remains a classic.

José Clemente Orozco (1883–1949) Born in what today is known as Ciudad Guzmán, Jalisco, Orozco is considered one of the "Big Three" muralists along with Diego Rivera and David Alfero Siquieros. His gloomy, angry, but powerful works project his bitter view of politics. His years of struggle included a stint painting street signs and doll faces in the U.S. On one trip north across the border U.S. Customs destroyed his brothel series of paintings. Alma Reed, who owned Delphic Studios in New York, took him under her wing, promoting his career. His best-known murals appear in Guadalajara and the many of his easel works are in the Alvaro Carrillo Gil Museum in Mexico City. He is buried in the Rotunda de los Ilustres of the Dolores Cemetery in Mexico City.

Antonio López de Santa Anna (1794–1876) One of the most scorned characters in Mexican history, he was president of Mexico 11 times between 1833 and 1855. Audacious, pompous, and self-absorbed, his outrageous exploits disgust and infuriate Mexicans even today, but none more than his role in losing half the territory of Mexico to the United States. Defeated and captured at the Battle of San Jacinto outside Houston, Texas, in 1836, among other things he agreed to allow Texas to be a separate republic and to mark the boundary at the Rio Grande. When the U.S. voted to annex Texas, it sparked the Mexican-American War which the U.S. won in 1848. In the Treaty of Guadalupe Hidalgo which followed between the two nations, the U.S. paid Mexico $15 million for Texas, New Mexico, California, Arizona, Nevada, Utah, and part of Colorado. Eventually Santa Anna was exiled, but returned 2 years before he died, poor, alone, and forgotten. He is buried in the Guadalupe Cemetery behind the Basilica de Guadalupe, Mexico City.

3. ART, ARCHITECTURE & LITERATURE

ART & ARCHITECTURE

Mexico's art and architectural legacy began more than 3,000 years ago. Until the fall of the Aztec empire after the Spanish conquest of Mexico in 1521, art, architecture, politics, and religion in Mexico were inextricably intertwined and remained so to a different extent through the colonial period.

World-famous archeological sites in Mexico—more than 1,500 of them—are individually unique even when built by the same groups of people. Each year scholars decipher more information about those who built these cities, using information they left in bas-relief carvings, sculptures, pottery, murals, and hieroglyphics.

Mexico's pyramids are truncated platforms, not true pyramids, and come in many different shapes. At Tzintzuntzán, near Lake Pátzcuaro, in Michoacán state, the buildings, called *yacatas*, are distinguished by semicircular buildings attached to rectangular ones. Many sites have circular buildings, usually called the observatory and dedicated to Ehécatl, god of the wind. Few pre-Hispanic buildings remain in either Colima or Jalisco although exquisite pottery examples are preserved in museums in both states.

Pottery played an important role and different indigenous groups are distinguished by their use of color and style in pottery. In Tonalá near Guadalajara, pottery traditions begun in pre-Hispanic times continue today and the National Museum of Ceramics in that village contains many good samples of Jalisco pottery as well as pieces from around Mexico. Ancient Jalisco pottery was both off-white and dark red and often decorated with black or red. Many of the figures show the workaday world of unknown peoples, carrying children or water jugs and at play. Good examples are on display at the small museum of anthropology in Guadalajara, across from Agua Azul Park. Both Jalisco and Colima are riddled with underground burial chambers and much of the dark red pottery was found in these multiroomed vaults. Near Colima City visitors can go to some of these underground tombs. Colima is also famous for clay pieces formed into the shapes of potbellied hairless dogs, many of them dancing. But the pottery also took the shape of vegetables, especially squash.

IMPRESSIONS

The revolution gave us self-confidence and a conscience for our existence and our destiny.
—José Clemente Orozco

... Mexico is a country as richly set with architecture as an Elizabethan gown with pearls. Obviously they are not all jewels, but all have their places in the great network from which such buildings as the parish church of Taxco, San Agustín Acolman, the cathedreal of Puebla, the Palacio del Gobierno in Guadalajara, or the Casa de los Azulejos in Mexico City stand out.
—Elizabeth Wilder Weismann, *Art and Time in Mexico*, 1985

Excellent museums in Colima display the unusual work of pre-Hispanic peoples of that area. Besides the museums mentioned above, prime samples from this area are in the Museum of Anthropology in Mexico City.

With the arrival of the Spaniards a new form of architecture came to Mexico, which, for the next 300 years is known as the Viceregal era, when Spain's appointed viceroys ruled Mexico. Many sites that were occupied by indigenous groups at the time of the conquest were razed, and in their place appeared Catholic churches, public buildings, and palaces for conquerors and the king's bureaucrats. Indian artisans, who formerly worked on pyramidal structures, were recruited to give life to these structures, often guided by drawings of European buildings the Spanish architects tried to emulate. Frequently left on their own, the indigenous artisans sometimes implanted their symbolism on the buildings. They might sculpt a plaster angel swaddled in feathers reminiscent of the god Quetzalcoatl or the face of an ancient god surrounded by corn leaves or use the pre-Hispanic calendar counts or the 13 steps to heaven or the nine levels of the underworld to determine how many flowerettes to carve around the church doorway. Good examples of native symbolism are at the church in Xochimilco near Mexico City and Santa María Tonanzintla near Puebla. Native muralists had a hand in painting a knight in tiger skin on the Augustinian monastery in Ixmiquilpan, Hidalgo.

To convert the native populations, New World Spanish priests and architects altered their normal ways of building and teaching. Often before the church was built, an open-air atrium was first constructed so that large numbers of parishioners could be accommodated for service. *Posas* (shelters) at the four corners of churchyards were another architectural technique unique to Mexico, again for the purpose of accommodating crowds during holy sacraments. Because of the language barrier between the Spanish and natives, church adornment became more graphic. Biblical tales came to life in frescoes splashed across church walls and Christian symbolism in stone supplanted that of pre-Hispanic times. Out went the eagle (sun symbol), feathered serpent (symbol of fertility, rain, earth, and sky), and jaguar (power symbol) and in came Christ on a cross, saintly statues, and Franciscan, Dominican, and Augustinian symbolism on church facades. The talents of native master stone- and wood-carvers were turned to Christian subjects. It must have been a confusing time for the indigenous peoples, which accounts for the continued intermingling of Christian and pre-Hispanic ideas as they tried to make sense of it all by mixing preexisting ideas with new ones. The convenient apparition of the Virgin Mary on former pre-Hispanic religious turf made it "legal" to return there to worship and build a "Christian" shrine. Baroque became even more baroque in Mexico and was dubbed *Churrigueresque*. Excellent Mexican baroque examples are in Guadalajara in the Chapel of Our Lady of Aranzaú, and Guadalajara's Regional Museum, as well as Santa Prisca Church in Taxco and San Cayetano de la Valencia Church near Guanajuato. The term *Plateresque* was given to facade designs resembling silver design, but more planted on a structure than a part of it. Acolman convent near the ruins of Teotihuacán has one of the best Plateresque facades in Mexico. The Viceregal Museum in Tepozotlán, north of Mexico City, holds a wealth of artwork from Mexican churches during this period.

Running concurrently with the building of religious structures, the public buildings took shape, modeled after those in European capitals. Especially around

Puebla the use of locally made colorful tile, a fusion of local art and Talavera style from Spain, decorated public walls and church domes. The hacienda architecture sprang up in the countryside, resulting in often massive, thick-walled, fortresslike structures built around a central patio. Remains of haciendas, some still operating, can be seen in almost all parts of Mexico. The San Carlos Academy of Art was founded in Mexico City in 1785, taking after the renowned academies of Europe. Though the emphasis was on a Europeanized Mexico, by the end of the 19th century, the subject matter of easel artists was becoming Mexican: Still lifes with Mexican fruit and pottery, clearly Mexican landscapes with cacti and volcanoes appeared, as did portraits, whose subjects wore Mexican regional clothing. José María Velasco (1840–1912), the father of Mexican landscape painting, emerged during this time. His work and that of others of this period are at the National Museum of Art in Mexico City.

With the late 19th-century entry of Porfirio Díaz into the presidency came another infusion of Europe. Díaz idolized Europe and during this time he lavished on the country a number of striking European-style public buildings, among them opera houses still used today. He provided European scholarships to promising young artists who later returned to Mexico to produce clearly Mexican subject paintings using techniques learned abroad. While the Mexican Revolution, following the resignation and exile of Díaz, ripped the country apart between 1911 and 1917, the result was the birth of Mexico, a claiming and appreciation of it by Mexicans. In 1923 Minister of Education José Vasconcelos was charged with educating illiterate masses. As one means of reaching many people he started the muralist movement when he invited Diego Rivera and several other budding artists to paint Mexican history on the walls of the Ministry of Education building and the National Preparatory School in Mexico City. From then on, the "Big Three" muralists, David Siquieros, Guadalajara-born José Clemente Orozco, and Rivera, were joined by others in bringing Mexico's history in art to the walls of public buildings throughout the country for all to see and interpret. The years that followed eventually brought about a return to easel art, an exploration of Mexico's culture, and a new generation of artists and architects who are free to invent and draw upon subjects and styles from around the world. Among the 20th-century greats are the Big Three muralists, as well as Rufino Tamayo, Gerardo Murillo (Dr. Atl), José Guadalupe Posada, Saturnino Herrán, Francisco Goitia, Frida Kahlo, Roberto Montenegro, José María Velasco, Pedro and Rafael Coronel, Miguel Covarrubias, Olga Costa, and José Chávez Morado. Among the important architects during this period is Luis Barragán, of Guadalajara, who incorporated design elements from haciendas, and Mexican textiles, pottery, and furniture, into sleek, marble-floored structures splashed with the vivid colors of Mexico. His ideas are used by Mexican architects all over Mexico today.

LITERATURE

By the time Cortés arrived in Mexico, the cultures of Mexico were already masters of literature, recording their poems and histories by painting in fanfold books (codices) made of deer skin and bark paper or carving on stone. To record history, gifted students were taught the art of book making, drawing, painting, reading, and writing. After the conquest the Spaniards deliberately destroyed native books. However, several Catholic priests, among them Bernardo de Sahugun and Diego de Landa (who was one of the book destroyers) encouraged the Indians to record their customs and history. These records are among the best we have that document life before the conquest. During the conquest Cortés wrote his now-famous five letters to Charles V, which give us the first printed conquest literature, but it was spare by contrast to the work of Díaz de Castillo. Enraged by an inaccurate account of the conquest written by a flattering friend of Cortés, 40 years after the conquest Bernal Díaz de Castillo, one of the conquerors, wrote his lively and very readable version of the event, *True History of the Conquest of Mexico;* it's regarded as the most accurate. The first printing press appeared in Mexico in 1537 and was followed by a proliferation of printing mostly on subjects about science, nature, and getting along in Mexico. The most important literary figure during the 16th century was Sor Juana Inés de la Cruz, child prodigy and later poet-nun whose works are still treasured. The first Spanish novel written in Mexico was *The Itching Parrot* by José Joaquín Fernández de Lizardi about 19th-century Mexican life. The first daily newspaper appeared in 1805. Nineteenth-century writers produced a plethora of political fiction and nonfiction. Among the more explosive was *The Presidential Succession of 1910* by Francisco Madero (who later became president) which contributed to the downfall of Porfirio Díaz and *Regeneración,* a weekly anti-Díaz magazine published by the Flores Mignon brothers. Among 20th-century writers of note are Octavio Paz, author of *The Labyrinth of Solitude* and winner of the 1991 Nobel Prize for literature, and Carlos Fuentes, who wrote *Where the Air Is Clear.* Books in Mexico are relatively inexpensive to purchase but editions are not produced in great quantity. Newspapers and magazines proliferate, but the majority of those who read devour comic-book novels, the most visible form of literature.

4. RELIGION, MYTH & FOLKLORE

RELIGION

Mexico is a predominantly Catholic country, a religion introduced by the Spaniards during the conquest of Mexico. Despite the preponderance of the Catholic faith, in many places it has pre-Hispanic overtones. One need only visit the *curandero* (folk healing) section of a Mexican market, or attend a village festivity featuring pre-Hispanic dancers to understand that supernatural beliefs often run parallel to Christian ones.

Mexico's complicated mythological heritage from pre-Hispanic literature is jammed with images derived from nature—the wind, jaguars, eagles, snakes, flowers, and more, all intertwined with elaborate mythological stories that explain the universe, climate, seasons, and geography. So strong were the ancient beliefs in their mythological dieties that Mexico's indigenous peoples built their cities according to the cardinal points, with each direction assigned a particular color (the colors might vary from group to group). The sun, moon, and stars took on godlike meaning and their religious, ceremonial, and secular calendars were arranged to show tribute to these omnipotent gods.

Most groups believed in an underworld (not a hell) usually of nine levels and heaven of 13 levels, so the numbers nine and 13 become mythologically significant.

IMPRESSIONS

Jalisco is not only a state but also a magic name. The scenes for many of Mexico's modern movies and popular novels are set in Jalisco and often have the name in the title; practically all of the ranchero songs are about Jalisco or about Guadalajara, its capital. This popularity is probably traceable to a nostalgia for the good old days of Mexico which Jalisco once represented.
—Herbert Cerwin, *These Are the Mexicans*, 1947

Jalisco is rich in ancient remains. Burial places are constantly discovered, though the material unearthed falls, at least to a great extent, into the hands of shrewd dealers, who sell it to tourists and thus scatter it over the earth.
—Carl Lumholtz, *Unknown Mexico*, 1902

The solar calendar count of 365 days and the ceremonial calendar of 260 days are numerically significant. How one died determined where one wound up after death, in the underworld, heaven, or at one of the four cardinal points. Everyone had to first make the journey through the underworld.

One of the richest sources of mythological tales is the *Popol Vuh*, a Maya bible of sorts, that was recorded after the conquest. The *Chilam Balam*, another such book, existed in hieroglyphic form at the conquest and was recorded using the Spanish alphabet into Mayan words that could be understood by the Spaniards. The *Chilam Balam* differed from the *Popol Vuh* in that it is the collected histories of many Maya communities.

Each of the ancient cultures had its set of gods and goddesses and while the names might not cross cultures, their characteristics or purpose often did. Chac, the hook-nosed rain god of the Maya, was Tlaloc, the mighty-figured rain god of the Aztecs; Quetzalcoatl, the plumed serpent god/man of the Toltecs, became Kukulkán of the Maya. The tales of the powers and creation of these deified personages make up Mexico's rich mythology. Sorting out the pre-Hispanic pantheon and mythological beliefs in ancient Mexico can become an all-consuming study (the Maya alone had 166 deities), so below is a list of some of the most important gods.

Chac Maya rain god
Cinteotl Huastec corn god
Coatlíque Huitzilopochtli's mother, whose name means "she of serpent skirt," goddess of death and earth
Cocijo Zapotec rain god
Ehécatl Wind god whose temple is usually round; another aspect of Quetzalcoatl
Huitzilopochtli War god and primary Aztec god, son of Coatlíque
Itzamná Maya god above all, who invented corn, cocoa, and writing and reading
Ixchel Maya goddess of water, weaving, and childbirth
Kinich Ahau Maya sun god
Kukulkán Quetzalcoatl's name in the Yucatán
Mayahuel Goddess of pulque
Ometeotl God/goddess all powerful creator of the universe, ruler of heaven, earth, and underworld.
Quetzalcoatl A mortal who took on legendary characteristics as a god (or vice

versa). When he left Tula in shame after a night succumbing to temptations, he promised to return; he reappeared in the Yucatán. He is also symbolized as Venus, the morning star, and Ehécatl, the wind god.

Tezcaltipoca Aztec sun god known as "Smoking Mirror"
Tláloc Aztec rain god
Tonantzin Aztec motherhood goddess
Xochipilli Aztec god of dance, flowers, and music
Xochiquetzal Flower and love goddess

5. CULTURAL & SOCIAL LIFE

The population of Mexico is 85 million, with 15% white (most of Spanish descent), 60% mestizo (mixed Spanish and Indian), and 25% pure Indian (descendants of the Maya, Aztecs, Huastecs, Otomies, Totonacs, Huichol, and other peoples). Added to this ethnic mix are Africans brought as slaves; European merchants and soldiers of fortune; and the lingering French influence from the time of Maximilian's abortive empire in the New World.

Although Spanish is the official language, about 50 indigenous languages are still spoken, mostly in the Yucatán peninsula, Oaxaca, Chiapas, Chihuahua, Nayarit, Puebla, Sonora and Veracruz, Michoacán, and Guerrero.

Modern Mexico clings to its identity while embracing outside cultures, so Mexicans enjoy the Bolshoi Ballet as readily as a family picnic or village festival. Mexicans have a knack for knowing how to enjoy life, and families, weekends, holidays, and festivities are a priority. A weekend holiday stretched into 4 days is called a *puente* (bridge) and with the whole family in tow, Mexicans flee the cities to visit relatives in the country, picnic, or relax at resorts.

The Mexican workday is a long one; laborers begin around 7am and get off at dusk; office workers go in around 9am and, not counting the 2- to 3-hour lunch, get off at 7 or 8pm. Once a working career is started, there is little time for additional study. School is supposedly mandatory and free through the sixth grade, but many youngsters quit long before that, or never go at all.

Sociologists and others have written volumes trying to explain the Mexican's special relationship with death. It is at once mocked and mourned. Day of the Dead, November 1 and 2, is a good opportunity to see Mexico's relationship with the concept of death.

6. PERFORMING ARTS

MUSIC & DANCE

One has only to walk down almost any street or attend any festival to understand that Mexico's vast musical tradition is inborn; it predates the conquest. Musical instruments were made from almost anything that could be made to rattle, produce a rhythm, or a sound—conch-shell trumpets, high-sounding antler horns, rattlers from seashells and rattlesnake rattlers, drums of turtle shell as well as upright leather-covered wood (*tlalpanhuéhuetl*) and horizontal hollowed logs (*teponaztli*), bells of gold and copper, wind instruments of hollow reeds or fired clay, and soundmakers from leather-topped armadillo shells and gourds. Many were elaborately carved or decorated befitting the important ceremonies they accompanied. So important was music that one of Moctezuma's palaces, the Mixcoacalli, was devoted to the care and housing of musical instruments which were guarded around the clock. In Aztec times, music, dance, and religion were tied together with literature. Music was usually intended to accompany poems which were written for religious ceremonies. Children with talent were separated and trained especially as musicians and poets, two exacting professions in which mistakes carried extreme consequences. The dead were buried with musical instruments for the journey into the afterlife.

Music and dance in Mexico today is divided into three kinds, pre- and post-Hispanic, and secular. Pre-Hispanic dancing may be seen at the Ballet Folklórico de Mexico which, among other places, performs in Guadalajara. Many pre-Hispanic dances are still performed in regional village fiestas; examples are the dances of the Huicholes and Coras of Jalisco and Nayarit. Post-Hispanic music and dance first evolved to teach the native inhabitants about Christianity. "Los Santiagos" is about St. James battling heathens, and "Los Moros" shows Moors battling Christians. Others, like "Los Jardineros," were spoofs on pretentious Spanish life. Secular dances are variations of Spanish dances, characterized by lots of foot tapping, skirt-swishing, and flirtatious gestures. No Mexican fiesta night would be complete without the "Jarabe Tapatío," the national folk dance of Mexico, created in Guadalajara.

Besides the native music and dances, there are regional, state, and national orchestras. On weekends state bands often perform free in central plazas. Mexicans have a sophisticated enjoyment of performing arts from around the world and world-class auditoriums in which they perform. Any such performance will be a sell-out, so it's possible to find national as well as international groups touring most of the year but especially in conjunction with the Cervantino Festival which takes place in Guanajuato in October and November. Invited groups perform throughout the country before and after the festival.

7. SPORTS & RECREATION

The precise rules of the ball game played by pre-Hispanic Mexicans aren't known, but it is fairly well established that some of the players were put to death when the game was over. Stone carvings of the game left on the walls of ballcourts throughout Mesoamerica depict heavily padded players elaborately decked out. With that interesting beginning, team sports are still popular in Mexico.

Bullfighting, introduced by the Spaniards, is performed countrywide today. Jai alai, another Spanish game, is played in arenas in Mexico City and Tijuana. By the 18th century the Mexican gentleman cowboy, the charro, displayed skillful horsemanship during the "charreada" a Mexican-style rodeo. Today charro associations countrywide compete all year, usually on Sunday mornings. Although supposedly illegal, in many places cockfights are held in specially built arenas. Probably the most popular spectator team sport today is soccer; turn on the TV almost any time to catch a game.

Mexico has numerous golf courses, especially in the resort areas, but also excellent ones in Mexico City and Guadalajara. It is sometimes easier to rent a horse in Mexico than a car, since it is a pastime enjoyed by many people at beach resorts as well as in the country. Sport bicycling has grown in popularity so it isn't unusual to see young men making the grind of steep mountain passes during cycling-club marathons.

Tennis, racquetball, squash, waterskiing, surfing, and scuba diving are all sports visitors can enjoy in Mexico. There's good scuba diving on the Pacific, but the best place for that sport is Mexico's Yucatán Caribbean coast. Mountain climbing and hiking volcanoes is a rugged sport where you'll meet like-minded folks from around the world.

8. FOOD & DRINK

Mexican food served in the United States isn't really Mexican food; it's a transported variation that gets less Mexican the farther you get from the border. True Mexican food usually isn't fiery hot; hot spices are added from sauces and garnishes at the table. While there are certain staples like tortillas and beans that appear almost universally, Mexican food and drink varies considerably from region to region; even the beans and tortillas sidestep the usual in some areas just to keep you on your toes.

DINING CUSTOMS

Who you are and what you do makes a difference on when you eat. If you are a businessperson you may grab a cup of coffee or *atole* and a piece of sweet bread just before heading for work around 8am. Around 10 or 11am it's time for a real breakfast and that's when restaurants usually fill with people eating hearty breakfasts that may look more like lunch with steak, eggs, beans, and tortillas. Between 1 and 5pm patrons again converge for lunch, the main meal of the day, that begins with soup, then rice, then the main course with beans and tortillas and maybe a meager helping of a vegetable, followed by dessert and coffee. Workers return to their jobs until 7 or 8pm. Dinner is late, usually around 9 or 10pm. Although you may see many Mexicans eating in restaurants at night, big evening meals aren't traditional; a typical meal at home would be a light one with leftovers from breakfast or lunch, perhaps soup, or tortillas and jam, or a little meat and rice.

Foreigners searching for an early breakfast will often find that nothing gets going in restaurants until around 9am; that's a hint to bring your own portable coffeepot and coffee and buy bakery goodies the night before and make breakfast yourself. Markets however are bustling by 7am and that's the best place to get an early breakfast. Though Mexico grows flavorful coffee in Chiapas, Veracruz, and Oaxaca, a jar of instant coffee is often all that's offered, especially in budget restaurants.

Some of the foreigner's greatest frustrations in Mexico have to do with getting and retaining the waiter and receiving the final bill. If the waiter arrives to take your order before you are ready, you may have trouble getting him again when you are ready. Once an order is in, ordinarily the food arrives in steady sequence. Getting the check is another matter. It's considered rude for the waiter to bring it before it's requested, so you have to ask for it (sometimes more than once, when at last you've found the waiter). To summon the waiter, waive or raise your hand, but don't motion with your index finger, a demeaning gesture that may even cause the waiter to ignore you. Or if it's the check you want, a smile and a scribbling motion into the palm of your hand can send the message across the room. In many budget restaurants, waiters don't clear the table of finished plates or soft-drink bottles because they use them to figure the tab. Always double-check the addition.

REGIONAL CUISINE

Mexico's regional foods are a mixture of pre-Hispanic, Spanish, and French cuisines and at their best are among the most delicious in the world. Recipes developed by nuns during colonial times to please priests and visiting dignitaries have become part of the national patrimony, but much of Mexico's cuisine is derived from pre-Hispanic times. For the visitor, finding hearty, filling meals is fairly easy on a budget, but finding truly delicious food is not as easy. However, some of the best food is found in small inexpensive restaurants where regional specialties are made to please discerning locals. Explanations of specific dishes are found in the Appendix. Although the foods mentioned below originated in a particular part of the country, they frequently cross state lines and appear on menus countrywide.

Tamales are one of Mexico's traditional foods, but regional differences make trying them a treat as you travel. In northern Mexico they are small and thin with only a tiny sliver of meat inside. Chiapas has many *tamal* types, but all are plump and usually come with a sizable hunk of meat and sauce inside. A *corunda* in Michoacán is a triangular-shaped tamal wrapped in a corn leaf rather than the traditional corn husk. In Oaxaca traditional tamales come steaming in a banana leaf. The *zacahuil* of coastal Veracruz is the size of a pig's leg (which is in the center) and pit-baked in a banana leaf. *Molote,* a tiny football-shaped tamal, is a specialty around Papantla, Veracruz.

Tortillas, another Mexican basic, are not made or used equally. In northern Mexico flour tortillas are served more often than corn tortillas. Blue-corn tortillas, once a market food, have found their way to gourmet tables throughout the country. Oaxaca state boasts a large assortment of tortillas, including a hard, thick one with holes used like a cracker, and the huge tlayuda that holds an entire meal. Tortillas are fried and used as garnish in tortilla and Tarascan soup. Filled with meat they become tacos. A tortilla stuffed, rolled, or covered in a sauce and garnished results in an enchilada. A tortilla filled with cheese and lightly fried is a quesadilla. Rolled into a narrow tube, stuffed with chicken, then deep fried, it's known as a flauta. Leftover tortillas cut in wedges and crispy fried are called totopos and used to scoop beans and guacamole salad. Yesterday's tortillas mixed with eggs, chicken, peppers, and other spices are called chilaquiles. Small fried corn tortillas are delicious with ceviche or when topped with fresh lettuce, tomatoes and sauce, onions, and chicken they become tostadas. Each region has a variation of these tortilla-based dishes.

Northern Mexico is known for charro beans, made with beer, *cabrito* (roast kid), *machacada* (shredded beef), Mennonite cheese, and, around Saltillo, pulque bread, made with the alcoholic drink made from maguey.

Around Tapalpa, Jalisco, roast lamb is the specialty. Birria, both red and white, are specialties of Colima and Jalisco.

Besides being known for tamales, Oaxaca has delicious regional cheeses and green, yellow, red, and black *mole*.

Puebla is known for the many dishes created by colonial-era nuns, among them traditional *mole poblano*, Mexican-style barbecue, lamb *mixiotes*, *tinga*, and the eggnoglike rompope. Rompope is a local specialty sold widely in the mountains of Jalisco.

Regional drinks are almost as varied as the food in Mexico. Tequila comes only from the blue agave grown near Guadalajara. Hot *ponche* (punch) is found often at festivals and is usually made with fresh fruit and spiked with tequila or rum. Baja California and the region around Querétaro is prime grape-growing land for Mexico's wine production. The best pulque supposedly comes from Hidalgo state. Beer is produced in Guadalajara, Monterrey, the Yucatán, and Veracruz. Delicious fruit-flavored waters appear on tables countrywide made from hibiscus flowers, ground rice and melon seeds, watermelon, and other fresh fruits. Sangría is a spicy orange juice–and pepper-based chaser for tequila shots.

9. RECOMMENDED BOOKS, FILMS & RECORDINGS

BOOKS

There is an endless supply of books written on the history, culture, and archeology of Mexico and Central America. I have listed those that I especially enjoyed.

HISTORY

A Thumbnail History of Guadalajara (Editorial Colomos, 1983) by José María Muriá Rouret, can be purchased in Guadalajara in English. It provides excellent background on the city's early trials and architecture. *A History of Mexico* (American Heritage Library, 1969), by Henry Bamford Parkes, is a concise, colorfully written historical account. A remarkably readable and thorough college textbook is *The Course of Mexican History* (Oxford University Press, 1987) by Michael C. Meyer and William L. Sherman. *The Conquest of New Spain* (Shoe String Press, 1988), by Bernal Díaz, is the famous story of the Mexican conquest written by Cortés's lieutenant. *The Crown of Mexico* (Holt Rinehart & Winston, 1971) by Joan Haslip, a biography of Maximilian and Carlota, reads like a novel. *Ancient Mexico: An Overview* (University of New Mexico, 1985), by Jaime Litvak is a short, very readable history of pre-Hispanic Mexico. *The Wind That Swept Mexico* (University of Texas Press, 1971), by Anita Brenner, is a classic illustrated account of the Mexican Revolution. Charles Flandrau wrote the classic *Viva Mexico: A Traveller's Account of Life in Mexico* (Eland Books, 1985) early this century, a blunt and humorous description of Mexico. Most people can't put down Gary Jennings's *Aztec* (Avon, 1981), a superbly researched and colorfully written fictionalized account of Aztec life before and after the conquest.

CULTURE

Five Families (Basic Books, 1959) and *Children of Sanchez* (Random House, 1979), by Oscar Lewis, are sociological studies written in the late 1950s and early 1960s about typical Mexican families. *Mexican and Central American Mythology* (Peter Bedrick Books, 1983), by Irene Nicholson, is a concise illustrated book that simplifies the subject.

A good but controversial all-around introduction to contemporary Mexico and its people is *Distant Neighbors: A Portrait of the Mexicans* (Random House, 1984), by Alan Riding. Patrick Oster's *The Mexicans: A Personal Portrait of the Mexican People* (Harper & Row, 1989) is a reporter's insightful account of ordinary Mexican people. Another book with valuable insights into the Mexican character is *The Labyrinth of Solitude* (Grove Press, 1985), by Octavio Paz.

For some fascinating background on northern and western Mexico and the Copper Canyon, read *Unknown Mexico* (Dover Press, 1987), written by Carl Lumholtz, an intrepid writer and photographer around the turn of the century.

The best single source of information on Mexican music, dance, festivals, customs, and mythology is Frances Toor's *A Treasury of Mexican Folkways* (Crown, 1967). *Life in Mexico: Letters of Fanny Calderón de la Barca* (Doubleday, 1966), edited and annotated by Howard T. Fisher and Marion Hall Fisher, is as lively and entertaining today as when it first appeared in 1843, but the editor's illustrated and annotated update makes it even more contemporary. Scottish-born Fanny was married to the Spanish ambassador assigned to Mexico.

ART, ARCHEOLOGY & ARCHITECTURE

The Mexican Codices and Their Extraordinary History (Ediciones Lara, 1985) by María Sten tells the story of the native peoples' "painted books." *Mexico Splendors of Thirty Centuries* (Metropolitan Museum of Art, 1990), the catalog of the 1991 traveling exhibition, is a wonderful resource on Mexico's art from 1500 B.C. through the 1950s. Another superb catalog, *Images of Mexico: The Contribution of Mexico to 20th Century Art* (Dallas Museum of Art, 1987) is a fabulously illustrated and detailed account of Mexican art gathered from collections around the world. *Art and Time in Mexico: From the Conquest to the Revolution* (Harper & Row, 1985), by Elizabeth Wilder Weismann, illustrated with 351 photographs, covers Mexican religious, public, and private architecture with excellent photos and text. *Casa Mexicana* (Stewart, Tabori & Chang, 1989) by Tim Street-Porter takes readers through the interiors of some of Mexico's finest homes-turned-museums or public buildings and private homes using color photographs. *Mexican Interiors* (Architectural Book Publishing Co., 1962), by Verna Cook Shipway and Warren Shipway, uses black-and-white photographs to highlight architectural details from homes all over Mexico.

FOLK ART

Chloë Sayer's *Costumes of Mexico* (University of Texas Press, 1985) is a beautifully illustrated and written work. *Mexican Masks* (University of Texas Press, 1980), by

Donald Cordry, remains a definitive work on Mexican masks based on the author's collection and travels. Cordry's *Mexican Indian Costumes* (University of Texas Press, 1968) is another classic on the subject. The two-volume *Lo Efímero y Eterno del Arte Popular Mexicano* (Fondo Editorial de la Plastica Mexicana, 1974), produced during the Echeverría presidency, is out of print, but it's one of the most complete works ever produced on Mexican folk art and customs. Carlos Espejel wrote both *Mexican Folk Ceramics* and *Mexican Folk Crafts* (Editorial Blume, 1975 and 1978), two comprehensive books that explore crafts state by state. *Folk Treasures of Mexico* (Harry N. Abrams, 1990) by Marion Oettinger, curator of folk art and Latin American art at the San Antonio Museum of Art, is the fascinating illustrated story behind the 3,000-piece Mexican folk art collection amassed by Nelson Rockefeller over a 50-year period, as well as much information about individual folk artists.

NATURE

Peterson Field Guides Mexican Birds (Houghton Mifflin, 1973), by Roger Tory Peterson and Edward L. Chalif, is an excellent guide to the country's birds. *A Guide to Mexican Mammals & Reptiles* (Minutiae Mexicana, 1989), by Norman Pelham Wright and Dr. Bernardo Villa Ramírez, is a small but useful guide to some of the country's wildlife.

FILMS

Mexico's first movie theater opened in 1897 in Mexico City. Almost immediately men with movie cameras began capturing everyday life in Mexico as well as what later became news, including both sides of the Mexican Revolution. All these early films are safe in Mexican archives. As an industry, it had its Mexican start with the 1918 film *The Gray Automobile Gang* (La Banda del Automóvil Gris) by Enrique Rosas Priego, based on an actual cops-and-robbers event in Mexico, but the industry's heyday really began in the 1930s and lasted only until the 1950s. Themes revolved around the Mexican Revolution, handsome but luckless singing cowboys, and helpless, poor-but-beautiful maidens all against a classic Mexican backdrop, at first rural or village (*rancho*) and later city neighborhood. Classic films and directors from that era are *Alla en el Rancho Grande* and *Vamonos Con Pancho Villa,* both by Fernando de Fuentes; *Champion Without a Crown* (*Campeón sin Corona*) a true-life boxing drama, by Alejandro Galindo; *The Pearl* (*La Perla*), by Emilio Fernández based on John Steinbeck's novel; *Yanco,* by Servando Gonzalez about a poor, young boy of Xochimilco who learned to play a violin; and the sad tale of *María Candelaria* also set in Xochimilco, another Fernández film starring Dolores del Río. Comedian Cantinflas starred in many Mexican films, and became known in the U.S. for his role in *Around the World in Eighty Days.* If Mexico's golden age of cinema didn't last long, Mexico as subject matter and location has had a long life. The Durango mountains have become the film-backdrop capital of Mexico. *The Night of the Iguana* was filmed in Puerto Vallarta, putting that seaside village on the map. *Old Gringo* was filmed in Zacatecas and *Viva Zapata* and *Under the Volcano* were both set in Cuernavaca.

RECORDINGS

While Mexico's homegrown cinema may have hit a snag, it's recording industry has not; Mexicans take their music very seriously—just notice tapes for sale almost everywhere, nearly ceaseless music in the streets, and bus-driver collections of tapes to entertain passengers by. For the collector there are numerous choices from contemporary rock to ballads from the revolution, ranchero, salsa, and sones, and romantic trios. You'll arrive and leave the states of Jalisco and Colima with the sound of mariachi music playing. Among the top recording artists is Mariachi Vargas. No mariachi performance is complete without *Guadalajara, Las Mañanitas,* and *Jarabe Tapatío*. For trio music, some of the best is by Los Tres Diamantes, Los Tres Reyes, and Trio Los Soberanos. If you're requesting songs of a trio, good ones to ask for are *Sin Ti, Usted, Adios Mi Chaparita, Amor de la Calle,* and *Cielito Lindo*. Traditional ranchero music to request, which can be sung by soloists or trios, are *Tu Solo Tu, No Volveré,* and *Adios Mi Chaparita*. Music from the Yucatán would include the recordings by the Trio Los Soberanos and Dueto Yucalpeten. Typical Yucatecan songs are *Las Golondrinas Yucatecas, Peregrina, Ella, El Pajaro Azul,* and *Ojos Tristes*. Heartthrob soloists from years past include Pedro Vargas, Hector Cabrera, Lucho Gatica, Pepe Jara, and Alberto Vazquez. Marimba music is popular in Veracruz, Chiapas, and the Yucatán. Peña Ríos makes excellent marimba recordings. Though marimba musicians seldom ask for requests, some typical renditions would include *Huapango de Moncayo,* and *El Bolero de Ravel*. Mariachi music is played and sold all over Mexico. One of the best recordings of recent times is the Royal Philharmonic Orchestra's rendition of classic Mexican music titled *Mexicano;* it's one purchase you must make. In a more popular vein Los Broncos's *Cuentame, Cuentame* is played so often you'd think it was the national song.

CHAPTER 2
PLANNING A TRIP TO THE REGION

1. **INFORMATION, ENTRY REQUIREMENTS & MONEY**
- **WHAT THINGS COST IN PUERTO VALLARTA**
- **WHAT THINGS COST IN MANZANILLO**
- **WHAT THINGS COST IN GUADALAJARA**
2. **WHEN TO GO—CLIMATE, HOLIDAYS & EVENTS**
- **CALENDAR OF EVENTS**
3. **HEALTH & INSURANCE**
4. **WHAT TO PACK**
5. **TIPS FOR THE DISABLED, SENIORS, SINGLES, FAMILIES & STUDENTS**
6. **ALTERNATIVE/ADVENTURE TRAVEL**
7. **SHOPPING**
8. **GETTING THERE & DEPARTING**
9. **GETTING AROUND**
- **FAST FACTS: MEXICO**

In this chapter, the where, when, and how of your trip is discussed—the advance planning that gets your trip together and takes it on the road.

Most of the questions people ask before traveling to Mexico are discussed here. This chapter addresses such important issues as when to go, whether or not to take a tour, what pretrip health precautions should be taken, what insurance coverage to investigate, and where to obtain additional information.

1. INFORMATION, ENTRY REQUIREMENTS & MONEY

SOURCES OF INFORMATION

The **State of Jalisco** provides information through **Casa Jalisco,** State Government Promotion Office, 118 Broadway, Suite 639, San Antonio, TX 78205 (tel. 512/227-2887; fax 512/227-2889).

Mexican Government Tourism Offices throughout the world include the following:

In the **United States:**

Chicago: 70 E. Lake St., Suite 1413, Chicago, IL 60601 (tel. 312/565-2786).

Houston: 2707 N. Loop West, Suite 450, Houston, TX 77008 (tel. 713/880-5153).

Los Angeles: 10100 Santa Monica Blvd., Suite 224, Los Angeles, CA 90067 (tel. 213/203-8191).

Miami: 128 Aragon Ave., Coral Gables, FL 33134 (tel. 305/443-9167).
New York: 405 Park Ave., 14th Floor, New York, NY 10022 (tel. 212/755-7261).
San Antonio: Mexican Government Tourism Office, for surface travel to Mexico only, Centre Plaza Building 45 NE Loop 410, San Antonio, TX 78216 (tel. 512/366-3242; fax 512/366-1532).
Washington, D.C.: 1911 Pennsylvania Ave. NW, Washington, DC 20006 (tel. 202/728-1750).

In **Canada:**
Montréal: One Place Ville-Marie, Suite 2409, Montréal, PQ H3B 3M9 (tel. 514/871-1052).
Toronto: 2 Bloor St. West, Suite 1801, Toronto, ON, M4W 3E2 (tel. 416/925-0704).

In **Europe:**
Frankfurt: Weisenhüttenplatz 26, 06000 Frankfurt-am-Main 1 (tel. 4969/25-3541).
London: 60 Trafalgar Sq., 3rd floor, London WC2 N5DS (tel. 441/839-3177).
Madrid: Calle de Velázquez 126, Madrid 28006 (tel. 34/261-1827).
Paris: 4 rue Notre-Dame-des-Victoires, 75002 Paris (tel. 331/40-210-0734).
Rome: Via Barberini 3, 00187 Roma (tel. 396/474-2986).

In **Asia:**
Tokyo: 2.15.1 Nagata-Cho, Chiyoda-Ku, Tokyo 100 (tel. 813/580-2961 or 580-5539).

The following newsletters may be of interest to readers who want to keep up with Mexico between visits: **Sanborn's News Bulletin,** Dept. FR, P.O. Box 310, McAllen, TX 78502. It's a free newsletter produced by Sanborn's Insurance, offering tips on driving conditions, highways, hotels, economy and business, RV information, fishing, hunting, and so forth.

Travel Mexico, Apdo. Postal 6-1007, Mexico, D.F. 06600, is published six times a year by the publishers of *Traveler's Guide to Mexico*—the book frequently found in hotel rooms in Mexico. The newsletter covers a variety of topics from news about archeology, to hotel packages, new resorts and hotels, and the economy. A subscription costs $15.

Mexico Meanderings, P.O. Box 33057, Austin, TX 78764, is a new six-to-eight page newsletter with photographs featuring off-the-beaten-track destinations in Mexico. It's aimed at readers who travel by car, bus, or train, and is published six times annually. A subscription costs $18.

For other newsletters, see also "Retiring," below.

ENTRY REQUIREMENTS

DOCUMENTS

You'll need a Mexican Tourist Permit, issued free at the border, at any Mexican consulate, at any of the Mexican tourist offices listed above, or by the airline when you check in.

To qualify for the tourist permit you must show proof of citizenship, such as naturalization papers, an official birth certificate with a raised seal (not a photocopy), current voter's registration, or valid passport. This proof of citizenship may also be requested to reenter the U.S. Children traveling without a parent must have an original (not a photocopy) of a notarized letter of consent for travel from the absent parent or parents.

The tourist permit is more important than a passport in Mexico, so guard it carefully—if you lose it, you may not be permitted to leave the country until you can replace it; that bureaucratic hassle takes several days or a week at least. A tourist permit can be issued for up to 180 days, and although your stay south of the border may be less than that, you should get the paper for the maximum time, just in case. Sometimes the officials don't ask, they just stamp a time limit, so be sure and say "6 months," or at least twice as long as you think. You may decide to stay, and you'll eliminate hassle by not needing to renew your papers. This hint is especially important for people who take cars into Mexico.

LOST DOCUMENTS

To replace a lost passport or other necessary travel document contact your embassy or nearest consular agent listed below in "Fast Facts." You must establish a record of your citizenship, and fill out a form requesting another Mexican Tourist Permit. If the Mexican Tourist Permit is lost as well, you can't leave the country; and without an affidavit regarding your passport and citizenship, you may have hassles at Customs when you get home. So you must get it all cleared up before trying to leave.

CUSTOMS

When you enter Mexico, Customs officials are tolerant as long as you have no drugs (marijuana, cocaine, etc.) or firearms. You're allowed to bring two cartons of cigarettes, or 50 cigars, plus a kilogram (2.2 lb.) of smoking tobacco; the liquor allowance is two bottles of anything, wine or hard liquor.

U.S. citizens are allowed up to $400 in purchases outside the country every 30 days. After $400, the first $1,000 is taxed at 10%. Any number of times a year Canadian citizens are allowed $20 in purchases after 24 hours' absence from the country or $100 after 48 hours or more.

Reentering the U.S., federal law allows a carton (200) of cigarettes, or 50 cigars, or 2 kilograms (total, 4.4 lb.) of smoking tobacco, or proportional amounts of these items, plus 1 liter of alcoholic beverage (wine, beer, or spirits). Also remember that you are restricted by the quotas set by the state in which you reenter the U.S. Liquor restrictions are most strictly applied at the border posts, less strictly at airports far from the border.

Canadian returning-resident regulations are similar to the U.S. ones: a carton of cigarettes, 50 cigars, 2 pounds (not kilos) of smoking tobacco, 1.1 liters (40 oz.) of wine or liquor, or a case of beer (8.2 liters). All provinces except Prince Edward Island and the Northwest Territories allow you to bring in more liquor and beer—up to 2 gallons (9 liters) more—but the taxes are quite high.

MONEY

CASH/CURRENCY

Mexican peso coins come in denominations of 20, 50, 100, (occasionally 200), 500, and 1000. Bills come in denominations of 2,000, 5,000, 10,000, 20,000, and 50,000.

Small bills and change are hard to come by even in stores, so collect as much as possible as you travel. The 500 and 1,000 peso coins and 2,000, 10,000, and 20,000 peso bills are the best to keep on hand.

The dollar sign ($) is used to indicate pesos in Mexico. A Mexican menu will list a glass of orange juice for $1,500 and that means 1,500 pesos. To avoid confusion, I will use the dollar sign in this book only to denote U.S. currency.

Many establishments dealing with tourists also quote prices in dollars. To avoid confusion, they use the abbreviations "Dlls." for dollars, and "m.n." (*moneda nacional*, or national currency) for pesos, so "$1,000.00 m.n." means 1,000 pesos.

Inflation in Mexico is increasing 20% to 30% per year. Every effort is made to provide the most accurate and up-to-date information in this book, but further changes are inevitable.

EXCHANGE

For the fastest and least complicated service, its best to carry traveler's checks. Cash can sometimes be difficult to exchange because counterfeit dollars have been circulated recently in Mexico, and merchants and banks are wary. In some small towns, banks may refuse to accept cash. Personal checks may delay you for weeks since a bank will wait for the check to clear before giving you your money. But I always carry one blank check, just for an emergency.

Banks often give a rate of exchange below the official daily rate. Hotels usually exchange below the bank's daily rate as well. Canadian dollars seem to be most easily exchanged for pesos at branches of Banamex and Bancomer.

In Mexico, banks are open Monday through Friday from 9am to 1:30pm; a few banks in large cities offer extended afternoon hours. Although they open earlier, you'll save time at the bank or currency-exchange booths by arriving no earlier than 10am. Generally they don't receive the official rate for that day until shortly before then and they won't exchange your money until they have the daily rate.

Large airports have currency-exchange counters that sometimes stay open as long as flights are arriving or departing.

TRAVELER'S CHECKS

Mexican banks pay you more for traveler's checks than for dollars in cash, but Casas de Cambio (exchange houses) pay more for cash than traveler's checks. All are examining dollars carefully. Some banks, but not all, charge a service fee, as high as 5%, to cash either dollars or traveler's checks. Sometimes banks post the service charge amount so you can see it, but they might not, so it pays to ask first and shop around for a bank without a fee.

CREDIT CARDS

You'll be able to charge some hotel and restaurant bills, almost all airline tickets, and many store purchases. You can get cash advances of several hundred dollars on your card, but there may be a wait of 20 minutes to 2 hours. However, you can't charge gasoline purchases in Mexico.

VISA (Bancomer in Mexico), MasterCard (Carnet in Mexico), and less widely, American Express, are the most accepted cards. The Mexican bank named Bancomer, with branches throughout the country, has inaugurated a system of automatic teller machines linked to VISA International's network. If you are a VISA customer, you may be able to get peso cash from one of the Bancomer ATMs.

WHAT THINGS COST IN PUERTO VALLARTA — U.S. $

Collective van from the airport to downtown	$5.00–$6.00
Local telephone call	.10–.50
Double at the Garza Blanca (very expensive)	$260.00–$505.00
Double at the Quinta Real (expensive)	$140.00–$240.00
Double at the Playa Los Arcos (moderate)	$50.00–$60.00
Double at the Chez Elena (budget)	$25.00–$35.00
Three-course dinner for one at Bogart's (expensive)	$75.00
Three-course lunch for one at La Casa del Almendro (moderate)	$25.00
Three-course lunch for one at Restaurant Juanita (budget)	$5.00–$10.00
Beer	$1.00–$2.00
Margarita	$2.00–$4.50
Half day of deep-sea fishing	$160.00–$200.00
Half day of diving (per person)	$45.00–$50.00

WHAT THINGS COST IN MANZANILLO — U.S. $

Collective van from the airport to downtown	$4.00–$5.00
Local telephone call	.10–.50
Double at Las Hadas (very expensive)	$225.00–$357.00
Double at the Sierra Manzanillo (expensive)	$105.00–$300.00
Double at the La Posada (moderate)	$50.00–$60.00
Double at the Hotel Colonial (budget)	$30.00–$35.00
Three-course dinner for one at Legazpi (expensive)	$50.00–$75.00
Three-course lunch for one at La Plazuela (moderate)	$15.00–$20.00
Three-course lunch for one at La Perlita (budget)	$4.00–$5.00
Beer	$1.00–$2.00

	US$
Margarita	$2.00–$4.50
Half day of deep-sea fishing	$200.00

WHAT THINGS COST IN GUADALAJARA — U.S. $

Collective van from the airport to downtown	$6.00
Local telephone call	.10–.50
Double at La Quinta Real (expensive)	$160.00–$200.00
Double at Hotel de Mendoza (moderate)	$70.00
Double at the Hotel San Francisco (budget)	$35.00
Three-course dinner for one at El Méson del Chef (expensive)	$35.00
Three-course dinner for one at Acropolis Café (moderate)	$15.00
Two-course dinner for one at Los Itacates Fonda (budget)	$8.00
Beer	$1.00–$2.00
Margarita	$2.00–$3.00
Admission to the bullfights	$1.50–$65.00
Ticket to the Degollado Theater Ballet Folklórico	$1.00–$6.00

BRIBES

Called propina (tip), mordida (bite), or worse, the custom is probably almost as old as humankind. Bribes exist in every country but in third world countries the amounts tend to be smaller and collected more often. You will meet with bribery, so you should know how to deal with it.

With the administration of President Salinas de Gortari, border officials have become more courteous, less bureaucratic, and less inclined to ask/hint for a bribe. I'm still wary, however, so just so you're prepared here are a few hints based on the past. If you don't offer a tip of a few dollars to the man who inspects your car (if you're driving), he may ask for it, as in "Give me a tip (*propina*)." Some border officials will do what they're supposed to do (stamp your passport or birth certificate and inspect your luggage) and then wave you on through. If you're charged for it, ask for a receipt. If you get no receipt, you've paid a bribe.

Officials don't ask for bribes from everybody. Travelers dressed in a formal suit and tie, with pitch-black sunglasses and a scowl on the face, are rarely asked to pay a bribe.

Those who are dressed for vacation fun, seem good-natured and accommodating, are charged every time. You may not want the bother of dressing up for border crossings, but you should at least act in a formal manner, and be rather cold, dignified, and businesslike, perhaps preoccupied with "important affairs" that are on your mind. Wear those dark sunglasses. Scowl. Ignore the request. Pretend not to understand. Don't speak Spanish. But whatever you do, avoid impoliteness, and absolutely never insult a Latin American official! When an official's sense of machismo is roused, he can and will throw the book at you, and you may be in trouble. Stand your ground—politely.

SCAMS

The **shoeshine scam** is an old trick that seems to happen most often in Mexico City. Here's how it works. A tourist agrees to a shine for, say, 3,000 pesos. When the work is complete the vendor says, "that'll be 30,000" and insists the shocked tourist misunderstood. A big brouhaha ensues involving bystanders who side with the shoeshine vendor. The object is to get the bewildered tourist to succumb to the howling crowd and embarrassing scene and fork over the money. A variation of the scam has the vendor saying the price quoted is per shoe. To avoid this scam, ask around about the price of a shine, and when the vendor quotes his price, write it down and show it to him *before* the shine.

Tourists are suckered daily into the **iguana scam,** especially in Puerto Vallarta and nearby Yelapa beach. Someone, often a child, strolls by carrying a huge iguana and says "wanna take my peekchur." Photo-happy tourists seize the opportunity. Just as the camera is angled properly, the holder of the iguana says (more like mumbles) "one dollar." That means a dollar per shot. Sometimes they wait until the shutter clicks to mention money.

Because hotel desk clerks are usually so helpful, I hesitate to mention the **lost-objects scam** for fear of tainting them all. But here's how it works. You "lose" your wallet after cashing money at the desk, or you leave something valuable such as a purse or camera in the lobby. You report it. The clerk has it, but instead of telling you that he does, he says he will see what he can do; meanwhile, he suggests that you offer a high reward. This one has all kinds of variations. In one story a reader wrote about, a desk clerk in Los Mochis was in cahoots with a bystander in the lobby who lifted her wallet in the elevator.

Another scam readers have written about might be called the **infraction scam.** Officials, or men presenting themselves as officials, demand money for some supposed infraction. Never get into a car with them. I avoided one with a bona-fide policeman-on-the-take when my traveling companion feigned illness and began writhing, moaning, and pretending to have the dry heaves. It was more than the policeman could handle.

Legal and necessary car searches by military personnel looking for drugs are mentioned elsewhere. But every now and then there are police-controlled yet illegal roadblocks where motorists are allowed to continue after paying.

Along these lines, if you are stopped by the police, I also suggest that you avoid handing your driver's license to a policeman. Hold it so that it can be read, but don't give it up.

My advice is intended to help you to be aware of potential hazards and how to deal with them. I log thousands of miles and many months in Mexico each year without serious incident, and I feel safer there than at home. (See also "Fast Facts"—"Emergencies" and "Safety," below.)

2. WHEN TO GO — CLIMATE, HOLIDAYS & EVENTS

From Puerto Vallarta south to Huatulco, Mexico offers one of the world's most perfect winter climates—dry, balmy, with temperatures ranging from the 80s by day to the 60s at night. From Puerto Vallarta south you can swim year round. Temperatures range from 72° to 86°F year round along the coasts of Jalisco and Colima.

High mountains shield Pacific beaches from *nortes* (northers—freezing blasts out of Canada via the Texas Panhandle). In summer the difference between west coast and Gulf coast temperatures is much less. Both areas become warm and rainy. Of the two regions the gulf is far rainier, particularly in the states of Tabasco and Campeche. Jalisco and Colima, like most of Mexico, have the most rain from May through September, with the rainiest months being June through August. There is a handy temperature-conversion chart in the Appendix to this book.

HOLIDAYS

Banks, stores, and businesses are closed on national holidays. Hotels fill up quickly, and transportation is very crowded. Mexico celebrates the following national holidays:

January 1	New Year's Day
February 5	Constitution Day
March 21	Birthday of Benito Juárez
March–April (movable)	Holy Week (Good Friday through Easter Sunday)
May 1	Labor Day
May 5	Battle of Puebla, 1862 (Cinco de Mayo)
September 1	President's Message to Congress
September 16	Independence Day
October 12	Columbus Day (Mexico: Day of the Race)
November 1–2	All Saints' and All Souls' Days (Day of the Dead)
November 20	Mexican Revolution Anniversary
December 11–12	Day of the Virgin of Guadalupe (Mexico's patron saint)
December 24–25	Christmas Eve (evening), Christmas Day

MEXICO CALENDAR OF EVENTS

JANUARY

- **Three Kings Day** Commemorates the Three Kings bringing of gifts to the Christ Child. On this day the Three Kings "bring" gifts to children. January 6.

FEBRUARY

- **Candlemas Day** On January 6, Rosca de Reyes, a round cake with a hole in the middle is baked with a tiny doll inside representing the Christ Child. Whoever gets the slice with the doll must give a party on February 2. Northwest of Guadalajara in San Juan de los Lagos, Jalisco, and Buenavista near Lagos de Moreno, Jalisco, with pilgrims coming from all over Mexico to honor the Virgen de San Juan de los Lagos. Also in Tecomán south of Manzanillo.
- **Ash Wednesday** The start of Lent and time of abstinence. It's a day of reverence nationwide, but some towns honor it with folk dancing and fairs. Movable date.

○ **CARNAVAL** *Three days before Ash Wednesday. In some towns there will be no special celebration, in others a few parades.*
Where: Especially celebrated in Tepoztlán, Morelos; Huejotzingo, Puebla; Chamula, Chiapas; Veracruz, Veracruz; Cozumel, Quintana Roo; and Mazatlán, Sinaloa. When: Date variable, but always the 3 days preceding Ash Wednesday. How: Transportation and hotels will be clogged, so it's best to make reservations 6 months in advance and arrive a couple of days ahead of the beginning of celebrations. The latter three resemble a U.S. festival–type atmosphere. In Chamula, however, the event harks back to pre-Hispanic times with ritualistic running on flaming branches. On Tuesday before Ash Wednesday, in Tepoztlán and Huejotzingo, masked and brilliantly clad dancers fill the streets.

MARCH

- **Benito Juárez Birthday** Celebrated with small hometown celebrations countrywide, but especially in Juárez's birthplace, Gelatao, Oaxaca.

○ **HOLY WEEK** *Celebrates the last week in the life of Christ from Good Friday through Easter Sunday with almost nightly somber religious processions, spoofing of Judas, and reenactments of specific biblical events, plus food and craft fairs. Businesses close and Mexicans travel far and wide during this week.*
When: March or April. How: Reserve early with a deposit. Airlines into and out of the country will be reserved months in advance. Buses to these towns or almost anywhere in Mexico will be full, so try arriving on the Wednesday or Thursday before Good Friday. Easter Sunday is quiet.

MAY

- **Labor Day** Worker's parades countrywide and everything closes. May 1.
- **Holy Cross Day** Día de la Santa Cruz. Workers place a cross on top of unfinished buildings and have food celebrations, bands, folk dancing, and fireworks around the work site. Celebrations are particularly colorful in Tequila, Jalisco. May 3.
- **Cinco de Mayo** A national holiday that celebrates the defeat of the French at the Battle of Puebla. May 5.
- **Feast of San Isidro** The patron saint of farmers is honored with a blessing of seeds and work animals. May 15.

JUNE

- **Navy Day** Celebrated by all port cities. June 1.
- **Corpus Christi Day** Honors the Body of Christ—the Eucharist—with religious processions, mass, food. Celebrated nationwide. Variable date 66 days after Easter.

JULY

- **Saint Peter** Día de San Pedro, is celebrated wherever St. Peter is the patron saint and honors anyone named Pedro or Peter. It's especially festive at San Pedro Tlaquepaque, near Guadalajara, with numerous mariachi bands, folk dancers, and parades with floats. June 29.

JULY

- **Virgin of Carmen** A nationally celebrated religious festival centered at churches nationwide. July 16.
- **Saint James Day** Día de San Juan, is observed countrywide wherever St. James is patron saint, and by anyone named Juan or John, or any village with Santiago in the name, often with rodeos, fireworks, and dancing. July 25.

AUGUST

- **Assumption of Virgin Mary** Venerated throughout the country with special masses and in some places processions. August 15-16.

SEPTEMBER

- **Independence Day** Celebrates Mexico's independence from Spain. A day of parades, picnics, and family reunions throughout the country. At 11pm on September 15, the president of Mexico gives the famous independence "grito" (shout) from the National Palace in Mexico City. Guadalajara has a weeklong fair and market in the central plaza. September 16 (parade day).

OCTOBER

- **Cervantino Festival** Begun in the 1970s as a cultural event bringing performing artists from all over the world to the Guanajuato, a picturesque village northeast of Mexico City, now the artists travel all over the republic after appearing in

MEXICO CALENDAR OF EVENTS • 39

Guanajuato. Check local calendars for appearances. Mid-October through November.
- **Feast of San Francisco de Asis** Anyone named Frances or Francis or Francisco, and towns whose patron saint is San Francisco, celebrate with barbecue parties, regional dancing, and religious observances. October 4.
- **Día de la Raza** Day of the Race, or Columbus Day (the day Columbus discovered America), commemorates the fusion of two races—Spanish and Mexican. October 12.
- **Feast of San José** This festival honors Saint Joseph and anyone named Joseph (José in Spanish). Ciudad Guzmán, Jalisco, between Guadalajara and Manzanillo, celebrates with a fair, processions, and regional dancing. October 21.

NOVEMBER

◎ **DAY OF THE DEAD** What's commonly called Day of the Dead is actually 2 days. November 1, All Saints' Day, honors saints and deceased children. November 2 is All Souls' Day, honoring deceased adults. Relatives gather at cemeteries countrywide, carrying candles and food, often spending the night beside graves of loved ones. Weeks before, bakers begin producing bread formed in the shape of mummies or round loafs decorated with bread shaped like bones. Decorated sugar skulls emblazoned with glittery names are sold everywhere. Many days ahead homes and churches erect special altars laden with Day of the Dead bread, fruit, flowers, candles, and the favorite foods as well as photographs of saints and of the deceased. On the 2 nights children dress in costumes and masks, often carrying mock coffins through the streets and pumpkin lanterns into which they expect money will be dropped. Often there are solemn processions to the cemetery, where villagers settle in for the night.

- **Revolution Day** Commemorates the start of the Mexican Revolution in 1910, with parades, speeches, rodeos, and patriotic events. November 20.

DECEMBER

◎ **DÍA DE GUADALUPE** Throughout Mexico, the Virgin of Guadalupe, patroness of Mexico, is honored, with religious processions, street fairs, dancing, fireworks, and masses. The Virgin appeared to a small boy, Juan Diego, in December 1531, on a hill near Mexico City. He convinced the bishop that the apparition had appeared by revealing his cloak upon which the Virgin was emblazoned. It's customary for children to dress up as Juan Diego, wearing mustaches and red bandanas.
  Where: The most famous and elaborate celebration takes place at the Basílica of Guadalupe, north of Mexico City, where the Virgin made her appearance. But every village in Mexico celebrates this day, often with processions of children carrying banners of the Virgin, and frequently with charreadas, bicycle races, dancing, and fireworks as well. In Jalisco this event has especially interesting celebrations in Tapalpa and El Grullo.
  When: December 12.

- **Christmas Posadas** Each night for 12 days before Christmas it's customary to reenact the Holy Family's search for an inn, with door-to-door candlelit processions in cities and villages nationwide.
- **Christmas** Mexicans extend this celebration and leave their jobs, often beginning 2 weeks before Christmas all the way through New Year's. Many businesses close and resorts and hotels fill up.
- **New Year's Eve** As in the U.S., New Year's Eve is the time to gather for private parties of celebration and to explode fireworks and sound off noisemakers.

3. HEALTH & INSURANCE

HEALTH PREPARATIONS

Of course, the very best ways to avoid illness or to mitigate its effects are to make sure that you're in top health and that you don't overdo it. Travel tends to take more of your energy than a normal working day, and missed meals mean that you get less nutrition than you need. Make sure you have three good, wholesome meals a day, get more rest than you normally do, and don't push yourself if you're not feeling in top form.

TURISTA Turista is the name given to the pervasive diarrhea, often accompanied by fever, nausea, and vomiting, that attacks so many travelers to Mexico on their first trip. Doctors, who call it traveler's diarrhea, say it's not just one "bug," or factor, but a combination of different food and water, upset schedules, overtiring, and the stresses that accompany travel. Being tired and careless about food and drink is a sure ticket to turista. A good high-potency (or "therapeutic") vitamin supplement, and even extra vitamin C, is a help; yogurt is good for healthy digestion, and it's becoming more available in Mexico.

How To Prevent It The U.S. Public Health Service recommends the following measures for prevention of traveler's diarrhea:

Drink only purified water. This means tea, coffee, and other beverages made with boiled water; canned or bottled carbonated beverages, including carbonated water; beer and wine; or water that you brought to a rolling boil or otherwise purified. Avoid ice, which is often made with untreated water.

Choose food carefully. In general, avoid salads, uncooked vegetables, and unpasteurized milk or milk products (including cheese). Choose food that is freshly cooked and still hot. Peel fruit yourself. Don't eat undercooked meat, fish, or shellfish.

The Public Health Service does not recommend that you take any medicines as preventatives. All the applicable medicines, including antibiotics, bismuth subsalicylate (as in Pepto-Bismol), and difenoxine (as in Lomotil), can have nasty side effects if taken for several weeks. The best way to prevent illness is to take care with food, water, and rest, and don't overdo it.

How To Get Well If you get sick, there are lots of medicines available in Mexico which can harm more than help. You should ask your doctor before you leave home what medicine he or she recommends for traveler's diarrhea, and follow his or her advice.

The Public Health Service guidelines are these: If there are three or more loose stools in an 8-hour period, especially with other symptoms such as nausea, vomiting, abdominal cramps, and fever, it's time to go to a doctor.

The first thing to do is go to bed and don't move until it runs its course. Traveling makes it last longer. Drink lots of liquids: tea without milk or sugar, or the Mexican *té de manzanilla* (chamomile tea), is best. Eat only *pan tostada* (dry toast). Keep to this diet for at least 24 hours, and you'll be well over the worst of it. If you fool yourself into thinking that a plate of enchiladas can't hurt, or that beer or liquor will kill the germs, you'll have a total relapse.

The Public Health Service advises that you be especially careful to replace fluids and electrolytes (potassium, sodium, etc.) during a bout of diarrhea. Do this by drinking glasses of fruit juice (high in potassium) with honey and a pinch of salt added; and also a glass of pure water with ¼ teaspoon of sodium bicarbonate (baking soda) added.

ALTITUDE SICKNESS At high altitudes it takes about 10 days or so to acquire the extra red blood corpuscles you need to adjust to the scarcity of oxygen. At very high-altitude places, your car won't run very well, you may have trouble starting it, and you may not even sleep well at night.

This ailment results from the relative lack of oxygen and decrease in barometric pressure that come from being at high altitudes (5,000 ft./1,500m, or more). Symptoms include shortness of breath, fatigue, headache, and even nausea.

Avoid altitude sickness by taking it easy for the first few days after you arrive at high altitude. Drink extra fluids, but avoid alcoholic beverages, which not only tend to dehydrate you, but also are more potent in a low-oxygen environment. If you have heart or lung problems, talk to your doctor before going above 8,000 feet.

BUGS AND BITES Mosquitoes and gnats are prevalent along the coast. Insect repellent (*rapellante contra insectos*) is a must, and it's not always available in Mexico. If you're sensitive to bites, pick up some antihistamine cream from a drugstore at home (Di-Delamine is available without a prescription). Rubbed on a fresh mosquito bite, the cream keeps down the swelling and reduces the itch. In Mexico, ask for "Camfo-Fenicol" (Campho-phenique), the second-best remedy.

Most readers won't ever see a scorpion, but if you're stung, it's best to go to a doctor.

MORE SERIOUS DISEASES You don't have to worry about tropical diseases too much if your journey is for less than 3 months, and if you stay on the normal tourist routes (that is, you don't head out into the boondocks to camp with the locals for a week).

You can also protect yourself by taking some simple precautions. Besides being careful about what you eat and drink, do not go swimming in polluted waters. This includes any stagnant water such as ponds, and slow-moving rivers. Avoid mosquitoes because they carry malaria, dengue fever, and other serious illnesses. Cover up, avoid going out when mosquitoes are active, use repellent, sleep under mosquito netting, and stay away from places that seem to have a lot of mosquitoes. The most dangerous areas seem to be on Mexico's west coast, away from the big resorts (which are relatively safe).

To prevent malaria if you go to a malarial area, you must get a prescription for antimalarial drugs, and begin taking them before you enter the area. You must also continue to take them for a certain amount of time after you leave the malarial area.

Talk to your doctor about this. It's a good idea to be inoculated against tetanus, typhoid, and diphtheria, but this isn't a guarantee against contracting the disease.

The following list of diseases should not alarm you, as their incidence is rare among tourists. But if you become ill with something more virulent than traveler's diarrhea, I want you to have this information ready at hand:

Dengue Fever Transmitted by mosquitoes, it comes on fast with high fever, severe headache, and joint and muscle pain. Three or 4 days after the onset of the disease, there's a skin rash. Highest risk is during July, August, and September. Risk for normal tourists is low.

Dysentery Caused by contaminated food or water, either amoebic or bacillary in form, it is somewhat like traveler's diarrhea, but more severe. Risk for tourists is low.

Hepatitis, Viral This virus is spread through contaminated food and water (often in rural areas), and through intimate contact with infected persons. Risk for tourists is normally low.

Malaria Spread by mosquito bites, malaria can be effectively treated if caught soon after the disease is contracted. Malaria symptoms are headache, malaise, fever, chills, sweats, anemia, and jaundice.

Rabies This virus is almost always passed by bites from infected animals or bats, rarely through broken skin or the mucous membranes (as from breathing rabid-bat-contaminated air in a cave). If you are bitten, wash the wound at once with large amounts of soap and water—this is important! Retain the animal, alive if possible, for rabies quarantine. Contact local health authorities to get rabies immunization. This is essential, as rabies is a fatal disease which can be prevented by prompt treatment.

Schistosomiasis This is a parasitic worm, passed by a freshwater snail larva which can penetrate unbroken human skin. You get it by wading or swimming in fresh water where the snails are, such as in stagnant pools, streams, or cenotes. Two or 3 weeks after exposure, there's fever, lack of appetite, weight loss, abdominal pain, weakness, headaches, joint and muscle pain, diarrhea, nausea, and coughing. Six to 8 weeks after infection, the microscopic snail eggs can be found in the stools. Once diagnosed (after a very unpleasant month or two), treatment is fast, safe, effective, and cheap. If you think you've accidentally been exposed to schistosomiasis-infected water, rub yourself vigorously with a towel, and/or spread rubbing alcohol on the exposed skin.

Typhoid Fever You can protect yourself by having a typhoid vaccination (or booster, as needed), but protection is not total; you can still get this very serious disease from contaminated food and water. Symptoms are similar to those for traveler's diarrhea, but much worse. If you get typhoid fever, you'll need close attention by a doctor, perhaps hospitalization for a short period.

Typhus Fever You should see a doctor for treatment of this disease, which is spread by lice. Risk is very low.

INSURANCE

HEALTH/ACCIDENT/LOSS

It can happen anywhere in the world—you discover you've lost your wallet, your passport, your airline ticket, and your tourist permit. Whether the loss is from your negligence or by theft, you'll want to report it. Always keep a photocopy of these documents in your luggage—it makes replacing them easier. To be reimbursed for insured items once you return, you'll need to report the loss to the Mexican police and get a written report. If you don't speak Spanish, take along someone who does. The report-making involves much typewriter clacking and question answering.

If you lose official documents, you'll need to contact both Mexican and U.S. officials in Mexico before you leave the country. See "Information, Entry Requirements, and Money," above, specifically the section on "Documents."

Before leaving home ask your insurance agent what health coverage is in force while you are out of the country. Several credit-card companies include accident and trip-cancellation insurance coverage as a benefit for charging airline tickets on a charge card.

For additional coverage you may want to consider policies from the following companies:

Health Care Abroad, 243 Church Street NW, Vienna, VA 22180 (tel. 703/255-9800, or toll free 800/237-6616), for trips lasting 10 to 90 days. Coverage includes accident and sickness, and insurance against luggage loss and trip cancellation can be added.

Access America, Inc., 600 Third Avenue, New York, NY 10163 (tel. 212/490-5345, or toll free 800/851-2800) also offers medical and accident insurance as well as coverage for luggage loss and trip cancellation.

EMERGENCY EVACUATION

For extreme medical emergencies there's a service from the United States that will fly people to American hospitals: Air-Evac, 24-hour air ambulance. Call collect 24 hours, 713/880-9767 in Houston, 619/278-3822 in San Diego, 305/772-0003 in Miami.

4. WHAT TO PACK

CLOTHING   High-elevation cities such as Mazamitla and Tapalpa, both in the mountains of Jalisco, require warm clothing. For the coastal areas, however, bring lightweight cottons. The temperatures aren't high, usually less than 90°F, but the humidity often reaches 100%. In summer, generally speaking, throughout Mexico it rains almost every afternoon or evening between May and October—so take rain gear. An easily packable rain poncho is most handy, since it fits in a purse or backpack and is ready for use in an instant. Guadalajara and other nonresort cities and villages tend to be conservative in dress, so save shorts and halter tops for seaside resorts. For

44 • PLANNING A TRIP TO THE REGION

dining out in a nice restaurant in conservative Guadalajara, a jacket and tie for men and nice dress or suit for women is appropriate. In Puerto Vallarta nice restaurants are more casual even when they are expensive. A cool dress for women and slacks and shirt for men will do fine.

GADGETS First-class hotels generally provide washcloths, but if you're staying in moderately priced or budget hotels, bring your own, or better yet a sponge (which dries quickly)—you'll rarely find washcloths in a budget-category hotel room. A bathtub plug (one of those big round ones for all sizes) is a help since fitted plugs are frequently missing, or don't work even in expensive hotels. Blow-up (inflatable) hangers and a stretch clothesline are handy. I never leave home without a luggage cart, which saves much effort and money, and is especially useful in small towns where there are no porters at bus stations. Buy a sturdy one with at least 4-inch wheels that can take the beating of cobblestone streets, stairs, and curbs. A heat-immersion coil, plastic cup, and spoon are handy for preparing coffee, tea, and instant soup. For power failures, a small flashlight is a help. A combo pocketknife (for peeling fruit) with screwdriver (for fixing cameras and eyeglasses), bottle opener, and corkscrew is a must.

5. TIPS FOR THE DISABLED, SENIORS, SINGLES, FAMILIES & STUDENTS

FOR THE DISABLED

Travelers whose disability involves the legs, those who are unable to walk, or who are in wheelchairs or on crutches discover quickly that Mexico is one giant obstacle course. Beginning at the airport on arrival you may encounter steep stairs before finding a well-hidden elevator or escalator—if one exists. Airlines will often arrange wheelchair assistance for passengers to the baggage area. Porters are generally available to help with luggage at airports and large bus stations and once you've cleared baggage claim. Escalators (and there aren't many in the country) are often not operating. The Guadalajara airport has an up escalator to the restaurant, but no down escalator or elevator. Few handicapped-equipped rest rooms exist, or when one is available, access to it may be via a narrow passage that won't accommodate a wheelchair or someone on crutches. Many five-star and Gran Turismo hotels (the most expensive) now have rooms with handicapped bathrooms and handicap access to the hotel. For those traveling on a budget, stick with one-story hotels, or those with elevators. Even so, there will probably still be step obstacles somewhere. Stairs without handrails abound in Mexico. Intracity bus drivers generally don't bother with the courtesy step upon boarding or disembarking. On city buses the distance between the street and the bus can require considerable force to board. Generally speaking, no matter where you are, someone will lend a hand, although you may have to ask for it.

FOR SENIORS

HAZARDS Handrails are often missing. Unmarked or unguarded holes in sidewalks countrywide present problems for all visitors.

RETIRING Mexico is a popular country for retirees, although income doesn't go nearly as far as it once did. Successful transplants do several things before venturing south permanently: Stay for several weeks in any place under consideration. Rent before buying. Check on the availability and quality of health care, banking, transportation, and rental costs. How much it costs to live depends on your life-style and where you choose to live. Car upkeep and insurance, clothing and health costs are important variables to consider.

The Mexican government requires foreign residents to prove a specific amount of income before permanent residence is granted, but you can visit for 6 months on a tourist visa and renew it every 6 months without committing to a "legal" status. Mexican health care is surprisingly inexpensive. You can save money by living on the local economy: Buy food at the local market, not imported items from specialty stores; use local transportation and save the car for long-distance trips. Among the most popular places for retirement in Mexico or long-term stays are Guadalajara, Lake Chapala, Ajijic, and Puerto Vallarta, all in the state of Jalisco, and Manzanillo, Colima, where U.S. condo owners abound. The following newsletters are written to inform the prospective retiree about Mexico:

AIM, Apdo. Postal 31-70, Guadalajara, Jal. 45050, Mexico, is a well-written, plain talking, and very informative newsletter on retirement in Mexico. Recent issues reported on retirement background and considerations for Lake Chapala, Aguascalientes, Alamos, Zacatecas, west coast beaches, Acapulco, and San Miguel de Allende. It costs $16 to the U.S. and $19 to Canada. Back issues are three for $5.

Retiring in Mexico, Apdo. Postal 5-409, Guadalajara, Jal. (tel. 36/21-2348 or 47-9924), comes in three editions—a large January edition and smaller spring and fall supplements, all for $12. Each newsletter is packed with useful information about retiring in Guadalajara. It's written by Fran and Judy Furton who also sell other packets of information as well as host an open house in their home every Tuesday for $12.

Sanborn Tours, 1007 Main Street, Bastrop, TX 78602 (tel. toll free 800/531-5440) offers a "Retire in Mexico" Guadalajara orientation tour.

FOR SINGLE TRAVELERS

Mexico may be the land for romantic honeymoons, but it's also a great place to travel on your own without really being or feeling alone. Although combined single and double rates is a slow-growing trend in Mexico, most of the moderately priced and budget hotels mentioned in this book offer singles at cheaper rates. There's so much to see and do that being bored needn't be a problem. Mexicans are very friendly and it's easy to meet other foreigners and take up with them for a day or two or meal along the way if you desire. Certain cities like Acapulco, Manzanillo, and Huatulco have such a preponderance of twosomes that single travelers there may feel as though an appendage is missing. On the other hand, singles can feel quite comfortable in Puerto Vallarta and San Blas. In those places you'll find a good combination of beachlife, nightlife, and tranquillity, whichever is your pleasure. Guadalajara, too, is easy on the single traveler. If you don't like the idea of traveling alone, you might try **Travel Companion Exchange,** P.O. Box 833, Amityville, NY 11701 (tel. 516/454-0880; fax 516/454-0170), which brings prospective travelers together. Members complete a profile, then place an anonymous listing of their travel interests in the newsletter.

Prospective traveling companions then make contact through the exchange. Membership costs $36 to $66 for 6 months.

FOR WOMEN

As a frequent female traveler to Mexico, most of it alone, I can tell you firsthand that I feel safer traveling in Mexico than in the U.S. And no, I'm not afraid. That answers the first two questions most people ask me. Mexicans are a very warm and welcoming people and I'm not afraid to be friendly wherever I go. But I use the same common-sense precautions I use traveling anywhere else in the world: I'm alert to what's going on around me.

Mexicans in general, and men in particular, are nosy about single travelers, especially women. They want to know with whom you're traveling, whether you're married or have a boyfriend, and how many children you have. My advice to anyone exchanging these details with taxi drivers or other people whose paths you'll never cross again or with whom you don't want to become friendly, is to make up a set of answers regardless of the truth: I'm married, traveling with friends, and I have three children. Being divorced may send out a wrong message about availability or imagined degree of loneliness. Drunks are a particular nuisance to the lone female traveler; even when they can hardly walk they still muster up a "staggering" amount of machismo to speak, stumble along with you, or become a pest. Don't try to be polite, just leave or duck into a public place.

Generally women alone will feel comfortable going to a hotel lobby bar, but are asking for trouble or a hassle going into a pulquería or cantina. In restaurants, as a general rule, single women are offered the worst table and service. You'll have to be vocal about your preference and insist on service. Service may improve (but don't count on it) if you dine at off-peak hours. Tip well if you plan to return. Don't tip at all if service is bad.

And finally, remember, Mexican men learn charm early. The chase is as important as the conquest (maybe more so). Despite whatever charms *you* may possess, think twice before taking personally or seriously all the adoring, admiring words you'll hear.

FOR MEN

I'm not sure why, perhaps because it's a challenge or because non-Spanish-speaking, foreign men appear innocent or weak, but they seem to be special targets for scams and pickpockets. So if you fit this description, whether traveling alone or in a pair, exercise special vigilance.

FOR FAMILIES

Mexico has a high birthrate, so small children make up a large part of the population. Mexicans travel extensively with their families, so your child will feel very welcome. Hotels will often arrange for a baby-sitter. Hotels in the mid- to upper range have small playgrounds for children and hire caretakers on weekends to oversee them and the children's pool so the parents can relax. Few budget hotels offer these amenities.

Before leaving for Mexico, you should check with your doctor and get advice on medicines to combat diarrhea and other ailments. Bring a supply, just to be sure. Disposable diapers are made and sold in Mexico (one popular brand is Kleen Bebé). The price is about the same as at home, but the quality is lower. Also, Gerber's baby foods are sold in many stores. Dry cereals, powdered formulas, baby bottles, and purified water are all easily available in midsize to large cities.

Cribs, however, may present a problem. Except for the largest and most luxurious hotels, few Mexican hotels provide cribs.

Many of the hotels we mention, even in noncoastal regions, have swimming pools, which can be dessert at the end of a day traveling with a child who has had it with sightseeing.

FOR STUDENTS

Students traveling on a budget may want to contact the student headquarters in the various cities that can supply information on student hostels. Maps and local tourist information are also available. The office in Mexico City is at Hamburgo 273 (tel. 5/514-4213); in Guadalajara, it's Terranova 1220 (tel. 36/42-0025); and in Monterrey, at Padre Mier Poniente 665 (tel. 83/44-9588).

6. ALTERNATIVE/ADVENTURE TRAVEL

EDUCATIONAL/STUDY TRAVEL
SPANISH LESSONS

A dozen towns south of the border are famous for their Spanish-language programs. Mexican National Tourism offices (see "Information, Entry Requirements, and Money," above) may have information about schools. Go anytime of year—you needn't really wait for a "semester" or course year to start. It's best to begin on a Monday, however.

Don't expect the best and latest in terms of language texts and materials. Many are well out-of-date. Teachers tend to be underpaid and perhaps undertrained, but very friendly and extremely patient. Seek out Mexican students of English and exchange conversation with them. This is how the best friendships are made.

Try living with a Mexican family. Pay in advance for only a week or 10 days, and if things are going well, continue. If your "family stay" ends up being little more than a room rental, feel free to go elsewhere. Family stays are not particularly cheap, by the way, so you should get your money's worth in terms of interaction and language practice.

The National Registration Center for Studies Abroad (NRCSA), 823 North 2nd Street, Milwaukee, WI 53203 (tel. 414/278-0631), has a catalog ($5) of schools in Mexico. They will register you at the school of your choice, arrange for room and board with a Mexican family, and make your airline reservations, all for no extra fee. Contact them and ask for a (free) copy of their newsletter.

HOMESTAYS Spanish-language schools frequently provide lists of families who offer rooms to students. Often the experience is just like being one of the family.

ADVENTURE/WILDERNESS TRAVEL

Besides a lack of funds, Mexico is behind in its awareness and commitment to tourists' interest in ecology-oriented adventure and wilderness travel. As a result, most

48 • PLANNING A TRIP TO THE REGION

of the national parks and nature reserves are understaffed and/or not staffed by knowledgeable persons. Most companies offering that kind of travel are U.S. operated and trips are specialist-led. The following companies offer a variety of off-the-beaten-path travel experiences.

Victor Emanuel Tours, P.O. Box 33008, Austin, TX 78764 (tel. toll free 800/328-8368 in the U.S.), is an established leader in birding and natural history tours.

Toucan Adventure Tours, 3135 East 4th Street, Long Beach, CA 90814 (tel. 213/438-6293; fax 213/438-6228), organizes short Mexico hotel tours and 2-week overland camping tours of Mexico and Guatemala by 15-passenger van.

Wings, Inc., P.O. Box 31930, Tucson, AZ 85751 (tel. 602/749-1967), has a wide assortment of trips including birding in Oaxaca, Chiapas, Colima, and Jalisco.

7. SHOPPING

The charm of Mexico is no better expressed than in arts and crafts. Hardly a tourist will leave this country without having bought at least one of these handcrafted items. Mexico is famous for pottery, textiles, ceramics, baskets, and onyx and silver jewelry, to mention only a few.

This guide is designed to help the traveler know some of the crafts and the regions where they can be found. Many of these items can be found in markets and shops in both Guadalajara, Puerto Vallarta, and to a lesser extent in Manzanillo and around Lake Chapala. Jalisco's craft villages include Tonala and Tlaquepaque near Guadalajara, Ajijic and Jocotepec near Lake Chapala, and Tapalpa in the mountains south of Lake Chapala. Colima makes furniture and reproductions of pre-Hispanic pottery. I have listed the cities or villages where the item is sold (and often crafted), the first place listed being the best place to buy. The larger cities, especially Guadalajara, Puerto Vallarta, and Mexico City will have many crafts from other regions in addition to crafts from Jalisco and Colima. Tables of metric conversions and clothing sizes are in the Appendix. I would add that it is very helpful to visit a government fixed-price shop before attempting to bargain. There are two government-operated Casas de Artesanías in Guadalajara. This will give you an idea of the cost versus quality of the various crafts. Following are the various crafts, in alphabetical order.

BASKETS Woven of reed or straw—Oaxaca, Copper Canyon, Toluca, Yucatán, Puebla, Mexico City.

BLANKETS Tapalpa, Jalisco, as well as Saltillo, Toluca, Santa Ana Chiautempan, north of Puebla, Oaxaca, and Mitla (made of soft wool with some synthetic dyes; they use a lot of bird and geometric motifs). Make sure that the blanket you pick out is in fact the one you take since often the "same" blanket in the wrapper is not the same.

CANTERA STONE Guadalajara and Zacatecas.

EQUIPALE FURNITURE Tlaquepaque and Tonalá in Jalisco state and also Nayarit state.

GLASS Hand-blown and molded—Tlaquepaque, Jalisco, and also Monterrey and Mexico City.

SHOPPING • 49

GUITARS Made in Paracho, 25 miles north of Uruapan in the state of Michoacán on Highway 37 not far from the Jalisco state line.

HAMMOCKS AND MOSQUITO NETTING Mérida, Campeche, Mazatlán.

HATS Mérida (Panama), made of sisal from the maguey cactus; finest-quality weaving; easy to pack and wash. Also San Cristóbal de las Casas, Chiapas.

HUARACHES Leather sandals often with rubber-tire soles—abundant in Guadalajara's Mercado Libertad and San Blas.

HUIPILS Handwoven, embroidered, or brocaded overblouses indigenous to almost all Mexican states but especially evident in Yucatán, Chiapas, Oaxaca, Puebla, Guerrero, and Veracruz. Most of the better huipils are in fact used ones that have been bought from the village women. Huipils can be distinguished by villages; look around before buying; you'll be amazed at the variety.

LACQUER GOODS Olinala, Guerrero, northeast of Acapulco, is known for ornate lacquered chests and other lacquered decorative and furniture items. Pátzcuaro and Uruapan, in Michoacán state, are also known for gold-leafed lacquered trays.

LEATHER GOODS Guadalajara, Monterrey, Saltillo, León, Mexico City, San Cristóbal de las Casas, and Oaxaca.

MASKS Wherever there is locally observed regional dancing you'll find maskmakers. The tradition is especially strong in the states of Guerrero, Chiapas, Puebla, Oaxaca, and Michoacán.

ONYX Puebla (where onyx is carved), Querétaro, Matehuala, Mexico City.

POTTERY Tlaquepaque and Tonalá and whimsical daily-life figures in Santa Cruz de las Huertas near Tonalá, all in the state of Jalisco. Reproductions of Colima pottery in Colima City. Also Oaxaca, Puebla, Michoacán, Coyotepec, Izúcar de Matamoras, Veracruz, Copper Canyon, Dolores Hidalgo, and Guanajuato.

REBOZOS Sold in most markets. Woman's or man's rectangular woven cloth to be worn around the shoulders, similar to a shawl—Oaxaca, Mitla, San Cristóbal de las Casas, Mexico City, and Pátzcuaro. Rebozos are generally made of wool or a blend of wool and cotton and sometimes silk, but synthetic fibers are creeping in, so check the material carefully before buying. Also compare the weave from different cloths since the fineness of the weave is proportional to the cost.

SERAPES Heavy woolen or cotton blankets with a slit for the head, to be worn as a poncho—Tapalpa, Jalisco (3 hours south of Guadalajara or the same distance north of Manzanillo), Santa Ana Chiautempan (30 miles north of Puebla near Tlaxcala), San Luis Potosí, Santa María del Río (25 miles south of San Luis Potosí), Chiconcoac (1 hour's drive northeast from Mexico City, near Texcoco), Saltillo, Toluca, Mexico City.

SILVER Taxco, Mexico City, Zacatecas, and Guadalajara. Sterling silver is indicated by "925" on the silver, which certifies that there are 925 grams of pure silver per kilogram, or that the silver is 92.5% pure. In Mexico they also use a spread-eagle hallmark to indicate sterling. Look for these marks or otherwise you may be paying a high price for an inferior quality that is mostly nickel, or even silver plate called alpaca.

STONES Chalcedony, turquoise, lapis lazuli, amethyst—Querétaro, San Miguel del Allende, Durango, Saltillo, San Luis Potosí. Opals are sold in the village of Margarita off Highway 15 west of Tequila. The cost of turquoise and silver is computed by weight, so many pesos per carat.

SWEATERS Beautifully made and designed sweaters using natural dyes are a cottage industry in Tapalpa, Jalisco.

TEXTILES Oaxaca, Chiapas, Santa Ana near Puebla, Guerrero, and Nayarit are known for their excellent weaving, each culturally distinct and different. Ajijic and Jocotepec, both near Lake Chapala in Jalisco state, are weaving villages.

TORTOISE SHELL It's illegal to buy in Mexico and to bring into the U.S.

8. GETTING THERE & DEPARTING

From the U.S., how you choose to get to Mexico will depend on the amount of time and money you have. Air travel is generally quicker. Train travel can be less harried, and bus travel can be inexpensive, long, and variable in comfort.

BY PLANE

The airline situation is changing rapidly with many new regional carriers offering scheduled service to areas previously not served or underserved. Besides regularly scheduled service, charter service direct from U.S. cities to resorts is making Mexico much more accessible.

The main airlines operating direct or nonstop flights from the U.S. to points in Mexico with U.S. toll-free 800 numbers are: **Aero California** (tel. 800/237-6225), **Aeromexico** (tel. 800/237-6639), **Air France** (tel. 800/237-2747), **Alaska Airlines** (tel. 800/426-0333), **American** (tel. 800/433-7300), **Continental** (tel. 800/231-0856), **Delta** (tel. 800/221-1212), **Lacsa** (tel. 800/225-2272), **Lufthansa** (tel. 800/645-3880), **Mexicana** (tel. 800/531-7921), **Northwest** (tel. 800/225-2525), and **United** (tel. 800/241-6522). **Southwest Airlines** serves the U.S. border (tel. 800/531-5601).

The main departure points for U.S. airlines are Chicago, Dallas/Fort Worth, Denver, Houston, Los Angeles, Miami, New Orleans, New York, Orlando, Philadelphia, Raleigh/Durham, San Antonio, San Francisco, Seattle, Toronto, Tucson, and Washington, D.C.

Regional airlines operating within Mexico, with appropriate telephone numbers, are as follows: **Aero Cancún** (see Mexicana); **Aero Caribe** (see Mexicana); **Aero Leo López,** headquartered in El Paso (tel. 915/778-1022; fax 779-3534); **Aerolitoral** (see Aeromexico); **Aeromar** (tel. toll free 800/950-0747, or see Mexicana); **Aero Monterrey** (see Mexicana); **Aero Morelos,** headquartered in Cuernavaca (tel. 73/17-5588; fax 17-2320); **Aerovias Oaxaqueñas,** based in

Oaxaca (tel. 951/6-3824); **Noroeste** in Phoenix (tel. 602/275-7950) or Hermosillo (headquarters; tel. 621/7-5007). An airline called **Aero Jalisco** is in the talking stages and if organized it will fly from U.S. cities to points within Jalisco state (Guadalajara, Puerto Vallarta, etc.)

Bargain hunters rejoice! Excursion and package plans proliferate, especially in the off-season. A good travel agent will be able to give you all the latest schedules, details, and prices for both airlines, but the changes in regional airlines is ongoing, so you may have to sleuth those for yourself. The least expensive airline prices are midweek, in the off-season (after Easter to December 15). Sample off-season, midweek, round-trip fares are as follows: A round-trip excursion fare from New York to Guadalajara is $370; to Puerto Vallarta, $384; and Manzanillo, $556. From Los Angeles to Guadalajara a typical fare runs from $283; to Puerto Vallarta, $296; and Manzanillo, $345. From Denver, a round-trip fare to Guadalajara is $361; to Puerto Vallarta, $220; and to Manzanillo, $439. But never pay these prices without first pricing packages that include air and hotel.

CHARTERS

Charter service is growing and usually is sold as a package combination of air and hotel. Charter airlines, however, may sell air only, without hotel. **Taesa Airline**, through Universal Destinations in Houston, has charters from San Antonio to Puerto Vallarta and Guadalajara and may in the future inaugurate charters from Minneapolis and New York to Puerto Vallarta. **Latur** has charters from New York to Puerto Vallarta and Acapulco.

Tour companies operating charters include: Club America Vacations, Asti Tours, Apple Vacations, Friendly Holidays, Gogo Tours, and Mexico Tourism Consultants (MTC).

BY TRAIN

For getting to the border by train, call Amtrak (tel. toll free 800/872-7245 in the U.S.) for fares, information, and reservations.

BY BUS

Greyhound-Trailways, or its affiliates, offers service from the U.S. to the border, where passengers disembark, cross the border, and buy a ticket for travel into the interior of Mexico. At many border crossings there are scheduled buses from the U.S. bus station to the Mexican bus station.

BY CAR

Driving is certainly not the cheapest way to get to Mexico, but it is the best way to see the country.

Using your own car in Mexico, you will find that Mexican fuel prices, though a little lower than those in the U.S. and Canada, are in reality not that much of a bargain because the fuel tends to be of much lower octane. Remember, it's not just how much a gallon of gas costs, it's how far you can go that's important; and 82-octane Mexican Nova doesn't get you as far as 91-octane American regular.

Insurance costs are high (see below). Parking is a problem in the cities. Unless you have a full carload, the bus and train come out cheaper per person, and with public transport you don't have to undertake the tedious amount of driving needed to see a country this big.

If you want to drive to the Mexican border, but not into Mexico, border-area chambers of commerce or convention and visitors bureaus can supply names of secured parking lots. You can leave your car there while you see the country by rail, bus, or plane.

CAR PAPERS

You will have to provide proof that you own the car. Registration papers are sufficient for this. If the car ownership is in two names, then bring a notarized letter from the other owner giving permission to drive the car to Mexico. A change in procedures now simplifies getting the permit to drive a car into Mexico. Instead of a separate car permit attached to your tourist permit, there is now a stamp on the tourist permit.

The car papers will be issued for the same length of time as your tourist permit was issued for. It's a very good idea to greatly overestimate the time you'll spend in Mexico when applying for your permit, so that if something unforeseen happens and you have to (or want to) stay longer, you don't have to go through the long hassle of getting your papers renewed. The maximum term for tourist permit and temporary vehicle importation permit is 6 months.

You must carry your vehicle permit and tourist permit in the car at all times. Remember, too, that the driver of the car will not be allowed to leave the country without the car (even if it's wrecked or stolen) unless he or she satisfies Customs that the import duty will be paid. In an emergency, if the driver of the car must leave the country without the car, the car must be put under Customs seal at the airport and have the driver's tourist permit stamped to that effect. There may be storage fees.

MEXICAN AUTO INSURANCE

You must purchase Mexican insurance, as U.S. or Canadian insurance is not valid in Mexico, and any party involved in an accident who has no insurance (or ready proof of it) is automatically sent to jail and the car is impounded until all claims are settled. This is true even if you just drive across the border to spend the day; and it may be true even if you are injured.

Those with insurance are assumed to be good for claims and are released. The agency where you purchase your Mexican insurance will show you a full table of current rates and will recommend the coverage it thinks adequate. The policies are written along lines similar to those north of the border. It's best to overestimate the amount of time you plan to be in Mexico, because if you stay longer, it's a real runaround to get your policy term lengthened in Mexico. Any part of the term unused will be prorated and that part of your premium refunded to you in cash at the office on the American side on return, or by mail to your home. Be sure the policy you buy will pay for repairs in either the U.S. or Mexico and that it will pay out in dollars, not pesos.

One of the best insurance companies for south of the border travel is **Sanborn's**

Mexico Insurance, with offices at all of the border crossings in the U.S. I never drive across the border without Sanborn's insurance. It costs the same as the competition, and you get a **Travelog** that's almost like a mile-by-mile guide along your proposed route. Information occasionally gets a bit dated, but for the most part it's like having a knowledgeable friend in the car telling you how to get in and out of town, where to buy gas (and which stations to avoid), highway conditions, and scams. It's especially helpful in remote places. Most of Sanborn's border offices are open Monday through Friday, and a few are staffed on Saturday and Sunday. You can purchase your auto liability and collision coverage by phone in advance and have it waiting at a 24-hour location if you are crossing when their office is closed. As for costs, a car with a value of $10,000 costs $119 to insure for 2 weeks, or $61 for 1 week. For information contact Sanborn's Mexico Insurance, P.O. Box 310, Dept. FR, 2009 South 10th, McAllen, TX 78502 (tel. 512/686-0711; fax 512/686-0732). AAA auto club also sells insurance.

YOUR CAR

Know the condition of your car before you cross the border. Parts made in Mexico may be inferior, but service generally is quite good and relatively inexpensive. Your cooling system should be in good condition, with the proper mixture of coolant and water. Don't risk disaster with an old radiator hose, and carry a spare fan belt. In summer for long drives, an air conditioner is not a luxury, but a necessity. You might want a spare belt for this, too, just in case. Mexican gasoline is not up to high standards, even the best of it, so it's good to be sure your car is in tune to handle it.

Remember that Mexico is a big country, and that you may put several thousand miles on your tires before you return home—can your tires last a few thousand miles on Mexican roads? Take simple tools along if you're handy with them, also a flashlight or spotlight, a cloth to wipe the windshield, toilet paper, and a tire gauge. Mexican filling stations generally have air to fill tires, but no gauge to check the pressure. If you don't carry your own gauge you'll have to find a tire repair shop to get your tires checked, then return to the gas station for air. When driving I always bring along a combination gauge/air compressor sold at U.S. automotive stores. It plugs into the car cigarette lighter, making it a simple procedure to check the tires every morning and pump them up at the same time.

Not that many Mexican cars comply, but Mexican law requires that every car have **seat belts** and a **fire extinguisher.** Be prepared.

CROSSING THE BORDER

After you cross the border into Mexico from the U.S., you'll stop to get your tourist/car permit (now all in one), and a tourist decal will be affixed to a rear window. After that you'll come to a Mexican Customs post somewhere between 12 and 16 miles down the road. In the past every motorist had to stop and present travel documents. Now there is a new system that stops some motorists (chosen at random) for inspection. If the light is green go on through. If it's red, stop for inspection. In the Baja peninsula the procedures may differ slightly—first you get your tourist permit, then on down the road you stop for the car permit. Theoretically, you should not be charged for your tourist permit, auto permit, and inspection, but the uniformed officer may try to extract a bribe from you (see "Bribes," above).

A last word: When you cross back into the U.S. after an extended trip in Mexico, the American Customs officials may inspect every nook and cranny of your car, your bags, even your person. They're looking for drugs, which includes illegal diet pills.

BY SHIP

Numerous cruise lines serve Mexico. Taking one, especially if it's a first time to Mexico, is one way to canvas beach resorts for a return trip. But keep in mind that a brief port call barely skims the surface. Possible trips include: from California down to the Baja peninsula (including specialized whale-watching trips), and to ports of call down the Pacific coast including Ixtapa/Zihuatanejo, Puerto Vallarta, Manzanillo, and Acapulco. Among the many cruise lines with Pacific coast itineraries is **Princess Cruises,** 10100 Santa Monica Boulevard, Los Angeles, CA 90067 (tel. toll free 800/344-2626 in the U.S.). Several cruise-tour specialists arrange substantial discounts on unsold cabins at the last minute. One such company is **The Cruise Line, Inc.,** 260 NE 17th Terrace, Suite 201, Miami, FL 33132 (tel. toll free 1-800/777-0707 or 327-3021 in the U.S.). **AAA** members receive cruise discounts on many different lines.

PACKAGE TOURS

Package tours offer some of the best values to the coastal resorts especially during high season from December until after Easter. Off-season packages can be real bargains. But to know for sure if the package is a cost saver you must price the package yourself by calling the airline for round-trip flight costs, and the hotel for rates. Add in the cost of transfers to and from the airport (which packages usually include) and see if it's a deal. Packages are usually per person, and single travelers pay extra. In the high season a package may be the only way of getting there because wholesalers have blocked airline seats. The airline may be completely booked when you call, but a travel agent can get you there through a package purchase. The cheapest package rates will be those in hotels in the lower range, always without as many amenities or as beautiful rooms as more costly hotels. But you can go to the public areas and beaches of any other hotel and spend the day without being a guest there. Use this book to read up on the hotels and make your selection. Travel agents, airlines, and hotels have information on specific packages.

9. GETTING AROUND

BY PLANE

U.S. and international airlines can fly to and from Mexico letting off and picking up passengers. But to fly from point to point within the country you'll rely on Mexican airlines. Mexico has two privately owned, large national carriers, **Mexicana** and **Aeromexico,** which fly from the U.S. to Mexico as well as within the country, and several up-and-coming regional carriers. Mexicana is Latin America's largest air carrier, dating back to 1921, and has the most extensive service within the country. Several of the new regional carriers are operated by, or can be booked through, Mexicana **(Aero Caribe, Aero Cozumel, Aeromar,** and **Aeromonterrey)** and

Aeromexico **(Aerolitoral)**. The regional carriers are expensive, but they go to places that were once difficult to reach. Look for this trend to continue. In each of the sections in this book, I've mentioned the regional carriers and the major ones with all pertinent telephone numbers.

Because major airlines can book some regional carriers, read your ticket carefully to see if a connecting flight is on one of these smaller carriers since they may leave from a different airport or check-in at a different counter.

AIRPORT TAXES

Mexico charges an **airport tax** on **all departures.** Passengers leaving the country on an **international departure** pay $12 in cash—dollars or the peso equivalent—to get out of the country. Each **domestic departure** you make within Mexico costs around $5 unless you are on a connecting flight and already paid at the start of the flight—you shouldn't be charged again if you have to change planes for a connecting flight.

RECONFIRMING FLIGHTS

Although airlines in Mexico say it is not necessary to reconfirm a flight, I always do. On several occasions I have arrived to check in with a valid ticket only to discover my reservation had been canceled. Now I leave nothing to chance. Also be aware that airlines routinely overbook. To avoid getting bumped, check-in for an international flight the required 1½ hours in advance of travel. That will put you near the head of the line.

BY TRAIN

Train travel is safer and more comfortable than going by bus. However, it is slower, costs more, and schedules are likely to be less convenient. I don't recommend traveling segunda (second class) anywhere, as it is usually hot, overcrowded, dingy, and unpleasant. Primera (first class) can be the same way unless you are sure to ask for **Primera Especial (first-class reserved seat)** a day or so in advance, if possible. In Primera Especial there is rarely the crowding and disorder of other classes. The top-of-the-line accommodations on trains, cheaper than flying but more expensive than the bus, are Pullman compartments (alcoba or camarín) for overnight travel.

Mexico has added first-class service to a number of trains under a general title of **Servicio Estrella (Star Service).** *Important Note:* Although this service is described here, and I've given specific information by town, Estrella Service is undergoing drastic changes this year, and the timetables could be altered considerably and service interrupted for a time. Please double-check before planning an itinerary around train travel. Estrella trains are more expensive but they are superior to regular trains in comfort; the price difference between Estrella and regular trains is small compared to what you get. At least one light snack is usually served at your seat, airline style, and is included in the price of the ticket. There may also be a dining car.

To reserve a place in an Estrella chair car, be sure to specify Primera Especial and not simply Primera, which may also be offered. Service and cleanliness may vary dramatically on the Estrella trains, but generally I've found them to be a delightful experience. This qualified statement means that the cars will be clean at the start of the journey, but little may be done en route to keep them that way. Trash may accumulate, toilet paper vanishes, the water cooler runs dry or has no paper cups, and the temperature may vary between freezing and sweltering. Conductors range from solicitous to totally indifferent. Considering the overall comfort though, they are a good value. Baggage is carried on and stored over your seat.

A **sleeping compartment** comfortable enough for one person, called a *camarín*, and an *alcoba* for two, with two beds, are available on overnight journeys on many trains. These convert to private sitting rooms during the day. Cramming more people than this in either size compartment is very uncomfortable, and not recommended even though tickets are sold for more than one or two in each.

There are two major train hubs—Mexico City and Guadalajara. If you plan to get on and off before your final destination, you must tell the agent your exact on-off schedule at the time of your ticket purchase, and there's usually a surcharge for the stops. Estrella trains are often filled, especially on holidays or with tour groups. Here is a summary of the major rail connections.

MEXICO CITY HUB

Regiomontaño: Runs between Nuevo Laredo at the Texas border through Monterrey and Saltillo to Mexico City.

El Constitucionalista: From Mexico City north and west to Querétaro, Irapuato, and Guanajuato.

El Tapatío: Mexico City to Guadalajara overnight.

El Oaxaqueño: Suspended but may be reinstituted—overnight between Mexico City and Oaxaca.

El Jarocho: Mexico City overnight to Veracruz passing Fortín de las Flores, Orizaba, and Córdoba en route.

El Purepecha: Suspended but may be reinstituted—overnight between Mexico City and Morelia, Pátzcuaro, and Uruapan.

El San Marqueño-Zacatecano: Northward between Mexico City through Irapuato, León, Lagos de Moreno, Aguascalientes, Zacatecas, and Juárez.

GUADALAJARA HUB

El Colimense: Suspended but may be reinstituted—from Guadalajara through Colima to Manzanillo on the Pacific coast.

El Tren del Pacífico: From Guadalajara along the Pacific coast to a dozen cities including Tepic, Mazatlán, Culiacán, Obregón, Hermosillo, Nogales, Puerto Peñasco, and Mexicali at the California border.

El Sinaloense: From Guadalajara to Tepic, Mazatlán, Culiacán, and Los Mochis.

OTHER TRAINS

El Nuevo Chihuahua-Pacífico: Begins at both Los Mochis and Chihuahua City and passes through Mexico's beautiful Copper Canyon.

El Rapido de la Frontera: From Chihuahua to Ciudad Juárez at the Texas border.

If you purchase your ticket at the train station, do it as soon as your plans are firm. In cities served by Estrella trains, you may find travel agents that will arrange your tickets, but they usually charge a service fee of up to 25% of the price of the ticket.

For advance planning using Estrella trains, your most secure bet is **Mexico by Rail,** Box 3508, Laredo, TX 78044, or call toll free 800/228-3225 in the U.S. Given 15 days' notice they will prepurchase your Estrella service train ticket and mail it to you. For holiday travel, make plans 45 days ahead. If you leave from Nuevo Laredo, the company will arrange secured parking, a prestamped tourist card, and transfers across the border. They charge a percentage on top of the regular price of the train ticket.

To contact the railroad directly for fares and schedule information in Mexico City, phone 5/547-6593, 547-1097, or 547-1084.

When deciding whether to use Mexico by Rail or another agent, consider the cost of going to the train station yourself and the uncertainty of space if you wait until you get there to reserve a seat. Although they seldom reply to mail, for the latest train itinerary or other questions, you can try writing well in advance to Commercial Passenger Department, National Railways of Mexico, Buenavista Grand Central Station, Mexico, D. F. 06358, or call 5/547-8972. For the Pacific Railroad Company write Tolsa 336, Guadalajara, Jal. Both companies have special personnel and divisions to handle group train travel. With enough lead time, they'll even put on extra cars.

TRAVEL TIME ON TRAINS

From Mexicali, the fast train takes 30 hours to Guadalajara, 45 to Mexico City. Pacific coast trains are notorious for running as much as 24 hours behind time. In general though, they take off on time.

BY BUS

Except for the Baja and Yucatán peninsulas, where bus service is not well developed, buses are frequent, readily accessible, and can get you to almost anywhere you want to go. More than a dozen Mexican companies operate large air-conditioned Greyhound-type buses between most cities. The cost is very reasonable, working out to around $1 an hour. Modern buses have replaced most of the legendary "village buses" that growled and wheezed when they were overloaded, which was often. Today it's best to buy your reserved-seat ticket, often via a computerized system, a day in advance on many long-distance routes. Schedules are fairly dependable, so be at the terminal on time for departure.

New buses are being added all over the country featuring large windows with an unobstructed view from every seat. **Omnibus de Mexico** has added **Executive Service** from several cities. Buses of that type cost much more than regular buses, carry half the number of passengers, have stewards, and include a club and movie section, similar to a train club car.

Many Mexican cities, including Guadalajara, now have new central bus stations that are much like sophisticated airport terminals rather than the bewildering array of tiny private company offices scattered all over town—such as Puerto Vallarta. I've included information on bus routes along my suggested itineraries. Keep in mind that routes, times, and prices may change, and as there is no central directory of schedules for the whole country, current information must be obtained from local bus stations or travel offices.

For long trips, carry some food, water, toilet paper, and a sweater (in case the air conditioning is too strong).

See the Appendix for a list of helpful bus terms in Spanish.

BY CAR

Most Mexican roads are not up to northern standards of smoothness, hardness, width of curve, grade of hill, or safety marking. Cardinal rule: Never drive at night if you can avoid it. The roads aren't good enough; the trucks, carts, pedestrians, and bicycles usually have no lights; you can hit potholes, animals, rocks, dead ends, or bridges out with no warning. Enough said.

You will also have to get used to the spirited Latin driving styles, which tend to depend more on flair and good reflexes than on system and prudence. Be prepared for new procedures, as when a truck driver flips on his left-turn signal when there's not a crossroad for miles. He's probably telling you that the road's clear ahead for you to pass—after all, he's in a better position to see than you are. It's difficult to judge, however, if he really means that he intends to pull over on the left-hand shoulder.

You may have to follow trucks without mufflers and pollution-control devices for miles. Under these conditions drop back and be patient, take a side road, or stop for a break when you feel tense or tired.

Take extra care not to endanger pedestrians. People in the countryside are not good at judging the speed of an approaching car, and often panic in the middle of the road even though they could easily have reached the shoulder.

Be prepared to pay tolls on some of Mexico's expressways and bridges. Tolls are high in this country, at least as high as in the U.S. The word for "toll" in Spanish is *cuota*.

CAR RENTALS

With some trepidation I wander into the subject of car-rental rules, which change often in Mexico. The best prices are obtained by reserving your car a week in advance from the U.S. Guadalajara and most other large Mexican cities have several rental offices representing the various big firms and some smaller ones. You'll find rental desks at the airports, at all major hotels, and at many travel agencies. The large firms like Avis, Hertz, National, and Budget have rental offices on main streets as well.

Cars are easy to rent if you have a credit card (American Express, VISA, MasterCard, etc.), are 25 or over, and have a valid driver's license and passport with you. One exception: Budget will hold a car reservation only with an American Express or Diner's Club credit card, but you can pay the rental with another card. Without a credit card you must leave a cash deposit, usually a big one. Rent-here/leave-there arrangements are usually simple to make, but are very costly.

Make sure you are guaranteed the quoted rate even if the size car reserved isn't available when you arrive. Take the name of the person you spoke with and ask for your confirmation number and keep it handy. Take a copy of the confirmation with you. When reserving from home do it directly with the car-rental firm rather than through a travel agent. If there is any discrepancy in the price between the time you reserve and when you arrive in Mexico, your quoted price came directly from the company and it can't be argued that your travel agent quoted an old price. Experience speaks.

Shop for a good price before renting, as there is a great variation between the quoted prices. Pay attention to insurance deductibles. Let's hope you don't have an accident, but if you do, one company may charge you the first $250 in damages while another may charge $1,000. Be sure to double-check all math on the rental form; if you were quoted rates in the States, be sure they are the same after the peso conversion appearing on the form. Return the car with the same level of gas; rental companies sock it to you on gas charges.

If you select to take mileage included, your completed estimate should look something like this for a VW Beetle rented from Avis:

Basic daily charge	$38.00
Collision/Damage and personal accident insurance	$15.00
Subtotal	$53.00
IVA tax 10%	$ 5.30
Grand Daily Total	$58.30

If you purchase Budget's collision/damage insurance the deductible is $250 if the car is reparable; $400 if unreparable.

A car rented for 7 days in either Puerto Vallarta, Guadalajara, or Manzanillo through Avis, which from the U.S. only rents with unlimited mileage, would be:

Basic weekly rental	$159.00
Insurance	$ 15.00 (daily)
Subtotal	$264.00
IVA tax 10%	$ 26.40
Total	$290.40 ($41.49 a day)

The Avis deductible is 5 days of the basic car rental, which in this case would be $5 \times \$38 = \$190$, if you buy their insurance.

Deductibles vary greatly, so don't fail to get that information.

If you pay for your car rental on a credit card, you may be entitled to waive the insurance, which may be covered by the credit-card company. Before assuming that it is, check with the credit-card company, and get a letter stating the terms. If you have an accident in Mexico, all parties can be carted off to jail until it's determined who is at fault or until you can show proof of insurance. If you buy the insurance with the car rental, that is usually sufficient proof. If that area is blank on the rental form, you may have to do a lot of explaining about the perks associated with your credit card. A letter from the credit-card insurer written in Spanish may help, so you can show it if you have an accident. Or you may have to pay for repairs, get a police report of the accident, and settle up with the credit-card insurer later.

From the U.S., Avis quotes prices with unlimited mileage; Hertz quotes with or without mileage. If you plan to do a lot of traveling, unlimited mileage rates can be a great bargain. Either way, you'll find that it still costs between $50 and $70 a day, after you add on gas, tolls, parking, etc. Presently, I find the best deals are through Avis, but even they can have problems. They have a selection of VW Beetles in Guadalajara, but few in Manzanillo, and in Manzanillo there may be no replacement cars in case of breakdown.

Read the fine print on the back of your rental agreement and note that insurance is invalid if you have an accident while driving on an unpaved road.

One last recommendation. Before starting out with a rental car, be sure you know their **trouble number.** The large firms have toll-free numbers, which may not be well staffed on weekends.

GASOLINE

There's one government-owned brand of gas and one gasoline station name throughout the country—Pemex (Petroleras Mexicanas). Each station has a franchise owner who buys everything from Pemex. There are two types of gas in Mexico—Nova, an 82-octane leaded gas, and Magna Sin, 87-octane unleaded gas. Magna Sin is sold from brilliantly colored pumps and costs around $1.20 a gallon. Nova costs around $1 per gallon. In Mexico, fuel and oil are sold by the liter, which is slightly more than a quart (40 liters equals about 10½ gallons). Nova is readily available. Magna Sin is now available in most areas of Mexico, along major highways and in the larger cities. Even in areas where it should be available, you may have to hunt around. The usual station may be out of Magna Sin for a couple of days—weekends especially. Or you may be told that none is available in the area, just to get your business. Plan ahead: Fill up every chance you get; keep your tank topped off. Pemex publishes a helpful Atlas de Carreteras (road atlas), which includes a list of filling stations with Magna Sin gas, although there are some inaccuracies in the list. No credit cards are accepted for gas purchases.

Here's what to do when you have to fuel up: Drive up to the pump, close enough so that you will be able to watch the pump run as your tank is being filled. Check that the pump is turned back to zero, go to your fuel filler cap and unlock it yourself, and watch the pump and the attendant as the gas goes in. Though many service station attendants are honest, most are not. It's good to ask for a specific peso amount rather than saying "full." This is because the attendants tend to overfill, splashing gas on the car and anything within range.

As there are always lines at the gas pumps, attendants often finish fueling one vehicle, turn the pump back quickly (or don't turn it back at all), and start on another vehicle. You've got to be looking at the pump when the fueling is finished, because it may show the amount you owe for only a few seconds. This "quick draw" from car to car is another good reason to ask for a certain peso-amount of gas. If you've asked for 20,000 pesos' worth, the attendant can't charge you 22,000 for it.

Once the fueling is complete, let the attendant check the oil, or radiator, or put air in the tires. Do only one thing at a time, be with him as he does it, and don't let him rush you. Get into these habits, or it'll cost you.

If you get oil, make sure that the can that is tipped into your engine is a full one. If in doubt, have the attendant check the dipstick again after the oil has supposedly been put in. Check your change, and again, don't let them rush you. Check that your locking gas cap is back in place.

DRIVING RULES

If you park illegally, or commit some other infraction, and you are not around to discuss it, police are authorized to remove your license plates (*placas*). You must then trundle over to the police station and pay a fine to get them back. Mexican car-rental agencies have begun to weld the license tag to the tag frame; you may want to devise a method of your own to make the tags difficult to remove. Theoretically, this will make the policeman move on to another set of tags easier to confiscate. On the other hand, he could get his hackles up and decide to have your car towed. To weld or not to weld is up to you.

Be attentive to road signs. A drawing of a row of little bumps means that there are speed bumps (*topes*) across the road to warn you to reduce your speed while driving through towns or villages. Slow down when coming to a village whether you see the sign or not—sometimes they install the bumps but not the sign!

Kilometer stones on main highways register the distance from local population centers. There is always a shortage of directional signs, so check quite frequently that you are on the right road. Other common road signs include:

Camino en Reparación Road Repairs
Conserva Su Derecha Keep Right
Cuidado con el Ganado, el Tren Watch Out for Cattle, Trains
Curva Peligrosa Dangerous Curve
Derrumbes Earthquake Zone
Deslave Caved-in Roadbed
Despacio Slow
Desviación Detour
Disminuya Su Velocidad Slow Down
Entronque Highway Junction
Escuela School (zone)
Grava Suelta Loose Gravel
Hombres Trabajando Men Working
No Hay Paso Road Closed
Peligro Danger
Puente Angosto Narrow Bridge
Raya Continua Continuous (Solid) White Line
Tramo en Reparación Road under Construction
Un Solo Carril a 100 m. One-lane Road 100 Meters Ahead
Zona Escolar School Zone

BREAKDOWNS

Your best guide to repair shops is the yellow pages. For specific makes and shops that repair them, look under *Automoviles y Camiones: Talleres de Reparación y Servicio;* auto-parts stores are listed under *Refacciones y Accessorios para Automoviles.* On the road often the sign of a mechanic simply says *Taller Mechanico.*

I've found that the Ford and Volkswagen dealerships in Mexico give prompt, courteous attention to my car problems, and prices for repairs are, in general, much lower than in the U.S. or Canada. I suspect that other big-name dealerships—General Motors, Chrysler, etc.—give similar, very satisfactory service. Often they will take your car right away and make repairs in just a few hours, sometimes minutes.

If your car breaks down on the road, help might already be on the way. Green, radio-equipped repair trucks manned by uniformed, English-speaking officers patrol the major highways during daylight hours to aid motorists in trouble. The "Green Angels" will perform minor repairs and adjustments free, but you pay for parts and materials.

MINOR ACCIDENTS

Most motorists think it best to drive away from minor accidents if possible. Without fluent Spanish, you are at a distinct disadvantage when it comes to describing your version of what happened. Sometimes the other person's version is exaggerated, and you may end up in jail or spending days straightening out things that were not even your fault. In fact, fault often has nothing to do with it. See "Mexican Auto Insurance," above.

PARKING

When you park your car on the street, lock up and leave nothing within view inside (day or night). I use guarded parking lots especially at night, to avoid vandalism and break-ins. This way you also avoid parking violations. When pay lots are not available, dozens of small boys will surround you as you stop, wanting to "watch your car for you." Pick the leader of the group, let him know you want him to guard it, and give him a peso or two when you leave. Kids may be very curious about the car and may look in, crawl underneath, or even climb on top, but they rarely do any damage.

CAMPING

It's easy and relatively cheap to camp south of the border if you have a recreational vehicle or trailer. It's more difficult if you only have a tent. Some agencies selling Mexican car insurance in the U.S. (including Sanborn's) will give you a free list of campsites if you ask. The AAA also has a list of sites. *RV Park & Campground Directory* (previously published by Rand McNally, now published by Prentice Hall, New York) covers Mexico.

Campgrounds here tend to be slightly below U.S. standards (with many attractive exceptions to this rule, though). Remember that campgrounds fill up just like hotels during the winter rush-to-the-sun and at holiday times. Get there early. It is not wise to camp on a beach or any other remote, unofficial place.

OTHER OPTIONS

BY RV Touring Mexico by recreational vehicle is a popular way of seeing the country. Many hotels have hookups. RV parks, while not as plentiful as in the U.S., are available throughout the country.

BY FERRY Ferries connect Baja California at La Paz and Santa Rosalía with the mainland at Topolobampo and Mazatlán.

HITCHHIKING You see Mexicans hitching rides at crossroads after getting off a bus, for example, but as a general rule hitchhiking isn't done. It's especially not wise for foreigners since they may be suspected of carrying large amounts of cash.

  MEXICO

In this section I have tried to anticipate some of the questions that you may find yourself asking. You will probably think of many other listings yourself; if so, I would appreciate hearing about them. Such listings will be included in future versions of this book.

Abbreviations Dept.—apartments; Apdo.—post office box; Av.—Avenida; Calz.—calzada or boulevard. C on faucets stands for caliente (hot), and F stands for fría (cold). In elevators, PB (planta baja) means "ground floor."

American Express Wherever there is an office, I've mentioned it.

Business Hours In general Mexican businesses in larger cities are open between 9am and 7pm. Smaller towns may close between 2 and 4pm. Most are closed on Sunday. Bank hours are 9 or 9:30am to 1pm Monday to Friday. A few banks in large cities have extended hours.

Camera/Film Both are more expensive in Mexico than in the U.S.; take full advantage of your 12-roll film allowance by bringing 36 exposures per roll, and bring extra batteries. AA batteries are generally available, but AAA and small disk batteries for cameras and watches are rarely found. A few places in resort areas advertise color-film developing, but it might be cheaper to wait until you get home.

If you're a serious photographer, bring an assortment of films at various speeds as you will be photographing against glaring sand, in gloomy Maya temples, and in dusky jungles. Proper filters are a help.

Cigarettes Cigarettes are much cheaper in Mexico, even U.S. brands, if you buy them at a grocery or drugstore and not a hotel tobacco shop.

Climate See "When to Go," above.

Crime See "Safety" and "Legal Aid," below, and "Scams" and "Bribes," above.

Currency See "Information, Entry Requirements, and Money," above.

Customs Mexican Customs procedures have been streamlined. At most crossings entering tourists are requested to punch a button. If the resulting light is green you go through without inspection. If it's red your luggage or car may be inspected thoroughly or briefly.

Doctors/Dentists Every embassy and consulate is prepared to recommend local doctors and dentists with good training and modern equipment; some of the doctors and dentists even speak English. See the list of embassies and consulates under "Embassies/Consulates," below, and remember that at the larger ones a duty officer is on call at all times. Hotels with a high clientele of foreigners are often prepared to recommend English-speaking doctors. Almost all first-class hotels in Mexico have a doctor on call.

Documents Required See "Information, Entry Requirements, and Money," above.

Driving Rules See "Getting Around," above.

Drug Laws Briefly, don't use or possess illegal drugs in Mexico. Mexicans have no tolerance of drug users and jail is the solution with very little hope of getting out until the sentence (usually a long one) is completed or heavy fines or bribes are paid. *Important Note:* It isn't uncommon to be befriended by a fellow user, only to be turned in by that "friend," who then collects a bounty for turning you in. It's no win. Bring prescription drugs in their original containers. If possible pack a copy of the original prescription with the generic name of the drug. I don't need to go into detail about the penalties for illegal drug possession upon return to the U.S. Customs officials are also on the lookout for diet drugs sold in Mexico, possession of which could also land you in jail in the U.S. where they are illegal. If you buy antibiotics over the counter (which you can do in Mexico), say, for a sinus infection and still have some left, you probably won't be hassled by U.S. Customs.

Drugstores Drugstores **(farmacias)** will sell you just about anything you want, with prescription or without. Most are open Monday through Saturday from 8am to 8pm.

If you need to buy medicines after normal hours, you'll have to search for the *farmacia de turno*—pharmacies take turns staying open during the off-hours. Find any drugstore, and in its window may be a card showing the schedule of which farmacia will be open at what time.

Electricity Current in Mexico is 110 volts, 60 cycles, as in the U.S. and Canada, with the same flat-prong plugs and sockets. Some light bulbs have bayonet bases.

Embassies/Consulates They provide valuable lists of doctors, and lawyers, as well as regulations concerning marriages in Mexico. Contrary to popular belief, your embassy cannot get you out of a Mexican jail, provide postal or banking services, or fly you home when you run out of money. Consular officers can provide you with advice on most matters and problems, however. Most countries have a representative embassy in Mexico City and many have consular offices or representatives in the provinces.

Australia: The Australian Embassy in Mexico City is at Jaime Balmes 11, Plaza Polanco (tel. 5/395-9988); open Monday through Friday from 8am to 1pm.

Canada: The Canadian Embassy in Mexico City is at Schiller 529, in Polanco (tel. 5/254-3288); open Monday through Friday from 9am to 1pm and 2 to 5pm; at other times the name of a duty officer is posted on the embassy door. In Acapulco, the Canadian consulate is in the Hotel Club del Sol, Costera Miguel Alemán, at the corner of Reyes Catolicos (tel. 748/5-6621); open 8am to 3pm.

France: The French Embassy and the French Consulate-General is at Havre 15, between Reforma and Hamburgo, in the Zona Rosa (tel. 5/533-1360); open Monday through Friday from 8:30am to 1:00pm.

Germany: The Embajada de la República Federal de Alemania is at Lord Byron 737 (tel. 5/545-6655); open Monday through Friday from 9am to noon.

Netherlands: The Embajada Real de los Países Bajos is at Monte Urales 635 at Reforma, Col. Lomas (tel. 5/540-7788). Hours are Monday through Friday, 9am to 2pm.

New Zealand: The New Zealand Embassy is on the eighth floor of the building at Homero 229 (tel. 5/250-5999); open Monday through Thursday from 9am to 2pm and from 3 to 5pm, Friday from 9am to 2pm.

United Kingdom: The British Embassy in Mexico City is at Lerma 71, at Río Sena (tel. 5/207-2089 or 207-2186). Hours are 8:30am to 3:30pm Monday through Friday. There are **honorary consuls** in the following cities: Acapulco, Hotel Las Brisas, Carretera Escenica (tel. 748/4-6605 or 4-1580); Ciudad Juárez, Calle Fresno 185 (tel. 161/7-5791); Mérida, Calle 58 no. 450 (tel. 99/21-6799); Monterrey, Privada de Tamazunchale 104 (tel. 83/78-2565); Veracruz, Avenida Morelos 145 (tel. 29/31-0955); Guadalajara (tel. 36/35-8295); Tampico (tel. 12/12-9784).

United States: The American Embassy in Mexico City is right next to the Hotel Maria Isabel Sheraton at Paseo de la Reforma 305, corner of Río Danubio (tel. 5/211-0042, or for emergencies, 5/211-4536).

There are **U.S. consulates** in Ciudad Juárez (tel. 1/613-4048), Guadalajara (tel.

3/25-9202), Hermosillo (tel. 6/217-2382), Matamoros (tel. 891/12-5251), Mazatlán (tel. 667/81-2685), Mérida (tel. 9/925-5011), Monterrey (tel. 8/345-2120), Nuevo Laredo (tel. 8/714-0696), and Tijuana (tel. 6/681-7400).

In addition, **consular agents** reside in Acapulco (tel. 748/3-1969 or 485-7207); Cancún (tel. 988/4-1437), open from 10am to 2pm and 4 to 7pm; Durango (tel. 181/1-4445), open weekdays from 8am to 3pm; Mulege (tel. 685/3-0111); Oaxaca (tel. 951/6-0654); Puerto Vallarta (tel. 322/2-5769); San Luis Potosí (tel. 481/7-2510), open weekdays from 9am to 1pm and 4 to 7pm; San Miguel de Allende (tel. 465/2-2357), open Monday and Wednesday from 9am to 2pm and 4 to 7pm, Tuesday and Thursday from 4 to 7pm, and by appointment on Friday, Saturday, and Sunday; Tampico (tel. 121/3-2217); and Veracruz (tel. 29/31-0142).

Emergencies The 24-hour Tourist Help Line in Mexico City is 5/250-0151 and for legal assistance 5/525-9380 or 525-9384. See also "Legal Aid," below.

Etiquette As a general rule, Mexicans are very polite. Foreigners who ask questions politely, and say please and thank you, will be rewarded. Mexicans are also very formal; an invitation to a private home no matter how humble is an honor. And although many strangers will immediately begin using the familiar form of the verb "tu" for you, if you want to be correct, the formal "usted" is still preferred until a friendship is established. How long it takes to establish a friendship varies. I know neighbors in Mexico who are still on formal terms after 10 years. When in doubt use the formal and wait for the Mexican to change to the familiar. Mexicans are normally uncomfortable with our "Dutch treat" custom of dining and will usually insist on paying. It can be touchy, and you don't want to be insulting. But you might offer to get the drinks or insist on paying the tip. If you're invited to a home it's polite to bring a gift, perhaps a bottle of good wine or flowers.

Guides Most guides in Mexico are men. Many speak English (and occasionally other languages) and are formally trained in history and culture to qualify for a federally approved tourism license. Hiring a guide for a day at the ruins, or to squire you around Mexico City may be a worthwhile luxury *if* you establish boundaries in the beginning. Be specific about what you want to do, and how long you want the service. The guide will quote a price. Discussion may reduce the initial quote. If your guide is using his own car, is licensed (something he can prove with a credential), and speaks English, the price will be higher and is generally worth it. If you are together at lunch, it's customary to buy the guide's meal. When bus tours from the U.S. diminished a few years ago, many licensed English-speaking guides became taxi drivers, so it isn't unusual to find incredibly knowledgeable taxi drivers who are experienced guides. In Mexico City these licensed guides/taxi drivers often have a permanent spot outside the better hotels and are available for private duty. If the service has been out of the ordinary, a tip is in order—perhaps 10% of the daily rate. On tours, the recommended tip is $1.50 to $2 per day per person.

Hitchhiking Generally speaking hitchhiking is not a good idea in Mexico. Take a bus; they are cheap and go everywhere.

Holidays See "When to Go," above.

Information See "Information, Entry Requirements, and Money," above, and specific city for local information offices.

Language The official language is Spanish, but there are at least 50 Native American languages spoken and more than four times that many dialects. English is most widely spoken in resort cities and in better hotels. It's best to learn some basic Spanish phrases.

Laundry See information in various cities.

Legal Aid Proseco (Procuraduría Federal de Consumidor), Calle Doctor Navarro 210, 4th Piso, Col. de los Doctores, Mexico D.F. 06720 (tel. 525/761-4546; fax 525/761-3885), is a contact for tourists with legal problems. **International Legal Defense Counsel,** 111 South 15th Street, Packard Building, 24th floor, Philadelphia, PA 19102 (tel. 215/977-9982) is a law firm specializing in legal difficulties of Americans abroad. See also "Embassies/Consulates" and "Emergencies," above.

Liquor Laws See "Entry Requirements, Customs," above.

Mail Mail service south of the border tends to be slow (sometimes glacial in its movements) and erratic. If you're on a 2-week vacation, it's not a bad idea to buy and mail your postcards in the arrivals lounge at the airport to give them maximum time to get home before you do.

For the most reliable and convenient mail service, have your letters sent to you c/o the American Express offices in major cities, which will receive and forward mail for you *if* you are one of their clients (a travel-club card or an American Express traveler's check is proof). They charge a fee if you wish them to forward your mail.

If you don't use American Express, have your mail sent to you care of *Lista de Correos,* followed by the city, state, and country. In Mexican post offices there may actually be a "lista" posted near the Lista de Correos window bearing the names of all those for whom mail has been received. If there's no list, ask, and show them your passport so they can riffle through and look for your letters. If the city has more than one office, you'll have to go to the central post office—not a branch—to get your mail. By the way, in many post offices they return your mail to sender if it has been there for more than 10 days. Make sure people don't send you letters too early. See the Appendix for a list of postal terms.

Maps AAA maps to Mexico are quite good and available free to members at any AAA office in the U.S. Guia Roji also has good maps.

Newspapers and Magazines The English-language newspaper *The News,* published in Mexico City, carries world news and commentaries, and a calendar of the day's events including concerts, art shows, and plays.

Newspaper kiosks in larger Mexican cities will carry a selection of English-language magazines.

Passports See "Information, Entry Requirements, and Money" in this chapter.

Pets Taking a pet into Mexico, entails a lot of red tape. Consult the Mexican Government Tourist Office nearest you.

Police Police in general in Mexico are to be suspected rather than trusted; however, you'll find many who are quite helpful with directions, even going so far as to lead you where you want to go.

Radio/TV Many hotels now have antennae capable of bringing in U.S. TV channels. Large cities will have English-language stations and music.

Rest Rooms The best bet in Mexico is to use rest rooms in restaurants and hotel public areas. Always carry your own toilet paper and hand soap, neither of which is in great supply in Mexican rest rooms. Public facilities, usually near the central market, vary in cleanliness and usually have an attendant who charges a few pesos for toilet use and a few squares of toilet paper. Pemex gas stations have improved the maintenance of their rest rooms along major highways. No matter where you are, even if the toilet flushes with paper, there'll be a waste basket for paper disposal. Many people come from homes without plumbing and are not accustomed to toilets that take paper, and throw paper on the floor rather than put it in the toilet—thus you'll see the basket no matter what quality of place you are in. On the other hand the water pressure in many establishments is so low that paper won't go down. There's often a sign saying "do" or "don't" flush paper.

Safety Whenever you're traveling in an unfamiliar city or country, stay alert. Be aware of your immediate surroundings. Wear a moneybelt and don't sling your camera or purse over your shoulder. This will minimize the possibility of your becoming a victim of crime.

Crime is more of a problem in Mexico than it used to be. Although you will feel physically safer in most Mexican cities than in comparable big cities at home, you must take some basic, sensible precautions.

First, remember that you're a tourist, and an obvious target for crime. Beware of pickpockets on crowded buses, the Metro, in markets. Guard your possessions very carefully at all times; don't let packs or bags out of sight even for a second (the big first-class bus lines will store your bag in the luggage compartment under the bus, and that's generally all right, but keep your things with you on the less responsible village and some second-class buses on country routes.

Next, if you have a car, park it in an enclosed or guarded lot at night. Vans are a special mark. Don't depend on "major downtown streets" to protect your car—park it in a private lot with a guard, or at least a fence.

Women must be careful in cities when walking alone, night or day. Busy streets are no problem, but empty streets (even if empty just for afternoon siesta) are lonely places.

Important Warning: Agreeing to carry a package back to the States for an acquaintance or a stranger could land you in jail for years and cost a lot of money to get you out. Never do it no matter how friendly, honest, or sincere the request. Perpetrators of this illegal activity prey on innocent-looking single travelers and especially senior citizens.

Seasons/Booking Those planning to be in resorts like Puerto Vallarta, Manzanillo, San Blas, and Barra de Navidad, should make hotel reservations on major holidays (Mexican as well as international). Christmas, New Year's and Easter week are the worst for crowding. If you discover it's a holiday when you're en route to the resort, plan to arrive early in the day.

Several readers have written to me about difficulties they encountered in making reservations by mail, and even by toll-free reservation numbers. Some report no answer or no record of their request (or deposit check) when they've arrived. Or they are quoted a higher price than one they might have paid by just arriving without a reservation. I've experienced the same frustrations. Here's a suggestion: Only make reservations during high season if you are going to a beach area. Off-season just arrive and find out what's available by calling when you arrive.

Sightseeing As a general rule museums and archeological sites in Mexico are free on Sunday and they are free at all times to those age 13 and below, or over age 60.

Taxes There's a 10% tax on goods and services in Mexico and it's supposed to be included in the posted price.

Telephone/Telex/Fax *Important Note:* Area codes were gradually being changed as this book went to press. Usually the change affects area code and first digit, or area code only. But some cities such as Veracruz are adding exchanges and changing numbers. If you have difficulty calling long distance, ask the operator for assistance.

In 1990 Telefonos de Mexico reduced long-distance rates by 40%, and at the same time raised local rates. *Long-distance calls are still exorbitantly expensive,* especially out of the country, and now so are local calls.

Public pay phones for local use come in two types: In one, the slot at the top holds the 100-peso coin in a gentle grip until your party answers, then it drops; if there's no answer or a busy signal you can pluck your coin from the slot. With the other type, you insert a coin which disappears into the bowels of the machine, and drops into the cashbox when your call goes through, or into the return slot if it doesn't (after you hang up). This type of phone is often jammed, and your coin won't drop, so that when your party answers you will hear them but they won't hear you. Try from another pay phone.

For **long-distance calls** there are several ways to go: The most expensive is through a hotel switchboard, which may add a service charge to your already expensive bill. The least expensive way is to use Ladatel phones found increasingly in bus stations, airports, and downtown public areas of major cities and touristic zones. (See how to use the Ladatel below.) Next in cost, and often faster and more convenient, is the *caseta de larga distancia* (long-distance telephone office), found all over Mexico. Most bus stations and airports now have specially staffed rooms exclusively for making long-distance calls and sending faxes. Often they are efficient and inexpensive, providing the client with a computer printout of the time and charges. Long-distance operators are notoriously hard to reach, so no matter what method is used, the process can be time-consuming.

To call the U.S. or Canada collect, dial 09, and tell the *operadora* that you want *una llamada por cobrar* (a collect call), *teléfono a teléfono* (station-to-station), or *persona a persona* (person-to-person). Collect calls are the least expensive of all, but sometimes caseta offices won't make them, so you'll have to pay on the spot.

To make a long-distance call from Mexico to another country, from a caseta or Ladatel phone first dial 95 for the U.S. and Canada, or 98 for anywhere else in the world. Then dial the area code and number you are calling. If you need the international (English-speaking) operator after all, dial 09.

To call long distance (abbreviated "lada") within Mexico, dial 91, the area code, then the number. Mexican area codes (*claves*) are listed in the front of the telephone directories, and in the hotel listings for each area in this book. For Mexico City, it's 5; for Acapulco, 74. (See also beginning paragraph regarding gradual changes in area codes.)

You can save considerably by calling in off-peak periods. The cheapest times to call are daily after 11pm and before 8am, and all day Saturday and Sunday. The most expensive times are Monday through Friday from 8am to 5pm.

Ladatel call stations are at major transportation termini and other public places of importance. These special pay telephones allow you to dial direct long-distance calls to anywhere in Mexico or the world, at reasonable prices.

To use a Ladatel phone, first, have a good supply of 100-peso coins. Next, find out the approximate rate per minute for your call by picking up the handset and punching in the long-distance code (91 for Mexico, 95 for the U.S. and Canada, 98 for the rest of the world), plus the area or country and city codes for the destination of your call. The charge per minute in pesos will appear on the LCD display. For instance, if you press 95-212, you'll get the charge-per-minute for a call to Manhattan. Once you know the charge per minute, count your coins or tokens, make sure you have as many as you'll need, then dial your number and insert coins. The display will keep you informed of when more coins are needed. Instructions on Ladatel phones are in Spanish, English, and French. Be patient, though; reaching an international telephone operator may take a long time.

Mexico's area codes and numbers are sometimes shorter than North American ones.

To place a call to Mexico from your home country: dial the international service (011), then Mexico's country code (52), then the Mexican area code (for Mexico City it's 5), then the local number. Thus to call the Secretaría de Turismo's information number in Mexico City, you'd dial 011-52-5-250-0123. To dial the SECTUR information office in Acapulco, you'd dial 011-52-74-82-2170.

Keep in mind that calls to Mexico are quite expensive, even if dialed direct from your home phone. As a rule of thumb, it's usually much cheaper to call Europe or the Middle East than it is to call Mexico.

The telegraph office may be in a different place from the post office in many cities. Telex works out to be much cheaper than long distance calls, but you must know the telex number you want to call. Many businesses, particularly in the travel industry (travel agents and hotels), have telex numbers.

The effects of reducing long-distance rates while hiking local rates means that hotels have begun to charge for local calls made from hotel-room phones. Until now these calls were free. So far, most of the inexpensive hotels listed in this book do not have the equipment to track calls made from individual rooms and, therefore, telephone-use charges are not added to the room bill. But hotels with more sophisticated telephone systems are charging 35¢ to 50¢ per call. To avoid checkout shock, ask at check-in if local calls are extra.

Time Central standard time prevails throughout most of Mexico. The west-coast states of Sonora, Sinaloa, and parts of Nayarit are on mountain standard time. The state of Baja California Norte is on Pacific standard time, but Baja California Sur is on mountain time.

Note that daylight saving time is not used in Mexico, except in Baja California Norte (late April to late October).

Tipping Throw out the iron-clad 15% rule right away in budget restaurants south of the border, no matter what other travel literature may say. Do as the locals do: for meals costing under $3, leave the loose change; for meals costing from $4 to $5, leave 6% to 10%, depending on service. Above $5, you're into the 10% to 15% bracket. However, in above-average restaurants and exclusive places, the 15% rule holds. But don't tip on top of the 15% tax which is automatically included in your bill. Some of the more crass high-priced restaurants will actually add a 15% "tip" to your bill.

Bellboys and porters will expect about 25¢ per bag. You needn't tip taxi drivers unless they've rendered some special service—carrying bags or trunks.

Tourist Offices See "Information, Entry Requirements, and Money," above, and also specific city chapters.

Villas/Condos Renting a private villa or condominium home for a vacation is a popular vacation alternative. The difference between the two, of course, is that villas are usually freestanding and condos may be part of a large or small complex. Often the villas are true private homes in exclusive neighborhoods and rented out seasonally by their owners. Condominiums, on the other hand, may seem more like a hotel, although the secluded ones feel more exclusive. Either accommodation ordinarily comes with private kitchen and dining area, maid service, and pool. Often a full-time cook, maid, or gardener/chauffeur are on duty. I've seen prices as low as $80 a night to a high of $500. Prices are seasonal with the best deals between May and October. Of course, depending on the number of bedrooms, you can get a group together and share the cost. Four companies specializing in this type of vacation rental are: **Creative Leisure,** 951 Transport Way, Petaluma, CA 94954-1484 (tel. 707/778-1800, toll free 800/426-6367); **Travel Resources,** P.O. Box 1042, Coconut Grove, FL 33133 (tel. 305/444-8583; fax 305/445-5729); and **Mexico Condo Reservations,** 5801 Soledad Mountain Road, La Jolla, CA 92037 (tel. toll free 800/262-4500 in the U.S., 800/654-5543 in Canada). All have brochures with photographs of potential properties.

Water Most hotels have decanters or bottles of purified water in the rooms and the better hotels have either purified water from regular taps or special taps marked "Agua Purificada." In the resort areas, hoteliers are beginning to charge for in-room bottled water. Virtually any hotel, restaurant, or bar will bring you purified water if you specifically request it, but you'll usually be charged for it.

CHAPTER 3
GETTING TO KNOW PUERTO VALLARTA

1. ORIENTATION
- DID YOU KNOW...?
2. GETTING AROUND
- FAST FACTS: PUERTO VALLARTA

Puerto Vallarta (pop. 250,000) is gorgeous, with its tropical mountains right beside the sea, its coves and beaches, and its Mexican town of white buildings with red-tiled roofs. Puerto Vallarta's development—mostly on the outskirts of the original town—has lent prosperity without destroying charm.

Once an agricultural village on the Bay of Banderas, far from roads, airports, electricity, and tourism, Puerto Vallarta ceased to be a secret with the making of *Night of the Iguana*. Elizabeth Taylor bought a house in the village, and the growth of a booming resort started with a good highway and a jetport.

1. ORIENTATION

ARRIVING

BY PLANE **Aero California** has nonstop or direct flights from Phoenix and San Diego. **Aeromexico** flies from Los Angeles as well as Guadalajara, La Paz, León, Mexico City, and Tijuana. **Alaska Airlines** flies from Los Angeles and San Francisco. **American Airlines** has direct flights from Dallas/Fort Worth. **Continental** flies nonstop from Houston. **Delta** flies nonstop from Los Angeles. **Mexicana** has direct or nonstop flights from Chicago, Dallas/Fort Worth, Denver, Los Angeles, and San Francisco, plus Guadalajara, Mazatlán, and Mexico City. The regional airline **Aero Vallarta** flies to and from Manzanillo November through Easter. **Taesa** charter airline (through Universal Destinations in Houston) has flights from San Antonio to Puerto Vallarta and Guadalajara. Check with a travel agent regarding charter service; charters from New York, Los Angeles, Minneapolis, and other cities are anticipated during 1992.

The airport is close to the north end of town on the main highway, only about 6 miles from the downtown, where most of the budget hotels are located. Upon arriving, take the airport minivan (*colectivo*) for around $5 (the exact fare depends on where you're going); or you can walk a block to the highway and catch a city bus for about 35¢.

DID YOU KNOW...?

- To be legally married in Mexico a civil ceremony is required; church ceremonies are optional.
- No monuments honor Hernan Cortés in Mexico.
- The poinsettia is named after Joel Poinsett, first United States Minister to Mexico in 1823.
- Elizabeth Taylor wasn't a member of the cast in *The Night of the Iguana*, which was filmed in Puerto Vallarta and starred Ava Gardner and Richard Burton.
- Pirates once roamed the waters off the port of San Blas.

BY BUS Getting to Puerto Vallarta from Mexico City, Guadalajara, or points north and south along the coast is not difficult, as it is served by a whole slew of bus lines: **Tres Estrellas de Oro** (first class), **Estrella Blanca** (first class), **Transportes del Pacífico** (first and second class), and **Transportes Norte de Sonora** (first and second class), and **Autotransportes del Pacífico** (second class).

When you arrive by bus, you'll be south of the river on Madero, Insurgentes, or Constitución streets and close to many of our hotel selections. The locations of the bus "stations" (most are small offices or waiting rooms) of the various lines are as follows: **Autotransportes del Pacífico,** Constitución and Madero; **Tres Estrellas de Oro,** Insurgentes 210; **Transportes Norte de Sonora,** Madero 343 near Insurgentes; **Transportes del Pacífico,** Insurgentes 160; **Estrella Blanca,** Insurgentes 180.

BY CAR From Mazatlán to the north (6 hr.) or Manzanillo to the south (3.5 hr.), the only choice is the coastal highway. From Guadalajara (8 hr.), take Highway 15 to Tepic, then Highway 200 south.

BY FERRY Ferry service between Puerto Vallarta and Cabo San Lucas in Baja California has been suspended for the past few years. Inquire at the tourist office for the latest information or call the **SEMATUR** ferry office in Mexico City (tel. 5/53-7957).

DEPARTING

BY PLANE Airline offices: **Aero California,** Plaza Caracol, Marina no. 23G (tel. 1-1571; airport 1-1444); **Aeromexico,** Juárez 255 (tel. 1-1897, 2-5898, or 2-0031; airport 2-1055 or 2-1204); **Alaska Airlines,** airport (tel. 3-0350 or 3-0351, toll free 95-800/426-0333 in Mexico); **American Airlines,** airport (tel. 1-1927, 2-3788, 2-3878, or 2-3787); **Continental,** airport (tel. 2-3095 or 2-3096); **Delta,** airport (tel. 2-4032 or 2-3919, toll free 91-800/9-0221 in Mexico); **Mexicana,** Juárez 202 (tel. 2-5000); **Aero Vallarta,** Zaragoza and Juárez (tel. 2-2210; airport 2-0999 or 2-5354).

BY BUS Until the new bus terminal near the airport is completed, riders must make do with finding the "station" (most are small offices or waiting rooms) of their choice south of the river along Madero, Insurgentes, and Constitución streets.

The second-class **Autotransportes del Pacífico,** at the corner of Constitución and Madero (tel. 2-3436), has hourly buses to Manzanillo from 5am to 6pm (a 6-hr. trip), and service almost as frequent to Melaque (a 4.5-hr. trip). It also has four buses a day to Guadalajara between 8am and 10pm. Buy your ticket an hour before departure or even a day ahead. This is the best line for Manzanillo and Melaque.

The first-class **Tres Estrellas de Oro,** Insurgentes 210 (tel. 2-1019), offers 12 buses daily for the 12-hour trip to Guadalajara, for which you can buy a reserved-seat ticket the day before. It also has **de paso** buses to Culiacán, Mazatlán, and Manzanillo. The station is small and understaffed and what staff there is tends to be surly and gleefully unhelpful.

Transportes Norte de Sonora, at Madero 343 near Insurgentes (tel. 3-1322), has one bus to Tepic at 6am (a 3-hr. trip). In addition, it offers a 3pm bus to Mexico City and two to Guadalajara, including a first-class bus at 11pm. The remainder are second-class buses.

Transportes del Pacífico, Insurgentes 160 (tel. 2-1015), has both first- and second-class service to Guadalajara and Mexico City and second-class to Tepic. Its Tepic buses depart almost hourly from 5am to 9pm (a 3.5-hr. trip). **Estrella Blanca** (first class), Insurgentes 180 (tel. 2-0613), goes to Tepic (at 10am and 5pm), Irapuato, Mexico City (3 buses daily), and Guadalajara (4 buses daily).

CITY LAYOUT

From the center of old town nearly everything in the central village is within walking distance. The seaside promenade, or *malecón,* follows the rim of the bay from north to south, and the town stretches back into the hills a half dozen blocks. Coming in from the airport, north of town, you'll pass the town pier, the Marina Vallarta development, and many luxury hotels; downtown the malecón is lined with shops and restaurants.

NEIGHBORHOODS IN BRIEF

The areas of Puerto Vallarta below begin in order from north to south.

Nuevo Vallarta Nuevo Vallarta, a master-planned resort, is just north of Puerto Vallarta, the airport, and Marina Vallarta and across the Ameca River in the state of Nayarit (about 8 miles north of downtown). It also has small hotels, condominiums, the Jack Tar Resort Village, a yacht marina, plus a convention center under construction. Another new complete resort complex is on the drawing board for Nuevo Vallarta and we'll be hearing more about it. For now though, Nuevo Vallarta is difficult to reach by public transportation; taxis charge $6 one-way to or from Puerto Vallarta proper.

Marina Vallarta Marina Vallarta, a resort-city-within-a-city, is at the northern edge of the hotel zone not far from the airport. It boasts a half dozen luxury hotels and condominium projects, a huge marina with 400 yacht slips, a golf course, restaurants and bars, an office park, and a shopping plaza.

Hotel Zone North of old town to the airport many luxury hotels, such as the Krystal, Sheraton, and Fiesta Americana, line a strip of beach.

North of the Río Cuale/old town The area north of the Río Cuale is the oldest part of town—the original Puerto Vallarta. The waterfront is lined with shops and restaurants and the town plaza and church are here.

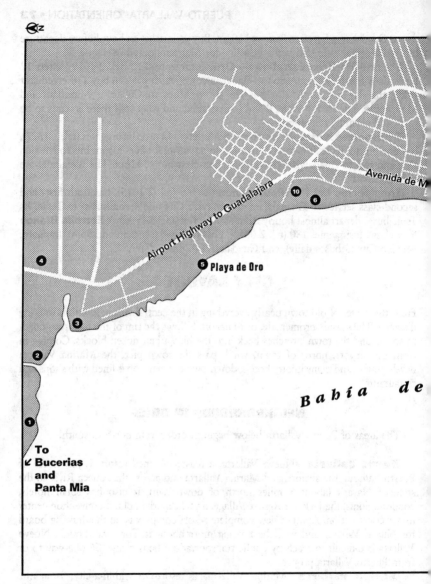

Airport ❷
Bullring ❹
Cruise Pier ❸
John Necomb Tennis Center ❻
Market ❽
Nueva Vallarta ❶
Playa de Oro ❺
Playa Olas Altas ❾
Tourist Office ❼
Villa Vallarta Cente
Zócalo ❼ₐ

PUERTO VALLARTA ORIENTATION

Río Cuale
Libramiento (Bypass)
Río Cuale

Market

The Malecón

7A
7

8

9
Playa Olas Altas

Banderas

To Manzanillo →

Los Arcos

To Yelapa and Tomatlan

Río Cuale The Cuale river divides north town from south town. In the middle of the river is an island now built up with numerous restaurants and shops.

South of the Río Cuale The area south of the river used to be only beach, but in the last decade it has become as built up as the old town. Today the best budget lodgings are here, as well as the bus "stations."

Mismaloya Beach South of town about 6 miles lies Mismaloya Beach, where *Night of the Iguana* was filmed, and the Jolla de Mismaloya Resort & Spa, which marks the farthest development to the south. Between it and the downtown are more five-star hotels such as the Camino Real and Garza Blanca Resort either on the beach or mountainside.

2. GETTING AROUND

By Bus City buses run from the airport through the expensive hotel zone along 31 de Mayo (the waterfront street), across the Río Cuale and inland on Vallarta, looping back through the downtown hotel and restaurant districts, on Insurgentes and several other downtown streets. These will serve just about all your transportation needs frequently and cheaply—about 35¢ a ride.

By the way, all the local buses leave from the same plaza, **Lázaro Cárdenas,** a few blocks south of the river at Cárdenas and Suárez. Hours are generally from 6am to 8 or 9pm. The ones heading north leave from the beach side of the plaza, on Olas Altas. If you want to go north to the airport, take a bus marked "Ixtapa" or "Junta."

If you want to go south, take the no. 02 minivan (*colectivo*), which leaves from the east side of the plaza, away from the beach, every 10 to 15 minutes all day until 5pm, then every half hour until 8 or 9pm. Be sure to ask if you want to go to Mismaloya Beach; another no. 02 goes farther to Boca de Tomatlán (a fishing village) and may not stop at Mismaloya. Otherwise there are few regular stops—you just tell the driver where you want to get out. As a rule, locals riding the buses and minivans are very helpful to tourists. The fare is about 50¢.

IMPRESSIONS

The west coast beach towns Puerto Vallarta and San Blas, once completely isolated, are now booming. Every tourist tells the next one that these places are the real Mexico, off the beaten track, tranquil, and despite a certain squalidity, also delightful. And tourists are already beginning to go there by the hundreds. Within four or five years we will probably have half a dozen rivals for Acapulco, which, with the present great influx of North Americans, has practically ceased to be a Mexican town.
—JOHN A. CROW, *MEXICO TODAY*, 1957

At the present moment the only way to reach Puerto Vallarta is by plane . . . Although a road is sketched upon maps, only some ungainly open-air, high-wheeled buses make the trip. It takes them about 2 days [from Guadalajara] to make the 200 mile trip."
—JAMES NORMAN, *TERRY'S GUIDE TO MEXICO*, 1965

By Boat The town pier (*muelle*), where you'll catch pleasure boats to Yelapa and for fishing excursions, is north of town near the airport and a convenient, inexpensive bus ride from town. Just take any bus marked "Pittalal" and tell the driver to let you off at the muelle. Do not confuse the town pier with the new pier south of the river at Playa Olas Altas.

By Taxi They cost $2 to $3 for most trips downtown, $8 to $10 to or from Mismaloya Beach to the south. But with such good bus service there's little reason to use them.

FAST FACTS: PUERTO VALLARTA

American Express The office is located in the Villa Vallarta shopping center on the main highway to the airport (Carretera Aeropuerto, km 2.5), north of downtown (tel. 2-6876, toll free 91-800/00-333).

Area Code The area code is 322.

Climate Hot and humid; rain most afternoons June through August.

Consulates The U.S. Consular Agency is at Miramar and Libertad on the second floor of Parián del Puente 12B, just north of the river bridge near the market (tel. 322/2-0069, 24 hours a day for emergencies). Open Monday, Wednesday, and Friday from 9am to 1pm; Tuesday and Thursday from 10am to 1pm.

Holidays See "Special Events" in Chapter 5; also see "Where to Go" in Chapter 2.

Information The State Tourism Office, Juárez and Independencia (tel. 322/2-0242, 2-0243, or 3-0744), is in a corner of the white Presidencia Municipal building near the main square. This is also the office of the "tourist police" who hear tourist complaints. Open Monday to Friday from 9am to 9pm, Saturday from 9am to 1pm.

Important note: Beware of "tourist information" booths along the street—they are usually time-share hawkers offering "free" or cheap Jeep rentals, cruises, breakfasts, etc., as bait. If you are suckered in, you may or may not get what is offered and the experience will cost at least half a day of your vacation.

Laundry Lavandería Nelly on Guerrero near Matamoros will wash and dry a load of clothes for about $3. Open Monday to Friday from 9am to 1:30pm and 4 to 8pm, Saturday from 9am to 1:30pm.

Telephone See "Fast Facts: Mexico" in Chapter 2.

CHAPTER 4
WHERE TO STAY & DINE IN PUERTO VALLARTA

1. **WHERE TO STAY**
- FROMMER'S SMART TRAVELER: HOTELS
2. **WHERE TO DINE**
- FROMMER'S SMART TRAVELER: RESTAURANTS

The hotel and restaurant listings in this chapter begin in Marina Vallarta at the far north end of Puerto Vallarta's developed area and end past downtown at Mismaloya, the farthest development south.

1. WHERE TO STAY

MARINA VALLARTA

The Marina Vallarta is the northern extension of the "Hotel Zone" and is located just before the airport. The hotels below are built around the new 400-slip marina and 18-hole golf course designed by Joe Finger. All except the Quinta Real are on the beach.

MARRIOTT CASAMAGNA, Marina Vallarta, Puerto Vallarta, Jal. Tel. 322/1-0004, toll free 800/228-9290 in the U.S. 433 rms and suites (all with bath). A/C TV TEL MINIBAR

$ Rates: High season $201 single or double sunset view; $230 single or double ocean view; $402 suite.

You're first impressed with the splendid openness of this grand hotel which debuted in 1990; the enormous lobby soars and baronial hallways lead to the rooms and beach; from the lobby to the beach you cross a small artificial pond. The sound of fountains is ever present throughout the hotel. Rooms are accented in pale sienna and pale ocher and all have ocean views and balconies, hairdryers, ironing boards and irons, and in-room safety-deposit boxes. Rooms with king-size beds have a couch; those with two double beds have an easy chair and game table.

Dining/Entertainment: Mikado, the Japanese restaurant, is open for dinner; La Estancia, open for all three meals; and Las Casitas, a poolside restaurant, is open for breakfast and lunch.

Services: Laundry, room service, travel agency, car rental, beauty salon, barber

> **FROMMER'S SMART TRAVELER: HOTELS**
>
> 1. Purchasing a package which includes either hotel alone or airfare usually saves considerable money.
> 2. Never pay the public rate without first investigating package deals from your home country before arrival in Puerto Vallarta.
> 3. Consider travel time to and from Puerto Vallarta before purchasing a 2- or 3-day package (you could spend half your time traveling).
> 4. Most of the bargain hotels are in town, south of the Río Cuale.
> 5. More expensive hotels are in the Hotel Zone, Marina Vallarta, and south to Mismaloya.
> 6. Travel during May, August, and September—the slowest months of the off-season (post-Easter to mid-December). Always ask about discounted rates or special packages in those months.
> 7. Prices go up anywhere from 25% to 50% from mid-December through Easter week, when all the best rooms are generally booked.
> 8. It's best to have reservations in high season, but if you don't, arrive early in the day and start your search. If you are told that the rooms are full, ask if you can leave your name and return at checkout time to see if anyone has vacated.

shop, gift shop, summer children's program (ages 5 to 12) at extra cost, 14 security cameras.

Facilities: Huge oceanside pool, coed gym, 5 tennis courts (3 lighted for night play), volleyball court.

MELIA PUERTO VALLARTA, Marina Vallarta, Puerto Vallarta, Jal. 48300. Tel. 322/1-0200, toll free 800/336-3542 in the U.S. 403 rms. A/C TV TEL MINIBAR

$ Prices: High season $115 single, $127 double.

The new Melia Puerto Vallarta boasts an enormous swimming pool, a vast stretch of beach, and a football field–sized entrance courtyard illuminated by 49 tower skylights. The nine-story hotel was designed by the architect of the Barcelona Olympics facilities and it's so high-tech that it looks more like an industrial complex than a resort hotel. However, the lushly landscaped grounds, with clusters of flower beds and wide brick walkways, help soften the ultramodern feeling. Guest rooms have diagonal views of the marina or bay, landscaped private terraces, and bedside lighting control plus marble floors, wood and wicker furnishings, and brass accents. Despite its size the beach area is seldom used due to a retaining wall and steps that make access difficult. Watch out for the undertow.

Dining/Entertainment: The hotel's formal restaurant, Ailem (Melia spelled backwards) specializes in haute cuisine and grilled seafood. It's open from 6pm to 11pm. The coffee shop, Quetzal Café, is open from 7am to midnight. The beachfront restaurant, El Patio, serves sandwiches and drinks during pool hours. One of the two lounges has nightly entertainment.

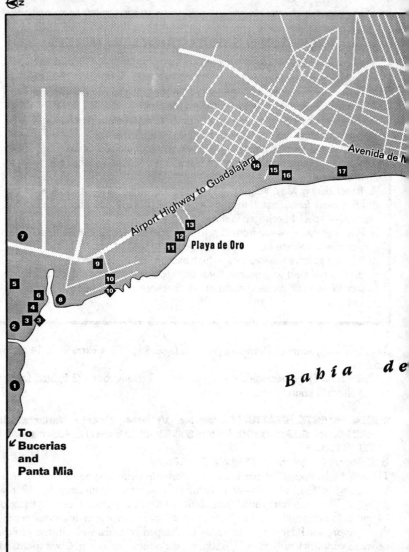

ACCOMMODATIONS:
Buenaventura 18
Camino Real 27
Casa Magna 3
Casa Panoramica 24
Casa Pilitas 26
Fiesta Americana 13
Fiesta American Plaza 16
Garza Blanca 28

Holiday Inn 11
Hyatt Coral Grand 29
La Jolla Mismolaya 30
Krystal 10
Melia Vallarta 6
Nuevo Rosita 19
Omni Vallarta 12
Playa de Oro 9
Plaza Las Glorias 15

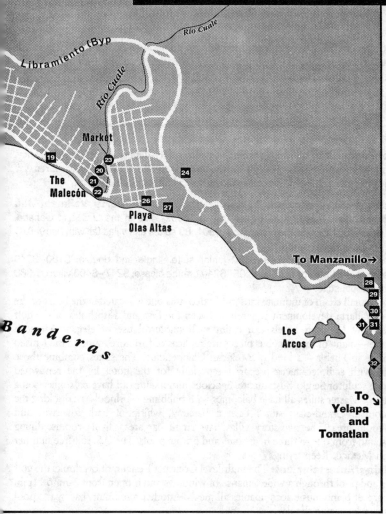

PUERTO VALLARTA ACCOMMODATIONS & DINING

Sheraton 17
Quinta Real 5
Velas Vallarta 4

DINING:
Casa Magna 3
Chico's Paradise 32
Krystal Restaurant 10
Tomatlán 31

POINTS OF INTEREST:
Airport 2
Bullring 7
Cruise Pier 8
Market 23 John Newcomb Tennis Center 16
Nueva Vallarta 1
Tourist Office 21
Villa Vallarta Center 14
Zócalo 22

IMPRESSIONS

There are a number of apartments for rent in town [Puerto Vallarta]. They range in price from $125 to $150 per month, including maid, utilities, etc.
—James Norman, Terry's Guide to Mexico, 1965

It becomes a virtue, almost a necessity, to do some loafing. The art of leisure is therefore one of Mexico's most stubbornly defended practises [sic] and one of her subtle appeals; a lesson in civilization which we of the hectic north need very badly to learn.
—Anita Brenner, Your Mexican Holiday, 1932.

Services: Laundry, room service, in-room safety-deposit boxes, travel agency, car rentals, shopping arcade, water sports, and supervised activities for children.
Facilities: Large pool, 2 tennis courts, volleyball, and table tennis.

QUINTA REAL, Pelicanos 311, Marina Vallarta, Puerto Vallarta, Jal. 48300. Tel. 322/1-0800, toll free 800/362-9170 in the U.S. and Canada, 91-800/3-6015 in Mexico. Fax 322/1-0801. 80 suites and villas (all with bath). A/C TV TEL

$ Rates: High season $140–$160 junior suite single and double; $160–$240 master suite single or double; $205–$240 grande classe; $247–$400 villa; $1,380 presidential suite.

One of a small chain of intimate inns in Mexico, this one is located in the heart of the Marina Vallarta development squarely between the first and 18th holes of the golf course. Few Mexican hotels can claim such masterful use of elegant Mexican furniture—many of the gorgeous pieces are replicas of furniture found in the Museo Alfenique in Puebla—a kind of Mexican Chippendale. The suites combine those designs with sculpted faces prepared especially for the hotel by the renowned Mexican sculptor Sergio Bustamante. Spacious junior suites all have balconies (some have two). Master suites all have balconies with bubbling whirlpools overlooking the golf course. Grand-class suites have a balcony, whirlpool bath for two, and living-room area. The two-story villas have small bar areas, living rooms, dining rooms, and from one to three bedrooms and private pools. The U.S. toll-free number rings in Mexico. Keep trying.

Dining/Entertainment: The multilevel Gourmet Restaurant overlooks the golf course and pool through a wide expanse of windows and is open from 7am to 11pm. Live harp or piano music accompanies all meals. Another restaurant/bar by the pool serves snacks during the day.

Services: Laundry, room service, car rental, travel agency. Grande classe guests receive champagne and fresh juice on arrival, have separate check-in and access to the hotel's fax and secretarial services.

Facilities: Large gorgeous pool facing the golf course; 46 private pools.

VELAS VALLARTA GRAND SUITE RESORT, Marina Vallarta, Puerto Vallarta, Jal. 48300. Tel. 322/1-0091, toll free 800/659-8477 in the U.S. and Canada. 361 suites (all with bath). A/C TV TEL

$ Rates: High season $173 single; $310 double.

This large, sprawling all-suite hotel is set on 10 beachfront acres built in a U shape with two wings of one- and two-bedroom suites and a central area with a lobby, restaurants, bar, and shops. A colonnaded arcade separates the lobby from the lushly landscaped pool area which meanders with waterfalls and has plenty of lounging areas. Though all the spacious units are privately owned, approximately half are used for hotel purposes (the upper three floors). All have ocean views, marble floors, large living rooms, full kitchens with coffee makers, microwaves, and blenders—the works. The large bedrooms open onto terraces running the width of the suite. Two-bedroom suites have two bathrooms, a dining table for eight, a set of doors leading to the terrace, and a small empty room ideal for a child's bedroom. All are decorated with rattan furniture in light tones and pastel fabrics.

Dining/Entertainment: The restaurant Andrea is open from 7am to 10:30pm and serves international cuisine featuring flaming dishes and crêpes. The Gourmet Nook, an intimate eatery featuring nouvelle Mexican cuisine, serves dinner from 6pm to midnight. The palapa-covered Beach Club by the pool serves sandwiches and crêpes from 11am to 5pm and cocktails until 7pm. The lobby bar, La Alhambra, is open from 5pm to 1am and features live entertainment nightly. There's usually a Mexican Fiesta Night once a week by the pool with live entertainment and dancing.

Services: Laundry, room service, travel agency, baby-sitting, concierge, beauty shop, car rental, and activities program for children.

Facilities: 3 interconnected swimming pools and children's pool, 4 tennis courts (3 lighted) with tennis pro on duty, game room and video arcade, indoor and outdoor parking.

HOTEL ZONE

The main street from town and fronting the hotel zone is Avenida de las Garzas, but it's also known as the airport road—a handy piece of information to keep in mind when reading addresses.

FIESTA AMERICANA PUERTO VALLARTA, Av. de las Garzas s/n, Puerto Vallarta, Jal. 48300. Tel. 322/2-2010, toll free 800/223-2332 in the U.S. 363 rms and suites. A/C TV TEL MINIBAR

$ Rates: High season $195 single or double deluxe room. **Parking:** Free.

The Fiesta Americana's enormous thatched palapa lobby is a landmark along hotel row and is equally impressive once you enter the spacious lobby. With lots of plants, splashing fountains, breezes, and sitting areas, the lobby sets a casual South Seas tone. The nine-story building embraces a large plaza with pool facing the beach. Marble-trimmed rooms in neutral tones with pastel accents come with pretty carved headboards and comfortable furniture. All have private balconies with sea views.

Dining/Entertainment: Chula Vista is open from breakfast through dinner, La Pergola is open from 7am to 11pm, and El Morocco is open for fine dining from 7pm to midnight. There's live music nightly in the lobby bar. Friday López is the popular disco, open from 10:30pm to 3am.

Services: Laundry, room service, travel agency, beauty shop, in-room hairdryers.

Facilities: Pool, 6 tennis courts, tennis privileges at the Fiesta Americana Plaza Vallarta, health club with sauna and massages.

FIESTA AMERICANA PLAZA VALLARTA TENNIS & BEACH RESORT, Av. de las Garzas (km 2.5 on airport highway), Puerto Vallarta, Jal.

48300. **Tel. 322/2-4448,** toll free 800/223-2332 in the U.S. and Canada. 438 rms and suites. A/C TV TEL MINIBAR

$ Rates: High season $115–$150 single or double. **Parking:** Free.

An airy atrium lobby surrounded by two-story stucco arches marks the contemporary hacienda style of this five-story beachfront hotel. Its wings frame a huge courtyard with a large free-form pool facing the beach. The medium-sized rooms are decorated in earth tones and pastels with attractive cane and wood furniture, marble-trimmed baths (with shower and tub), and private balconies. Most rooms have ocean views.

Dining/Entertainment: The elegant Place Vendôme, open from 6pm to 11pm, features French/Cajun/Creole cuisine and live piano music. Condesa del Mar specializes in gourmet continental fare and is open from 11am to 5pm. Los Cantaros serves American and Mexican favorites from 7am to 9pm. In the evening the Lobby Bar has live music for dancing.

Services: Laundry, room service, business center, travel agency, shopping arcade, concierge, baby-sitting.

Facilities: John Newcombe Tennis Club with 4 lighted indoor courts and 4 outdoor clay courts (see "Sports and Recreation" in Chapter 5), large pool, sauna, massage by appointment.

KRYSTAL VALLARTA, Av. de las Garzas s/n, Puerto Vallarta, Jal. 48300. **Tel. 322/2-1041,** toll free 800/231-9860 in the U.S. and Canada. 359 rms, suites, and villas (all with bath). A/C TV TEL MINIBAR

$ Rates: High season $138 deluxe room single or double; $185 junior suite single or double; $325–$460 master suite; $475–$1,035 villa.

Built to resemble a Mexican village with cobblestone streets, this completely self-contained resort oasis is spread out over 37 plant- and fountain-filled acres with a prime beachfront location. Interwoven in this setting are the accommodations in one- and two-story buildings. Although the resort is large, there is still a sense of seclusion, with many shaded interior walkways linking the various pool areas and restaurants. In fact, with seven restaurants and numerous bars, you can dine and drink without ever leaving the place, should that be your choice. All the guest rooms were completely refurnished and renewed in 1991. The four varieties of accommodations include 38 three-bedroom villas with private pools, 22 suites with spacious living rooms, 48 junior suites, and 251 deluxe rooms. Trios of villas share a private pool; large suites come with refrigerators. All come with tile floors, area rugs, tasteful loomed bedspreads, and balconies or patios. Electric carts take guests to and from their rooms, for, depending on where your room is, it can be a long walk within the grounds. The hotel is not far from the main pier and airport.

Dining/Entertainment: Seven restaurants are open daily including: Bogart's, one of the finest restaurants in Puerto Vallarta, open from 6pm to midnight; Kamakura, an excellent Japanese restaurant, open from noon to midnight; Tango, featuring specialties from Argentina, open from 6pm to midnight; La Terrazza, for Mexican food, open from 7 to 11:30pm; El Palmara, open for breakfast from 8 to 11am; Rarotonga, seafood restaurant by the pool, open from 7 to 10:30am and noon to 5:30pm; and La Noria coffee shop, open 24 hours. Among the six bars, the lobby bar has live music nightly. For evening entertainment there's Christine's disco, open from 10:30pm to 3am; Fiesta Brava, is held Thursday in winter, and guests are seated for a Mexican dinner at tables overlooking a bullring where the show is held.

PUERTO VALLARTA: WHERE TO STAY • 85

Services: Laundry, room service, travel agency, shops, baby-sitting with 12 hours' advance notice, wedding arrangements with advance notice, car rental.

Facilities: Olympic-size pool, 2 free-form pools, 38 private pools, 2 tennis courts, racquetball court, fitness center with whirlpool and exercise equipment.

OMNI PUERTO VALLARTA HOTEL AND GRAND SPA, Av. de las Garzas s/n, Puerto Vallarta, Jal. 48300. Tel. 322/2-3959, toll free 800/843-6664 in the U.S. 248 rms and suites (all with bath). A/C TV TEL

$ Rates: $100–$115 standard; $115–$140 deluxe; $120 Omni Club; $432–$490 ambassador suite. Ask about spa packages.

The central 14-story hotel is flanked on both sides by five stories of rooms leading to the beach and overlooking the pool and ocean. Opened in 1989, its exclusive calling card is the 12,000-square-foot, fully equipped and staffed spa—the only one in Puerto Vallarta. The rooms are wonderfully large, with high ceilings, natural tone furniture, and pastel fabrics and walls. Standard rooms are in the five-story wings, deluxe rooms are on the first nine floors of the main tower. The 26 Omni Club rooms, on the penthouse floors, have additional amenities (see below). Spa services can be purchased separately as a 3- or 7-day package in three varieties—beauty and pampering, anti-stress management, and weight and fitness control. Spa packages include all spa meals. The hotel is next to the Hotel Fiesta Americana Puerto Vallarta.

Dining/Entertainment: La Terraza, a sunny restaurant facing the pool, is open for all meals. The Beach Club, outdoors, is open daylight hours. The Villalinda is the hotel's fine-dining restaurant open in the evening and serving international food. Spa guests can request a special spa menu.

Services: Laundry, room service, travel agency, beauty shop. Omni Club guests receive robes in each room, daily continental breakfast, afternoon hors d'oeuvres, express registration, and concierge assistance.

Facilities: Large outdoor pool. Spa facilities include 22 Universal weight stations, 6 computerized bicycles, and an aerobics room with scheduled classes and circuit training. Professional nutritional and fitness evaluations are offered, with herbal wrap, salt-glow loofah, mud pack, hour massage, shiatsu massage, facial, anti-aging treatment, mini-lifting mask, and mud mask. Spa services are separate for men and women and include whirlpool, cold plunge, sauna, eucalyptus steam room, pressure showers, and locker rooms.

PLAZA LAS GLORIAS PUERTO VALLARTA, Av. de las Garzas s/n, Puerto Vallarta, Jal. 48300. Tel. 322/2-2224. Toll free 800/342-2644 in the U.S. 374 rms, suites, and villas. A/C TV TEL MINIBAR

$ Rates: High season $105–$160 single or double. **Parking:** Free.

Designed in a contemporary Mediterranean style with white stucco, terra-cotta tile, and handcrafted Mexican touches, this four-story hotel is arranged around a palm-shaded pool area facing the sea. Individual palapas line its beach. The standard rooms are small- to medium-size, with cool marble floors, ivory walls, blond rattan furniture, and usually balconies. The 140 villas include kitchenettes. It's adjacent to the Plaza Vallarta shopping center, which has 100 shops.

Dining/Entertainment: Las Pergolas restaurants offers international cuisine and La Terraza is the poolside restaurant for snacks. Of the three bars, the one at the pool features live music from 7 to 11pm.

Services: Laundry, room service, travel agency, car rental, shops, concierge, baby-sitting.

Facilities: 2 pools, sauna, massage by appointment, tennis privileges at the nearby Fiesta Americana Plaza Vallarta.

NORTH OF THE RÍO CUALE

This is the real center of town, where the market, principal plazas, church, and town hall all lie. Budget lodgings are scarce here, although most of the hotels are moderately priced.

MODERATE

HOTEL BUENAVENTURA, Av. Mexico 1301, Puerto Vallarta, Jal. 48350. Tel. 322/2-3737, toll free 800/227-0212 in California, 800/458-6888 elsewhere in the U.S. 210 rms. A/C TEL

$ **Rates:** High season $60 single, $70 double, $80 triple; off-season $40 single, $45 double, $50 triple.

⭐ The giant palapa roof of the hotel lobby and restaurant set the tone for the breezy, jungle-lush interior filled with *equipales* leather furniture. Somewhat off the beaten tourist track, the Buenaventura holds its place in the market with appealing prices, comfort, and its beautiful beachfront. The attractive rooms have beam-and-brick ceilings and tiled floors, and some have balconies. There's also a swimming pool next to the beach. Only fourth-floor rooms have color TV with U.S. channels. It's on the beach about 6 blocks north of the malecón at Nicaragua.

BUDGET

CHEZ ELENA INN, Matamoros 172, Puerto Vallarta, Jal. 48350. Tel. 322/2-0161. 17 rms. FAN

$ **Rates:** High season $35 single or double; off-season $25.

A quiet secluded cozy inn set on a hillside overlooking Banderas Bay, the rooms are built around a small central patio off the restaurant (see "Where to Dine," below). Access is up a flight of stairs to a second floor, where breezes keep rooms cool. The different colored rooms are decorated with simple Mexican furnishings and accented with local crafts. There's a rooftop deck for sunning. Located on a hill above the cathedral in the central part of town, it's ideal for those who want peace and quiet and an excellent restaurant.

HOTEL ENCINO, Juárez 122, Puerto Vallarta, Jal. 48380. Tel. 322/2-0051. Fax 322/2-2573. 75 rms. A/C TEL

$ **Rates:** $22 single; $26 double.

🅢 The hotel's spotless rooms are cheerfully decorated with turquoise-blue furniture and other bright touches, white walls, and tiled floors. Most have their own private balconies with sliding glass doors and views of the ocean, river, or mountains and town. Rooms also come with radios. Especially nice are the rooftop swimming pool and the restaurant/bar, Vista Cuale, which enjoy lovely vistas of mountains and sea. To find it head south on Juárez to the place where Vallarta crosses the river; it's next to the bridge.

SOUTH OF THE RÍO CUALE

VERY EXPENSIVE

CASA PILITAS, Santa Barbara 428 (Apdo. Postal 114), Puerto Vallarta, Jal. 48300. Tel. 322/2-0496, toll free 800/745-7085. 4 rms (all with bath). FAN

$ Rates: For eight people daily, Nov–May $460; June–Oct $375.

A private eight-level villa on Los Muertos beach with four bedrooms, it climbs a verdant hillside from the beach to the entry at the top level. You enter by way of a tiled outdoor terrace with a panoramic view (great for watching sunsets in winter). The living room, dining room, kitchen level is furnished in white with vibrant accents and has a live, caged macaw. The next level holds the cozy den. Bedroom one on the next level has twin beds, while bedroom two on the level following has a king-size bed and private terrace. Below was the owner's original living room, and the bedroom, with a double bed, is reached via a spiral staircase. The final living level has a private balcony overlooking the pool and terrace level, which are nearest the beach. Fireplaces throughout are functional, but hardly necessary in balmy Puerto Vallarta.

Services: A cook, maid, and gardener are included in the price, and guests provide their own food. (The staff will do the shopping.) There's an extra deposit for use of the phone, which can be refunded.

Facilities: Pool, two large terraces.

EXPENSIVE

CASA PANORAMICA, Hwy. 200 to Mismaloya, km 1 (Apdo. Postal 114), Puerto Vallarta, Jal. 48300. Tel. 322/2-3656, toll free in the U.S. 800/745-7805. 7 rms (all with bath). FAN

$ Rates (including breakfast): Nov–May $98; June–Oct $110.

Nestled in a jungle hillside this 24 room villa was once a private home that has become a handsome bed-and-breakfast. As you enter the wrought-iron gate, the spacious pool terrace is on the left, with its own kitchen, bar, and a sheltered and unsheltered lounge area. The second level has two bedrooms (Hibiscus and Poinsettia) each with a king-size bed. Level three has two bedrooms (Copa de Oro and Aves de Paraiso) with two double beds and a king-size bed, respectively. These levels can be rented by the room or as a four-bedroom house. Next up is level three with one bedroom (Mariposa), a completely separate suite with kitchen and private balcony, next to a lovely terrace with a gas grill. On the top level is a bedroom (Margaritas) with a queen-size bed, living room, and kitchen, and another bedroom (Orquidias) with a living room and terrace garden. The latter two are adjacent to the hotel's panoramic terrace with the best views in the house. Breakfast is served here under a thatched palapa roof. Rooms have white brick walls and tile floors and colonial-style furniture using light colored fabrics and colorful Mexican accents. The house can be rented in its entirety, by the individual room, or as a four-bedroom, two-bedroom, or one-bedroom house. Each room has a private entry. Most bathrooms have sunken tubs and all have tub/shower combinations.

Dining: Breakfast is served daily on the upper terrace.

Services: Breakfast cook, maid, gardener/houseboy. On request, coffee can be served in your room before breakfast. A full-time cook can be arranged for an extra cost.

Facilities: Pool, several terraces.

MODERATE

CASA CORAZON, 326 Amapas (Apdo. Postal 66), Puerto Vallarta, Jal. 48380. **Tel.** 322/2-1371 at the restaurant. 12 rms (all with bath). FAN

$ Rates (including breakfast): High season $55–$60 single or double; off-season $20–$25 single or double. *Note:* No children under 12.

Perched on a hill beside the beach Playa del Sol, this four-story villa has been converted by its American owners into a delightful bed-and-breakfast inn. It prides itself on its friendly, casual atmosphere, where guests get together over the complete breakfast served on the expansive terrace. The front gate opens onto the beach, where the inn has a bar and restaurant.

To get there, walk 10 blocks south of the river on Vallarta, turn right onto Pilita for 3 blocks, then left for ½ block on Amapas. For reservations write to P.O. Box 937, Las Cruces, NM 88004 (tel. 505/523-4666 or 522-4684).

HOTEL MOLINO DE AGUA, Vallarta 130 (Apdo. Postal 54), Puerto Vallarta, Jal. 48380. **Tel.** 322/2-1907 or 2-1957, toll free 800/423-5512 in California, 800/826-9408 elsewhere in the U.S., Fax 322/2-6056. 20 rms, 16 suites, 29 cabins (all with bath). A/C

$ Rates: High season $55–$85; low season $35–$70. **Parking:** Free.

This complex of luxury cabins and small buildings, reached by winding walkways, is nestled into lush tropical gardens beside the river and sea. Although on a main street and centrally located, with all its big trees and open space it's a completely tranquil oasis. Some units are individual bungalows with private patios and there's a small two-story building near the beach. Amenities include a Jacuzzi beside the pool and an excellent restaurant/bar, the Aquarena. Parking is protected. It's ½ block south of the river on Vallarta.

HOTEL FONTANA DEL MAR, Dieguez 171, Puerto Vallarta, Jal. 48380. **Tel.** 322/2-0583 or 2-0712, toll free 800/458-6888 in the U.S. 27 rms, 15 suites (all with bath). A/C TV TEL

$ Rates: High season $35 single, $40 double; off-season $25 single, $30 double; $5–$7 more for suite.

One of the best budget hotels in the area is on a quiet side street in downtown Vallarta, only 2 blocks from the beach, Playa del Sol. The inviting decor includes curly white iron and royal blue. The clean, comfortable rooms overlook the plant-filled courtyard with more frilly iron trim. All rooms have showers, and the suites come with balconies or kitchenettes. Guests can use the small rooftop swimming pool or the pool and beach-club facilities at the Hotel Playa Los Arcos a block away.

PLAYA LOS ARCOS, Olas Altas 390, Puerto Vallarta, Jal. 48380. **Tel.** 322/2-1583, toll free 800/458-6888 in the U.S. Fax 322/2-0583. 135 rms, 10 suites (all with bath). A/C TEL

$ Rates: Dec 18–Easter $40–$50 single, $50–$60 double; $70–$90 suite; off-season $46 double. Ask about further discounts in June and Sept–Oct.

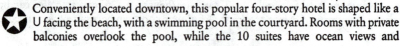
Conveniently located downtown, this popular four-story hotel is shaped like a U facing the beach, with a swimming pool in the courtyard. Rooms with private balconies overlook the pool, while the 10 suites have ocean views and

kitchenettes. The standard rooms are small but pleasantly decorated with pink floral spreads and carved wooden furniture painted pale pink—two double beds, a dresser, a table, and two chairs. On the premises there are tennis courts, a restaurant, coffee shop, and beachside bar with occasional live entertainment. It's 7 blocks south of the river.

To find it, walk 5 blocks south of the river on Vallarta, then right on Badillo 2 blocks, then left on Olas Altas.

BUDGET

HOTEL MARSOL, Rodriguez 103 (Apdo. Postal 4), Puerto Vallarta, Jal. 48380. Tel. 332/2-1365 or 2-0865. 138 rms, 22 apartments (all with bath). A/C (22 apartments) FAN
$ Rates: $28 single; $36 double; $46 apartment for one or two.

Right on Playa del Sol beach, this large, airy hotel has nothing but a row of coconut palms and a retaining wall between its veranda and the beach, while oceanside restaurants are a mere 50 yards away. The apartments have balconies facing the sea and aging kitchenettes. The other rooms face the mountains and town. There's also a pool.

To get there walk 7 blocks south of the river on Vallarta, then right on Rodriguez to the beach.

POSADA RIO CUALE, Serdan 242 (Apdo. Postal 146), Puerto Vallarta, Jal. 48380. Tel. 322/2-0450 or 2-0914. 21 rms (all with bath). A/C
$ Rates: $31 single; $36 double.

This delightful two-story hotel occupies one of the town's busiest intersections. Its large rooms have arched brick windows and wooden shutters; the quietest are away from Calle Vallarta. At night the swimming pool becomes a lighted fountain, and the courtyard around it is part of the popular Restaurant Gourmet, which has mariachi music on Friday, Saturday, and Sunday nights from 8 to 10:30pm. Park in front on the street.

Walk 1 block south of the river at Serdan and Vallarta.

HOTEL POSADA DE ROGER, Badillo 237, Puerto Vallarta, Jal. 48380. Tel. 322/2-0836 or 2-0639. 52 rms (all with bath). A/C (24 rms) FAN TEL
$ Rates: $20 single; $23 double. Extra person $4.

$ This former pension is now a hotel with simple but homey, comfortable, and spotless rooms at a good price. Guests enjoy the small, second-floor swimming pool and choose from several levels of terraces with tropical plants and bougainvillea. The hotel has retained its friendly ambience, and guests still gather in the attractive courtyard for conversation and entertainment. The hotel's restaurant/bar, El Tucán, is downstairs.

To get here walk 5 blocks south of the river on Vallarta, then right on Badillo ½ block.

SOUTH TO MISMALOYA

VERY EXPENSIVE

GARZA BLANCA, Hwy. 200 south to Mismaloya, km 7.3 (Apdo. Postal 58), Puerto Vallarta, Jal. Tel. 322/2-1023, toll free 800/331-0908 in the

U.S. and Canada; 213/216-2900 in Los Angeles. 59 rms, suites, casitas, villas. A/C TEL MINIBAR

$ Rates: $260 beachfront suite; $315 chalet suite; $340–$435 1- or 2-bedroom casita; $505 2- or 3-bedroom villa. Ask about tennis and golf packages.

This intimate and exclusive resort, 4½ miles from downtown, caters to a clientele who value rest and relaxation over action and activity. Nestled on a hillside and around beautiful Palo María beach south of town, there's a rustic-tropical feeling, with natural materials used simply yet elegantly—roughly carved wood, driftwood, stone walls, and leather furniture. From the one-bedroom, two-story suites you step from your door onto the beach. Private pools come with the one-bedroom, chalet suites which are set into the hillside overlooking the bay. The villas and casitas also perch on the hill but are larger, with one, two, or three bedrooms. The Mexican hacienda-style interiors of the casitas and chalets are split-level with tile floors, high ceilings, substantial wood furniture, large windows, lots of plants, and ceramic art and accessories; each has a private garden patio and pool overlooking the sea. Rooms also have ceiling fans and vast ocean views. Jeeps or vans take guests to and from the hillside accommodations.

Dining/Entertainment: The Café, by the pool, is open daily from 8:30am to 4pm. The Restaurante, an open-air restaurant by the beach, is open from 7:30 to 11pm daily and offers an international menu.

Services: Laundry, room service, gift shop, and weddings (ask for their wedding information sheet).

Facilities: 6 hard-surface tennis courts with tennis pro, central pool and several private pools, golf privileges at the Marina Vallarta Club de Golf.

EXPENSIVE

CAMINO REAL, Hwy. 200 south to Mismaloya, km 3.2. Tel. 322/2-0002, toll free 800/228-3000 through Westin Hotels in the U.S. and Canada. 337 rms and suites (all with bath). A/C TV TEL MINIBAR

$ Rates: $185–$207 single or double main building; $230–$276 single or double Royal Beach Club; $300 Fiesta Suite.

Not so long ago the Camino Real was the farthest hotel or establishment of any kind, 2½ miles south of town. Though it has neighbors now, on down the highway, it's still set apart with a lush mountain backdrop and retains that exclusivity that made it popular from the beginning. The hotel is actually two buildings: the 250-room main hotel curving gently with the shape of the Playa Las Estacas (beach), and the new 11-story, 87-room Royal Beach Club, also on the beach. Rooms in the main building are large, some with sliding doors facing the bay, and others with balconies. Royal Beach Club rooms from the sixth floor up have balconies with whirlpool spas. The top floor is divided among six two-bedroom Fiesta Suites with whirlpool spas on the balcony, and each has a private swimming pool. All rooms are accented with the vibrant colors of Mexico and come with hairdryers, remote control TV (with U.S. channels), and in-room safe-deposit boxes. Royal Beach Club rooms have robes besides other amenities mentioned below.

Dining/Entertainment: Restaurants, all open daily include: La Perla, open from 7pm to midnight, features nouvelle-French cuisine; Azulejos, on a patio terrace by the beach, is open from 7am to midnight; La Brisa, on the north end of the beach, open from 11am to 6pm, serves seafood specialties; and the Snack Shack near the pool serves drinks and sandwiches from 11am to 6pm. The lobby bar, with a view of the bay, opens from 5pm to 1am with live bands each evening and dancing on weekends.

Services: Laundry, room service, travel agency, car rental, children's program December, June, July, and August.

Facilities: 2 swimming pools, 2 lighted tennis courts, health club with weights, sauna, steam room, and weekday aerobic classes, boutiques, and convenience store. Royal Beach Club guests enjoy separate check-in and concierge, daily complimentary continental breakfast, and evening cocktails and hors d'oeuvres.

HYATT CORAL GRAND, Hwy. 200, km 8.5 (Apdo. Postal 448), Puerto Vallarta, Jal. 48300. Tel. 322/3-0707 or 2-5191, toll free in U.S. and Canada 800/233-1234. 120 suites (all with bath). A/C TV TEL MINIBAR

$ Rates: High season $190 standard single or double; $210 deluxe; $690 Coral Grand.

Overlooking a beautiful beach 5 miles south of town, this 10-story white hotel has window boxes spilling over with vines and bougainvillea. The open-air lobby is accessed from a bridge that connects it to the street four stories above the beach. Inside, waterfalls cascade through a lush courtyard; outside a pretty blue-tiled terrace is perfect for watching the waves. There's a serene, intimate ambience here. Spacious suites are done in white with pastel accents, tasteful art, comfortable furniture, and queen or double beds; each has a living room with a couch that makes into a bed, and small balconies provide a view of the ocean. Superior and deluxe suites have Jacuzzis, king-size beds, robes, and hairdryers. Master suites have two bedrooms and a whirlpool, and the Coral Grand suite has an indoor tile swimming pool with adjacent Jacuzzi, a waterfall, and a steam room.

Dining/Entertainment: El Coral, the gourmet restaurant, open from 6pm to midnight, serves international cuisine by candlelight while a piano plays softly. The Colibri restaurant, open from 7am to 6pm, specializes in seafood. The outdoor Oyster Bar faces the ocean and is open for lunch only. La Cascada, the poolside bar, is open daylight hours and the Lobby Bar opens midday, with live entertainment in the evenings.

Services: Laundry, room service, travel agency, concierge, baby-sitting.

Facilities: Large pool, children's pool, tennis court lighted at night, Ping-Pong and pool tables, board games, children's game room, water sports, gym with massage service and steam baths.

LA JOLLA DE MISMALOYA, Hwy. 200 south to Mismaloya, km 10.5 (Apdo. Postal 158B), Puerto Vallarta, Jal. Tel. 3-0660, toll free 800/322-2343 in California, 800/322-2344 elsewhere in the U.S. 394 suites. A/C TV TEL

$ Rates: $145 1-bedroom suite; $295 2-bedroom suite. Prices are higher Christmas and Easter week.

This hotel's three nine-story buildings are arranged around beautiful Mismaloya Beach, where *Night of the Iguana* was filmed. One building is set into a cliff overlooking the cove, while the two buildings on the beach are connected by a U-shaped arcade that frames a large courtyard of interlaced pools, palapas, patios, and lush gardens facing the sea. Shops, restaurants, and lounges are intermingled in this courtyard and arcade area. White stucco and large arches create the feeling of a spacious modern hacienda. Each of the guest quarters is a spacious suite equipped with kitchenettes with a counter that doubles as a bar with high stools. The majority have one bedroom with bath, but 31 have two baths and 15 have two bedrooms, two baths, and two kitchens. All have ocean views and balconies and are decorated in a luxurious contemporary style in whites and pastels with marble counters and floors. On a hill above the cove you can still see the ruins of the movie set. The hotel is 6½ miles south of town.

Dining/Entertainment: The Patio Restaurant, in the courtyard with a view of the beach, is open from 8am to 11pm. The Beach Club is open for lunch near the pool and features sandwiches and drinks. Bariloche, the fine-dining restaurant, offers specialties from Argentina and is open from 7 to 11pm. La Jolla, open from 8am to 11pm, features Mexican food from its perch on the cliff overlooking the cove. Iggy's disco, which shows *Night of the Iguana* every night at 7pm, is open from 7pm to 1am. Terrace of the Stars lounge, connected to Iggy's, has marvelous views of the cove and is open from noon to 1am. On Tuesday night the hotel holds a Beach Party with open bar, buffet, and live music from 7 to 10pm for $25; on Saturday night, from 7 to 10pm, it hosts a Mexican Fiesta with open bar, buffet, mariachis, folkloric dancing, and fireworks for $25.

Services: Laundry, room service, travel agency, concierge, purified tap water, travel agency, beauty shop, car rental, shopping arcade, baby-sitting.

Facilities: 5 pools (one for children), 3 tennis courts (with resident pro), 4 outdoor Jacuzzis, gym with steambath, and massages and facials are available, water sports on the beach. It's also possible to take small boats from Mismaloya Beach to Playa Yelapa (see "Sports and Recreation" in Chapter 5).

2. WHERE TO DINE

Although eating out in Puerto Vallarta has become more expensive, some bargains and good values remain.

MARINA VALLARTA

EXPENSIVE

MIKADO RESTAURANT, Marriott CasaMagna Hotel, Marina Vallarta. Tel. 1-0004.
   Specialty: JAPANESE.
$ Prices: Sushi appetizers $3–$10; main courses $18–$35.
   Open: Daily 8pm–11pm.

Puerto Vallarta's newest Japanese eatery is truly elegant. Though it offers the same type of grilled-at-the-table food as others of its kind, that's where the resemblance ends. The setting is royal Japanese, featuring high ceilings, elegant chandeliers, porcelain vases, and marble everywhere. Ferns and a generous use of wood and a collection of silk kimonos grace the walls. Food and service are superb. The menu features grilled seafood, with shrimp and lobster specialties, plus an extensive sushi

FROMMER'S SMART TRAVELER: RESTAURANTS

1. South of the river is the best area for finding inexpensive-to-moderate restaurants. One cluster centers around the street Olas Altas, quite close to the beach; another edges Vallarta. But the hottest new food street is Badillo, fast becoming the south side's unofficial "restaurant row."
2. North of the river, a nice snack as you stroll along the malecón is an *elote* (corn-on-the-cob) served on a stick either roasted or broiled, sold at little stands in the evening. Try it with mayonnaise and cheese, or with lemon, salt, and chile, the way the Mexicans like it.
3. You can pick up inexpensive fruit, vegetables, and picnic fixings at the municipal market beside the Río Cuale where Libertad and Rodriguez meet. You can also eat upstairs at one of the many little *loncherías*—just choose what is freshly cooked and hot.
4. Restaurants fronting the malecón and those on the beach will be more expensive and not necessarily better in quality than others in less prime locations.
5. Fine dining in Puerto Vallarta, however, can be just as exquisite but much less expensive than the equivalent in the U.S.

menu. Each selection is presented as a beautiful artistic arrangement complemented by fresh ginger and mustard.

HOTEL ZONE

EXPENSIVE

BOGART'S, Krystal Vallarta Hotel, Av. de las Garzas s/n. Tel. 2-1459.
  Specialty: CONTINENTAL/ECLECTIC.
  $ Prices: Full meal $75.
  Open: Daily 6pm–midnight.

Pointed Moorish arches, murmuring fountains, a silky tent ceiling, and high-backed peacock chairs create the mysterious mood of Casablanca in this softly lighted, sumptuous restaurant. A pianist plays in the background while waiters out of *Arabian Nights* serve such delicacies as Persian Crêpes (sour cream, cheese, and caviar), escargots, sorbet between courses, and flambéed Shrimp Krystal. For a big splurge or a special occasion, a dinner in this fantasy place is unforgettable. It's north of town near the main pier; take the "Muelle" bus. Bogart's is on the front of the hotel property, facing the main boulevard.

NORTH OF THE RÍO CUALE

MODERATE

LA CASA DEL ALMENDRO, Galeana 180. Tel. 2-4670.
  Specialty: MEXICAN.

$ Prices: Appetizers $2–$5; main courses $5–$12.
Open: Daily 11am–4pm and 5–11pm.

Built around the beautiful interior patio of a 19th-century home shaded by a huge almond tree in the middle, this charming restaurant is said to be the oldest house in Puerto Vallarta; it retains the atmosphere of a Mexican home and family members provide excellent service. Meals are served upstairs or down. At night candlelight flickers on checkered tablecloths. There's a downstairs bar as well. It's known for its seafood and has some of the best ceviche in town, and to honor its name, the restaurant serves almond-stuffed lobster and almond-cream pie. You'll find the restaurant just off the malecón 1 block inland on Galeana.

CHEZ ELENA, Matamoros 172. Tel. 2-0161.
Specialty: INDONESIAN/MEXICAN.
$ Prices: Appetizers $2–$4; main courses $5–$12.
Open: Daily 6pm–11pm.

Perched on a hillside with a magnificent view of the ocean, this exclusive little restaurant is part of a cozy inn (See "Where to Stay," above). The atmosphere is cool and quiet, more like someone's home than a commercial restaurant. The menu is filled with delicious (often fiery hot) Indonesian dishes as well as Mexican and seafood dishes. Regular menu items include a Mexican plate, an Indonesian plate with satay (peanut) sauce, and chicken Java with curry sauce; there's usually a seafood special also. Specialty coffees are served. It's located on a hill above the cathedral in the central part of town.

BRAZZ, Morelos and Galeana. Tel. 2-0324.
Specialty: MEXICAN.
$ Prices: Appetizers $2.50–$6; main courses $7–$17; breakfast $5–$6; seafood casseroles $10.
Open: Daily 8am–1am; live music nightly 7pm–1am.

Lunch bargains are served in the air-conditioned dining room, surrounded by a large open-air bar with leather equipales furniture. Festive *papel picado* (cut-out paper) and bits of painted fabric hang from the bar's high ceiling and flutter in the breeze. In the evening mariachis and marimbas play. You'll find it 1 block inland off the south end of the malecón.

EL OSTIÓN FELIZ, Libertad 177. Tel. 2-2508.
Specialty: MEXICAN/SEAFOOD.
$ Prices: Appetizers $4.50–$7; main courses $8–$17; seafood salad $6; crab tacos $4; seafood casseroles $10; oyster cocktail or stew $6.
Open: Daily 10am–midnight or 1am.

Across from the Hotel Río, "The Happy Oyster" serves a cornucopia of seafood, including a salad of squid, octopus, frogs' legs, conch, and shark. Choose from seven different seafood casseroles or be macho and go for the shark ceviche! Crayfish from local rivers is available in season. It's just 1 block north of the river on Libertad just off Morelos.

BUDGET

HELADOS BING, Juárez 280. Tel. 2-1627.
Specialty: ICE CREAM.
$ Prices: Single cone 90¢; special sundae $3.

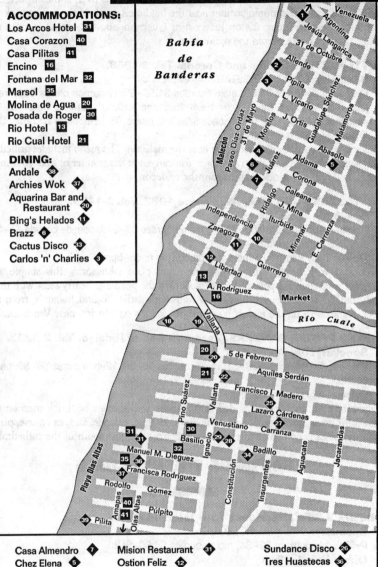

Open: Daily 8:30am–10:30pm.

The most popular ice-cream shop in town has a long list of flavors to choose from. It also has branches at Cárdenas and Constitución south of the river; at the airport; and at Villa Vallarta, the shopping center near the big hotels north of town. Just look for its pink-and-white decor. It's on Juárez near Guerrero, about 2 blocks in from the malecón and ½ block from the main plaza.

TUTTI FRUTTI, Morelos and Corona. Tel. 2-1068.
   Specialty: HEALTH/VEGETARIAN/AMERICAN.
$ Prices: Appetizers $1.50; main courses $1.50–$5; cinnamon coffee 50¢; fresh juices or licuados made with fresh fruit and milk or purified water $1.50; sandwiches $1.50–$2; three quesadillas and beans $3; hamburger and fries $4.
   Open: Mon–Sat 8am–10pm.

This is a good spot for a quick snack near the malecón. The menu includes grilled or cold sandwiches with all the trimmings. You can eat at the counter or take your meal out. You'll find it 1 block inland from the malecón.

RESTAURANT JUANITA, Av. Mexico 1067. Tel. 2-1458.
   Specialty: MEXICAN.
$ Prices: Appetizers $1.50–$2.50; main courses $3–$10; comida corrida $3–$4; pozole $2; giant shrimp $10.
   Open: Daily 8am–10:30pm; comida corrida noon–5pm.

Decorated with bright piñatas, paintings, and plaid tablecloths, this simple and cheerful restaurant is open to the sidewalk. Try the pozole (a hearty stew with meat and hominy) or splurge on the giant shrimp with garlic. To find Juanita's, from the river, walk north on the malecón several blocks; it's on Mexico near Venezuela.

PIETRO PASTAS & PIZZAS, Zaragoza 245 at Hidalgo. Tel. 2-3233.
   Specialty: ITALIAN.
$ Prices: Appetizers $3.50–$7; main courses $6–$8; 12-inch pizzas $6–$8; pasta $6.50.
   Open: Daily noon–midnight.

Italian music and swags of braided garlic on the wall above a big brick oven set the mood for menu offerings: ravioli, cannelloni, lasagne, calzone, and, of course, pizza. And the pasta is homemade. It's across the street and just south of the cathedral.

SOUTH OF THE RÍO CUALE

MODERATE

ARCHIE'S WOK, Rodriguez 130. Tel. 2-0411.
   Specialty: ORIENTAL/ECLECTIC.
$ Prices: Appetizers $2–$4; main courses $4.50–$12.
   Open: Daily 1–10pm.

After training as a chef in California, Archie Alpenia brought his family to Puerto Vallarta and ended up as chef to the late John Huston, director of *Night of the Iguana*. Today Archie's Wok stirs up delightfully eclectic Asian fare: Filipino eggrolls, Thai coconut fish, chicken Singapore, and spicy red curry, to name but a few dishes. Desserts surprise with homemade fudge brownies, lime pie, and carrot cake. To find it, walk 7 blocks south of the river on Vallarta, then left on Rodriguez 2½ blocks.

PUERTO VALLARTA: WHERE TO DINE • 97

RESTAURANT/BAR AQUARENA, Hotel Molino de Agua, Vallarta 130.
Tel. 2-1907 or 2-1957.
Specialty: MEXICAN/SEAFOOD.
$ Prices: Appetizers $3.50–$6; main courses $3.50–$6 at lunch, $7–$15 at dinner; breakfast $3–$6; grilled seafood platter for two $30; Sat night cookout $10–$18.
Open: Daily 7:30am–11pm; breakfast to 11:30am; happy hour 6–9pm.

Have a relaxing meal in the beautiful dining room decorated with bamboo, or on the shady terrace looking out on the pool and tropical gardens. While the pianist plays every night from 6 to 9:30pm (during high season), savor well-executed margaritas followed by the grilled seafood platter—a large tray of succulent lobster, shrimp, fish, and tender squid—the latter in a velvety, exquisitely spiced *adobo* sauce. For lunch the tortilla soup is a filling and budget-wise winner. Afterward, take a stroll around the romantic gardens. It's immediately south of the river on Vallarta.

FONDA LA CHINA POBLANA, Insurgentes 222. Tel. 2-4049.
Specialty: MEXICAN.
$ Prices: Appetizers $2–$6; main courses $3–$8; tacos $3; breakfast $2–$2.50.
Open: Daily 24 hours.

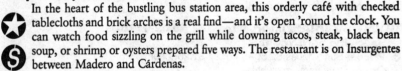

In the heart of the bustling bus station area, this orderly café with checked tablecloths and brick arches is a real find—and it's open 'round the clock. You can watch food sizzling on the grill while downing tacos, steak, black bean soup, or shrimp or oysters prepared five ways. The restaurant is on Insurgentes between Madero and Cárdenas.

EL DORADO, Pulpito s/n. Tel. 2-1511.
Specialty: MEXICAN.
$ Prices: Appetizers $2.50–$7; main courses $4.50–$12; green salad or sandwiches $3.50–$7; breakfast $1.50–$5.
Open: Daily 8am–9pm.

This open-air, palapa-roofed restaurant on the beach is a local favorite, especially for a hearty breakfast by the sea. Try the Huevos Motulenos—Yucatecan-style eggs on tortillas with black beans, cheese, and a tangy *salsa*. In the late afternoon watch the surfers and parasailors while sipping a cool drink. Seafood is another specialty, and iced tea is always available. To find it, walk 9 blocks south of the river on Vallarta, then right on Pulpito to its end at the beach.

PIZZA JOE, Badillo 269. Tel. 2-2477.
Specialty: ITALIAN.
$ Prices: Salad $4; main courses $5–$17; large pizza (14 inch) with everything $17; lasagne $8; pasta $5–$7; slice of cheesecake $2.50.
Open: Mon–Sat 2–11pm.

Behind a high brick wall lies a garden patio with twinkle lights in the trees, soft music, and red-checked tablecloths, where you can *mangi* under the stars on some of the best Italian *cucina* in town. Besides pizza there's a good range of pastas, as well as vegetarian and meat lasagne. The simply decadent homemade cheesecake comes in several flavors: lemon-lime, orange, Kahlúa, and chocolate-almond. The young American-Canadian couple who own it, Joe and Clara, make everyone feel welcome. It's on Badillo, left, ½ block from Vallarta.

PUERTO NUEVO, Badillo 284. No phone.
Specialty: MEXICAN/SEAFOOD.
$ Prices: Appetizers $3–$6; main courses $6–$13; daily special $11.
Open: Daily 12:30pm–11pm.

Owner and chef Roberto Castellon presents seafood with inventive flair: Try the crab enchiladas, shrimp "filet mignon," or smoked marlin—or the unusual manta ray tacos. Dine inside or in the roofed, open-air sidewalk area hung with plants for a jungly effect. You'll find it 5 blocks south of the river off Vallarta, ½ block on Badillo.

BUDGET

PATACHU PASTELERÍA, Vallarta 179.
Specialty: FRENCH BAKERY.
$ Prices: Bread, pastries, and quiche by the piece 25¢–$2.
Open: Daily 9am–9pm.

The young Parisian Frédéric Leborgne came all the way to Puerto Vallarta to open his French bakery. It's the real thing—selling authentic baguettes (both white and whole wheat), flaky croissants, individual fruit tarts, pies, and quiche (whole or by the slice). Drop in for a pastry with coffee or to get picnic supplies. It's 2 blocks south of the river on Vallarta.

TOMMY'S TORTAS, Insurgentes 323. Tel. 2-0175.
Specialty: SANDWICHES.
$ Prices: Sandwiches $2.50–$4; fries $1.25; beer $1.25.
Open: Daily 8am–midnight.

On the southern edge of the bus district, this neat new restaurant turns out delicious Mexican *tortas* (sandwiches made with various combinations of meat and cheese) and french fries, which diners wash down with beer or soft drinks. It's painted in dusky Santa Fe pastels and has three open arches across the front, with indoor and sidewalk tables. You'll find it 4 blocks south of the river on Insurgentes between Cárdenas and Carranza.

THE PANCAKE HOUSE [CASA DE HOTCAKES], Badillo 289.
Specialty: AMERICAN/MEXICAN BREAKFAST.
$ Prices: Breakfast $3.50–$6.
Open: Tues–Sun 8am–2pm.

For a hearty, American-style breakfast or brunch, stop at "the only pancake house on the west coast of Mexico." Mouth-watering pancakes and waffles are imaginatively mixed with fruit, chocolate, nuts, and even peanut butter. You can also pig out on eggs Benedict, cheese blintzes, breakfast burritos, or Belgian waffles. Owner and travel writer Memo Barroso and his Canadian wife recently remodeled the place with lots of tile and white stucco in a style suggesting an airy, contemporary hacienda. To find it walk 5 blocks south on Vallarta, then left on Badillo 1 block.

SPECIALTY DINING

JUNGLE RESTAURANTS

One of the unique attractions of Puerto Vallarta is its "jungle restaurants," located to the south, toward Mismaloya. Each one offers open-air dining in a magnificent tropical setting, by the sea or beside a mountain river. Determine the distance from town by the kilometer in the address. For minivan transportation see "Getting Around" in Chapter 3.

CHICO'S PARADISE, Hwy. 200, km 20. Tel. 2-0747.
  Specialty: MEXICAN/SEAFOOD.
  $ Prices: Appetizers $3–$11; main courses $8–$25; soups $3–$6; barbecued ribs $10; grilled seafood platter for two $50.
  Open: Daily 11am–7pm.

Lunch at this lively tropical place, perched on the edge of a clear boulder-framed river gorge under a big thatched roof, can easily be a day's outing. Arrive early (noon) to get a good table, then enjoy the river view and the mariachis. Among the tasty dishes are barbecued ribs, fish *sarandeado* (grilled in a special way), seafood *cazuelas* (casseroles), black bean soup, and the seafood platter for two. After dining, hike down to the river to swim and sunbathe, or explore the crafts and souvenir shops on the premises. Don't forget to bring your swimsuit, tennis shoes, and beach towels!

Chico's is about 13 miles south of town on the main highway. *Note:* round-trip cab fare is about $30 (get a group of four to share). Or take the no. 02 minivan (50¢) to Boca de Tomatlán, a fishing village, then get a taxi from there—a relatively short distance. (See "Getting Around" in Chapter 3.)

CHINO'S PARAISO, Hwy. 200, km 6.5. Tel. 3-0102.
  Specialty: GRILLED LOBSTER/CRAYFISH/STEAK.
  $ Prices: Appetizers $8; main courses $11–$20.
  Open: Daily noon–5pm.

Tucked into some rock formations, this jungle restaurant offers five open-air terraces overlooking a clear green river. Guests often take a dip in the swimming holes and waterfalls before or after eating. The setting is usually shady and cool, and quite festive when the marimbas play, which is usually 1 to 3pm. To get there take a cab or minivan as far as the entrance to La Jolla de Mismaloya Resort, then hike about a mile on the dirt road on the mountain side of the highway.

EL EDÉN, off Hwy. 200 between the Camino Real and La Jolla Mismaloya. No phone.
  Specialty: GRILLED SEAFOOD.
  $ Prices: Main courses $15–$25.
  Open: Daily 10am–5:30pm.

With just enough jungle cleared in this luxuriant spot beside a clear river to set up movie cameras, a crew shot scenes here for *The Predator,* starring Arnold Schwarzenegger. Then the current owner turned the set into a restaurant. Guests can dine while watching other guests dropping into the inviting green river Tarzan-style from a rope swing. Corn tortillas made on the spot usually come with the dinners. It's 3 miles off the highway on the mountain side, between the Hotel Camino Real and La Mismaloya. This is the most difficult jungle restaurant to reach, for not all taxi drivers want to drive the long and bumpy dirt road. It has no phone, so check first with a travel agent or at the tourist office to confirm it is open.

LE KLIFF, Hwy. 200, km 17. Tel. 2-5725 or 2-2733.
  Specialty: NOUVELLE SEAFOOD/INTERNATIONAL.
  $ Prices: Appetizers $4–$7; main courses $10–$20.
  Open: Lunch daily noon–5pm; dinner daily 6–11pm.

Shaded by a huge thatched palapa, diners are scattered among several intimate tiers of terraces stepping down a cliff towards the surf. Open to the breezes, this elegant and romantic restaurant serves excellent cuisine on blue tablecloths while soft music plays in the background. Try the cold avocado and crab soup or the tequila shrimp with red and green peppers and cilantro, plus the pistachio flan for dessert! This makes a fine sunset spot, too. It's about 6 miles beyond La Jolla Mismaloya Resort. Take a taxi all the way (very expensive), or the minivan as far as Tomatlán and a taxi from there.

EL SET, Conchas Chinas, Hwy. 200, km 2.5. Tel. 2-1056 or 2-0302.
   Specialty: GRILLED SEAFOOD, MEAT/INTERNATIONAL.
$ **Prices:** Appetizers $3–$8; main courses $10–$28.
   Open: Breakfast and lunch on the beach daily 8am–4pm; dinner in the restaurant daily 5–11pm.

This charming informal restaurant has been a favorite of visitors for years. Terraces lush with palms, shady manzanillo trees and bougainvillea on a cliff above the sea and sturdy leather tables and chairs create a relaxed tropical mood. Spectacular sunsets and Conchas Chinas Casserole are the specialties of this place. Live music accompanies dinners of grilled steaks and seafood, spareribs, soups, and salads. It's beside the Conchas Chinas Hotel and near the Hotel Camino Real.

RESTAURANT PRIMITIVO, Boca de Tomatlán, Hwy. 200, km 18 south of town.
   Specialty: SEAFOOD.
$ **Prices:** Full meal $8–$20.
   Open: Daily 8am–7pm.

★ Another out-of-town restaurant by the sea, this one, however, is relatively undiscovered, definitely less expensive than the others, and exudes that rustic jungle chic visitors like to discover. In fact it bills itself as "The way Puerto Vallarta was." Select main courses from the seafood menu and dine on a terrace overlooking the Boca de Tomatlán Bay. I haven't tried breakfast here, but I'm told it's terrific. The undeveloped beach is the equivalent of a block away (but there are definitely no blocks out here in the boonies), so it's possible to spend the day by the water and use the restaurant as a base. It's almost 11 miles south of Puerto Vallarta approximately 2 miles past La Jolla de Mismaloya Hotel. To get here take the no. 02 minivan (50¢) to Boca de Tomatlán, an oceanside village; the village is also where the vans turn around to return to PV.

CHAPTER 5

WHAT TO SEE & DO IN PUERTO VALLARTA

- SUGGESTED ITINERARIES
1. ORGANIZED TOURS
2. SPORTS & RECREATION
- FROMMER'S FAVORITE PUERTO VALLARTA EXPERIENCES
3. SHOPPING
4. EVENING ENTERTAINMENT
5. EASY EXCURSIONS

Puerto Vallarta's beaches are its main attraction. The Tourism offices and travel agencies can provide information on what to see and do. Puerto Vallarta is above all a place to relax and enjoy yourself.

SUGGESTED ITINERARIES

IF YOU HAVE 2 DAYS

Day 1 Relax, amble along the beach, and have a peaceful dinner.

Day 2 Sleep late, then stroll around the central village. Have lunch at one of the beachside restaurants, and later select a good sunset spot from one of the restaurants mentioned in Chapter 4 and stay on for dinner.

IF YOU HAVE 3 DAYS

Days 1 and 2 Spend these days as outlined above.

Day 3 Take one of the boats to Yelapa and spend the day or afternoon on the beach with lunch and refreshments at one of the palapa-topped restaurants there. In the evening find a refreshing outdoor restaurant, enjoy one of the festive Mexican entertainment nights that usually include folkloric dancing, dinner, and refreshments.

IF YOU HAVE 5 DAYS

Days 1, 2, and 3 Spend these days as outlined above.

Day 4 Sleep in, then head for one of the jungle restaurants with a pool or nearby beach and spend the day. Or spend the day diving at the numerous interesting spots not far off shore. Or if it's Saturday, take the House and Garden Tour. In the evening take a sunset cruise and you'll be back before dark with plenty of time to sample Puerto Vallarta's growing nightlife, be it disco, lobby bar with live music and dancing, or one of the lively restaurants that double as nightspots.

Day 5 On the last day, just relax.

1. ORGANIZED TOURS

The State Tourism Office (see "Fast Facts" in Chapter 3) and travel agencies can provide information on what to see and do, and travel agencies can arrange tours, car rentals, and other activities. I highly recommend the agencies Viajes Toucan Tours (tel. 2-4600 or 2-4646) and Viajes Marely (tel. 2-5973).

TOURS

City tours, jungle tours, and **horseback riding tours** at several different ranches in the country can be arranged through Viajes Marely (tel. 2-5973) and other travel agencies. They cost from $15 to $35 per person.

A **house and garden tour** of four private homes in town is offered every Saturday at 11am by the International Friendship Club for a donation of $12 per person. The tour bus departs from the main plaza by the State Tourism Office (which has information about this event). Proceeds are donated to local charities.

BOAT TRIPS

Puerto Vallarta offers a number of different boat trips, including **sunset cruises and excursions to Yelapa** (a tiny town on a lovely cove), **Las Animas Beach, La Manzanilla Beach,** and **Quimixto Falls.** Some make a stop at the **Los Arcos rock** formations for **snorkeling,** some include lunch, and most provide music and an open bar on board. Prices range from $20 for a sunset cruise to $50 for an all-day outing. Viajes Toucan Tours (tel. 2-4600 or 2-4646) and other travel agencies have tickets and information. Operadura Buenaventura (tel. 3-0309) offers relaxing sunset dinner cruises on the *Tuna I* through the **mangrove lagoons** and **canals** north of Puerto Vallarta. *Note:* The town pier/marina used by most pleasure boats is north of downtown near the airport. Do not confuse it with the new pier at Playa Olas Altas south of the river.

2. SPORTS & RECREATION

THE BEACHES

Puerto Vallarta's beaches start well north of town, out by the airport, with **Playa de Oro,** and extend all around the broad Bay of Banderas. The most popular are **Playa Olas Altas,** also known as Playa Muertos or Playa del Sol, just off Calle Olas Altas, south of the Río Cuale; and **Playa Mismaloya,** in a beautiful sheltered cove about 6 miles south of town along Highway 200. It was at Mismaloya that *Night of the Iguana* was filmed. You can still see and hike up to the stone buildings that were constructed for the movie, on the point framing the south side of the cove. The Jolla de Mismaloya Resort is on this beach, as well as several rustic seafood restaurants; this and all beaches in Mexico are public.

To get to Mismaloya, take the no. 02 minivan from Plaza Lázaro Cárdenas (see "Getting Around" in Chapter 3). Along this route to Mismaloya are many other fine beaches, including **Punta Negra,** with soft white sand, an enjoyable view, and a little palapa restaurant. You can ask the driver to let you off at any point and explore the area for yourself.

Around the rocky point **south of Playa Olas Altas** are quite a number of small, sheltered coves that get very little use and are much nicer than the Coney Island atmosphere of the main beach.

Waterskiing, parasailing, and other water sports are available at many beaches along the Bay of Banderas.

BULLFIGHTS

Bullfights are held from November through April on Wednesday afternoons at the bullring La Paloma, across the highway from the town pier. Tickets can be arranged through a travel agency or through Foto Taurina (tel. 2-1158).

DIVING

While Puerto Vallarta is not the diving mecca that Cozumel is, there's enough here to make it worthwhile. Three diving areas are of interest: Las Mariettas Islands, where there are caves; Quimixto, where there's good visibility and lots of fish; and Los Arcos (a rock formation), which is shallow with good color changes. Local travel agencies can make arrangements and the cost is around $50 per person.

FISHING

For **deep-sea fishing,** September through November is best for sailfish; marlin, dorado, and roosterfish are found all year. Cost is around $160 for ½ day and $200 to $500 for a full day depending on how far out you go, and the boat and provisions

---

IMPRESSIONS

A remote charming fishing village [Puerto Vallarta] on Bahia de Banderas, one of the west coast's most beautiful bays. The town, climbing up the slopes of mountains that surround the bay is Mexico's nearest equivalent to a quiet Mediterranean village, even to the tourists who are beginning to discover it. How to get there: Daily flights . . . from Guadalajara, or by mail plane from Tepic. There is no railway, first-class bus or good road communication.
—JAMES NORMAN, *TERRY'S GUIDE TO MEXICO,* 1965.

chosen. **Freshwater fishing** is available at the Cajon de Peña Reservoir, 70 miles south of Puerto Vallarta, a 7,000-acre artificial lake stocked with **bass;** the fishing is good all year. Since the lake also irrigates local crops, depending on the season, you'll see rice, sorghum, corn, and tropical fruit orchards. Ask local travel agents for details.

GOLF

Puerto Vallarta has two golf courses: an 18-hole private course at Marina Vallarta for members only; and the 18-hole Los Flamingos Club de Golf 5 minutes north of Nuevo Vallarta (tel. 2-5025, ext. 1203). Golf packages are available through several hotels including the Villas Quinta Real and Marriott CasaMagna, both in Marina Vallarta, and Hotel Garza Blanca south of Puerto Vallarta.

HUNTING

Near the Cajon de Peña Reservoir (see "Fishing," above) there are three hunting seasons: duck and dove, October 23 to February 21; quail, January 2 to April 10; chachalaca, November 27 to January 24; and wild boar, December and January. It's illegal (with stiff penalties) to hunt deer, mountain lion, jaguar, and ocelot. Cost for a day of hunting is $80 for the day, to $150 overnight. Ask a local travel agent for details.

TENNIS

Besides the hotels mentioned in "Where to Stay" above which have tennis courts, there's also the **John Newcombe Tennis Center** with four outdoor (clay) and four indoor courts. It's next to the Hotel Fiesta Americana Plaza Vallarta, not to be confused with the Fiesta Americana Puerto Vallarta. Nonguests of the hotel pay $12 an hour for court use; guests pay $8. A tennis pro is on duty for lessons at an extra charge. It's open daily from 7am to 9pm. For reservations call 2-4448, extension 500.

WHALE WATCHING

Whales are often seen offshore during February and March from Punta Mita, north of Puerto Vallarta.

A STROLL THROUGH TOWN

Puerto Vallarta's tightly knit cobblestone streets are a delight to explore (with good walking shoes!), full of tiny shops, rows of windows edged with curling wrought iron, and vistas of red-tiled roofs and sea. Start with a walk up and down the *malecón*, the seafront boulevard. Among the sights not to miss is the **municipal building** on the main square (next to the State Tourism Office), which has a large **mural by Manuel Lepe** inside in its stairwell.

Nearby, up Independencia, sits the **cathedral** topped with its curious crown; on its steps women sell colorful herbs and spices to cure common ailments. Here Richard Burton and Elizabeth Taylor were married the first time—she in a Mexican wedding

PUERTO VALLARTA ATTRACTIONS

0 — 200 m / 220 y

Bahía de Banderas

Río Cuale

ATTRACTIONS:
- Burton-Taylor bridge ⓭
- Cactus Disco ㊵
- Cathedral ⓫
- Franzi Café ㉒
- Gringo Gulch (neighborhood) ⓬
- La Iguana Nightclub ㉜
- Market ⓲
- Museo del Río Cuale ㉑
- Plaza Cárdenas ㉝
- Sundance Disco ㉞
- Tourist Office ⓰
- Zócalo/Main Square ⓳

FROMMER'S FAVORITE
PUERTO VALLARTA EXPERIENCES

Beach Lazing Spend a day or more lazing on any of Puerto Vallarta's fine wide beaches dozing, reading a book, and watching the waves.

Sunset Watching Search out just the right place to see the sunset—an important part of a Puerto Vallarta vacation.

Sunset Cruise End the day aboard one of the several cruise boats offering sunset dinner cruises. My favorite goes north of Puerto Vallarta among the mangroves and canals.

Yelapa Beach Let the boat you came on leave without you, pick one of the palapa restaurants as a base for refreshments, and spend the day on the beach. Use your ticket for the last boat back.

Deep-Sea Fishing A half day or day far out at sea can be a thrilling and relaxing experience, especially if the fishing is good to great. Bring back your catch and have one of the restaurants prepare it for dinner.

Jungle Restaurants Spend an afternoon at one of the jungle restaurants swimming, relaxing, and eating.

House and Garden Tour Join the Saturday tour to see what's behind the walls of Puerto Vallarta's elite homes.

---

dress, he in a Mexican charro outfit. Of course afterward they had fireworks! Three blocks south of the church, head uphill on **Libertad,** lined with small shops and pretty upper windows; it brings you to the **public market** on the river.

After exploring the market, cross the bridge to the **island in the river;** sometimes a painter is at work on its banks. Walk down the center of the island towards the sea, and you come to the tiny **Museo del Cuale,** which exhibits pre-Columbian ceramics and local artists; it's open daily from 9am to 2pm and 3pm to 8pm. Then retrace your steps to the market and Libertad, and climb up steep **Miramar to Zaragoza;** at the top is a magnificent view over rooftops to the sea. Up Zaragoza to the right 2 blocks is the famous pink-arched bridge that once connected **Richard Burton's and Elizabeth Taylor's houses.** This area is known as **Gringo Gulch,** where many Americans have houses.

SPECIAL EVENTS

The week leading up to **December 12**—the "birthday" of Mexico's patron saint, the **Virgin of Guadalupe**—this is an important day all over Mexico, and is celebrated with processions of "Las Peregrinas" (religious pilgrims) and much merrymaking.

3. SHOPPING

Excellent quality merchandise is brought to Puerto Vallarta from all over Mexico and sold in hundreds of little shops all over town. The prices here are higher than in the places of origin, so if you're planning to visit other parts of Mexico, you might want to wait and make your purchases at the sources. In Guadalajara, 6 hours away by bus, prices are considerably lower.

Puerto Vallarta's **municipal market** is just north of the Río Cuale where Libertad and Rodriguez meet. The mercado sells clothes, jewelry, serapes, shawls, leather accessories and suitcases, papier-mâché parrots, stuffed frogs and armadillos, and of course T-shirts. Be sure to do some comparative shopping before buying. It's open daily from 8am to 8pm.

Calle Libertad next to the market is the place to buy *huaraches*—comfortable, practical sandals made of leather strips and rubber-tire soles. Buy a pair that fits very tightly—they stretch out quickly and can become too floppy.

CRAFTS & FOLK ART

ARTE MAGICO HUICHOL, Corona 164. No phone.

This may be the best gallery of Huichol art in all of Mexico. It carries very fine large and small yarn paintings by recognized Huichol artists, as well as intricately beaded masks, bowls, and ceremonial objects. Open: Mon–Sat 10am–9pm.

GALLERY INDIGENA, Cárdenas 288. No phone.

More Mexican folk art and handmade wares await down the street from Olinala Gallery. Open: Mon–Sat 10am–2pm and 5–8pm.

NACHO'S, Libertad 160A. No phone.

Beautifully made silver jewelry from Taxco and lacquerware from Olinala are sold here. When buying sterling, always look for the .925 stamp on the back. Open: Mon–Sat 10am–2pm and 5–8pm.

OLINALA GALLERY, Cárdenas 274. Tel. 2-4995.

The fine indigenous Mexican crafts and folk art here include an impressive collection of authentic masks and Huichol beaded art. Priced from $45 to $2,000 for museum-quality pieces, most of the masks have been worn in ceremonies rather than created for tourists. Reference books and other literature are available in English, and the knowledgeable staff will gladly answer questions. Open: Mon–Sat 10am–2pm and 5–9pm.

QUERUBINES, Juárez 501-A. Tel. 2-3475.

"Cherubs" offers Guatemalan and Mexican wares, including embroidered and handwoven clothing, wool rugs, jewelry, straw bags, and Panama hats. Open: Mon–Sat 9am–9pm.

LA REJA, Juárez 501. Tel. 2-2272.

A great selection of Mexican ceramics and some lovely Guatemalan fabrics are among the crafts here. Open: Mon–Sat 9am–2pm and 4–8pm.

CONTEMPORARY ART

The galleries below carry contemporary Mexican and/or foreign artists.

FITZPATRICK/DE GOOYER, Morelos 589. Tel. 2-1982.
Among the works featured here is that of Marta Gilberta, a local artist whose reputation as an artist is growing. Open: Mon–Sat 10am–2pm and 4–8pm.

GALERÍA PACÍFICO, Juárez 519. Tel. 2-6768.
Open: Mon–Sat 10am–9pm.

SERGIO BUSTAMANTE GALLERY, Juárez 275. Tel. 2-1129.
Fantastic creatures emerging from eggs and other colorful, surreal images in three-dimensional ceramics are Bustamante's trademark. Open: Mon–Sat 9am–9pm.

GALERÍA UNO, Morelos 561. Tel. 2-0908.
Open Mon–Sat 10am–9pm.

FLOWERS & EDIBLE GIFTS

BLOSSOMS VALLARTA, Calle Colombia 1438-12. Tel. 2-6568.
If you want to surprise someone with a gift delivery while you're in Vallarta, Elia Behena of Marely Travel will deliver gift baskets to hotels, condos, and ships. The assortment includes baskets of flowers, wine and champagne, or of candy, assembled with other edible goodies and including wine or champagne. The most popular gift is the 2-foot-high donkey piñata carrying a load of fresh flowers.

4. EVENING ENTERTAINMENT

Wander down the malecón after dark and you'll hear music pouring out from half a dozen inviting restaurant/bars with their windows open to the sea. The beach doesn't go to sleep at night, either. Bands play under the palapas and there's dancing on the beach. Restaurants with live music, such as Brazz, (see "Where to Dine" in Chapter 4), can also provide a pleasant evening.

RESTAURANT/BARS

ANDALE, Olas Altas 425. Tel. 2-1054.
South of the river, Andale can be the one of the wildest watering holes in town for youthful vacationers. Drinks are reasonably priced and sometimes the Tequila Slammers are on the house. Its restaurant upstairs is a bit quieter, with tables overlooking the street. Open: Daily 4pm–midnight.
Admission: Free. **Prices:** Margaritas $2.50; beer $1.50.

CARLOS O'BRIAN'S, Paseo Díaz Ordaz 786 (the malecón) at Pipila. Tel. 2-1444.

The young-at-heart form a long line out front in the evening as they wait to get inside and join the party. Late at night the scene resembles a rowdy college party. Revelers have been known to dance on the tables and chairs. Open: Daily 11am–2am.
Admission: Free. **Prices:** Drinks $2.50–$6.

RESTAURANT/BAR VALLARTA CUALE, Río Cuale. No phone.

At the tip of the island where the river flows into the sea, this restaurant has a beautifully decorated terrace with leather furniture and scarlet tablecloths. Hit the bar for happy hour and sunset-watching, or in the evening when a romantic trio serenades diners. Food prices are a bit steep. Open: Daily 8am–11pm; happy hour 6–8pm (2-for-1 drinks); live music 7:30–10:30pm.
Admission: Free. **Prices:** Beer $1.50; margaritas $2–$4.

FRANZI CAFE, Río Cuale. No phone.

At this pleasant spot under shady trees on the island in the middle of the river, talented groups play live jazz in the evening. Dinner is expensive, but you can always stop by for drinks. The Sunday champagne brunch from 8am to noon also features live music (sometimes a harpist). Open: Daily 8am–midnight; live jazz nightly 8–11pm.
Admission: Free. **Prices:** Drinks $2.50; fancy coffee $6; Sun brunch $12.

MOGAMBO, Paseo Díaz Ordaz 644 (the malecón). Tel. 2-3476.

Live jazz lures in passersby to sit beneath the crocodiles and other stuffed creatures on the walls of this African-theme bar and restaurant. Open: Daily 8am–2pm; live jazz nightly 8pm–2am.
Admission: Usually free. **Prices:** Drinks $2–$4; fancy coffee $5.50.

RESTAURANT/BAR ZAPATA, Paseo Díaz Ordaz 522 (the malecón). Tel. 2-4748.

Photographs and memorabilia from the Mexican Revolution surround you as you listen to live South American music. You can sit at the bar on one of the revolving horse-saddle stools. Open: Nightly 7pm–1:30am; live music 7pm–midnight.
Admission: Free. **Prices:** National drinks $3.

DISCOS

The discos are loud and expensive, but a lot of fun. Admission is $5 to $10, and you'll generally pay $3 for a margarita, $2 for a beer, more for a whisky and mix. Keep an eye out for free disco passes frequently available in hotels, restaurants, and other tourist spots. Most discos are open from 10pm to 4am.

CACTUS, Dieguez and Vallarta. Tel. 2-6037 or 2-6077.

A current favorite, this large disco offers pounding music, sculpted cavelike walls sprouting trees and cactus, and several tiers of seating that frames the large, high-tech dance floor on three sides. Open: Nightly 10pm–5am.
Admission: $10. **Prices:** Drinks $2–$5.

CHRISTINE, Krystal Vallarta Hotel, Av. de las Garzas, north of downtown off airport road. Tel. 2-1459.

With its Victorian "streetlamps" and ceiling spangled with tiny lights, the interior resembles a cross between an octagonal jewel box and a turn-of-the-century gazebo in a park—until the opening light show. Then the stage fogs up, lights swing down and start flashing, and suddenly you're enveloped in booming classical music like you've *never* heard it before. After the show, video screens and disco sounds take over. Open: Nightly 10:30pm–4am; opening light show at 11pm.

Admission: $11. **Prices:** Drinks $2–$5. *Note:* No shorts for men, tennis shoes, or thongs.

FRIDAY LÓPEZ, Hotel Fiesta Americana Puerto Vallarta, north of downtown off the airport road. Tel. 2-2010.
Live bands and the upstairs-downstairs Spanish colonial–style setting keep everyone hopping in this festive night spot. Classic rock-and-roll "gold" is the music of choice. Open: Nightly 10:30pm–3am.

Admission: $8; women free on Wed. **Prices:** Drinks $2.50–$5.

IGGY'S, La Jolla de Mismaloya Resort, km 11 on the main highway south of town. Tel. 2-1374.
Every night at 7pm this disco shows the movie that put Puerto Vallarta on the map: *Night of the Iguana*. Afterward you can dance or enjoy the wonderful view of Mismaloya Beach below, where the movie was filmed. The remains of the movie set can be seen on the southern point above the beach. Open: Nightly 7pm–1am. No dress code. *Note:* The minivan no. 02 (50¢) runs up to Mismaloya until 9pm or so (see "Getting Around" in Chapter 3). A taxi back will cost around $8 (gather a group of four to share).

Admission: Free. **Prices:** Drinks $2–$3.

SUNDANCE, Cárdenas 329. Tel. 2-2296.
Columns, arches, and comfortable furniture surround the black-lighted dance floor in the middle of the large room. This nightspot is popular with well-heeled locals but draws its share of tourists, too. Open: Nightly 10pm–4am.

Admission: Free Sun–Thurs, $8 Fri–Sat. **Prices:** Drinks $2.50–$5.

MEXICAN FIESTAS & HOTEL EVENTS

LA IGUANA, Cárdenas 311 between Constitución and Insurgentes. Tel. 2-0105.
For a real extravaganza, go to La Iguana for an evening of entertainment that includes an open bar and an all-you-can-eat buffet. The owner-chef-showman-host, Gustavo Fong Salazar, was born in Mexico to a Chinese father and Mexican mother, went to school in Hong Kong, managed the American Club there, and served in the American armed services in China during World War II. Returning to Mexico 28 years ago, after seeing great shows in many parts of the world, he originated the concept of Mexican folk shows for tourists, which have since become popular all over the country. The show is as eclectic as its owner's experience, with Mexican folkloric dancing, mariachis, rope-twirling, piñatas, fireworks, and an orchestra for dancing. Open: Thurs and Sun 7pm–11pm.

Admission: $30.

KRYSTAL VALLARTA HOTEL, Av. de las Garzas, north of downtown off the airport road. Tel. 2-1459.

Mexican fiestas are held just about every night at major hotels around town and generally include a Mexican buffet, open bar, and live music and entertainment. One of the best is hosted by the Krystal Vallarta on Tuesday and Saturday at 7pm. The hotel also puts on a comic **"Charreada"**—a Mexican rodeo—with lots of audience participation (it also includes dinner and drinks) on Thursday at 7pm. The State Tourism Office and local travel agencies can provide information on these and other hotel events; agencies can arrange tickets.

Admission: $25–$35.

5. EASY EXCURSIONS

PLAYA YELAPA

A cove as inviting as a tropical fantasy is a 2-hour trip by boat down the coast. Go to the town marina and catch the 9am boat, the *Serape*, to Yelapa for $17 round-trip, returning around 4pm. The fare includes two drinks on board but you need to bring your own lunch or buy it in Yelapa. Several other boats and cruises go to Yelapa and include lunch and open bar for $30 to $35. Travel agencies can provide tickets and information.

At Yelapa you can lie in the sun, swim, eat fresh grilled crayfish or seafood at a restaurant right on the beach (try Vagabundo's), have your picture taken with an iguana (for $1 a shot!), let local "guides" take you on a tour of the town or up the river to see the waterfall, and hike up to visit Rita Tillet's crafts shop on the edge of the mountain.

WHERE TO STAY

For cheap accommodations ask around to see if residents are renting rooms; or rent a palapa hut with a dirt floor.

HOTEL LAGUNITAS, reservations through Sergio García in Puerto Vallarta. Tel. 322/2-1932. 20 cottages (all with bath). **Directions:** On the far left end of beach in Yelapa.

$ Rates: $18 single; $30 double (rate varies according to season and demand). The rock and stucco cottages with thatched roofs and screened windows are rustically agreeable. Services are unpredictable, but you might spend a blissful few days in these cottages. Beach palapa restaurants are steps away, but it wouldn't hurt to bring a supply of snacks and drinking water. There's electricity from 7 and 11pm. There are no telephones in Yelapa.

SAN BLAS

San Blas, Nayarit (pop. 10,000) is an easygoing fishing village and tourist town on a lush section of the Pacific Coast 150 miles north of Puerto Vallarta and 40 miles west of Tepic. It has beaches edged with coconut palms and palapa beach-shack restaurants selling fresh grilled fish, and its slow pace makes visitors want to linger. It is known for its excellent surfing (one beach is said to have the longest waves in the world), its great variety of birds (more than 300 species), and the idyllic jungle cruise up a river to the Tovara springs. Along the road into town watch for stands selling smoked fish and tiny houses woven of mangrove branches.

Most people get to San Blas by bus or train by way of Tepic, capital of the state of Nayarit. If you should have to stay overnight in Tepic, the most economical lodgings are on or near the main town plaza.

By bus from Puerto Vallarta **Transportes del Pacífico,** Insurgentes 160 (tel. 2-1015), has hourly service to Tepic. From Tepic to San Blas buses leave frequently. The bus station is conveniently located on the main square, Calle Sinaloa (tel. 5-0043).

By car from Puerto Vallarta, follow Highway 200 north to Tepic. From there take the four-lane toll road ("Cuota") north to the exit for San Blas; the toll is about $3. From here to the coast, the two-lane highway takes about an hour to wind through ever-lusher tropical country, finally emerging in San Blas.

As you enter the village of San Blas on the principal street, **Juárez,** the main square is on the right. At its far end sits the old church, with a new one next to it. Next door is the bus station, and on the other side of the churches, the mercado (market). After passing the square, the first one-way street to the left is **Batallón,** an important thoroughfare that passes a bakery, a medical clinic, several hotels, and Los Cocos Trailer Park, and ends at Borrego Beach, with its many outdoor fish restaurants.

Nearly everything is within walking distance, and there are public buses that go to the farther beaches, Matanchen and Los Cocos, on their way to the next village to the south, Santa Cruz.

The rainy season is May through October, though this usually means brief showers, with September and October the wettest months. The no-see-ums are worst during the rainy season, so bring plenty of repellent. Summer can be hot and steamy.

The **Tourist Office** is next door to McDonald's Restaurant on Calle Juárez, open daily (usually) from 4 to 6pm (no phone).

WHAT TO SEE & DO

After you've walked around the town and taken the river cruise, there is not a lot to do besides relax, swim, read, walk the beach, and eat fish—unless you're a serious birdwatcher or surfer. During the winter months, however, you can also look for **whales** off the coast of San Blas.

Port of San Blas

Like Acapulco, San Blas was once a very important port for New Spain's trade with the Philippines. Pirates would attempt to intercept the rich Spanish galleons headed for San Blas, and so the town was fortified. Ruins of the fortifications complete with cannons, the old church, and houses all overgrown with jungle are still visible atop the hill, **La Contadura.** The fortress settlement was destroyed during the struggle for independence in 1811, and has been in ruins ever since. From San Blas Father Junípero Serra also set out to establish missions in California during the 18th century.

The view from La Contadura is definitely worth the trouble of getting there: The entire surrounding area stretches out before you, a panorama of coconut plantations, coastline, town, and lighthouse at Playa Del Rey. To reach the ruins from San Blas, head east on Avenida Juárez about ½ mile, as if going out of town. Just before the bridge, take the stone path that winds up the hill to your right.

Beaches & Water Sports

One of the closest beaches is **Borrego Beach,** south from the town plaza on Batallón until it ends. This is a gray sand beach edged with palapa restaurants selling fish. For a more secluded place to swim, pay a fisherman to take you across El Pozo Estuary at the southwest edge of town to the "island," actually El Rey Beach. Walk to the other side of the island and you might have it all to yourself. Or try the beach on the other side of the lighthouse on this island. Bring your own shade, for there are no trees. The fisherman "ferry" charges about $1 one-way and operates from 6am to 6pm. Canoes and small boats can also be rented at the harbor on the west side of town, following Avenida Juárez.

About 3 miles south of San Blas is **Matanchen Bay.** If driving, head out Avenida Juárez towards Tepic, cross the bridge, and turn right at the sign to **Matanchen.** A bus also stops there on its way south to the village of Santa Cruz, departing from the bus station on the main square at 9am, 11am, 1pm, 3pm, and 5pm; check on the return stops at Matanchen Bay, which are generally an hour later. There's a little settlement here where you can have a snack or a meal, or rent a boat and guide for the jungle river cruise.

A half mile past the settlement is a dirt road to **Las Islitas Beach,** a magnificent swath of sand stretching for miles, with a few beach-shack eateries. This is the famous **surfing** beach of the mile-long waves, and real and would-be surfing champions come from Mexico and the U.S. to test their mettle here, especially during September and October, when storms create the biggest waves. If you don't have a surfboard, you can usually rent one from one of the local surfers for around $2 an hour. The bodysurfing at Islitas and Matanchen is good, too. A taxi to Islitas will cost about $4 from downtown San Blas.

Farther south from Matanchen is beautiful **Playa Los Cocos,** lined with coconut palms. It's also on the bus route to Santa Cruz, but double-check on stops and schedules before boarding in San Blas.

Jungle Cruise to Tovara Springs

Almost the moment you hit San Blas, you'll be approached by a "guide" who offers "a **boat ride** into the jungle." This can be exciting, but expensive as well, depending on how many people share the cost: about $40 for a boatload of one to four persons for the 3- to 4-hour trip from the bridge at the edge of town on Juárez. It's less (about $30) for the shorter, 2-hour trip from the Embarcadero near Matanchen Bay, out of town. Either way it's worth it if you take the early morning cruise—through shady mangrove mazes and tunnels, past tropical birds and cane fields, to the beautiful natural springs, La Tovara, where you can swim. There's a restaurant here, too, but stick to soft drinks or beer. This is one of the unique tropical experiences in Mexico, and to make the most of it, find a guide who will leave at 6:30 or 7am: the first boat on the river encounters the most birds, and the Tovara River is like glass then, unruffled by breezes.

Around 9am the boatloads of tour groups start arriving, and the serenity evaporates like the morning mist.

Note: The guide may also offer to take you to **"The Plantation"**—pineapple and banana plantations on a hill outside of town. The additional cost of this trip, for most people, is not worth it.

Birdwatching

As many as 300 species of birds have been sighted here, one of the highest counts in the Western Hemisphere. **Birders and hikers** should pick up a copy of the booklet, *Where to Find Birds in San Blas, Nayarit,* on sale at Hotel Las Brisas Resort. With maps and directions it details all the best birding spots and walks—including hikes to some lovely waterfalls where nonbirdwatchers can swim, too. Probably the best bilingual **guide to birds** and the area is **Manuel Lomelli,** who can be reached through Las Brisas Motel (tel. 321/5-0307 or 5-0558). A day's tour will cost around $100, which can be divided among the participants. Birding is best from mid-October to April.

WHERE TO STAY

For additional lodging choices, especially for a long stay, check the ads posted at McDonald's Restaurant.

Moderate

HOTEL LAS BRISAS RESORT, Calle Paredes Sur s/n, San Blas, Nay. 63740. Tel. 321/5-0480, 5-0307, or 5-0308. Fax 321/5-0112. 42 units (all with bath); 5 mini-suites. A/C (18 rms) FAN

$ Rates (including breakfast): $40 single, $50 with A/C; $47 double, $54 with A/C; more for suite. **Parking:** Free.

★ A block inland from the waterfront and nestled among pretty gardens of palms, hibiscus, and other tropical plants are the cottagelike four-plexes and other buildings (one with three stories) of this oasislike resort. The tranquil ambience, two pools (one for toddlers), and one of the best restaurant/bars in town all add to the appeal of the nicest place to stay in San Blas, while the rooms are modern, bright, and airy. Three have mini-kitchens. Another bonus is the manager, María Josefina Vazquez, one of the most knowledgeable and helpful people I've met on the Pacific Coast! To find it walk south from the square on Batallón about 6 blocks, then right on Campeche across from the Marino Inn, then left on the next street, Paredes Sur.

SUITES SAN BLAS, Matanchen and Las Palmas (Apdo. Postal 12), San Blas, Nay. 63740. Tel. 5-0047 or 5-0505. 23 suites. FAN

$ Rates: $30 suite for two; $35–$45 suite for four to six. Extra person $6.

This three-story apartment house has one- and two-bedroom suites with dark, Spanish-style furniture, multiple beds, kitchen, and balcony. There's a restaurant, swimming pool, children's pool, and a grassy children's playground with tall coconut palms. To get there walk south on Batallón about 7 blocks, then left on Las Palmas 1 block to Matanchen.

Budget

FLAMINGO HOTEL, Av. Juárez 105 Pte., San Blas, Nay. 63740. Tel. 321/5-0448. 25 rms (all with bath). FAN
$ Rates: $15 single; $17 double.
Built in 1863, this two-story hotel housed the German Consulate in its grander years. And it retains some of its colonial charm, despite its run-down condition. Some of the rooms are shabby (especially those upstairs), but those on either side of the courtyard are quite nice, with ceiling fans, 20-foot-high beamed ceilings, and barred windows. The quiet inner courtyard has high arches, a red-tiled floor, massive Spanish furniture, and lush tropical plants. Manager Jimmy Mendosa speaks perfect English. To find it walk 2 blocks west of the main square.

MISSION SAN BLAS HOTEL, Av. Cuauhtémoc 197, San Blas, Nay. 63740. Tel. 321/5-0023. 20 rms (all with bath). FAN
$ Rates: $15 single; $17 double. Extra person $4.
Formerly the Posada Casa Morales, this group of bungalows is within walking distance of town. Some of the bungalows have a view of the ocean, others overlook the pool and garden. The large rooms have cinderblock walls, with two double beds or three singles. It's on the waterfront at El Pozo Estuary.

CAMPING For camping, try the **Los Cocos Trailer Park** on Avenida Batallón and Calle José Azueta (tel. 321/5-0055), near the beach. It has 100 spaces and charges $6 single, $8 double per day for a basic hookup in its grassy park with palm trees. It also has a Laundromat and a bar.

WHERE TO DINE

For an inexpensive meal, try fresh grilled fish from one of the little shacks on the beach. A fairly large fish (filet or whole) with hot tortillas and fresh coconut milk to drink will cost about $5. The prices are the same at all of these places. From town, take Avenida Batallón south from the plaza follow your nose when you smell the fish grilling.

Moderate

RESTAURANT EL DELFÍN, Hotel Las Brisas Resort, Calle Paredes Sur s/n. Tel. 5-0112 or 5-0480.
Specialty: MEXICAN.
$ Prices: Appetizers $3–$6; main courses $7–$20.
Open: Daily 8am–9:30pm.

★ This hotel restaurant serves the best food in San Blas in an open-air dining room protected by screens and cooled by ceiling fans. Soft light, soft music, and comfortable captain's chairs add to the serene ambience. The chef masterfully plays from a wide repertoire of sauces: Try the steak with mustard sauce, the chicken "Orange," or the exquisite shrimp or fish with a creamy *chipotle* pepper sauce. Homemade soups and desserts deserve encores, too.

TONY'S LA ISLA, Mercado and Paredes s/n. Tel. 5-0407.

116 • WHAT TO SEE & DO IN PUERTO VALLARTA

Specialty: MEXICAN.
$ Prices: Appetizers $2–$4; main courses $4–$10.
Open: Tues–Sun 2–10pm.

Some swear the best seafood in San Blas is served at "Chef Tony's." A nautical decor of hanging shark jawbones, fishnets, and shells set the mood for the excellent shrimp, oysters, lobster, and fish. Or try the filet mignon with mushrooms. The restaurant is near the post office about 2 blocks south of the plaza.

Budget

MCDONALD'S, Juárez 36 Pte.
Specialty: MEXICAN.
$ Prices: Appetizers $2–$5; main courses $5–$10; beef and seafood shish kebab $7.
Open: Nov–June daily 7am–10pm; July–Oct Wed–Mon 7am–10pm.

This isn't what you're thinking—in fact this family-run restaurant, founded by Glenn McDonald of Iowa, has been operating in San Blas for 35 years. Specialties of the house include a seafood platter of fish, oysters, and shrimp; and a shish kebab of seafood and beef tenderloin. You'll find it 1 block west of the town square.

EVENING ENTERTAINMENT

At the moment, San Blas has two discotheques: **Disco Laffite** at the Hotel Los Bucaneros (tel. 5-0101) opens on weekends, while the **Marino Inn's disco** (tel. 5-0303) is open only during the Christmas and Easter (Holy Week) holidays. Both start around 10pm and close during the wee hours. But discos and their schedules come and go, so check locally upon arrival.

On most evenings (especially Sunday night), the plaza fills up with young people, talking and laughing while eating ice cream.

MIKE'S PLACE, Juárez s/n. Tel. 5-0432.

Live music is featured at this nightclub above McDonald's Restaurant, just west of the square. Here patrons can enjoy the view of the square and street from a balcony with tables. Manager Mike McDonald plays the organ and sings most nights from 9pm until 1 or 2am. When flamenco or folk groups perform, however, there's a cover charge. Open: Mon–Sat 6pm–2am, Sun noon–9pm; live music Wed–Sat.

Admission: Usually free. **Prices:** Drinks $2–$5.

VIEJANOS, Av. Batallón 25. No phone.

This bar a few doors south of the plaza offers recorded music, TV, and videos. The sign says "Ladies' Bar," but it's really more of a cantina and sports bar for men, though couples are fine. Open: Mon–Sat 9am–1am.

Admission: Free. **Prices:** Drinks $2.50.

LA FAMILIA, Av. Batallon 18. Tel. 5-0258.

This relatively new restaurant and video bar creates a festive mood with colorful tablecloths, bright *papel picado* hung here and there, and Mexican folk art and doodads on the walls. Open: Daily 7:30am–10pm.

Admission: Free. **Prices:** Drinks $2–$4.

SOUTH OF PUERTO VALLARTA

Several coastal resorts between Puerto Vallarta and Manzanillo are within reasonable driving distance from Puerto Vallarta. See "Easy Excursions" from Manzanillo in Chapter 8 for Las Alamandas, an exclusive small resort, and Hotel Careyes and Club Med Playa Blanca, all three of which are from 2½ to 3 hours from Puerto Vallarta.

CHAPTER 6
GETTING TO KNOW MANZANILLO

1. ORIENTATION
- DID YOU KNOW . . . ?
2. GETTING AROUND
- FAST FACTS: MANZANILLO

Today, Manzanillo, Colima (pop. 70,000), is the main seaport on the Pacific. The chief local industries are fishing, iron-ore mining, and tourism, which is beginning to boom. Nevertheless, it's slightly off the beaten path, 160 miles south of Puerto Vallarta and 167 miles southwest of Guadalajara. And it's still one of the Pacific coast's hidden jewels, since tourists don't come in droves the way they do to Puerto Vallarta and Acapulco. It's the ideal point from which to launch further explorations of the coast, especially the northern part halfway to Puerto Vallarta.

1. ORIENTATION

ARRIVING

BY AIR **Aeromexico** and **Mexicana** offer flights between Manzanillo and Mexico City, Guadalajara, and Los Angeles. There are connecting flights several times a week for Chicago, Dallas/Fort Worth, Monterrey, Reno, Sacramento, San Diego, San Francisco, and a few other cities. **Aero Vallarta** flies to Puerto Vallarta November through Easter.

The airport is a 45-minute ride north of town center. Colectivo vans meet each flight and you buy tickets ($4) inside the terminal. The train station is conveniently located downtown on the waterfront, within walking distance of several hotels. City buses stop in front. The bus station is several blocks inland.

BY TRAIN *El Colimense,* the first-class train running between Manzanillo, Colima, and Guadalajara, has been suspended, but may be reinstituted. Otherwise there's a slow (8 hr. or longer) second-class train.

BY BUS The service is very good to and from Manzanillo, up and down the coast and inland to Colima and Guadalajara.

Manzanillo's Central Camionera (bus station) is a few blocks east of town, at Vicente Suárez and Galeana, just off the road to Colima. Follow Hidalgo east until you come to Galeana and the bus station will be off to the right. **Auto Transportes Colima** goes to Colima every 15 minutes and the trip takes 2 hours on a *de paso/ordinario* and 1½ hours on a *directo*. **Tres Estrellas de Oro** has six buses

MANZANILLO: ORIENTATION • 119

? DID YOU KNOW...?

- Colima is derived from the Náhuatl word "Coliman" which has many interpretations—place of the mountain, place of the volcano, place of the god of fire, or place of our ancestors.
- Manzanillo is named after a poisonous tree found growing where the port's first pier was built.
- In 1954 Manzanillo became "Mexico's Sailfish Capital" after a record catch of more than 300 sailfish in three days.
- The name Jalisco is a corruption of a Nahuatl word, "Xaliaco," meaning "sandy place."
- Before the conquest of Mexico, Jalisco was occupied by Purépecha and Nahuatl speaking tribes.
- The Revillagigedo Islands, south of Baja California belong to Colima.
- López de Legazpi set sail for the Philippines from Barra de Navidad in 1564 and began the trade route of the Spanish Galleons (Nao de China) which brought riches from the Orient to Mexico.
- The Volcán de Colima (Colima volcano) first erupted in 1576 and most recently in 1991.
- In 1959 a typhoon nearly destroyed Manzanillo and Cuyutlán.
- In pre-Hispanic times in Colima a small hairless dog was bred to eat and traveled along with nomadic traders as their "portable" provisions.
- Colima is the second smallest Mexican state after Tlaxacala.

daily to Guadalajara and one of them is an express (no stops). They also can get you to Mexico City, and back up the coast to Culiacán, Guaymas, Mazatlán, Puerto Vallarta, Mexicali, and Tijuana. **Norte de Sonora** (tel. 2-0432) has twice weekly service to Tepic, Los Mochis, and Mazatlán. The most frequent service to Guadalajara (6-7 hr.), Puerto Vallarta (6 hr.) via Melaque (San Patricio), and Barra de Navidad (1.5 hr.) is on **Auto Camiones de Pacífico** (tel. 2-0515) with first-class service 25 times a day and second-class service almost as frequently. **Autobuses de Occidente** has frequent service to Colima and express service to Mexico City via Morelia and Toluca and direct and express service to Guadalajara. **Flecha Amarilla** (tel. 2-0210) also has assigned-seat service to Guadalajara, and other buses inland to León and San Luis Potosí. **Primera Plus,** a new bus line running between Manzanillo, Colima, and Guadalajara, offers air conditioning, video movies, vending-machine snacks and drinks, and fewer seats than regular buses. It costs more but the service is worth it.

BY CAR Coastal Highway 200 leads from Acapulco and Puerto Vallarta. From Guadalajara take Highway 54 through Colima. Outside of Colima you have a choice of a toll road, which is faster but less scenic, into Manzanillo.

DEPARTING

BY PLANE Transportes Terrestres (tel. 3-2470), the colectivo airport service, picks up passengers at hotels. Call a day ahead for reservations. One-way, the cost is $4. The Manzanillo office of **Aeromexico,** between Quintero and Galindo, is in the Centro Comercial "Carrillo Puerto" (tel. 333/2-1267 or 2-1711). **Mexicana** is at Avenida Mexico 380 (tel. 333/2-1972 or 2-1009; airport 3-2323). The airport is 45 minutes northwest of town at Playa de Oro. A colectivo van will cost $4 from the airport to downtown Manzanillo.

CITY LAYOUT

NEIGHBORHOODS IN BRIEF

Downtown The town, which is less attractive than you might expect, is at one end of a 7-mile-long curving beach, facing Manzanillo Bay, with four beach

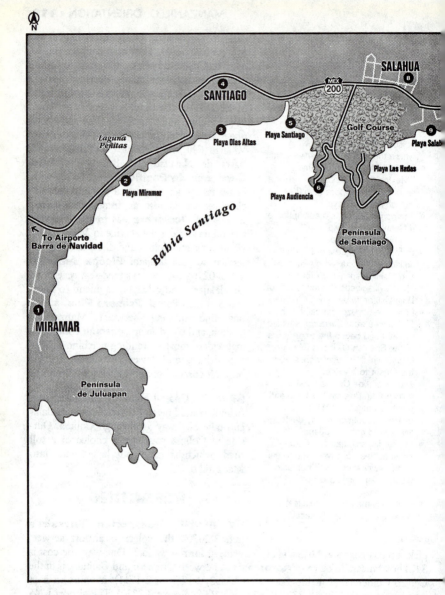

Central Plaza ⑯
Cruise Pier ⑮
Downtown Manzanillo ⑰
Las Brisas ⑬
Miramar ①
Playa Audencia ⑥
Playa Azul ⑪

Playa Las Brisas ⑫
Playa Las Hadas ⑦
Playa Miramar ②
Playa Olas Altas ③
Playa Salahua ⑨
Playa Santiago ⑤
Salahua ⑧

MANZANILLO AREA ORIENTATION

Tourism Office & Car Rental

Costera Miguel

Laguna las Garzas

MEX 200

To Colima →

MEX 200

Playa Azul ⓫

Laguna de San Pedrito

Playa Las Brisas ⓬

LAS BRISAS ⓭

Bahía Manzanillo

Costera Miguel de la Madrid

Train Station ⓮

Cruise Pier ⓯

⓰

DOWNTOWN MANZANILLO ⓱

Laguna de Cuyutlán

Santiago ❹
Tourism Office ❿
Train Station ⓮

sections—Playa Las Brisas, Playa Azul, Playa Salahua, and Playa Las Hadas. The northern terminus of the beaches is the Santiago Peninsula. Downtown activity centers around the plaza which has a brilliant poinciana tree with red blossoms, a fountain, kiosk, and a view of the bay. Train tracks parallel the street leading into the downtown area, then cut across the street to go inland. Large ships dock at the pier nearby. Avenida Mexico, the street leading out from the plaza's central gazebo, is the town's principal commercial thoroughfare. Walking along here you will find a few shops, small eateries, and juice stands. At night swallows by the hundreds come to roost on the telephone wires around the plaza.

Las Brisas Las Brisas peninsula fronts Manzanillo Bay and is separated from downtown by a cut large enough for ships to pass. It's between downtown and the Santiago Peninsula and it's reached by the Boulevard Costera Miguel de la Madrid (named for a president of Mexico born in the state capital of Colima). Turn back left at the Las Brisas intersection. A narrow paved road leads back down the peninsula past a row of small hotels fronting the beautiful Las Brisas beach.

Salahua Once you leave downtown the line of commercial buildings along the highway seems almost endless, and it's difficult to tell without a map when you've left one settlement and arrived at another. Salahua (the name means "salt water"), is one such settlement after Las Brisas and just before Santiago.

Lagoons **Laguna de Cuyutlán,** almost behind the city, stretches for miles south paralleling the coast. **Laguna de San Pedrito,** north of the city, parallels the Costera Madrid and it's behind Playa Las Brisas beach. **Playa del las Garzas,** a short distance farther north, is separated from Laguna San Pedrito by a small strip of land and is behind Playa Azul. All are good for birdwatching.

Santiago Peninsula Beyond the San Pedrito and Las Garzas lagoons is Santiago, the subdivision on the right, and the peninsula on the left, 7 miles from downtown. The high rocky mountain peninsula juts out into the bay separating Manzanillo Bay from Santiago Bay. It's the site of many beautiful homes, Las Hadas and Las Hadas's La Mantarraya Golf Course, and the best hotels in the area. The beach, Playa Las Hadas, is on the south side of the peninsula facing Manzanillo Bay and Playa Audiencia is on the north side facing Santiago Bay. Santiago and town are linked by the Costera Madrid. This stretch of road is also called the Santiago Highway, especially the extension beyond Santiago Peninsula.

IMPRESSIONS

Manzanillo, the main Pacific port for Guadalajara, Michoacan and Mexico City is a turn-of-the-century holdover, skipped over by main highways, tourists, airlines and tourist agents.
—JAMES NORMAN, *TERRY'S GUIDE TO MEXICO*, 1965

The place [Barra de Navidad] is tropically picturesque, has magnificent stretches of golden beach and is just beginning to develop as a tourist haven.
—JAMES NORMAN, *TERRY'S GUIDE TO MEXICO*, 1965

Bays **Manzanillo Bay** has the harbor, town, and beaches closest to town and it's separated by the Santiago Peninsula from the second bay, **Santiago,** which also has several beaches.

2. GETTING AROUND

By Bus The local buses (called camionetas) make a circuit from downtown along the lagoon opposite Playa Azul, and out along Manzanillo Bay to the Santiago Peninsula and the Bay of Santiago to the north. Buses marked Las Hadas go onto the peninsula and make a circuit by the hotels. This is a cheap way to see the coast to Santiago and take a tour of the peninsula.

By Taxi Taxis in Manzanillo supposedly have fixed rates for trips within town, as well as to points more distant, but they aren't posted; ask your hotel what a ride should cost to get a feel for what's right, then bargain.

 MANZANILLO

American Express Representative is Bahías Gemelas Travel Agency, Boulevard Costera Madrid, km 10 (tel. 3-2100; fax 3-0649).
Area Code The area code is 333.
Climate Manzanillo's tropical climate is hot and humid in the summer.
Holidays See "When to Go" in Chapter 2.
Information The **Tourism Office** (no phone yet) is in Salahua on the Costera Madrid (the main highway between Manzanillo Centro and Santiago), next to Avis and Budget car rentals. Hours are Monday through Friday from 9am to 3:30pm.
Laundry There's a Laundromat at the junction of the Manzanillo, Las Brisas, and Santiago roads called Lavandería Automática Gissy (*Hee*-see), in a little complex of shops.
Telephone See "Fast Fasts: Mexico in Chapter 2.

CHAPTER 7
WHERE TO STAY & DINE IN MANZANILLO

1. WHERE TO STAY
2. WHERE TO DINE

In Manzanillo where you stay tends to be your vacation experience more so than in other Mexican resort cities that have numerous side attractions. All areas are reasonably convenient to one another by either bus or taxi. Reservations are recommended for the Christmas, New Year's, and Easter holidays.

1. WHERE TO STAY

DOWNTOWN

BUDGET

HOTEL COLONIAL, Av. Mexico 100 and Gonzales Bocanegra, Manzanillo, Col. 28200. Tel. 333/2-1080 or 2-1134. 40 rms. A/C (25 rms) FAN (15 rms) TEL
$ Rates: $30–$35 single or double.

An old favorite, the three-story colonial-style hotel changes little from year to year—same minimal furniture, red-tiled floors, and basic comfort at ever-increasing prices. Higher prices are for rooms with air conditioning. In the central courtyard is a restaurant/bar. It's 1 block inland from the plaza on Galindo; the hotel is on corner right.

HOTEL EMPERADOR, Balvino Davalos 69, Manzanillo, Col. 28200. Tel. 333/2-2374. 28 rms. FAN
$ Rates: $10–$15 single bed; $17–$21 2 beds.

This very basic low-budget hotel offers clean, bare rooms with hot water and a fan. Most look out onto the tiny inner courtyard, which is more like an airshaft. It's 1 block west (left) of the plaza almost to the corner of Carrillo Puerto.

LAS BRISAS

Buses run out to Las Brisas from downtown. Look for "Brisas Direc" on the signboard. It's a 6-mile trundle around Manzanillo Bay, ultimately curving southward. Most hotels, bungalows, and condominiums are on the single main road.

MODERATE

CLUB VACACIONAL LAS BRISAS, Av. Lázaro Cárdenas 207, Las Brisas, Manzanillo, Col. 28200. Tel. 333/3-2075 or 3-1717. 56 bungalows. A/C (24rms) FAN (32rms) TEL

$ Rates: $30 bungalow for one; $44 bungalow for two. **Parking:** Free, in front.

This beachfront hostelry has plain but comfortable bungalows with kitchenettes surrounding a large pool and grassy interior lawn shaded by palms. Besides the pool there's one tennis court, and a restaurant open for all three meals. It's extremely popular with Mexican families on weekends. It's about halfway down the Las Brisas peninsula.

HOTEL LA POSADA, Av. Lázaro Cárdenas 201, Las Brisas (Apdo. Postal 135), Manzanillo, Col. 28200. Tel. and fax 333/3-1899. 24 rms. FAN

$ Rates (including breakfast): Off-season $45 single, $50 double; 10%–15% higher in high season.

Another longtime favorite of traveling cognoscenti, this small inn has a shocking-pink stucco facade with a large arch that leads to a broad tiled patio smack on the beautiful beach. The rooms have natural brick walls and simple but very tasteful furnishings. The atmosphere here is casual and informal—you can help yourself to beer and soft drinks all day long, and at the end of your stay, owner Bart Varelmann (a native of Ohio) will ask you how much you owe for refreshments. All three meals are served in the dining room or out by the pool. If you want to come for a meal, breakfast, served between 8 and 11am, costs around $5; lunch and dinner between 1:30 and 9pm cost about the same. It's at the far end of Las Brisas peninsula—the end closest to downtown.

SALAHUA

MODERATE

CONDOMINIOS ARCO IRIS, Costera Madrid, km 9.5 (Apdo. Postal 359), Manzanillo, Col. 28200. Tel. 333/30168. 21 rms. FAN

$ Rates: $70–$80 large quadruple; $35–$40 small double.

More like a motel with kitchenettes, than what we normally regard as condominiums, it's in a shaded parklike area set back off the busy Costera; the beach is close by the back of the property. Large quarters have two bedrooms and small ones have one bedroom. All the cottages have tile floors, kitchens, dining and living-room areas (some of which are in the kitchen), patios in front, screened windows, and small bathrooms. There's a pool in the center of the grounds. This is a popular place for

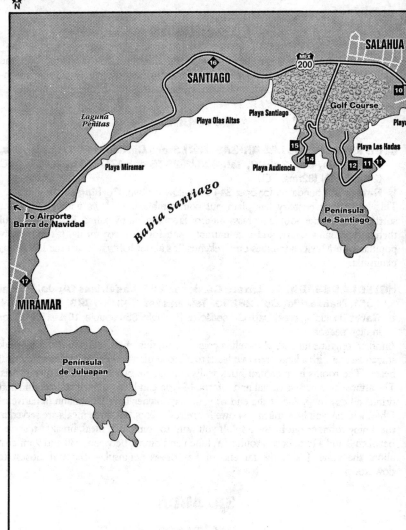

ACCOMMODATIONS:
Arco Iris 10
Fiesta Mexicana 7
La Posada 3
Las Hadas 11
Marlyn 15
Playya de Santiago 14
Plaza las Glorias 12
Sierra Manzanillo 13

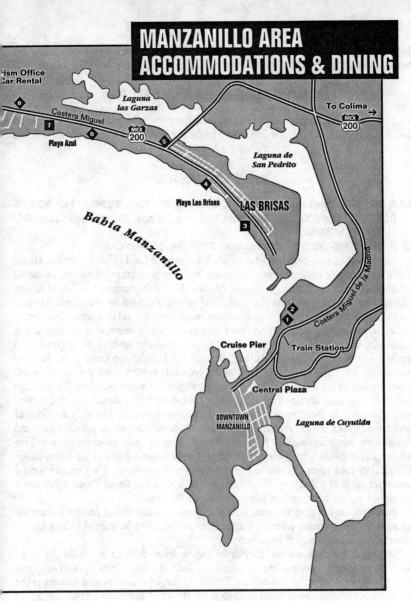

DINING:
Bugatti's ⑤
Carlos 'n' Charlies ⑥
Juanito's ⑯
Legazpi ⑪
Ly Chee ②
Manolo's ⑨
Oasis ⑰
La Perlita ①
La Plazuela ⑫
Teto's ⑧
Willy's ④

Mexican families on weekends and holidays, but midweek it's quite tranquil. It's beside Jalapeño's restaurant on the bay side, and the sign to it is easily missed.

SANTIAGO PENINSULA

Three miles north of Las Brisas crossroads is the peninsula and village of Santiago. Small city buses now go from downtown to the peninsula and back every 20 minutes or so.

VERY EXPENSIVE

LAS HADAS, Santiago Peninsula, Manzanillo, Col. 28200. Tel. 333/3-0000, toll free 800/228-3000 in the U.S. and Canada. 220 rms and suites. A/C TV TEL MINIBAR

$ Rates: $225–$295 single or double; $357 Royal Beach Club.

Anyone who has ever heard of Manzanillo has heard of Las Hadas; or say Las Hadas and a lot of people think that *is* Manzanillo. You may remember it from the movie *10* which featured Bo Derek and Las Hadas. The self-contained Eden that put Manzanillo on the map was the brainchild of the Bolivian entrepreneur Antenor Patino, featuring Moorish-style architecture that started a trend in Mexico, but hardly has an equal for lavishness. Built on the beach and up a half-moon shaped curve of the peninsula, the elegant white resort hotel is one of the most famous, popular, and exclusive in Mexico. The rooms, built around the hillside overlooking the bay, are connected by cobbled lanes lined with colorful flowers and palms. Covered, motorized carts are on call for transportation within the property. Though it's a large resort, it maintains an air of seclusion since rooms are large, spread out, and tucked here and there in short rows among the landscaped grounds. The six categories of accommodations are roughly divided among those with views or partial views and those with extra amenities. The understated, elegant, and spacious rooms have white-marble floors, sitting areas, and comfortably furnished balconies. Royal Beach Club guests have rooms on the upper tier with great bay views. They receive special amenities such as robes and hairdryers. Room 804 in the Royal Beach Club has a whirlpool on the patio with a fabulous view of the bay.

Entry, through a guarded gate, is to hotel guests, occupants of condominiums on an adjacent hill, patrons with restaurant reservations, or to bearers of tickets for the sunset cruise that takes off from here.

Dining/Entertainment: El Palmar, open from 5:30am to midnight is an open-air restaurant overlooking the pool. Los Delfínes, open from 1pm to 6pm and near the water, specializes in seafood. Elegant Legazpi Restaurant and Lounge is the formal place to dine, open from 6pm to midnight (see "Where to Dine," below). El Terral is open in winter only from 7pm to 1am and serves Mexican specialties. There are five lounges and bars with live entertainment somewhere on the property almost every evening, plus the disco, Cartouche, which opens at 10pm.

Services: Laundry, room service, shopping arcade, travel agency, beauty and barber shops, child care. Royal Beach Club guests have rapid check-in, continental breakfast, cocktails, concierge, preferred restaurant reservations, and late checkout.

Facilities: Club Las Hadas includes La Mantarraya, the hotel's 18-hole golf course, two pools, beach with shade tents, 10 tennis courts (8 hard-surface, 2 clay), marina for 70 vessels, water sports—scuba diving, snorkeling, sailing, and trimaran cruises. Royal Beach Club guests have an exclusive pool and reserved lounge chairs at the pool and beach.

HOTEL PLAZA LAS GLORIAS, Av. de Tesoro s/n, Santiago Peninsula, Manzanillo, Col. 28200. Tel. 3-0440 or 3-0550, toll free 800/342-2644 in the U.S. 86 rms (all with bath). A/C TV TEL

$ Rates: $95–$140 single or double. Prices vary with season or holiday.

The deep apricot-colored walls of this pueblalike hotel ramble over a hillside on Santiago Peninsula. From the restaurant on top and from most rooms, a broad vista unfolds below of other red-tiled rooftops, the palm-filled golf course, and bay. The spacious, stylishly furnished, and very comfortable units have, one, two, or three bedrooms, each with Saltillo tile floors, large living room, bar/kitchen, large Mexican tiled bathroom, and private patio with views. A few of the suites can be partitioned off and rented by the bedroom only. It's one of Manzanillo's hidden resorts, known more to wealthy Mexicans than to Americans. Try to get a room on the restaurant-and-pool level, otherwise there'll be a lot of stairs to climb. It's often full weekends and holidays, so make reservations early.

Dining/Entertainment: Las Plazuelas restaurant, a casual and informal restaurant in a half-moon shape, fronts the bay side to capture both the views and breezes. It's open for all three meals. Live musicians often serenade diners.

Services: Laundry, room service, elevator from bottom of property to top.

Facilities: Pool on the restaurant level. Golf privileges at La Mantarraya Golf Course.

HOTEL SIERRA MANZANILLO, Av. La Audiencia 1, Los Riscos, Manzanillo, Col. 28200. Tel. 333/3-2000, toll free 800/448-8355 in the U.S., 800/668-8355 in Canada; 402/398-3217 in Omaha, Neb. Fax 333/3-2272. 336 rms and suites (all with bath). A/C TV TEL MINIBAR

$ Rates: $105–$300 single or double; $1,150 Presidential Suite.

One of the most luxurious hotels in Mexico, it opened in 1990 with 21 floors overlooking La Audiencia beach. Architecturally it mimics the white Moorish style that has become so popular in Manzanillo. Inside it's palatial in scale and awash in pale gray marble. Room decor picks up the pale gray theme with washed gray armoires concealing the TV, minibar, glasses, and ice bucket. Standard rooms have two double beds or a king-size bed plus a small table, chairs, and desk. The 10 gorgeous honeymoon suites are carpeted and have sculpted shell-shaped headboards, king-size beds, and chaise longue. Junior suites have a sitting area with couch and large bathrooms. All rooms have balconies and ocean view.

Dining/Entertainment: La Hidra is an informal restaurant overlooking the pool and beach and open from 7am to 11pm. El Sol is on the pool terrace and has swim-up service from 10am to 6pm. La Palapa, next to the beach and tennis courts, serves snacks from noon to 6pm. Los Tibores an elegant formal restaurant on the seventh floor, serves international specialties from 6 to 11pm. Evenings from 8pm to 2am there's live music for dancing in the Bar Los Tibores, and live piano music in La Sierra, the lobby bar, from 1pm to midnight. La Porticada, an upper terrace bar, is open from 5 to 11pm.

Service: Laundry, room service, ice machine on each floor, in-room hairdryers, beauty salon, travel agency, 24-hour currency exchange.

Facilities: Grand pool on the beach, children's pool, 4 lighted tennis courts, exercise room with whirlpool, access to Las Hadas golf course.

MODERATE

HOTEL MARLYN, Santiago Península (Apdo. Postal 288), Manzanillo, Col. 28200. Tel. 333/3-0107. 42 rms and suites. A/C (4 suites) FAN (38 rms)
$ Rates: $30 single or double; $47 suite for four; $95–$100 bungalow for four.
White and airy, this hotel has a little swimming pool and a beachfront café. Some rooms have a sea view, but rates are much lower on the side facing inland. It's on the Audiencia Bay side of Santiago Peninsula. Taxis know the way.

HOTEL PLAYA DE SANTIAGO, Santiago Península (Apdo. Postal 90), Manzanillo, Col. 28200. Tel. 333/3-0055 or 3-0270. Fax 333/3-0344. 107 rms (all with bath), 24 bungalows. A/C TEL
$ Rates: $35 single or double. **Parking:** Free.
This is one of those 1960s-era hotels aimed at the jet set who've since migrated around the peninsula to Plaza Las Glorias and Las Hadas. You get the essence of glamour at a fraction of the price, but no beach—it's on a cliff overlooking the bay. Bungalows have kitchenettes. The restaurant and bar is positioned for views and there's a swimming pool and tennis court. The hotel is at the south end of the road just past the Hotel Marlyn and facing Audiencia Bay on Santiago Peninsula.

2. WHERE TO DINE

For picnic fixings there's a big supermarket, the Centro Comercial Conasuper on the road leading into town, ½ block from the plaza at Morelos. The huge store sells food, produce, household goods, clothes, hardware, and more. Open daily from 8am until 8pm.

DOWNTOWN
MODERATE

LY CHEE, Niños Heroes 397. Tel. 2-1103.
  Specialty: CHINESE.
$ Prices: Appetizers $8; main courses $4–$12.
  Open: Tues–Sun 2pm–10pm.
The most pleasurable waterfront restaurant faces the harbor under a huge palapa. The fare is mainly Chinese with main courses similar to any Chinese restaurant's, and several Mexican dishes are also offered. It's on the waterfront, catercorner from the train station and plaza.

BUDGET

CAFETERA/NEVERÍA CHANTILLY, Juárez and Madero (across from the plaza). Tel. 2-0194.
  Specialty: MEXICAN.
$ Prices: Breakfast $1.50–$3.50; comida corrida $4.40; main courses $2–$8.
  Open: Sun–Fri 7am–10pm.
Join the locals at this informal corner café facing the plaza. The large menu includes

club sandwiches, hamburgers, *carne asada a la Tampiqueña,* enchiladas, vegetable salads, and a daily lunch special—all moderately priced.

HELADOS BING, Av. Morelos and 21 de Marzo. No phone.
  Specialty: ICE CREAM.
  $ Prices: Single cones 70¢; double cones $1.50.
  Open: Daily 8am–10pm.

Look for Bing's pink-and-white awning on the northeast corner of the plaza opposite the harbor, and trundle over for the best ice cream in Mexico. Have it by the cone, in a cup, or piled with calories like the Bing special in a glass with fruit, hot chocolate, cream, and nuts, or a Bing roll, a 10-inch roll of cake and ice cream.

LA PERLITA RESTAURANT, Perlita Plaza. Tel. 2-2770.
  Specialty: MEXICAN.
  $ Prices: Main courses $2–$9; tacos, quesadillas, tortas (sandwiches), or french fries $2–$3.50; seafood $4–$15.
  Open: Daily 9am–midnight.

Look for the orange awnings at this economical fast-food stop on the waterfront where metal tables are set out on the shady plaza. Besides a good fast-food menu, they offer a full range of fruit and mixed drinks. Purified bottled water is used in the fruit drinks. It's next to the cruise ticket office. It's 1 block right of the plaza and opposite the train station.

Botaneros

Botaneros are a tradition almost exclusive to Manzanillo. For the price of a beer or soft drink, you receive delicious snacks—ceviche, soup, shark stew, pickled pigs' feet, tacos—the list goes on. The more you drink, the more the food appears. Bring a group of four or more and platters really arrive. It's customary to order at least two drinks and to tip the waitress well. She puts a box for your empties at your table and tallies the tab from its contents when you're ready to leave. Sometimes roving musicians come in to serenade; you pay per song, so settle on the price in advance. And most botaneros have a form of betting game, which you'll have to get a local to explain. Besides those below, there's also El Caporal and El Menudazo on the way to Santiago. Most are open daily from noon to 8pm and all charge about the same for a beer or soft drink.

BAR SOCIAL, facing the plaza.
  Specialty: DRINKS/SNACKS
  $ Prices: Beer or soft drink $1.50.
  Open: Mon–Sat noon–11pm.

More like a traditional Mexican cantina, with swinging doors and a room full of men, it's one of the original botaneros that's as popular with locals as it is with tourists. Women, however, will feel more comfortable in groups or with a male companion. Tables and booths are against the walls and an enormous bar takes up the center of the room. By early evening it gets noisy, crowded, and drunk inside, and tourists will probably want to exit before all that happens.

EL ÚLTIMO TREN, Niños Heroes. Tel. 2-3144.
  Specialty: DRINKS/SNACKS

$ Prices: Beer or soft drink $1.50
Open: Daily noon–8pm

Among the cheeriest of the botaneros, El Último Tren (the last train), is covered by a grand high palapa with ceiling fans to stir up the breeze. There's enough of a family feel to the place to bring older children, although technically they aren't allowed. It's not far from downtown proper, on the right, several blocks past the train station. Just in case—women's rest rooms are named *máquinas* (cars) and the men's room is a *garrotero* (signalman).

SANTIAGO ROAD
COSTERA MADRID

The restaurants below are on the Costera Madrid between downtown and the Santiago Peninsula and includes an area known as Salahua.

Expensive

CARLOS 'n' CHARLIES, Costera Madrid, km 6. Tel. 3-1150.
   Specialty: GRILLED SPECIALTIES. **Reservations:** Recommended after 6pm.
$ Prices: Lunch $9–$12; dinner $15.
   Open: Daily noon–1am; low season hours may vary.

This branch of the popular Anderson chain offers the same silliness and good food you find at the others around the country. Snorkeling fins, records, surfboards, hard hats, and cloth fish hang from the ceiling, and black-and-white photos from early in this century decorate walls. Eat inside or outside with a view of the bay—great for sunset. Seafood and beef are grilled outdoors but other specialties include beer-batter shrimp and "grande" margaritas. Come before 9pm for a good table. High season in the evening there may be a required minimum order for dinner, and a cover charge if you come just to drink.

MANOLO'S, Costera Madrid, km 10.5. Tel. 3-0475.
   Specialty: INTERNATIONAL.
$ Prices: Main courses $10–$18; salad bar $7.
   Open: Mon–Sat 6–11pm.

Another of Manzanillo's popular eateries, Manolo's carries on the popular trend of casual breezy dining under a palapa roof. Friendly owners Manuel and Juanita López and family do the serving, and cater to American tastes with "safe" salad dispensed from a boat-turned-salad-bar. Among the popular main courses is filet of fish Manolo on a bed of spinach with melted cheese Florentine-style, and frogs' legs in brandy batter. They claim the onion soup is "the best this side of Paris." And most people can't leave without first being tempted by the fresh homemade coconut or pecan pie. Coming from downtown, Manolo's is on the right about 3 blocks before the turn to Las Hadas.

OSTERÍA BUGATTI, Santiago and Las Brisas crossroad. Tel. 3-2999.
   Specialty: INTERNATIONAL. **Reservations:** Recommended after 8pm.
$ Prices: Appetizers $4–$6; Sonora steaks and seafood $14–$17; pasta $6.50–$8.
   Open: Daily 1pm–1am. **Closed:** Sept 15–27.

One of the best restaurants in town is in a dark, vaulted cellar with a brick ceiling and soft lighting. Your English-speaking waiter arrives bearing a platter laden with quality

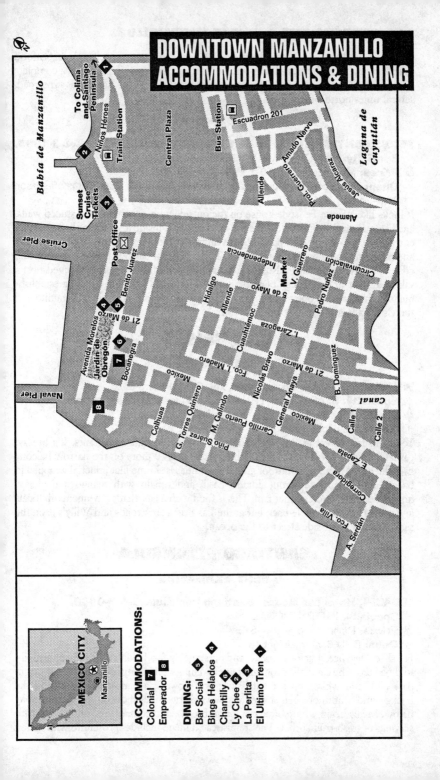

beef, pork, and seafood. Your selection will be cooked to your specifications. Seafood selections include lobster, red snapper, and shrimp. Air conditioning, plus a complete international bar, help to make this a popular place. It's at the Las Brisas crossroad, several miles north of town center.

Moderate

TETO'S CANTINA GRILL, Costera Madrid, km 9.5, Salahua. Tel. 3-1990.
  Specialty: MEXICAN/AMERICAN.
  $ Prices: Main courses $7.50–$11.50; beer $1.50.
  Open: In season bar opens daily at noon, restaurant 7pm–3am; off-season 8pm–3am.

It looks like a Santa Fe–style house on the outside with sienna-colored stucco walls, and vigas protruding just below the red-tiled roofline. Inside it's dark in the bar as you enter, but in back are walls painted with murals of old Mexico, lots of potted plants and tables around a small outdoor pool. The restaurant has two lives—in season and off-season. In season owner Rosabelia López de Salcedo serves up barbecued ribs, a salad bar, fish, and Mexican platters. But off-season it's strictly a drinking establishment. Either way it's open when everything else seems shut down in Manzanillo and there's usually a live soloist in the evening.

LAS BRISAS

EXPENSIVE

WILLY'S, Las Brisas crossroads. Tel. 3-1794 or 3-0023.
  Specialty: SEAFOOD/INTERNATIONAL. **Reservations:** Recommended.
  $ Prices: Appetizers $2.50–$7; main courses $7–$15.
  Open: Daily 7pm–midnight.

You're in for a treat at one of Manzanillo's most popular restaurants. It's breezy, casual, and small with perhaps 20 tables inside and 10 more on the narrow balcony over the bay. Among the outdoor grilled specialties is shrimp filet imperial wrapped in bacon, red snapper tarragon, dorado basil, and robalo with mango and ginger, homemade pâté, and coconut flan. This is food with a flair that's a winner with locals and tourists alike. Double back left at the Las Brisas crossroads and Willy's is on the right down a short side street to the ocean.

SANTIAGO PENINSULA

VERY EXPENSIVE

LEGAZPI, Hotel Las Hadas, Santiago Peninsula. Tel. 3-0000.
  Specialty: INTERNATIONAL.
  $ Prices: Dinner for one $50–$75.
  Open: Daily 6pm–midnight.

For sheer elegance, gracious service, and outstanding food, don't miss the opportunity to dine here. The candlelit room announces dining tranquillity with tables, covered in pale pink and white and set with silver and flowers; a pianist plays softly in the background. Enormous bell-shaped windows on two sides show off the sparkling bay below. Meals begin with a basket of warm breads, and courses are interspersed with servings of fresh-fruit sorbet. The sophisticated menu includes prosciutto with melon marinated in port wine, lobster bisque, broiled salmon, steak Diane, roast duck, lobster, or veal, and 32 flaming desserts from crêpes to Irish coffee. It's a dining experience you won't soon forget.

EXPENSIVE

LA PLAZUELA RESTAURANT, Hotel Plaza Las Glorias, Av. de Tesoro s/n, Santiago Peninsula. Tel. 3-0440 or 3-0550.
  Specialty: INTERNATIONAL.
  $ Prices: Lobster $18–$25; seafood grill $50.
  Open: Daily 8:30–11am, 1–5pm, and 7–11:30pm.

For a meal on an outdoor mountainside terrace with a fabulous bay view, try the restaurant here overlooking the golf course and bay. It's breezy, casual, and cool anytime of day but great for a night out with the city lights twinkling around the bay. Main courses include the usual grilled food with an emphasis on fresh seafood. It's on the Manzanillo Bay side of Santiago Peninsula near Las Hadas.

BEYOND SANTIAGO

EXPENSIVE

L' RÉCIFE RESTAURANT & BAR. Punta Juliapan, Hwy. 200 to Barra de Navidad. Tel. 3-0624.
  Specialty: STEAK/SEAFOOD. **Reservations:** Recommended.
  $ Prices: Appetizers $7.50–$10; main courses $15–$35.
  Open: Daily 1–5pm and 7–11:30pm. (Sept usually closed).

It's almost 20 miles beyond town to the turnoff to this mountaintop restaurant, but it's worth the drive. You'll see the sign pointing left on the highway. Follow that road for a couple of miles. The restaurant spreads out from a giant palapa covering around the terrace and swimming pool and overlooks a beautiful cove. It's a delightful place to come for a swim and lunch or for a romantic dinner. Among the specialties you'll find prime rib, chateaubriand, and duck. The seafood grill is excellent.

OASIS, Club Santiago. Hwy. 200 to Barra de Navidad, km 18. Tel. 3-0937.
  Specialty: SEAFOOD.
  $ Prices: Soup $3.50–$4.50; main courses $15–$30.
  Open: Daily 11am–2am.

Opened in 1991 by the owners of Willy's, the ambience here is entirely different. Enter through the great bamboo doors and you'll find rustic elegance while dining under this gigantic palapa overlooking the bay and open to the breezes. The menu is similar to Willy's except that it's primarily seafood with a few chicken, pork, and beef main courses. Among the specialties you'll find red snapper provençal, shrimp curry, and sea bass tarragon with apples. To find the Oasis go 10 miles from downtown and turn left at the Club Santiago sign. Turn left again at the first street and it's all the way to the end.

MODERATE

JUANITO'S, Costera Madrid, km 14. Tel. 3-1388.
  Specialty: HAMBURGERS/MEXICAN/AMERICAN.

$ Prices: Breakfast $1.50–$4; hamburgers $2; tacos and tostadas $1.60; ribs $8.
Open: Daily 8am–11pm.

The motto here is "come mucho, pague poco" (eat a lot and pay a little). I've watched this spotless, family-run restaurant grow and prosper over the years and their recipe for success is simple: Serve the most popular mainstays of the U.S. and Mexican cultures. John "Juanito" Corey and his wife, Esperanza, and children are always on duty serving hamburgers and fries, hot dogs, club sandwiches, fried chicken and barbecued ribs, tacos, tostadas, enchiladas, milk shakes and lemonade, pie and ice cream. There's hardly ever a lull. The hamburgers taste just like home, although they're a bit smaller and the portion of fries not as large as in the States. It's 8½ miles from downtown Manzanillo on the highway going to Barra de Navidad and it's before the Club Maeva resort.

CHAPTER 8

WHAT TO SEE & DO IN MANZANILLO

- SUGGESTED ITINERARIES
1. ORGANIZED TOURS
- FROMMER'S FAVORITE MANZANILLO EXPERIENCES
2. SPORTS & RECREATION
3. SHOPPING
4. EVENING ENTERTAINMENT
5. EASY EXCURSIONS

Activities in Manzanillo depend on where you stay. Most resort hotels here are completely self-contained, with restaurants and sports all on the premises. Manzanillo is a good jumping-off point for crossing into Jalisco state, north to Barra de Navidad and Melaque, to the individual beach resorts of Fiesta Americana Los Angeles Locos Tenecatita (yes, that's all one name), Hotel Tecuan, Hotel Careyes, Club Med Playa Blanca, and Las Alamandas, a new, luxurious and ultra-exclusive inn. The curvy drive through the mountains after passing Barra de Navidad is a beautiful one. It's also easy to make excursions southeast of Manzanillo, inland to Colima, capital of Colima state, an hour away, and on to the mountain resort towns of Tapalpa and Mazamitla, both a 3-hour drive from Manzanillo in Jalisco state (see "Easy Excursions" from Guadalajara in Chapter 11).

SUGGESTED ITINERARIES

IF YOU HAVE 2 DAYS

Day 1 Relax, take a dip in the ocean or pool. Have dinner at a nearby restaurant.

Day 2 Sleep late. Order room service breakfast and dine at leisure on your own patio. Spend the rest of the day by the pool or on the beach. In the evening take a sunset cruise, then have dinner at an outdoor restaurant such as L'Récife or Las Plazuelas.

IF YOU HAVE 3 DAYS

Days 1 and 2 Spend these days as outlined above.

Day 3 Rise early and take a side trip to see the museums in Colima, the state capital an hour away to the southeast. Or spend the day on the beach at the coastal village of Barra de Navidad 45 minutes south.

IF YOU HAVE 5 DAYS

Days 1, 2, and 3 Spend these days as outlined above.

Days 4 and 5 Explore the beautiful coast south of Manzanillo. Select from one or two of the resorts mentioned under excursions. Or in a completely different direction spend one or two nights at one of the chilly mountain resorts of Jalisco—Tapalpa or Mazamitla—3 hours southeast and covered under "Easy Excursions" in Chapter 11.

1. ORGANIZED TOURS

CITY TOURS/EXCURSIONS

Because Manzanillo is so spread out, you might consider a city tour, or one to Barra de Navidad. I highly recommend the services of Luis Jorje Alvarez at the **Viajes Lujo,** Avenida Mexico 143-2, Manzanillo, Col. 28200 (tel. 333/2-2919; fax 333/2-4075). Office hours are Monday to Friday 9am to 2pm and 4 to 7pm and Saturday 9am to noon, but tours in or out of town can be anytime. A ½-day city tour costs around $14; a trip to Barra de Navidad costs around $30 per person. He can also provide trips to the mountain resorts of Tapalpa and Mazamitla. He uses air-conditioned vans and speaks English.

SUNSET CRUISE

Many charter boats are available along the waterfront. For a sunset cruise, buy tickets downtown at La Perlita Dock (across from the train station) fronting the harbor.

FROMMER'S FAVORITE
MANZANILLO EXPERIENCES

Lazing Manzanillo's lack of good shopping and sightseeing attractions makes it easy to relax without that nagging feeling that you should be touring.

Terrace Dining Manzanillo excels in good restaurants where you can enjoy the view and soothing breezes.

Sunset Cruise There's nothing like winding up the day with the smell of fresh sea air and the sound of a ship skimming through the water while the sun goes down.

Deep-Sea Fishing Fishing is superb here, and a day spent far out at sea is synonymous with a Manzanillo vacation.

Tickets go on sale daily from 10am to 2pm and 4 to 7pm, and cost around $15, which includes two drinks. It's a good idea to buy the ticket a day ahead, since hotels and travel agencies in town also book this cruise.

2. SPORTS & RECREATION

BEACHES

La Audiencia Beach, on the way to Santiago, offers the best swimming, but **Playa Las Brisas,** shallow for a long way out, is the most popular because it is much closer to the downtown area. **Playa Miramar,** on the Bahía de Santiago, up past the Santiago Peninsula, is another of the town's most popular beaches, well worth the ride out there on the local bus from town. The major part of the **Playa Azul** drops off a little too steeply for safe swimming, and is not recommended for waders.

BIRDING

There are many lagoons along the coast. As you go from Manzanillo up past Las Brisas to Santiago, you'll pass the **Laguna de San Pedrito** and **Laguna de las Garzas (lagoon of the herons)** where herons, pelicans, and other coastal waterfowl congregate. The herons nest here in December and January. Back of town, on the road leading to Colima (the capital) is the **Laguna de Cuyutlán.** The toll road to Guadalajara crosses the lagoon and if you pull off after the bridge, you may spot many birds along the shoreline.

FISHING

Manzanillo is also famous for its **fishing**—marlin, sailfish, dolphin fish, sea bass, and manta ray. Competitions are held around the November 20 holiday, and in February.

GOLF

La Mantarraya Golf Club (tel. 3-0000), adjacent to Las Hadas, is open from 7am to 7pm and visitors are welcome to play. Greens fee is $50 for 18 holes or $30 for 9 holes. Carts rent for $27 to $36, clubs $24, caddies $10 to $16.

TENNIS

Several of the hotels mentioned in Chapter 7 have tennis courts with a resident pro. But you can also play at La Mantarraya Golf Club next to Las Hadas. The cost is $15 an hour during the day and $24 at night. Tennis classes at the club cost $33.

3. SHOPPING

Only a few shops carry Mexican crafts and clothing and almost all are downtown on the streets near the central plaza. You can also try exploring the new malls on the road to Santiago and the arcades of the better hotels, all of which have fashionable shops.

4. EVENING ENTERTAINMENT

Manzanillo's nightlife is centered around hotels and several restaurants with live music in the evenings. Among them are the **Hotel Sierra Manzanillo, Carlos 'n' Charlies, Teto's Cantina Grill,** and the disco **Cartouche** at Las Hadas.

5. EASY EXCURSIONS

BARRA DE NAVIDAD & MELAQUE

One of the most popular side trips from Manzanillo is to the coastal resort village of Barra de Navidad, 65 miles north of Manzanillo.

Buses from Manzanillo run the route up the coast frequently on their way to Puerto Vallarta and Guadalajara. Most stop in Barra de Navidad. By car, take coastal Highway 200 north.

In the 17th century, Barra de Navidad was a harbor for the Spanish fleet, and it was from here, in 1654, that galleons set off to conquer the Philippines. Located on a crescent-shaped bay with curious rock outcroppings, Barra de Navidad and neighboring Melaque (both on the same bay) boast a perfect beach, with a peaceful ambience unfettered with the trappings of jet-set Mexico. Barra has been "discovered," but only by a small number of people from December through Easter and on weekends in summer when it's packed. Most of the year it's a real getaway with a pick of rooms and a slow and easy pace. Recently Barra has been in the process of getting a face-lift which includes a new water and sewer system, new streets, and an extended waterfront with a new marina.

The bus will let you off in the town center near the central plaza in front of the bus station office, painted hot pink and lime green. The main beach street, **Legazpi,** and hotels are in front 2 blocks. Two blocks behind and to the right is the lagoon side with its main street, **Morelos/Veracruz,** and more hotels and restaurants. Few streets are marked, but 10 minutes of wandering will give you the village's entire layout.

The **Tourism Office** for both Barra de Navidad and Melaque is at Sonora 15 (tel. 333/7-0100), ½ block and around the corner from the Hotel Tropical. The office is open Monday through Friday from 9am to 7pm, and Saturday from 9am to noon or 1pm. They have good maps of Barra.

WHERE TO STAY

HOTEL CABO BLANCO, Pueblo Nuevo (Apdo. Postal 31), Barra de Navidad, Jal. 48980. Tel. 333/70168 or 7-0022. Fax 333/7-0168. 125 rms and condos/suites (all with bath). A/C TEL

$ Rates: $60 single; $65 double; $90 junior suite; $145 suite; $188 master suite. This inland hotel, 5 minutes from the beach, is Barra's best, built more for yacht owners than beach lovers. A marina harbors most vessels or owners can dock in the canal in front of the row of condos. The main hotel section is built around a large interior grounds and pool with swim-up bar, and edged by lawns, palms, and tropical

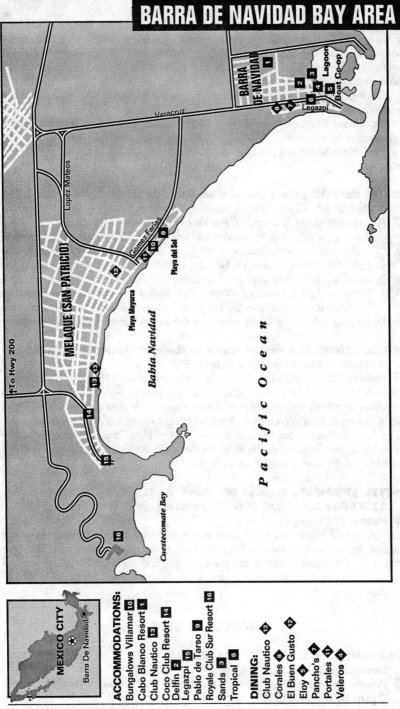

BARRA DE NAVIDAD BAY AREA

ACCOMMODATIONS:
- Bungalows Villamar 10
- Cabo Blanco Resort 1
- Club Nautico 13
- Coco Club Resort 14
- Delfin 2
- Legazpi 15
- Pablo de Tarso 9
- Royale Club Sur Resort 16
- Sands 3
- Tropical 6

DINING:
- Club Nautico 13
- Corales 8
- El Buen Gusto 12
- Eloy 5
- Pancho's 7
- Portales 11
- Veleros 4

foliage. The condo section is farther back with a separate pool. Hotel rooms have a patio or balcony facing either the pool or interior garden and each has a semicomplete kitchen with bar and sink. The condo section features one-, two-, and three-bedroom quarters, with as many stories. Each has a complete kitchen, living room, and bathrooms off each bedroom.

Dining/Entertainment: The hotel has two restaurants, one indoor and one outdoor.

Services: Laundry, room service, lobby TV with U.S. channels, travel agency, baby-sitting by reservation.

Facilities: Swimming pool for adults and one for children, 2 tennis courts, yacht marina.

HOTEL DELPHÍN, Calle Morelos 23, Barra de Navidad, Jal. 48987. Tel. 333/7-0068. 25 rms (all with bath), 3 apartments. FAN
$ **Rates:** $25 single; $35 double. **Parking:** Free, across street.

Among Barra's better-maintained hotels, this three-story hotel offers nice, well-cared-for rooms, each with red-tile floors and either double or two single beds. Outside each room are tables and chairs on the covered walkways. The courtyard with small pool and lounge chairs is shaded by an enormous tree. A breakfast buffet is served during high season on the lovely second-level breakfast terrace and costs $6. The menu includes banana hotcakes, a tradition at the Delphín. It's on the landward side of the lagoon about midway down.

HOTEL SANDS, Morelos 24, Barra de Navidad, Jal. 48987. Tel. 333/7-0018 or 7-0148. 43 rms (all with bath). FAN
$ **Rates:** $30 single; $38 double; $104 bungalow for six, $78 bungalow for four.

The colonial-style Sands offers small but homey rooms, with red-tiled floors, and windows with both screens and glass. Lower rooms look onto a public walkway and wide courtyard. Upstairs rooms are brighter. In back is a beautiful pool by the lagoon. The hotel is known for its high-season "happy hour" from 2 to 6pm at the pool-terrace bar. After 6pm, the hotel is quiet again. It's catercorner from the Hotel Delphín, on the lagoon side at Jalisco.

HOTEL TROPICAL, Legazpi 96, Barra de Navidad, Jal. 48987. Tel. 333/7-0020. Fax 333/7-0149. 57 rms (all with bath). FAN
$ **Rates:** $30 single; $38 double.

Located on the beach, this hotel offers nice rooms with either a view of the sea or lagoon. Rooms all have two double beds. Oceanview rooms have a narrow terrace and wall of windows, making the rooms bright and cheery. The breezy seaview terrace restaurant has a separate bar, and a tiny children's pool. It's at the far end of Legazpi facing the bay.

WHERE TO DINE

PANCHOS, Legazpi 53. Tel. 7-0176.
 Specialty: SEAFOOD.
$ **Prices:** Breakfast $1.50–$3; main courses $4–$12; deviled shrimp $8.
 Open: Daily 9am–11pm.

For the most popular place where locals hang out for the food and conversation, pull up a chair on the sand floor. Roving musicians drop in and bananas hang on a string. In the afternoon it's the place to chew the fat (besides the food), play a game of dominoes, and have a big lunch. You must try the spicy deviled shrimp that was invented here. The ground marlin ceviche is fabulous in a sauce of tomatoes and hot peppers. An order is plenty for two people. You'll find it towards the far end of Legazpi, next to Restaurant Pacífico.

VELEROS, Veracruz 64. No phone.
   Specialty: SEAFOOD/BEEF.
   Prices: Appetizers $1.75–$4; main courses $5–$10.
   Open: Low season daily noon–11pm; high season daily 8am–11pm.

At this restaurant on the lagoon, it's tranquilizing to watch fishermen float by. The ambience is clean, classy, and casual with cloth-covered tables, an ivy covered brick wall, impeccable service, and dependably good food. Seafood specialties include shrimp brochet and fish filet, but there's also peppersteak, filet mignon, and grilled chicken. It's on the lagoon, near the boat rental and Restaurant Eloy.

WHAT TO SEE & DO

Swimming and enjoying the lovely beach and bay view take up most people's time.

Boat trips

If you want a **boat ride,** go to your right, just about ½ block south of the Restaurant Eloy on Calle Veracruz, until you come to the tiny boatmen's cooperative, with fixed prices posted on the wall. Someone will take you wherever you want to go. A round-trip to the village of **Colimilla,** just across the lagoon, popular for its many pleasant restaurants, costs $9 for up to eight people and you stay as long as you like; for a 30-minute **tour around the lagoon,** it's $12; or out on the sea, $15.

Sportfishing

Deep-sea fishing costs $17 per hour and up to six people can share the cost. Waterskiing costs $50 an hour. Ask for boatman Sergio Barcena Monzalez, who speaks excellent English.

AN EXCURSION TO MELAQUE (SAN PATRICIO)

For a change of scenery you may want to wander over to Melaque (also known as San Patricio) 3 miles from Barra and on the same bay. You can walk to it on the beach from Barra or take one of the frequent local buses from the bus station near the main square in Barra. If you can imagine it, Melaque's pace is even more laid-back than Barra's, and though it's a larger village it seems smaller, has fewer restaurants and less going on. The paved road ends where the town begins. A few yachts bob in the harbor and the palm-lined beach is gorgeous.

If you come by bus from Barra, you'll be dropped off at the new bus station near town center a block from the beach. Restaurants and hotels line the beach and it's impossible to get lost, but a word of orientation will help. Coming into town from the main road, you'll be on the town's main street, **Avenida López Mateos.** You'll pass the main square and come down to the waterfront, where there's a trailer park. The street going left (southeast) along the bay is **Avenida Gomez Farías;** the one going right (northwest) is **Avenida Miguel Ochoa López.**

Where to Stay

The prices mentioned below are for low season (May to October). From November to the end of Easter week, prices may go up 25% to 30% in some hotels.

All along this seaside avenue, you'll see signs for hotels as well as bungalows. In Melaque, bungalows are rooms with a kitchen and sometimes a sitting room as well.

Be aware that the sound of the pounding surf in Melaque is loud enough to disturb a good night's sleep.

COCO CLUB MELAQUE, Miguel Ochoa López (Apdo. Postal 8), Melaque, Jal. 48940. Tel. 333/7-0001. Fax 333/7-03882. 236 rms and suites. A/C

$ Rates (including all meals and open bar): $90 single; $120 double; $67 suite per person.

Recently bought by the Club Maeva chain, this is Melaque's best hotel and it's located at the far end of the beach. The all-inclusive concept features buffet-style meals, open bar all day, a selection of water sports at no extra charge, plenty of loud music, and bikini-clad staff. There are only a few pieces of water-sports equipment, so there may be a wait. Rooms are decorated in soft apricot pastels with sculpted plaster shell headboards and all have balconies facing the ocean.

Dining/Entertainment: The large restaurant doubles as the entertainment arena in the evening when the staff puts on shows.

Facilities: Pool facing the beach; use of water-sports equipment included in the price.

CLUB NAUTICO MELAQUE, Madero 1, Melaque, Jal. 48980. Tel. 333/7-0239. 56 rms (all with bath). FAN

$ Rates: $30 single; $35 double.

One of Melaque's better inns, rooms are nicely furnished and immaculate. Some have private balconies. There's a swimming pool in front (street side) of the hotel. El Dorado, the hotel's huge breezy beachside palapa restaurant and bar with a total bay view is one of the nicest on the beach. Breakfast costs $1.50 to $3, seafood $6 to $9, and other main courses of chicken or beef are between $6 and $15. Try the amandine fish in an almond-butter sauce, which, like all their main courses comes with rice and vegetables. It's open from 7:30am to 10:30pm daily. To find it, walk right from the front of the bus station, it's on the left facing the beach.

HOTEL DE LEGAZPI, Av. de las Palmas, Melaque, Jal. 48980. Tel. 333/7-0397; in the U.S., call 317/846-2566 Apr–Nov (ask for owner Martin Curley). 14 rms (all with bath). FAN **Directions:** Walk through town past the Coco Club Melaque at the far end of the beach.

$ Rates: $25 single; $30 double.

American owned, this two-story hotel at the north end of the bay has a nice secluded location on a beautiful portion of beach. The large rooms are simply furnished and have tile floors. It's a 10-minute walk to town and there are several palapa-style restaurants nearby. There's lobby TV with U.S. channels, a community kitchen, and a swimming pool in front of the hotel.

ROYALE COSTA SUR, Cuaxtecomate Bay (Apdo. Postal 2), Melaque,

Jal. 48940. Tel. 333/7-0125. Fax 333/7-0085. Reservations in Guadalajara through the Monte Casino Agency (tel. 36/16-5962). 64 rms. A/C TV TEL

$ Rates (including all meals and open bar): $60 single; $120 double.

After driving 1½ miles west of Melaque on a windy mountain road you see the gorgeous azure Cuaxtecomate Bay with a few small homes and the Hotel Royale Costa Sur on the beach at water's edge. It's an all-inclusive hotel patterned after Club Med (without the sophistication). Rooms are located in both the multistory main-hotel section and meandering up the hill. All are comfortably but simply furnished and come with tile floors and views of the ocean. Taxis are on call for transportation to and from town. Though it's less than 2 miles from town, its remote mountain location makes it more suitable for those who have their own transportation, or those who like a mountain hike to town, and those who enjoy the tranquillity of staying in one place. It's a popular spot with Canadians escaping the cold in winter.

Dining/Entertainment: There are two restaurants, one inside and one outside under a thatched palapa by the pool. Open bar from 10am to midnight. The staff puts on comedy shows nightly.

Services: Free local calls to Barra de Navidad, Careyes, Melaque, and Chamela.

Facilities: Large pool by the beach; use of catamaran, snorkeling gear, rubber boat, kayak, windsurfing board included in price. Jet-ski at extra cost.

BUNGALOWS VILLAMAR, Hidalgo 1, Melaque, Jal. 48980. Tel. 333/7-0005. 5 bungalows (all with bath). FAN

$ Rates: $18 single bungalow; $25 double bungalow. Discounts for longer stays.

It's a quiet place where you can watch waves breaking and the palm trees swishing in the garden. Clean, but well used, the bungalows enjoyed a fresh coat of paint in 1990. Most have two bedrooms, living room and kitchen, bath, private patio out back, and a private sitting terrace with chairs out front by the garden. There is also an elevated terrace overlooking the beach and bay. Manager Roberto Ramirez speaks perfect English and is friendly and helpful. It's almost always full during winter months, so make reservations well ahead. It's on the corner, next to Posada Gaviotas.

POSADA PABLO DE TARSO, Gomez Farías 49, Melaque, Jal. 48980. Tel. 333/7-0117 or 7-0268; in Guadalajara tel. and fax 36/16-4850. 27 rms (all with bath). FAN (13 rms) A/C (14 rms)

$ Rates: $35 single, double $42 with A/C; $85 bungalow for six people with fan.

Parking: Free.

This two-level hotel offers exceptionally tidy rooms with fans. Two have kitchens and sitting rooms. There's a grassy courtyard, a seaside terrace and large swimming pool. Large bungalows sleep six people. To find it, walk left of the bus station; it's past the Motel Vista Hermosa.

Where to Dine

Besides the El Dorado restaurant mentioned above under Club Nautico, Avenida López Mateos has several little eateries which are good for light meals or snacks. There are also many rustic palapa restaurants right on the beach.

FONDA LOS PORTALES, Gomez Farías 358. Tel. 7-0268.

Specialty: SEAFOOD.

$ Prices: Breakfast $1.75–$2.25; seafood platters $5–$7.50.

Open: Daily 8am–6pm.

With its new brick floor and freshly painted chairs, the rough edges are gone and Los Portales looks more inviting. This simple family-run restaurant near the Posada Gaviotas is popular for its seafood platters at good prices. But there's fried chicken, too, and side orders of rice and vegetables.

EL BUEN GUSTO, López Mateos 18.
Specialty: MEXICAN. **Directions:** Walk ½ block from square going towards beach; it's at Mateos at Farías.

$ Prices: Soft drinks 40¢; beer 75¢; tamales 50¢; tacos 35¢; pozole $1.75; roast chicken $2.

Open: Daily 9am–11pm.

This eatery run by the Benjamin Macias Solis family, features metal tables and chairs and home-style food, which is why there's always a loyal following of Mexicans around. The bowl of *pozole* is large, tasty, and filling.

Evening Entertainment in Barra & Melaque

During high season there is always happy hour (from 2 to 6pm) at the Hotel Sands poolside/lagoonside bar in Barra.

DISCO EL GALLEON, Hotel Sands, Calle Morelos, Barra de Navidad.

Cushioned benches and cement tables encircle the round dance floor. It's all open air, but garden walls restrict air flow and there are few fans so you can really work up a sweat dancing the night away. They serve drinks only, no snacks. Open: Daily 8pm–2am.

Admission: Mon–Thurs $1.75–$2.50, Fri–Sat $3.50.

TANGA, Coco Club, Melaque. Tel. 7-0001.

Opened in 1991, it's located on a corner of the Coco Club Melaque Hotel. Open: Wed–Sun 10:30pm–3am.

Admission: $5.

TENACATITA

After Barra de Navidad and about 40 miles from Manzanillo you come to an obscure sign on the left pointing to Fiesta Americana Los Angeles Locos Tenacatita, an all-inclusive resort.

FIESTA AMERICANA LOS ANGELES LOCOS TENACATITA, Apdo. Postal 7, Melanque, Jal. Tel. 333/7-0220, toll free 800/223-2332 in the U.S. Fax 333/7-0229. 180 rms. A/C TV TEL

$ Rates (including all meals, domestic drinks, water sports, and activities): High season $820 per person, 7-night minimum; low season $700 per person, 3-night minimum.

Entrance to the hotel is via a winding cobblestone road through an Edenic coconut grove. Once past the guarded entry you see the hotel beside one of the Pacific coast's most beautiful beaches. There's a daily list of activities posted in the lobby including torpedo rides, aerobics and water exercises, windsurfing classes, water polo, jazz class and tennis clinic, snorkeling, and waterskiing. The travel agency can arrange excursions for deep-sea fishing and to Puerto Vallarta, Manzanillo, and Colima. Rooms are nicely furnished and all have balconies and ocean views. It's very popular with vacationing Mexican families and is likely to be booked for major Mexican holidays. The big drawback here (and it may not be for some people) is that you're miles from anything, and because of the minimum-stay requirement, if you don't like it, you're stuck. The hotel is approximately 30 miles north of the Manzanillo airport on Highway 200 to Barra–Puerto Vallarta.

Dining/Entertainment: Meals are served from 7 to 11:30am, 1 to 4:30pm, and 9 to 10pm.

Services: Laundry, travel agency.

Facilities: Large oceanside pool; all water-sports equipment; tennis, jazz, windsurfing, and aerobics classes.

TECUAN

About 45 minutes from Barra de Navidad and after the turnoff to Tenacatita, you'll see a white cone-shaped silo painted with a sign to El Tecuan. Turn left and drive 6½ miles on a curvy cobblestone road through a mango *ejido* (plantation). The road ends at the Hotel El Tecuan.

EL TECUAN, Hwy. 200, km 33.5. Tel. 333/7-0132. Fax 333/16-6615. Reservations: Garibaldi 1676, Guadalajara, Jal. 44680 (tel. 36/16-0183; fax 36/16-6615). 40 rms, suites, villas. A/C

$ Rates: $40 standard single, $50 standard double; $45 single, $56 double junior suite; $70–$95 villa.

Built on a hill overlooking a wide half-moon bay and beach, El Tecuan is a comfortable and moderately priced standby on this coast that's getting ever more expensive. Besides the wide bay spreading out in front of the hotel, there's a big, beautiful, natural lagoon to the left that's perfect for canoeing. The main building, made of stone and stucco, is built around the swimming pool and faces the bay. Suites and villas are connected via a boardwalk to the main section. Rooms have red-tiled floors and are comfortably furnished. Villas are two stories and have kitchens. Most rooms have ocean views. Like other hotels along this coast, what you see is the first part of a grand scheme of building that has yet to take place.

Dining: There's one restaurant serving all three meals from 8:30am to 10:30pm.

Facilities: Tennis court, swimming pool, basketball and volleyball courts. Bicycles, horses, and canoes for rent.

CAREYES

The next development after Tecuan is Careyes.

In 1972 a group of investors, most notably the Brignone family of Italy, selected 2,500 beautiful coastal acres for a resort development 65 miles north of Manzanillo and 100 miles south of Puerto Vallarta. Today, among the rocky promontories and beach-lined bays, are two developments, the 72-room Hotel Costa Careyes with its numerous casitas and privately owned villas spread over the magnificent bluffs, and in an opposite bay, the Club Med Playa Blanca, with its own private beach. The property runs more than 4 miles along the highway and has 8 miles of shoreline. It's about a 1½-hour drive north of Manzanillo on Highway 200, but only about an hour from the

Manzanillo airport. The two-lane paved road twists through the forested mountain, making it a beautiful, if quite curvy, drive. The area is rich in wildlife: 135 bird species have been counted in the Careyes area alone, four species of marine turtles nest on the beaches between July and December, 70 species of bats have been sighted, and there are fox, ocelot, and alligators among the jungle animals. Shortly before the turn (left) to the development you'll see a sign with one branch of the cobbled road going to Hotel Careyes and the other to Club Med. Taxis from Manzanillo charge around $60 one-way for the trip. There are car rentals at the Manzanillo airport.

HOTEL COSTA CAREYES, Hwy. 200, km 47, Careyes, Jal. Tel. 333/7-0010. Fax 333/7-0050 toll free 800/835-0139 in the U.S. Reservations: Efrain Gonzalez Lura 2123, Guadalajara, Jal. 44150. tel. 36/16-7248; fax 16-8979. 99 rms, suites, and casitas. A/C

$ Rates: High season Nov–Apr 15 single or double $140–$746; low season Apr 16–Nov 14 $110–$520.

Built in an enormous U with a forest of palms leading to the beach, it resembles a miniature Mediterranean village. Clientele is an interesting mix of wealthy Europeans and Americans. It's both sophisticated and rustic, with the room facades awash in bleached earth tones and trimmed in pale blue to match the sea, and each with a plant-filled balcony. Casitas are built on different levels along the beach behind the main hotel building. A covered arcaded walkway, lined with trendy shops of clothing and decorative arts, links the U and leads to rooms, the beachside restaurant, and pool. Standard rooms, one-bedroom suites, and two-bedroom apartments, are casually chic, with tile floors and loomed cotton bedspreads. Two casitas with two bedrooms have private pools.

Dining/Entertainment: Pelicanos, the main restaurant by the pool and beach, is open for all meals. Playa Rosa, a covered open-air restaurant on the adjacent beach, serves casita guests only. Mirador restaurant, on a hill overlooking the property, is open for dinner. Meals cost $15 to $35 each; in high season there are often set-price buffets costing $20 and up. Food isn't outstanding although the restaurants have great atmosphere and good service. There's a disco nightly at El Mirador restaurant and often live musicians serenade during dinner at Pelicanos.

Services: Laundry, purified tap water. Room service is available if arranged in advance since there are no in-room phones.

Facilities: Pool, 2 tennis courts (bring your own equipment), 2 polo fields, TV/paperback lending room, equipment for windsurfing, snorkeling, kayaking.

Special-Interest Activities: Turtle Watch—Named after the hawksbill turtle, which is *careyes* in Spanish, the hotel, with a staff biologist, sponsors a "save the turtle" program. Guests can participate in nightly turtle watch July through December when they come ashore at night to lay eggs. The hatchlings appear 45 days later so some guests may witness both events. Pacific Ridley, leatherback, black turtle, and hawksbill nest on Playa Teopa, a nearby beach belonging to the hotel and all are in danger of extinction. There's no guarantee you'll see a turtle nesting, but the hotel posts a "Turtle Probability Calendar" at the desk with dates when the possibility is best. **Birding**—Don't miss an opportunity to go to nearby Bird Island, a natural habitat for nesting boobies between July and September. You see the birds close-up sitting on their ground nests. The dry months of November to June are good for birding on the mainland since many fly over during migration, but there are no official birding walks; you're on your own. **Polo**—Polo clubs from around the world converge here for polo season, December through April, to play on the hotel's two polo fields. Polo Club membership ranges from $52 for a day to $2,875 for 3 months. There's an additional charge for horse rental, tournament fee, stable fee, boarding (if you bring your own horse), groom's quarters and food, and private lessons. The hotel has two polo fields. **Boat tours and deep-sea fishing**—Hour-long boat tours ($20) and ½-day boat and coastline tours with snorkeling and lunch on a private beach ($45) are offered as well as deep-sea fishing for $20 an hour. **Horseback riding**—Guests have a choice between the polo ponies or regular hotel horses.

CLUB MED PLAYA BLANCA. Tel. 333/2-0008, toll free 800/258-2633 in the U.S. and Canada. 558 rms (all with bath). A/C

$ Rates (including all meals and most sports and activities): $95–$125 per night; $950–$1,250 per week per person double, including air transportation. Higher rates on holidays.

On a beautiful bay opposite the Hotel Careyes, the sienna-colored hotel spills up and around and down a lovely, lushly landscaped hillside to the beach. After a recent remodeling, rooms are larger and brighter and have two full beds. Each Club Med has a different personality and clientele. This one has always been popular with active singles and young couples, which the extensive and innovative program of activities indicates. Children 12 and over are welcome. Prices are usually based on double occupancy, but certain times of year single reservations are accepted at no additional charge. Transportation from either Puerto Vallarta or Manzanilla is extra.

Dining/Entertainment: The main dining room, above the bar and pool, is open for all three buffet-style meals. El Pelicano on the beach serves extended breakfast and lunch buffets, or for two or more, seafood dinners are served to the table. El Zapata, also on the beach, serves steaks. Bars include one by the pool, a disco bar, and beach bar. The staff provides evening entertainment in a combination of shows and games that involve guests and there's disco dancing every night.

Services: In-room safes, irons and ironing boards available; telephone messages are posted.

Facilities: Olympic-size pool, 6 tennis courts (4 night lit); equipment for sailing, kayaking, snorkeling, archery, volleyball, basketball, Ping-Pong, bocce ball, and billiards. Fitness center with aerobics and calisthenics classes. Additional charge: arts-and-crafts materials, massage, deep-sea fishing, excursions to Manzanillo, Puerto Vallarta, etc.

Special-Interest activities: Rock Climbing—Dubbed the new sport of the '90s here you learn to scale vertical surfaces on an artificial wall. **Comedy workshops**—Improvisation workshops are free and led by the Chicago City Limits, but limited to 15 students weekly. Learn to create comedy scenes, songs, and stories, improvise characters, take pratfalls and deliver punch lines, then star in a show at the end of the week. Half-hour open workshops, available to all guests, offer a sample of comedy techniques. **Musicians workshop**—Come with musical talents and create working combos. There's a computer-music and graphic workshop, too. **Magicians workshop**—Learn secrets of sleight of hand. **Circus workshop**—Learn to fly from a high trapeze, trampoline, juggling, and highwire. **Scuba certification**—Free PADI or NAUI certification classes, but no exploration dives. **Intensive horseback riding**—For $15 an hour, create an individualized program to learn all aspects of riding with 2½ hours of daily ring instruction which leads to dressage and jumping. There are daily trail rides as well. Price includes all equipment plus you receive a videotape of yourself to take home. (For an extra charge you can use the same horse all week.)

LAS ALAMANDAS

In 1990, Isabel Goldsmith, granddaughter of Atenor Patino who developed Las Hadas, opened Las Alamandas, a super-exclusive hideaway between Manzanillo and Puerto Vallarta. It's intended as the beginning of a larger resort, but for now there are only five villas (four for rent) and no further construction is under way. Details on where it is and how to get there are given when guests make reservations. There's no sign on the highway. Entrance to the property is by prior request only. It's about 2 hours from Manzanillo and 2½ from Puerto Vallarta.

LAS ALAMANDAS, Hwy. 200 Manzanillo–Puerto Vallarta. Information and reservations in the U.S.: The Bel-Air Hotel Company (tel. 213/826-9453; fax 213/826-4601). In Mexico City: tel. 5/540-7657; fax 5/540-7658.

$ Rates (including breakfast and lunch): Casa del Sol high season $450 single, $1,000 house, low season $350–800. Casa del Domo high season, $450 single, $750 house; low season $350–$600. Casa Azul high season $1,060 entire 3-bedroom casa, $230–$350 individually; low season $850 entire casa, per bedroom $180–$280; Casita San Miguel high season $250; low season $200.

⭐ Part of a 1,500-acre estate and set on 70 acres against a low hill, the small cluster of buildings spreads almost to the wide clean beach. It's a beautifully landscaped spot, on an entirely private beach. Designed by Guadalajara architect Gabriel Nuñez, it's a mixture of Mediterranean, Mexico, and Southwest, and it's been featured in *Architectural Digest* and *Casa Gente*. The furnishings, selected by Isabel Goldsmith, are a fabulous blend of Mexican handcrafted furniture, pottery and folk art, with cushy sofas, beds, and pillows covered in bright textiles from Mexico and Guatemala, and give the rooms a relaxed, casual feel. The combined effect of architecture and furnishings is stunning, yet comfortable, and you definitely feel like kicking back here; since only 22 guests can be accommodated at any one time, the threat of crowds is nonexistent. All of the guesthouses are grouped around a small cobbled plaza, lush with vegetation. All villas have lavish use of space, high-pitched tiled roofs, cool tiled floors, and tiled verandas with sea views. And each guest bedroom has its own bathroom. Casa del Sol, at beach level, is painted bright yellow and has three bedrooms, a large, completely equipped kitchen, living room, and common entry foyer as well as separate entrances for each bedroom. Casa del Domo, painted hot pink, has a dome in the entry, two large bedrooms each with a private terrace, shared living room, and full kitchen. Casa Azul (blue house), on a hill, has great view and breezes, four bedrooms which can be rented individually or all together. All bedrooms in Casa Azul have their own entrance, oversize bath, private terrace, and a seating area. Casita San Miguel is part of Casa Azul.

Dining/Entertainment: Oasis is the festive, sheltered restaurant serving all three meals and featuring fresh grilled food and Mexican specialties. Honor bar.

Services: Private housekeeper and cook assigned to each villa except Casa Azul, which has individual suites and rooms. Laundry service, nightly turndown. Fishing, boat rides, and diving trips are arranged on request. Transportation to and from Manzanillo ($150 one-way) and Puerto Vallarta ($180 one-way) can be arranged.

Facilities: 60-foot swimming pool, lighted tennis court, fully equipped gym with treadmill, Stairmaster, Versclimber, and Lifecycle. Large-screen TV in the lobby. VCR in each villa, with video library for rentals. Private 3,000-foot paved landing strip, capable of accommodating a King Air turboprop. Make advance arrangements for landing.

CUYUTLÁN

Thirty miles south of Manzanillo and 5 miles east off Highway 200 is Cuyutlán. It's a small, tidy, budget-priced coastal village lined with modest hotels and restaurants. The attraction is the black-sand beach. A wood-slat path leads across the hot black sand to the rows of umbrella-covered chairs for rent lined up facing the ocean. Weekends and holidays the beach becomes crowded, but weekdays it's a tranquil place to be. The waves are big and strong here, so be very careful of the undertow. The Cuyutlán lagoon is behind the town a mile or more and it's a haven for many colorful birds. Ask a local to point the way.

COLIMA

Many Americans, who think Colima begins and ends with the popular port of Manzanillo, are missing a lot by overlooking the state's attractive capital, a balmy metropolis of 116,000 inhabitants only a 2-hour drive 60 miles southwest of Manzanillo and 165 miles southwest of Guadalajara. Its founder in 1523, was the conquistador Gonzalo de Sandoval, youngest member of Cortés's staff.

Although one of Mexico's smallest states, Colima has an incredible range of climate and topography. The northern part contains pine forests and part of Mexico's second-highest active volcano, Volcán de Colima (12,870 ft.), which last erupted in 1991. The rest of the volcano lies in Jalisco. While the capital, Colima, lies virtually at the foot of the volcano, its 1,640-foot altitude allows it to have a climate similar to Manzanillo's. An even higher mountain, visible if you come from Guadalajara, is the 14,000-foot Nevado de Colima, which, in spite of its name, lies entirely in the state of Jalisco.

You can get there by plane on Aero California from Tijuana and Mexico City, with connections to La Paz. The first-class train between Guadalajara and Manzanillo has been suspended. There's a second-class train from Manzanillo and Guadalajara, but it could take forever. The train station is south of the town center. By bus there's frequent service from Manzanillo and Guadalajara. The new, very comfortable Primera Plus bus costs more but it's air conditioned, has video movies, vending machine refreshments, and fewer seats than regular buses. Colima's new central bus station is out of town and there's taxi service to town, or get a city bus marked "Centro." If you come by car from Manzanillo, follow the signs out of town. After several miles you'll see the turnoff to Highway 54 and a few miles farther a choice of a toll road, or continuing on the nontoll road. They don't give you much warning and you may wind up entering the toll road whether you intended to or not.

Colima's beautiful central plaza, surrounded by the palatial colonial-era buildings, is one of the most handsome in Mexico. From the plaza Hidalgo and Madero go east and west of it and Reforma and Barrera go north and south.

The **State Tourist Office** Hidalgo 75 (tel. 2-4360 or 2-8360), is 1½ blocks from the plaza. You can get maps and brochures here, or make reservations to stay at the state-owned inn in the mountains outside of Comala. To find the tourist office, take the street down the right side of the Palacio from the main square. It's open Monday through Friday from 8:30am to 3pm and 5 to 9pm and Saturday from 9am to 1pm.

152 • WHAT TO SEE & DO IN MANZANILLO

Most sights are within walking distance of the central plaza.

WHERE TO STAY

Moderate

HOTEL AMERICA, Morelos 162, Colima, Col. 28000. Tel. 331/2-7488.
Fax 331/4-4425. 55 rms (all with bath). A/C TV TEL **Directions:** Walk 1½ blocks west of the plaza to Morelos; it's on the right ½ block down.
$ Rates: $45 single or double.

This downtown hotel offers large and tastefully furnished rooms. It's almost always full of traveling businesspeople, so get here early in the day if you want a room. There's laundry service, restaurant, and bar, and for men there's a gym with a sauna, hot tub, and vapor bath.

Budget

HOTEL CEBALLOS, Portal Medellin 12, Colima, Col. 28000. Tel. 331/2-4444. 60 rms (all with bath). A/C (6 rms) FAN (54 rms).
$ Rates: $20–$25 single or double.

On the east side of the main plaza, this hotel looks great from the outside, however, they've done a lot of squeezing to make more rooms, and the interior has lost much of its charm as well as its courtyard. The cell-like rooms are clean and freshly painted. The desk clerk will try to pressure you into taking a higher-priced room than you want. Insist that she tell you the lowest rate. Higher prices are for rooms with air conditioning, which really isn't necessary.

WHERE TO DINE

Moderate

LOS NARANJOS (The Orange Trees), Gabino Barrera 43. Tel. 2-0029.
  Specialty: MEXICAN.
$ Prices: Main courses $2–$6; tacos 75¢–$3.
  Open: Daily 8am–11:30pm.

The leading restaurant downtown is handsomely decorated with orange and white linens, light blue walls, and orange fruit designs hand-painted on the chairs. For the quality of decor you'd expect higher prices. I highly recommend the pollo caserola, a vegetable and meat stew of carrots, potatoes, and peas in a delicious tomato broth, all served in a clay casserole with a side order of fresh corn tortillas. It's enough for two. To find it, from the zócalo walk down Madero (left of the cathedral) and take the first street on the left.

Budget

LAS PALMAS, Callejon del Caco. Tel. 2-4444 or 4-0388.
  Specialty: MEXICAN.
$ Prices: Breakfast $1.75–$3.50; main courses $1.75–$5.
  Open: Mon–Sat 8am–10pm.

There's a sign on the sidewalk, directing you through a small interior mall to the back and the tranquil little restaurant. There's covered dining space as well as umbrella-shaded patio tables. The food is Mexican fast food such as tacos, quesadillas, and soup, plus hamburgers and french fries. It's behind the Hotel Ceballos (on the plaza) just off the pedestrian-only street.

WHAT TO SEE & DO

MUSEUM OF WESTERN CULTURES (Museo de Occidente de Gobierno de Estado), Galvan s/n. No phone.

Also known as the Museum of Anthropology, this is one of my favorite museums in the country. It has many pre-Hispanic pieces, including the famous clay dancing dogs of Colima. There are fine examples of clay, shell, and bone jewelry, exquisite clay human and animal figures, and diagrams of tombs showing unusual funeral customs. The museum is on Galvan at Ejercito Nacional.

Admission: Free.
Open: Daily 9am–7:30pm.

MUSEUM OF POPULAR CULTURE MARÍA TERESA POMAR, University of Colima, 27 de Septiembre and Gabino Barrera. Tel. 2-5140.

One of the city's most interesting museums contains regional costumes and musical instruments from all over Mexico, photographs showing the day-to-day use of costumes and masks, and folk art from Oaxaca, Guerrero, and elsewhere. The section devoted to Mexico's sweet bread (pan dulce) is set up like an authentic bakery with each bread labeled. At the entrance is a shop selling Mexican folk art.

Admission: 50¢.
Open: Tues–Sat 9am–2pm and 4–7pm, Sun 9am–2pm. **Directions:** From the Museum of Western Cultures go left out the front door. Walk 5 long and short blocks to the wide Av. Galvan at Ejercito. Cross it and the museum is on your right.

MUSEO DE HISTORIA DE COLIMA, Portal Morelos 1. No phone.

Opened in 1988, the city's newest showcase is dedicated to state history. The beautiful colonial building is the former Hotel Casino, the birthplace of former Mexican president Miguel de la Madrid Hurtado. It's on the plaza opposite the Hotel Ceballos. The collection includes pre-Hispanic pottery, baskets, furniture, and dance masks. More than 5,000 pre-Hispanic pieces are packed away awaiting the renovation of the upper floor. Between the pottery at this museum and the Museo Occidente, you'll begin to understand why the Aztec name for Colima meant "place where pottery is made." Colima is also known for the variety of pre-Hispanic tombs, and one of the best displays here shows drawings of many kinds of tombs. You may be asked to leave your purse or bag with the guard as you enter.

Admission: Free.
Open: Mon–Sat 10am–2pm and 4–8pm. Sun bookstore only, same hours.

COMALA

From the old Colima bus station buses go to Comala every 15 minutes. The trip takes 20 minutes and costs 15¢. By taxi it will cost $6. This picturesque little village is near a mysterious magnetic zone out on the highway. Get one of the taxi drivers on the square to run you out to this area, a few miles from town. When he gets there he'll kill the engine. Then the magnetic pull takes control and the car gathers speed uphill without engine power. The phenomenon was discovered by accident a few years ago when a motorist had car trouble, but couldn't get the vehicle to stop. If you keep going on this road you'll reach the Volcán de Colima, which disappears behind the mountain, then reappears, larger and larger with each loop around the curves—quite a twilight zone experience. There is a state-owned lodge here, where you can arrange to stay overnight in rustic cabins. Volcanic ash is everywhere.

Back in town, the village is liveliest on Sunday when roving bands of mariachis gather to serenade diners under the arcades around the central plaza. As many as five different groups sing at once. The food, drink, and atmosphere of this village make for a perfect day in Mexico. Get here before 3pm to get a good seat for all the wholesome revelry that really gets going around 3:30pm.

On the outskirts of town, an artisans' school is open Monday through Saturday. Visitors are welcome to come in and browse.

CHAPTER 9
GETTING TO KNOW GUADALAJARA

1. ORIENTATION
- DID YOU KNOW . . . ?
2. GETTING AROUND
- FAST FACTS: GUADALAJARA

Known as the "City of Roses," Guadalajara is a great metropolis, the second largest in Mexico. It is considered by many the most Mexican of cities. Given its charter as *muy leal y muy noble ciudad* ("most loyal and noble city") by none other than Emperor Charles V, it has held a prominent place in Mexican affairs ever since that time. Charles, who ran most of Europe and a lot of the world at the time, certainly knew what he was doing. Guadalajara (pop. 1,700,000), capital of the state of Jalisco, celebrates its 450th anniversary in February 1992. Sophisticated and beautiful though it is, the once very visible roses which decorated the city appear only occasionally these days.

As though to emphasize the great things that were expected of it, Guadalajara's Spanish builders gave the city not one but four beautiful plazas in its center. Today the city's leaders have given it a fifth, the enormous **Plaza Tapatía,** an ambitious stretch of urban redevelopment extending for about a mile through the urban landscape. Scattered with trees and monuments, sprinkled with fountains, the new super-plaza links the city's major colonial buildings, opens new perspectives for viewing them, and joins the past with the great new buildings of the present. This now-completed, ambitious project is very "Mexican" in its grand scope.

By the way, *tapatío* (or *tapatía*) is a word you'll come across often in this city. No one is certain quite where it originated, but tapatío means "Guadalajaran"—a thing, a person, even an idea. The way a charro (Mexican cowboy) gives his all, or the way a mariachi sings his heart out—that's tapatío!

Guadalajara is as sophisticated, and at least as formal as Mexico City. Dress is conservative; resort wear is out of place here.

1. ORIENTATION

ARRIVING

BY PLANE **Aero California** reaches Guadalajara through Tijuana and San Diego. **Aero Guadalajara** flies from Culiacán, San Luis Potosí, Zacatecas, and

Tampico five or six times a week. **Aeromar** flies to Guadalajara from Mexico City, San Luis Potosí, Tepic, and Monterrey. **Aeromexico** connects Guadalajara to the U.S. via Houston and Los Angeles. In Mexico, Aeromexico flies from Guadalajara directly to and from Acapulco, Cancún, Culiacán, Monterrey, Puerto Vallarta, and Torreón. **Alaska Airlines** has service from San Francisco and Los Angeles. **American Airlines** connects through Dallas/Fort Worth. **Continental Airlines** connects U.S. flights through Houston. **Delta** flies from Los Angeles. **Mexicana** has three Mexican hub cities—Mexico City, Monterrey, and Cancún—offering connections to most major and many minor destinations in the country.

Guadalajara's international airport is a 25-minute ride from the city. Collective minivans are lined up in front of the airport. Drivers will direct you to the correct van; you pay after you board. Tickets cost $6 to the downtown area. For the return trip, the company picks up at residences only, charging around the same. So to save money, pick a residence address anywhere in the downtown area and wait there for the van. Taxis charge around $13.

BY TRAIN Guadalajara is the country's second-largest train hub. The **National Railways of Mexico** (tel. 50-0826) link Mexico City and Guadalajara with other destinations on Mexico's new first-class train service. *Estrella* (for more information, see "By Train" in "Getting Around," below). Pacific coast trains are notoriously off-schedule. *El Tapatío* runs from Mexico City to Guadalajara leaving Mexico City at 8:40pm, arriving in Guadalajara at 8:10am. *El Sinaloence* arrives from Mazatlán at 10:05am. *El Colimense* to Colima and Manzanillo has been suspended, but may resume.

From **Mexicali,** on the California border, *El Tren del Pacífico* departs at 9am Pacific standard time, arriving in Guadalajara at 5pm the next day. From **Nogales,** Del Pacífico departs at 2:20pm and arrives in Guadalajara at 5pm a day later. *El Sinaloense* also goes along the Pacific coast from Los Mochis through Mazatlán and Tepic, but it isn't as good or convenient a train.

The train station on Calzada Independencia is within walking distance (with light luggage) of a couple of recommended hotels. Buses marked "Centro" go downtown, and those marked "Estación" go to the station from downtown. Otherwise you're at the mercy of the taxis that charge almost $5 to go the short distance anywhere between the station and the city center.

BY BUS The bus station is 6 miles south of the city center. **City buses** pick up passengers in front of each terminal building and can become incredibly crowded. Unless you get a seat, there will be no space for even a small suitcase. Any bus marked "Centro" goes downtown.

White **minivans (combis)** holding 16 or more passengers also serve the terminal and are more comfortable and convenient. Combi 40, with "Centro" or "Nva." or "Nueva Central" on the windshield, travels along Revolucíon and begins and ends its route on Calle Ferrocarril between 16 de Septiembre and Corona, just a few blocks from the Plaza Tapatía and many of our recommended hotels. Use these if your suitcase fits on your lap. Buses and minivans often empty at the beginning of the "U" where traffic enters in front of the Flecha Amarilla terminal. There it's easier to get a seat before they get crowded.

Buy fixed-price taxi tickets from a booth inside each terminal near the exit doors. Rates vary according to destination.

ORIENTATION • 157

BY CAR From Nogales on the California border, follow Highway 15. From Barra de Navidad, or southeast on the coast, take Highway 80. From Mexico City, Highway 90 leads to Guadalajara. Coming from Manzanillo or Colima on the Pacific coast, take Mex 110, either the new toll road or the free road. The toll road shortens the trip by 1½ hours and tolls cost around $20 one-way. The free road, which winds through the mountains, is in good condition.

DEPARTING

BY PLANE International flights require check-in 90 minutes before takeoff and domestic flights, at least 60 minutes before departure. **Auto Transportaciones Aeropuerto** (tel. 12-4278, 12-4308, or 12-9337) runs **minivans** between the airport and city 24 hours a day. **Aero California** (tel. 26-1901 or 26-1064; airport 89-0924). **Aeromar** (tel. 26-4656 or 26-4658). **Aeromexico** (tel. 25-2559; airport 89-0119). **Air France** (tel. 30-3721 or 30-3707). **Alaska Airlines** (tel. toll free 95/800-426-0333 in Mexico). **American Airlines** (tel. 89-0304; airport 30-0349). **Continental Airlines** (tel. 89-0433 and 89-0261). **Delta** (tel. 30-3530 or 30-3226). **Lufthansa** (tel. 16-3175 or 16-3249). **Mexicana** (tel. 47-2222; airport 89-0119). Travelers on any Mexicana international flight can receive a 25% discount on domestic flights in Mexico by asking for the VIMEX fare. Tickets for other destinations in Mexico must be purchased within 7 days of arrival in Mexico.

BY TRAIN Going to **Mexicali,** on the California border, *Del Pacífico* departs Guadalajara at 8:15am, arrives in Tepic at 1:55pm, Mazatlán at 6:50pm, and Mexicali at 4:30pm, the next day. For Nogales, near the Arizona border, *Del Pacífico* departs Guadalajara at 8:15am, arrives in Mazatlán at 6:50pm, and arrives in Nogales at 11am. There are no sleeping cars. *El Tapatío,* a train with overnight sleeping compartments, leaves Guadalajara at 8:55pm and arrives in Mexico City at 8:10am. This is a popular train; reserve a place early.

Most travel agencies will arrange tickets on *Del Pacífico* trains, but there may be a service charge. **MaCulls Travel Agency,** 361 López Cotilla, has up-to-date train information and will make reservations. Located next to the Hotel Universo downtown on the corner of Degollado, it's open Monday to Friday from 9am to 2pm and 4 to 7pm and Saturday from 9am to 2pm.

BY BUS Two bus stations serve Guadalajara—the old one near downtown and the new one 6 miles out on the way to Tonalá. A convenient place for bus information is **Servicios Coordinados,** 254 Calzada Independencia, a kind of "bus travel agency" located under the Plaza Tapatía. There travelers can make reservations, buy tickets, and receive information on the six main bus lines to all points in Mexico—much better than trekking out to the no-longer "central" Central Camionera (see below).

The Old Bus Station: For bus trips within a 60-mile radius of Guadalajara, including **Lake Chapala, Ajijic, and Jocotepec,** go to the **old bus terminal** on Niños Heroes off of Calzada Independencia Sur and look for **Transportes Guadalajara-Chapala** (tel. 19-5675), which has frequent buses and combi service beginning at 6am to Chapala and Ajijic. (For Tlaquepaque and Tonalá, see "Easy Excursions" in Chapter 11.)

The New Bus Station: The **Central Camionera,** about 6 miles and a 20-minute ride east of downtown toward Tonalá, provides bus service to or from virtually any point in Mexico. The new terminal resembles an international airport: Seven separate buildings are connected by a covered walkway in a U shape, with one-way traffic entering on the right. Each building houses several first- and second-class bus lines. And that's the only drawback—you must go to each one to find the line or service that suits you best. It's one of the nicest bus stations in Mexico, with amenities like shuttle buses, restaurants, gift shops, luggage storage (*guarda equipaje*), book and magazine shops, liquor stores, Ladatel long-distance telephones, and hotel information. There's also a large, new, budget hotel next door (see "Where to Stay" in Chapter 10). To get there by bus take the **Diagonal Tonalá** on 16 de Septiembre/Alcalde opposite the cathedral in downtown Guadalajara.

The price difference between first and second class is small, but the difference in speed, comfort, and convenience is sometimes, but not always, great. None of the buses from here are of the school-bus variety. To get you started here are a few hints on served areas. All the lines to **Aguascalientes** or **Zacatecas** are on the left and include Camiones de los Altos (tel. 57-6158 and 57-6151), Estrella Blanca (tel. 57-6158 and 57-6151), Transportes Chihuahenses (tel. 57-7431 or 57-8199), Transportes del Norte (tel. 57-8455), and Autobuses al Aguila (tel. 57-8128). To **Tepic** or **San Blas** on the Pacific coast, try Estrella Blanca. If to **Manzanillo,** try the first-class Primera Plus (tel. 57-7310) which costs more but has only 34 seats, self-serve refreshments, air conditioning, and video movies. Or try Flecha Amarilla (tel. 57-7316), Autobuses del Occidente (tel. 57-6460), or Unidos de la Costa (tel. 57-4933). Or to **Barra de Navidad** and **San Melaque** (San Patricio), then go to Auto Camiones del Pacífico (tel. 57-4805), or Unidos de la Costa (mentioned above). To **Pátzcuaro, Morelia,** or **Uruapan,** then go to Flecha Amarilla (tel. 57-7310), Autobuses del Occident (tel. 57-6460), or Tres Estrellas de Oro (tel. 57-6969 or 57-7225).

CITY LAYOUT

Guadalajara is not a difficult city to negotiate, but it certainly is big. While most of the main attractions are within walking distance of the historic downtown area, others, such as the nearby villages of Tonalá, Tlaquepaque, and farther away, Lake Chapala and Ajijic are accessible by bus.

Street names change at the cathedral.

NEIGHBORHOODS IN BRIEF

Historic Center The heart of the city takes in the Plaza de Armas, Plaza de los Laureles, Los Hombres Ilustres, Plaza Liberación, and the Plaza Tapatía. It's the tourist center and includes major museums, theaters, restaurants, hotels, and the largest covered market in Latin America, all linked by wide boulevards and pedestrian-only streets. It's bounded east and west by 16 de Septiembre/Alcalde and Prosperidad (across Calzada Independencia) and north and south by Hidalgo and Morelos.

Parque Agua Azul An enormous city park directly south (20 blocks) of the historic center, with a children's area and rubber-wheeled train. Nearby are the state crafts shop, performing arts theaters, and the anthropology museum.

GUADALAJARA & ENVIRONS

160 • GETTING TO KNOW GUADALAJARA

? DID YOU KNOW...?

- Guadalajara is Mexico's second largest city.
- Lake Chapala is the largest lake in Mexico.
- Jalisco is the sixth largest Mexican state.
- One of Mexico's "big three" muralists, José Clemente Orozco, was born in Guadalajara in 1883.
- The Jarabe Tapatío (Mexican Hat Dance) was developed in Guadalajara.
- The blue agave, from which tequila is made, grows only around Guadalajara near the town of Tequila.
- Mariachi music developed in Cocula, a small town near Guadalajara, where there are now no mariachis.
- During the 300 years that Mexico belonged to Spain, no Spanish king ever visited the country.

Chapultepec A fashionable neighborhood with shops and restaurants 25 blocks west of the historic center reached by Avenida Vallarta, with Chapultepec as the main artery through the neighborhood.

Minerva Circle Almost 40 blocks west of the historic center, the Minerva Circle is at the confluence of Avenidas Vallarta, López Mateos, and Circunvalación Washington. A fashionable neighborhood, it has several good restaurants and the Hotel Fiesta Americana, all reached by the Par Vial.

Plaza del Sol The largest shopping center in the city, south of the Minerva Circle and southwest of the historic center near the intersection of López Mateos and Mariano Otero.

Zapopan Once a separate village founded in 1542, now a full-fledged suburb 20 minutes northwest of the Plaza Tapatía via Avenida Avila Camacho. It's most noted for its 18th-century basilica and the revered 16th-century image of the Virgin of Zapopan made of corn paste and honored every October 12. The city's fashionable country club is just south of Zapopan.

Tlaquepaque Seven miles southeast of the historic center, a village of mansions-turned-shops fronting pedestrian-only streets and plazas.

Tonalá Four miles from Tlaquepaque, a village of more than 400 artists working in metal, clay, and paper, with a huge street market on Sunday and Thursday.

2. GETTING AROUND

By Bus Two bus routes will satisfy 90% of your intracity transportation needs. Buses bearing the sign **"Par Vial"** run a rectangular route going east along Hidalgo to the Mercado Libertad and then west along Juárez (becoming Vallarta) to the Glorieta Minerva, near the western edge of the city.

Many buses run north-south along the Calzada Independencia (not to be confused with Calle Independencia), but the **"San Juan de Dios–Estacion"** bus goes between the points you want: San Juan de Dios church, next to the Mercado Libertad, and the railroad station past Parque Agua Azul. This bus is best because most other buses on Calzada Independencia have longer routes (out to the suburbs, for instance) and thus tend to be more heavily crowded at all times.

For getting to Tlaquepaque and Tonalá by bus see "Easy Excursions" in Chapter 11.

When you want to get off a local bus, signal the driver to stop by pushing one of the buzzer buttons on the bus ceiling.

Electric trolleys run the same routes and are quieter, newer, and more pleasant to ride than buses—and cost the same—15¢ to 50¢.

By Colectivo Colectivos are minivans running throughout the city day and night picking up and discharging passengers at fixed and unfixed points. They are often a faster and more convenient way to travel than the bus. There are no printed schedules, and the routes and fixed stops change frequently. However, locals know the routes by heart and can tell you where and how to use the colectivos. Prices are only slightly higher than the bus.

By Taxi Taxis are an expensive way to get around town. A short 10- to 15-minute ride, for instance, from the Plaza de Armas to Las Margaritas restaurant costs an exorbitant $5.25, whereas a bus there costs only 15¢.

By Car All major car-rental agencies are represented with booths at the airport and at various locations in town. The least expensive rates are found by arranging the rental from your home country at least 7 days in advance of arrival in Guadalajara. As an example, Avis rates are $38 per day, plus $15 a day insurance and 15% tax. Weekly rates are $159 plus the daily insurance and tax. Both are with unlimited mileage. This rate may be higher if you pick up the car on a weekend or major holiday. As you chauffeur yourself around keep in mind several main arteries. The Periferico is a loop around the city that connects to most other highways entering the city. Traffic on the Periferico is slow because it is heavily potholed, filled with trucks, and is only a two-lane road. Several important freeway-style thoroughfares crisscross the city. Gonzalez Gallo leads south from town center and connects to the road to Tonalá and Tlaquepaque or leads straight to Lake Chapala. Highway 15 from Tepic intersects with both Avenida Vallarta and Calzada Lázaro Cárdenas. Vallarta then goes straight to the Plaza Tapatía area. Cárdenas crosses the whole city and intersects at the southern edge with the road to Chapala and to Tlaquepaque and Tonalá.

By Horse-drawn Carriage Take one of the elegant horse-drawn carriages for a spin around town. The cost is about $13 to $17, depending on the route and length of ride—usually about 45 minutes. Drivers congregate near the Mercado

---

IMPRESSIONS

The wonderful progress that Mexico has made within recent years is strikingly exemplified in the case of Guadalajara, which, less than twenty years ago, was a sleepy, backward place but little known to the outside world. The nearest railway was then some distance away, and travellers from the capital were obliged to make a large part of the journey in slow, uncomfortable stage-coaches. To-day, [sic] Guadalajara has become a busy, cosmopolitan city and an important railway center . . .
—W. E. CARSON, *MEXICO: THE WONDERLAND OF THE SOUTH*, 1909

Libertad and also behind the Plaza/Rotunda de Los Hombres Ilustres and other spots around town.

GUADALAJARA

American Express The office is at Vallarta 2440, Plaza Los Arcos (tel. 30-0200). It's open Monday to Friday from 9am to 2pm and Saturday from 9am to noon.

Area Code The area code is 36.

Baby-sitters Hotels can usually recommend baby-sitters; ask at the reception desk.

Bookstores Gonvil is a popular chain of bookstores throughout the city. There's one across from the Plaza de Los Hombres Ilustres on Alcalde and another a few blocks south at 16 de Septiembre 118 (Alcalde becomes 16 de Septiembre south of the cathedral).

Business Hours In Guadalajara most stores are open Monday to Friday from 10am to 7pm. Other offices such as travel agencies or other services may open at 9am. In Tlaquepaque and Tonalá, many shops close from 2 to 4pm.

Car Rentals Two to try are Auto-Rent de Guadalajara, Avenida Federalismo Sur 542-A (tel. 25-1515 or 26-2014), and Aguila, Avenida Juárez 845-A (tel. 25-9554 or 26-6098). Otherwise, there are many agencies in the airport arrivals area, or ask at your hotel.

Climate Guadalajara has a mild, pleasant, and dry climate year round. Bring a sweater for evenings during November through March. From June through September it's rainy and a bit cooler. The warmest months of March, April, and May are also hot and dry.

Currency Exchange Banks will change money and traveler's checks Monday to Friday from 9am to noon. Many travelers will be delighted/relieved to find handy **Pocket Tellers.** There's a 24-hour Pocket Teller that takes VISA, Cirrus and MasterCard at the Banamex bank at the corner of Corona and Juárez. Look for the seven-story gray building catercorner from the Café Madrid.

Dentist Call Ruben E. Moran, D.D.S., M. S. Angulo 1855 (tel. 52-1001). Or ask at your hotel lobby.

Doctors Contact Dr. William Fairbank, Juste Sierra 2515 (tel. 16-4851; emergency 13-6350).

Drugstores Farmacias Guadalajara are a chain throughout the city that offers late-night service. There's one near downtown on López Cotilla (tel. 14-2810 or 14-6657). Ask at your hotel where the closest pharmacy is. Farmacia Varela, Pedro Moreno 620, is open from 9am to 11pm (tel. 14-1433). Farmacia Corona, S. A. Hidalgo 601 (tel. 14-2201 or 13-2132) has delivery service.

Embassies/Consulates The world's largest American consular offices are here at 175 Progreso (tel. 25-9202 or 25-4445).

Emergencies For police call 17-5838 (state) or 21-7194 (highways). During the day, call the tourist office (tel. 14-0606, ext. 114). For extreme medical emergencies there's a service from the United States that will fly people to American hospitals: Air-Evac, 24-hour air ambulance; call collect 24 hours, 713/880-9767 in Houston, 619/278-3822 in San Diego, 305/772-0003 in Miami.

Etiquette Like most Mexicans, Guadalajarans are reserved and formal at first, but warm up quickly with a few words of conversation. I have found Guadalajarans generally to be among the most helpful of any city I visit. On several occasions over the years while trying to find my way by car alone, I have asked a fellow motorist directions (usually a family or woman) and been given not only the directions, but told "follow me, I'll lead you there." In every case, it was plain to see they took immense pleasure in helping the tourist.

Eyeglasses Look for the optic shop right across the plaza from the tourism office.

Holidays See "Special Events" in Chapter 11. February and October are the big festival months. On Christmas and Easter, many things are closed or have different hours, and the renowned Ballet Folklórico has no performances.

Hospitals Contact the Hospital Mexico-Ameriano, Colomos 2110 (tel. 41-0089).

Information The state of Jalisco's Tourist Information Office is at Morelos 102 (tel. 14-0606, ext. 114), in the Plaza Tapatía—at the crossroads of Paseo Degollado and Paraje del Rincón del Diablo. It's open Monday through Friday from 9am to 9pm, and Saturday from 9am to 1pm. The English-speaking staff provides good information and an excellent map.

For information on cultural happenings around town, check with the **Departamento de Bellas Artes,** located at Jesús García 720, on the Parque Alcalde (tel. 14-1614). The office is open Monday through Friday from 9am to 4pm and on Saturday from 9am to 1pm. **Instituto Cultural Cabañas** (tel. 18-6003, ext. 22), also has information on what's happening around town.)

Laundry/Dry Cleaning There are no laundries in the historic downtown area. Hotels generally offer this service (at a high price).

Lost Property Call the American consulate, police, or your bus company or airline (for property lost in transit).

Luggage Storage/Lockers Luggage storage is available in the main bus station, the Central Camionera and at the Guadalajara airport.

Newspapers/Magazines The Hotel Fénix (on the corner of Calle Corona and Avenida López Cotillo), has English-language newspapers and magazines and maps. It's also a good place to buy Guadalajara's English newspaper, ***The Colony Reporter,*** which is published every Saturday, if you don't spot it on a newsstand.

Police See "Emergencies," above.

Post Office It's at the corner of Carranza and Calle Independencia, about 4 blocks northeast of the cathedral. Standing in the plaza behind the cathedral and facing the Degollada Theater, walk to the left and turn left on Carranza. Walk past the Hotel de Mendoza, cross Calle Independencia, and look for the post office on the left-hand side.

Radio/TV Many English-speaking U.S. cable TV stations are broadcast in Guadalajara.

Religious Services Check *The Colony Reporter* newspaper.

Rest Rooms Use the facilities in a restaurant, museum, or hotel lobby area. Always carry your own paper and soap.

Safety As in any large city, don't be careless with belongings. Women should avoid walking around alone late at night.
Taxis See "Getting Around" in this chapter.
Transit Information See "Getting Around" in this chapter.

CHAPTER 10

WHERE TO STAY & DINE IN GUADALAJARA

- **1. WHERE TO STAY**
- **FROMMER'S SMART TRAVELER: HOTELS**
- **FROMMER'S SMART TRAVELER: RESTAURANTS**
- **2. WHERE TO DINE**

Guadalajara offers all the amenities in the way of hotels and restaurants of a major city. There are hotels for every budget, and restaurants offer cuisine from around the world.

1. WHERE TO STAY

EXPENSIVE

CARLTON HOTEL, Av. Niños Heroes and 16 de Septiembre, Guadalajara, Jal. 44190. Tel. 36/14-7272, toll free 91-800/3-6200 in Mexico. Fax 36/13-5539. 202 rms and suites (all with bath). AC TV TEL MINIBAR

$ Rates: $125 standard single or double; $150 junior suite; $165 master suite; $215 executive suite. Ask about weekend discounts.

Formerly the Sheraton Hotel, the Carlton is near Agua Azul Park and a short distance from the historic center. The nicely furnished rooms are unusually spacious. Standard rooms have either two double or one king-size beds. All have hairdryers and remote-control TV with U.S. channels. Master suites have a large living-room area, while junior suites have a small sitting area. Each of the fifth-floor executive suites includes terry robes, continental breakfast, afternoon coffee and sweets, and open bar in the early evening. The 10th floor is reserved for nonsmokers. You'll save money by purchasing a package for this hotel through a travel agent in the U.S.

Dining/Entertainment: La Pergula restaurant faces the pool with indoor or outdoor dining. There are two bars. Genesis Video Disco is open from 9:30pm to 1am daily.

Services: Laundry, room service, travel agency, purified tap water. For an extra charge guests may use the hotel's fax and copy machine.

Facilities: Large pool. Small, fully equipped fitness center for men.

FIESTA AMERICANA, Aurello Aceves 225, Glorieta Minerva, Guadalajara, Jal. 44100. Tel. 36/25-3434, toll free 800-223-2332 in the U.S. Fax 36/20-3725. 396 rms (all with bath). A/C TV TEL MINIBAR

$ Rates: $140 single or double; $175 Fiesta Club.

A 22-story luxury hotel on a grand scale, it caters to the exacting demands of travelers arriving for both business and pleasure. It's a bustling hotel with a 14-story lobby and popular lobby bar with ongoing live entertainment. Like the public areas of the hotel, the rooms are spacious and beautifully coordinated, all with TV with U.S. channels. The 27 exclusive Fiesta Club rooms and 7 suites on two floors, come with special amenities (see below).

Dining/Entertainment: The Chula Vista restaurant, open from 7am to 1am, offers an international menu, with a German buffet on Thursday evening and an Italian buffet on Friday evening. La Hacienda serves Mexican fare from 1pm to 1am, and Place de la Concorde is the French restaurant, open from 1pm to 1am. The lobby bar is open from noon to 2am. For more on the hotel's entertainment list see "Nightclubs and Cabarets" in Chapter 11.

Services: Laundry, dry cleaning, room service, travel agency.

Facilities: Heated rooftop swimming pool, two lighted tennis courts, with resident pro, and purified tap water. Fiesta Club guests key-only access to club floors, separate check-in and checkout, concierge, remote-control TV, continental breakfast and afternoon wine and hors d'oeuvres daily, as well as business services such as secretaries, fax, copy machine, and conference room.

HOLIDAY INN CROWNE PLAZA, López Mateos Sur 2500, Guadalajara, Jal. 45050. Tel. 36/31-5566, toll free 800/465-4329 in the U.S. Fax 36/31-9393. 300 rms and suites (all with bath). A/C TV TEL MINIBAR

$ Rates: $127 standard single or double; $155 Plaza Club; $506 presidential suite. Ask about summer discounts.

With a recent complete renovation this long-established hotel rose to the standard of the Crowne Plaza, the best of the Holiday Inn chain. There are two sections, the tower section in front and the two-story garden section in back. Although the tower section is the most popular, I prefer the tranquillity of the garden section. With the exception of the presidential suite, all rooms are basically furnished in the same beautifully coordinated furniture. They come with either two double beds or a king-size bed, love seat and two side chairs, balcony or terrace. The plush two-story presidential suite has

---

FROMMER'S SMART TRAVELER: HOTELS

1. Hotels in the "expensive" category often reduce prices on weekends, and weekdays especially in summer, meaning savings of as much as 50% off normal rates.
2. Hotels in the budget and moderate price category will often discount the quoted price if the hotel isn't full. It never hurts to ask.
3. Because of the daily devaluation of the peso, you will pay less in the long run if you use a credit card to pay the hotel bill.
4. Many budget-quality hotels don't accept credit cards even if there's a sticker on the window that says they do.
5. Although prices may vary from those quoted here, to avoid being overcharged, if a price seems too high when compared to the price quoted in this book, insist on seeing the official Secretaría de Turismo price sheet (*lista de tarifas*) and compare. This applies especially to budget-category hotels where clerks have been known to jack up the price and pocket the difference.

a handsome bar, separate dining and living room downstairs, and enormous bedroom upstairs with a giant jet tub in the bathroom. Plaza Club rooms are in the garden section and include separate check-in, concierge, valet, business center, continental breakfast, and afternoon drinks.

Dining/Entertainment: La Fuente Restaurant off the lobby is open 24 hours. El Kiosco is the outdoor restaurant near the pool. Jacarandas is the gourmet restaurant open from 1pm to 1am. Da Vinci discotheque opens between 10pm and 3am nightly. La Fiesta night club has live music, national and international shows, and is open from 10pm to 3am.

Services: Laundry, dry cleaning, room service, travel agency, safety-deposit box in each room. Guests on the commercial program have access to the hotel's fax and copier.

Facilities: Swimming pool, 2 lighted tennis courts, small gym with workout equipment, sauna separate for men and women, massage by appointment, play area for children, 2 handicapped rooms, and 32 no-smoking rooms.

HYATT REGENCY, Av. López Mateos at Moctezuma, Guadalajara, Jal. 45050. **Tel. 36/22-7778,** toll free 800/228-9000 in the U.S. and Canada, 91-800/5-077 in Mexico. Fax 36/22-9877. 347 rms and suites (all with bath). A/C TV TEL MINIBAR
$ Rates: $95 standard single or double; $265 junior suite; $156 Regency Club.
Parking: Free.

The elegant Hyatt Regency Hotel anchors one end of the Plaza del Sol, the city's largest and most fashionable shopping center. Glass elevators whish up and down the soaring lobby and guest rooms are as stylish as the hotel's public areas. Rooms vary in size but all are decorated in rose and green with natural wood furniture and all have a tub/shower combination. Four key-only floors are reserved for Regency Club guests who receive special amenities.

Dining/Entertainment: Arco Iris coffee shop opens for breakfast at 7am and closes at 1:30pm. The festive Hacienda La Moreña opens with a Mexican buffet breakfast from 7 to 11:30am, then reopens from 1:30pm to midnight. Aquarius snack bar is in the pool area. The lobby bar serves between 11am and 2am. There's live music in El Pueblito Cantina Monday to Thursday from 8pm to 3am and Friday and Saturday from 6pm to 3am.

Services: Laundry, dry cleaning, room service, beauty shop, travel agency, car rental, business center with bilingual secretarial services, and 24-hour doctor. Regency Club guests receive a daily newspaper, continental breakfast, and evening cocktails in the club's separate lounge.

Facilities: Swimming pool on the 12th floor, gym, sauna for men only, ice-skating rink.

QUINTA REAL, Av. Mexico 2727, Guadalajara, Jal. 44680. **Tel. 36/52-0000,** toll free 800/445-4565 in the U.S. and Canada; 91-800/3-6015 in Mexico. Fax 36/30-1797. 51 suites (all with bath). A/C TV TEL MINIBAR
$ Rates: $160 junior suite; $185 master suite; $200 grand-class suite; $640 presidential suite.

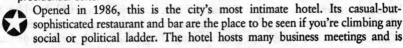

Opened in 1986, this is the city's most intimate hotel. Its casual-but-sophisticated restaurant and bar are the place to be seen if you're climbing any social or political ladder. The hotel hosts many business meetings and is frequently full. Each of the guest rooms is different: Eight have brick cupolas, some have balconies, several have conch-shaped headboards, and four come with whirlpool bath in the bathroom. All have elegant antique decorative touches, remote-control TV with U.S. channels, tub/shower combination, and king-size beds. It's located west of the city center 2 blocks from the Minerva Circle on Avenida Mexico at López Mateos.

Dining/Entertainment: The elegant off-lobby restaurant with both terrace and indoor dining is open for all meals. The adjacent bar opens from 1pm to 2am.

Services: Concierge, laundry and dry cleaning, massage by reservation, video players for rent, travel agency.

Facilities: Small heated pool.

EL TAPATÍO GRAN SPA & RESORT, Blvd. Aeropuerto 4275, Guadalajara, Jal. 45500 (Apdo. Postal 2953, Guadalajara, Jal. 44100). Tel. 36/35-6050, toll free 800/424-2440 in the U.S.; 914/632-0595 in New York. Fax 36/35-6664. 120 rms and suites (all with bath). A/C TV TEL MINIBAR

$ Rates: $135 standard single or double; $175 deluxe single or double. Spa packages available.

Located on a mountaintop between city center and the airport, no Guadalajara hotel exceeds this one for view or for getaway resort feeling, though the city is minutes away. Guests enter through guarded gates on a cobblestone lane that snakes up and around the mountain to the lobby and guest rooms. The hotel has been undergoing a complete refurbishing for several years and may be complete by the time you travel. All of the rooms are tastefully furnished and 34 are in the deluxe category with fireplaces, hot tubs on the terrace, hairdryers, robes, and remote-control TV. The new state-of-the-art spa should open in 1992. Besides being the hotel nearest the airport, it's also near both Tlaquepaque and Tonalá.

Dining/Entertainment: Los Laurales faces the pool and serves all three meals. Mesón del Chef is the elegant restaurant with an international menu and a panoramic view of Guadalajara below. It's open evenings only. There's a city view from the off-lobby bar, Puesta del Sol.

Services: Laundry, room service, and travel agency.

Facilities: General guest facilities include pool with swim-up bar near restaurants and rooms, horseback riding, racquet club with 10 clay tennis courts (4 lighted) and instructor, gymnasium, jogging track, sauna, steam and massage rooms, and pro shop. Spa guest facilities in a separate building include outdoor hot jet-air pools and chiller pool, hydrotherapy tubs, inhalation room, Turkish and Russian baths, Finnish sauna, herbal wraps, Loofa, salt-glow and soap rubs, massage, Scotch shower, aerobics, indoor gym, and juice bar.

MODERATE

HOTEL ARANZAZU, Av. Revolución 110, Guadalajara, Jal. 44100. Tel. 36/13-3232. 500 rms. A/C TV TEL

$ Rates: $48 single; $56 double. **Parking:** $6 per day.

Located near the intersection of Corona and Degollado, this comfortable hotel has a fine location within walking distance of all major downtown sights and restaurants. Check your bed, though; some mattresses sag. To get there from the Plaza de Las

GUADALAJARA: WHERE TO STAY • 169

Armas, walk 1 block east on Moreno and turn right (south) on Corona and walk 6 blocks.

Dining/Entertainment: Restaurant/bar and nightclub.
Services: Laundry and room service.
Facilities: Swimming pool, 1 children's pool.

HOTEL FRANCES, Maestranza 35, Guadalajara, Jal. 44100. Tel. 36/13-1190. 60 rms. FAN TV TEL

$ Rates: $49 single; $58 double.

With caution I mention this 379-year-old hotel, which is practically an institution in downtown Guadalajara. The downstairs disco is so loud that many readers have complained that it keeps them awake until the wee hours of the morning. Desk clerks seem indifferent to complaints. Thus forewarned, it's on a quiet side street off the Plaza Libertad and near the Degollado Theater—an excellent location. Though there's an air of elegance about the lobby, with marble floors, central court and fountain, and huge crystal chandelier, the rooms are basic and furnished with old-timey furniture. Some are carpeted and some have wood floors. To find it from the Plaza de Armas, walk 1 block east on Moreno to Maestranza and turn right. The hotel is on the left.

Dining/Entertainment: There's an off-lobby restaurant which serves all meals and Restaurant La Rosa which is open for dinner at 6pm. The disco, Maxim's, opens at 10:30pm nightly. In the lobby bar a piano soloist plays contemporary classics daily from noon to 8pm.

Services: Laundry and room service.

HOTEL DE MENDOZA, Carranza 16, Guadalajara, Jal. 45120. Tel. 36/13-4646. 104 rms. TV TEL

$ Rates: $55 single; $70 double. **Parking:** $2.25 a day.

This beautifully restored hotel is popular with foreigners for its quiet, colonial atmosphere and modern conveniences. It's at the corner of Hidalgo, only steps from Liberation Plaza and the Degollado Theater. Almost all of the large rooms have wall-to-wall carpeting, and some have a tub and a shower. Rooms face either the street or an interior court with a swimming pool. Rates may be higher if you call or reserve them from the U.S. Walk-in rates are cheaper—get them quoted in pesos. To get there from the Teatro Degollado, go to the left of the theater and look for Carranza, a block down on the left; turn left at the corner church, adjoining the hotel.

Dining/Entertainment: The hotel has one restaurant, La Forga, which is very good. El Campañario bar offers dance music.
Services: Laundry and room service.
Facilities: Swimming pool.

RÍO CALIENTE SPA, Primavera Forest, La Primavera, Jal. No phone. Reservations: Barbara Dane Associates, 480 California Terrace, Pasadena, CA 91105 (tel. 818/796-5577). 48 rms.

$ Rates (including all meals): patio area $65 single, double $115; pool area single $74, double $131. Discounts in Sept–Oct.

Word of mouth keeps this popular and very casual spa busy. Built along the hills of the Primavera forest and on a thermal water river, the setting, at 5,550 feet, is both rugged and serene. Temperatures average 80° F year round. Individual rooms are clustered in two areas. Those near the activity area are smaller and more simply furnished and cost less than the newer and more stylish rooms with patios near the river and pool. All have one double and one single bed, fireplace, full-length mirror, in-room safety-deposit box, desk, chest, and bedside reading lamps. Water is purified in the pools and kitchen, and jars of fresh purified water are supplied daily in each room. Extra spa programs vary throughout the year and might include special instructors for Spanish, nutrition, and electro-acupuncture face-lifts at an extra cost. A doctor comes daily. Huichol sell crafts on Sunday. To save money on transportation from the Guadalajara airport, take one of the airport's collective vans to the Fiesta Americana Hotel, then change to a yellow cab. If you're driving, follow Avenida Vallarta west which becomes Highway 15 with signs to Nogales. Go straight for almost 10½ miles and pass the village called La Venta del Astillero. Take the next left after La Venta and follow the rough road through the village of La Primavera for almost 5 miles. Keep bearing left through the forest until you see the hotel's sign on the left. There's no phone at the spa; reservations are through the U.S. only.

Dining/Entertainment: The help-yourself vegetarian meals are served in the cozy dining room. There's an activities room with nightly video movies or satellite TV, plus bingo and honor library.

Facilities: Two public-area outdoor thermal water pools and two private pools and sunning areas separate for men and women.

Services: Massage, with a choice of male or female massage therapist, mud wrap, anti-stress and anti-aging therapies, live cell therapy, horseback riding, sightseeing and shopping excursions are available at extra cost. Included in cost, besides meals, are daily guided hike, yoga and pool exercises, use of scented steam room with natural steam from underground river.

BUDGET

SUITES BERNINI, Av. Vallarta 1881, Guadalajara, Jal. 44140. Tel. 36/16-6736. 36 suites. TEL

$ Rates: $40 single or double. **Parking:** Free.

If you don't mind being a 10- or 15-minute bus ride (on the electric "Par Vial" bus) from the center of town, by all means try the Suites Bernini, on the corner of Union. (Avenida Juárez, one of the main streets in the center of town, changes names and becomes Avenida Vallarta as it heads west.) Marble steps, guarded by stone lions, lead to the entrance of this elegant 16-story tower. Each suite has a king-size bed, kitchen, and floor-to-ceiling windows, with a magnificent view. The rooms are decorated with potted palms, plush pale-blue carpeting, and artwork—really lovely and spotlessly clean. Choose one or two beds. To get there, take the "Par Vial" bus west on Avenida Juárez, 2 blocks south of the cathedral; it's at the corner of Union.

HOTEL DON QUIJOTE PLAZA, Heroes 91, Guadalajara, Jal. 44100. Tel. 36/58-1299. 32 rms, 1 suite. TV TEL

$ Rates: $35 single; $40 double.

This hotel, at Priciliano Sanchez, was converted from a huge, three-story town house. It's near the Hotel Aranzazu and the Hotel Posada San Francisco. You'd expect to pay much more for the rooms which are softly luxurious with heavy drapes, fashionable pastel furnishings, and wall-to-wall carpeting. The spacious suite has a corner balcony

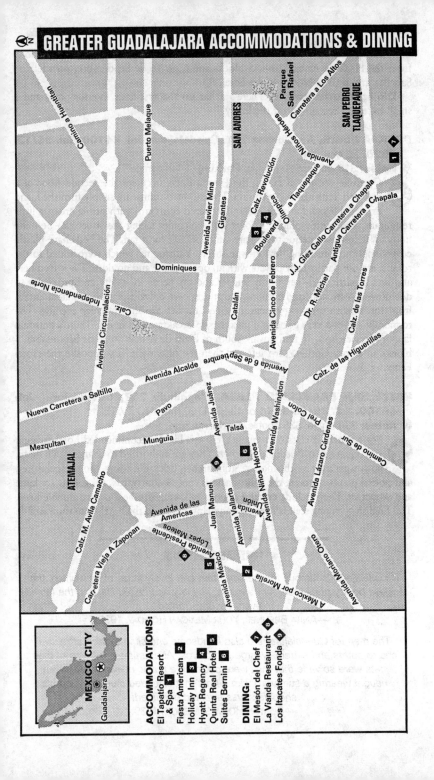

overlooking Priciliano Sanchez and would be an elegant splurge. To reach the hotel from the Plaza de Armas, walk 5 blocks south on 16 de Septiembre, turn left on Sanchez and walk 2 blocks to the hotel.

Dining/Entertainment: There's a bar on the first-floor interior patio and a small excellent restaurant off the lobby.

POSADA REGIS, Av. Corona 171, Guadalajara, Jal. 44100. Tel. 36/13-3026. 22 rms.

$ Rates: $18 single; $20 double. **Parking:** $6 in garage.

Opposite the Hotel Fénix, the Posada Regis occupies the second floor of a restored (long ago) old mansion. The carpeted rooms are simply furnished, and arranged around a large, tranquil covered courtyard with sitting areas, a little restaurant, and potted plants. Rooms with balconies facing the street can be quite noisy. Windowless interior rooms are stuffy, so ask for a fan. The beds have plastic covers and "nonbreathing" nylon-type sheets. Bathrooms, which were added to the rooms, are not particularly private with an open ceiling and no door. I've stayed here and find it particularly serves my budget and my needs for safety and proximity to downtown. A friendly and comfortable atmosphere prevails, with personal attention from the English-speaking manager. Video movies are shown every evening. The restaurant serves a very good and inexpensive breakfast and lunch. There's personal laundry service, too. To find it walk south of Plaza de Armas on 16 de Septiembre, 3 blocks to López Cotillo, turn left and then the next right. It's opposite the Hotel Fénix.

HOTEL SAN FRANCISCO PLAZA, Degollado 267, Guadalajara, Jal. 44100. Tel. 36/13-8954 or **13-8971.** 60 rms. A/C TV TEL

$ Rates: $30 single; $35 double. **Parking:** Free.

For a touch of class on a budget, try this highly recommended hotel facing a tiny square near Priciliano Sanchez. They are authorized to charge much more, so you get a lot for the money. Stone arches, brick-tile floors, bronze sculptures, and potted plants decorate the four spacious central courtyards. All rooms are large and attractive. They include either a double bed, king-size bed, or two double beds. The English-speaking staff is friendly and helpful. To find the hotel from the Plaza de

---

IMPRESSIONS

[Guadalajara] is famous for the small feet and lovely faces of its women, the reckless poetry of its men, for its music, its piety and its tequila, and the fame is in every case warranted.
—ANITA BRENNER, *YOUR MEXICAN HOLIDAY*, 1932

The men [of Guadalajara] are also handsome and cling to their attractive charro outfits and extremely large sombreros. At one time the brims of their hats were so wide that they were declared a public nuisance. Any man caught wearing a sombrero with a brim that extended much beyond his shoulders was arrested and fined.
—BURTON HOLMES, *MEXICO*, 1939.

Armas, walk 5 blocks south on 16 de Septiembre, turn left on Sanchez and walk 2 blocks to Degollado and the hotel. There's an off-lobby restaurant open from 7am to 11pm.

Near the Train & Old Bus Stations

Now that the central bus station has been relocated to near Tlaquepaque, there's little reason to stay in this area south of the town center, unless you can't find reasonably priced lodgings elsewhere or want to be close to the old bus station or the train station. It's a 25-minute walk to downtown.

HOTEL CANADA, Estadio 77, Guadalajara, Jal. 44440. Tel. 36/194014.
  120 rms. TEL
$ Rates: $10–$15 single; $12–$16 double.
My top pick in this area was recently remodeled, which added a bright, cheery feel to the lobby. The rooms got a face-lift as well, with fresh paint, and in most rooms new mattress and bedspreads. You probably wouldn't want to hang around the streets at night here, but it's decent enough for an economical multiday stay in the city. Desk clerks are helpful, but speak only Spanish. The hotel is ½ block from the old bus station and should not be confused with the Gran Hotel Canada, which faces the old bus station and is more expensive. To get there from the train station, go out the front door and walk straight on Independencia 4 long blocks, turn right on Estadio; it's on the left.

Near the New Bus Station

HOTEL EL PARADOR, Carretera a Zapotlanejo 1500, Guadalajara, Jal.
  Tel. 36/59-0142. 630 rms. TV TEL
$ Rates: $20 single; $25 double.
This new sprawling hotel is the only lodging near the new Central Camionera. Facilities include a 24-hour restaurant, two swimming pools, and saunas for men. Rooms are clean, simple, and comfortable, with two twin beds, but the tile hallways carry noise like a megaphone. You'll see the hotel's large sign as you exit the bus station.

 FROMMER'S SMART TRAVELER: RESTAURANTS

1. Stock up on fruit or bakery goods for an inexpensive breakfast.
2. Make lunch the main meal when prices are generally less expensive.
3. Fine dining is cheaper in Guadalajara than a comparable meal in the U.S., so this is the place for an all-out splurge.
4. For a meal in a bowl, try hearty soups like tlalpeño, tortilla, and pozole.
5. Drink Mexican-made liquor and wine which are inexpensive compared to any imported version.

2. WHERE TO DINE

Although the restaurants below serve food from around the world, I urge you to try a local dish—**birria**. It's a hearty soup of lamb, pork, or goat meat in a tasty chicken and tomato broth, lightly thickened with masa (corn meal) and spiced with oregano, garlic, onions, cumin, chiles, allspice, and cilantro. Restaurants around El Parián in Tlaquepaque have it on the menu daily.

For those on a truly low budget, the second floor of **Mercado Libertad** will look like heaven. You can get a comida corrida here for $2 at any of what seem like hundreds of little restaurant stands. There's a vegetarian section, too, and lots of places for tacos, tamales with atole, and enchiladas. But be careful about cleanliness—some people say you should never eat here. Nonetheless, hundreds of people do eat here every day, and seem to be surviving just fine—I've even done it myself. Check it out—it's a fascinating slice of Mexican life, even if all you end up doing is looking. If you're planning to eat, the best time to go is early in the morning, while the food is the freshest.

EXPENSIVE

LA COPA DE LECHE, Juárez 414. Tel. 14-5347 or 14-1845.
  Specialty: INTERNATIONAL.
  $ Prices: Appetizers $1.25–$4; main courses $4.50–$10; seafood $8–$10; comida corrida $7.50.
  Open: Daily 8am–midnight; comida corrida served noon–4pm.

Close to the cathedral, the most famous and long-lived restaurant in Guadalajara has a sidewalk café and balcony, plus upstairs and downstairs dining rooms. An organist playing live lunch music helps drown out the relentless din on Juárez. The eclectic menu includes Mexican, American, and continental specialties. A full-course dinner will run about $18, right up there with North American prices. To find the restaurant from the Plaza de Armas, walk 1 block to Juárez, turn right, and walk 1½ blocks. The restaurant is on the right.

EL MESÓN DEL CHEF, Hotel El Tapatío Spa & Resort, Aeropuerto 4275, Tel. 35-6050.
  Specialty: INTERNATIONAL.
  $ Prices: Full meal $35–$40.
  Open: Tues–Sun 8pm–midnight.

For the ultimate combination of view and elegant dining this hilltop restaurant in the Hotel El Tapatío can't be beat. There's a full wall of windows overlooking the city and at night, with the city lights and flickering candlelight and handsomely clad tables, it's a fitting place for a special night out. Service is polished and the menu includes beef, chicken, and fish specialties with a combination of preparations that includes Italian, French, and Mexican. The dessert selection is small but wonderful, and there's a good wine list.

ROSE CAFE, Hotel Frances, Maestranza 35. Tel. 13-1190.
  Specialty: INTERNATIONAL.

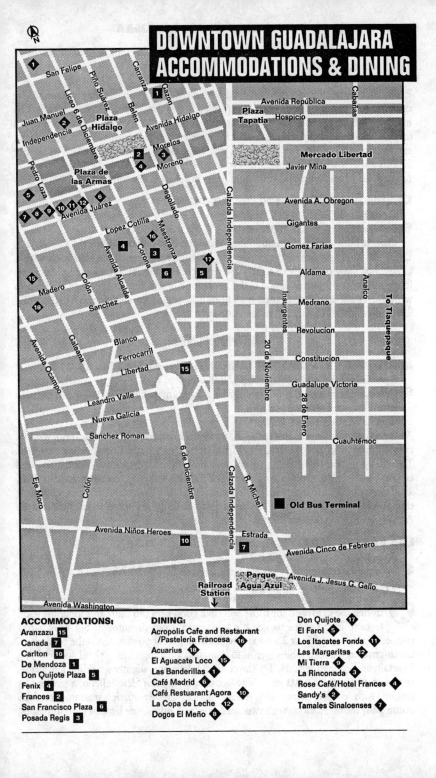

$ Prices: Appetizers $2.50–$6; main courses $3–$25 (chateaubriand for two); comida corrida $6.75.
Open: Daily 7am–10:30pm.

Each chair in the dining room is carved with a rose that is tinted slightly scarlet. The decor is soft pastel tones of rose, turquoise, and cream with art deco accents. The international cuisine here is a pleasant change; there's a lovely spaghetti primavera (natural carrot-and-spinach pasta with fresh vegetables and parmesan cheese), a steak sandwich, and coq au vin. For breakfast, each table receives a plate of miniature French pastries that are irresistible. From the Plaza de Armas, walk 1 block east on Moreno to Maestranza and turn right. The hotel is on the left.

LA VIANDA, Chapalita 120. Tel. 22-5926.
Specialty: FRENCH/CREOLE.
$ Prices: Full meal $25–$35.
Open: Mon–Sat 1–5pm and 7pm–midnight; Sun buffet 1–5pm.

Enjoy the lovely garden setting while you wait for your French-inspired food with a Creole twist that often gives a lightly spicy punch. Finding French cuisine in Mexico is fairly common, but combining it with Creole food is not. The end product is a success with interesting sauces combined with beef, fish, or chicken dishes, plus a delightfully flavored vegetable or salad. It's near López Mateos.

MODERATE

ACROPOLIS CAFE AND RESTAURANT, Corona 165. Tel. 13-2165.
Specialty: FRENCH PASTRIES/MEXICAN.
$ Prices: Breakfasts $3–$9; appetizers $2–$3; main courses $6–$7.50; pastries $1.50–$2; coffee/tea $1–$1.50.
Open: Mon–Sat 8am–9:30pm.

At the front of this restaurant is the **Pastelería Francesa** (French Bakery), with its colorful display of neapolitans, fresh fruit tarts, cream puffs, tortes, cakes, and pies. The dimly lit tearoom/dining room with pink tablecloths, brass chandeliers, and ceiling fans is a great place to revive. The English-language menu includes salads, sandwiches, and antojitos, plus grilled meats and fish. Fourteen breakfast combinations come with hash browns or beans and salad. To get there from the Plaza de Armas, walk 3 blocks south on 6 de Diciembre/Corona.

LAS BANDERILLAS, Av. Alcalde 833. Tel. 13-7926.
Specialty: MEXICAN/BEEF.
$ Prices: Appetizers 65¢–$6.75; main courses $3.50–$6.75.
Open: Mon–Sat 10am–1am.

Banderillas are the curved-hook picks used by bullfighters to weaken the bull during the fight, and for those who like good beef (no bull), this longtime local favorite is the place to go. It's a bit away from downtown, but only a few minutes by bus or a 15- or 20-minute walk. Bullfighting posters adorn the blue walls. Cloth-covered wooden tables surround a small stone bridge with a pond and trickling fountain among many plants. Try the cold and delicious, slightly sparkling lemonade, served in a huge terra-cotta mug. The house specialty is a filete relleno, a tender filet stuffed with cheese, ham, and tomato sauce. Freshly made, steaming tortillas accompany the meal, along with two delicious fresh salsas, one heaped with tomatoes, purple onions, and cilantro. To get to the restaurant from the cathedral, take one of the frequent buses headed north on Alcalde and get off at Avenida Jesús García (8 blocks). Cross Alcalde and look for the restaurant two doors from the corner and Goodyear Tires.

RESTAURANT DON QUIJOTE, Hotel San Francisco Plaza, Degollado 267. Tel. 13-8954 or 13-8971.
   Specialty: MEXICAN.
   $ Prices: Breakfasts $1–$4; appetizers 1¢–$1.75; main courses and antojitos $2.75–$5.75.
   Open: Mon–Sat 8am–9:30pm.

This amazingly reasonable and very nice hotel has a restaurant to match. High ceilings, paintings, and wooden tables and chairs make this an agreeable dining room, off a pretty patio filled with plants. The menu includes various Mexican specials, combination plates, and grilled meat and chicken. Those with a craving for mashed potatoes can satisfy it here. The local Guadalajaran beer, Estrella, costs less than a dollar. From the Plaza de Armas walk 5 blocks south on 16 de Septiembre, turn left on Sanchez and walk 2 blocks to Degollado. It's on the corner.

EL FAROL, Pedro Moreno 466. Tel. 13-0349.
   Specialty: MEXICAN/TAMALES.
   $ Prices: Tamales 90¢–$2.50; tacos $2.25 for four; main courses $3–$6.
   Open: Daily 9am–2am.

For a really authentic Mexican meal, try El Farol, upstairs, at the corner of Galeana. Pick a pleasant table by one of the balconies overlooking the pedestrian mall below. House specialties are the soft, rolled, corn-tortilla tacos—18 kinds to choose from. Diners are free to mix and sample the tacos, which come four to an order or, likewise, the tamales—three to an order. Save some room for the restaurant's famous specialty—cheese pie or one of the other tasty desserts. To reach the restaurant from the Plaza de Armas, walk 2 blocks west on Moreno. The restaurant is upstairs on the right.

CAFE MADRID, Juárez 264. Tel. 14-9504.
   Specialty: MEXICAN.
   $ Prices: Breakfasts $3–$5.25; appetizers $1.25–$3; main courses $6–$8; platillo tapatío $8; comida corrida $6.
   Open: Daily 8am–10:30pm; comida corrida 1–5 or 6pm.

★ Conveniently located, this popular café serves the best coffee in Guadalajara. The smell of coffee wafts outside the café in the morning—americano, espresso, cappuccino, and café con leche are all excellent eye-openers. Signs above the counter advertise chilaquiles and "ricos wafles" which are just that and served with warm syrup. For a light and inexpensive lunch, try the generous fruit cocktail, chilaquiles rojo or verde (red or green sauce), or a sandwich with french fries or salad. The extra-hearty platillo tapatío includes fried chicken, a chile relleno, an enchilada, potatoes, and salad. To reach the restaurant from the Plaza de Armas, walk 1 block to Juárez and turn left. It's on the left.

LAS MARGARITAS, López Cotilla 1477. Tel. 16-8906.
   Specialty: VEGETARIAN.

$ Prices: Soup $1.25; sandwiches $3.50–$4.50; main courses $3–$5; comida corrida $4.
Open: Mon–Sat 8am–9:30pm, Sun 8am–8pm; comida corrida noon–3pm.

A bit of a jaunt and an expensive taxi ride ($5), so take a bus to this upscale vegetarian restaurant just a few doors from Chapultepec. There's an attractive front terrace with tables, a dining room, or several more private dining rooms filled with potted plants. The comida corrida might include zucchini stuffed with cheese, brown rice, baked lentil casserole, and hot homemade bread, served with plenty of butter. The "Casarole Margaritas" is a very odd combination of rice, cheese, celery, tomatoes, green olives, and sprouts, yes, cooked right in with everything else and rather limp. There are 13 kinds of salads, lots of freshly made fruit and vegetable juices, ambrosia, and honey ice cream served in half a cantaloupe. To get there, take a "Par Vial" bus west on Juárez, get off at Chapultepec and walk left to López Cotilla. Turn right, and look for a green awning on the left.

RESTAURANT/BAR MI TIERRA, Juárez 590. Tel. 19-5943 or 14-1347.
Specialty: SEAFOOD/MEXICAN.
$ Prices: Appetizers $1.25–$10; main courses $4–$17; comida corrida $3.50.
Open: Daily 8am–11pm.

This open-air place has two floors of dining. Bright blue and green tablecloths, live music daily, and a large seafood menu help distract diners from the hubbub on Juárez. "Brocheta de Camarón," a shrimp brochet with all the extras, is one of the house specialties. Besides seafood, another house special is the "Tampiqueño," roast meat with rice, guacamole, beans, and salad. There's also a variety of seafood cocktails. The friendly dueña is out to please. From the Plaza de Las Armas walk 2 blocks south to Juárez, turn right, and the restaurant is about 3 blocks on the right, ½ block before Carmen Church.

SANDY'S RESTAURANT, 16 de Septiembre and Independencia. Tel. 14-4236.
Specialty: CREPES/MEXICAN.
$ Prices: Breakfasts $3.25–$7; sandwiches $4–$5; crêpes $4; appetizers $2–$5; main courses $6–$10.
Open: Daily 8am–10:30pm.

This second-story restaurant, formerly La Chalita, has balconies overlooking the Rotunda de Los Hombres Ilustres and the cathedral. Though a bit expensive, it's a nice place for breakfast, when the morning sun and mist play on the flowers and foliage in the park. For lunch, it's a slight escape from the bustle of city life below, and the menu includes niños pobres (poor boys, or subs), and assorted burgers and crêpes. The specialty of the house is crêpes, both dinner and dessert crêpes, and there's an extensive list of fancy drinks, including Irish coffee and cognacs. The restaurant is 2 blocks north of the cathedral on Alcalde, upstairs on the right, just past the Rotunda de los Hombres Illustres.

RESTAURANT LA RINCONADA, Morelos 86. Tel. 13-9914.
Specialty: MEXICAN/INTERNATIONAL.
$ Prices: Appetizers $3–$9; main courses $5–$10.
Open: Mon–Sat 12:30–10:30pm.

Housed in a beautiful old stone mansion on the Plaza Tapatía, La Rinconada draws diners in with live music, which is almost nonstop throughout the day. The dining room is set in the mansion's huge interior patio surrounded by arches and doors leading to smaller rooms with iron grill-covered windows. The setting is truly lovely, but the slow and inattentive service leaves something to be desired. Though some diners rave about the steaks, which are the house special, the Cornish hen, pasta, and soup were disappointing on my last visit. It's especially popular at lunch but the crowd thins out by late afternoon. It's an ideal place to relax after a performance at the Degollado Theater. To find it from the Plaza de Armas, walk 2 blocks east of the plaza along Morelos. Look for the restaurant behind the theater.

BUDGET

ACUARIUS, Prisciliano Sanchez 416. Tel. 12-6277.
Specialty: VEGETARIAN.
$ Prices: Comida corrida $4.50.
Open: Daily 1:30–8pm.

This tidy, airy little lunchroom has soft music playing, posters of Krishna, ads for yoga groups, and shelves of soy sauce and vitamins. The restaurant serves only a comida corrida daily, but it's a good one. There's a choice of two main dishes which you can sample first if you can't make up your mind. When I was there the choice was zucchini sautéed with mushrooms in a tangy tomato sauce or a mixed-vegetable stew. Whole-grain bread and whole-grain tortillas come with the meal, plus soup, fruit and yogurt or a salad, a tall, cool glass of fruit juice, plus dessert. From the Plaza de Armas, walk 4 blocks south on 16 de Septiembre and turn right on P. Sanchez. Walk 3½ blocks and it's on the right.

EL AGUACATE LOCO, Enrique Gonzales Martinez 126. No phone.
Specialty: VEGETARIAN.
$ Prices: Comida corrida $3.
Open: Mon–Sat 10am–8pm, Sun 10am–4pm.

Translated, this is the crazy avocado restaurant. Tiny and family operated, this hole-in-the-wall with no menu has the ultimate bargain/delicious vegetarian comida in town. The menu changes daily, but meals always begin with whole-grain tortillas and a tall, delicious glass of fresh jamaica juice (a dark, purple, mildly sweet drink), plus a huge plate of fresh bananas and papayas with lime. Next comes a tasty homemade soup—mine was a rich broth with spinach and whole grains. The main dish included perfectly cooked brown rice and vegetables with a tangy red sauce. Best of all was the moist, homemade banana cake for dessert. To find it from the Plaza de Armas, walk 2 blocks to López Cotilla, turn right, and walk 5 blocks to Martinez. Turn right and the restaurant is on the left.

CAFE RESTAURANT AGORA, Juárez 612. Tel. 14-3169.
Specialty: MEXICAN.
$ Prices: Breakfasts $1–$2; appetizers $2; sandwiches $1–$2; main courses $2–$5; espresso $1.
Open: Daily 8am–10pm.

Two covered patios next to the Ex-Convento del Carmen (across the street from the church) shelter a casual restaurant and café, which seems to be reorganizing into a coffeehouse: The formerly expansive menu is now tiny with only a few sandwich and main-dish offerings—including a chicken dish. The inexpensive huevos rancheros here, however, could be *the* breakfast deal in town. The restaurant is next to the Templo del Carmen. From the Plaza de Armas walk 1 block south to Juárez, turn right, and walk 3 or 4 blocks.

LOS ITACATES FONDA, Chapultepec Norte 110. Tel. 25-1106.
Specialty: MEXICAN.
$ Prices: Appetizers $1–$5; main courses $3–$6.
Open: Mon–Sat 8am–11pm, Sun 8am–7pm.

For an excellent meal, try this restaurant, which serves Mexican food "de la vieja cocina Mexicana" (from the old Mexican kitchen). There are three nice dining rooms, one on the patio near the fountain. One fun option here is to order "by the taco," so that you can sample a variety of very tasty dishes for just 45¢ each. To get there take the "Par Vial" bus line west on Juárez. Get off at Chapultepec and turn right. It's on the right.

TAMALES SINALOENSES, 45B Galvez at Juárez.
Specialty: TAMALES/MEXICAN.
$ Prices: Tamales 50¢–80¢ (less to go); pozole $2–$3; atole 50¢; coffee 45¢. No alcoholic beverages.
Open: Dinner daily 6:30–10:30pm.

This evening-only restaurant serves pozole and tamales, plus atole, a thick, lightly sweet corn drink traditionally eaten before bedtime and at breakfast. The tamales are huge, light, and tasty; one fills you up. They come with beef, pork, and chicken fillings, or in sweet varieties with raisins. The tamales are kept hot in large lidded cans, just the way they're sold in markets. Pozole comes in two sizes—large and small. The new restaurant is accented with tile and the stainless-steel kitchen is open to view. This is a good place to grab a bite before one of the frequent films, art openings, or concerts at the Carmen Convent just across Juárez. It's within easy walking distance of the Plaza de Armas. Walk 1 block to Juárez, turn right, and walk 3 or 4 blocks to the Templo del Carmen; the café is left of the templo facing the plaza.

CHAPTER 11

WHAT TO SEE & DO IN GUADALAJARA

- **SUGGESTED ITINERARIES**
1. **THE MAJOR ATTRACTIONS**
- **WALKING TOUR— MAJOR ATTRACTIONS**
2. **MORE ATTRACTIONS**
- **FROMMER'S FAVORITE GUADALAJARA EXPERIENCES**
3. **ORGANIZED TOURS**
4. **SPECIAL EVENTS**
5. **SPORTS & RECREATION**
6. **SHOPPING**
7. **EVENING ENTERTAINMENT**
8. **EASY EXCURSIONS**

Visitors to Guadalajara and surrounding villages discover a variety of sightseeing opportunities to satisfy most interests.

One of the best ways to see Guadalajara's top attractions is by taking a walking tour. A walk through the downtown area will acquaint visitors with the major historical, cultural, and architectural highlights of the city.

SUGGESTED ITINERARIES

IF YOU HAVE 2 DAYS

Day 1 Take my suggested walking tour of the historic downtown. Take your time browsing in the crafts section of the Libertad Market and walking the corridors of the Cabañas Cultural Institute and admiring Orozco's work there. Wind up the day with dinner near the Plaza Tapatía, then stroll over to Mariachi Square to hear the battle of singers.

Day 2 If it's Thursday combine trips for shopping at both Tlaquepaque and Tonalá and have dinner in Tlaquepaque or at the Hotel El Tapatío overlooking the city. On other weekdays, explore further the museums and other attractions in the city.

IF YOU HAVE 3 DAYS

Days 1 and 2 Spend these days as outlined above.

Day 3 Get an early start and spend the day at Lake Chapala, especially the lakeside villages of Chapala and Ajijic. Have breakfast in Chapala at one of the restaurants on the main street or on the malecón, then lunch at one of Ajijic's good restaurants. A sunset dinner at one of the lakeside restaurants is a nice way to wind up the day.

182 • WHAT TO SEE & DO IN GUADALAJARA

IF YOU HAVE 5 DAYS

Days 1, 2, and 3 Spend these days as outlined above.
Days 4 and 5 Set out early and spend 2 nights at the mountain resort towns of Mazamitla and Tapalpa.

1. THE MAJOR ATTRACTIONS

There is no better way to explore the museums and architecture of historic downtown Guadalajara than by taking a walking tour.

WALKING TOUR — MAJOR ATTRACTIONS

Start: Plaza de Armas.
Finish: Libertad Market.
Time: Approximately 3 hours, not including museum and shopping stops.
Best Times: After 10am when museums are open.
Worst Times: Monday or holidays when museums are closed.

Begin the tour in the plaza beside the main cathedral on Alcalde between Hidalgo and Morelos in the charming:

1. **Plaza de Armas.** Beside the main cathedral, on Alcalde between Moreno and Morelos, is this pleasant plaza with wrought-iron benches and walkways leading like spokes in a wheel to the ornate iron, French-made, central bandstand, directly in front of:
2. **The Palacio del Gobierno.** This eye-catching arched structure that dominates the plaza was built in 1774 and combines the Spanish/Moorish influences prevalent at the time. Go inside to view the spectacular mural of Hidalgo by José Clemente Orozco over the beautiful wooden-railed staircase to the right. The theme in the center, quite obviously, is social struggle. The panel to the right is called *The Contemporary Circus,* and the one on the left, *The Ghost of Religion in Alliance with Militarism.* Orozco was a native of Guadalajara and is held in high esteem here and countrywide. Wander across the courtyard and you might even catch a rare glimpse of a baby pigeon among the potted citrus trees. Going back out the front entrance, turn right and walk to the:
3. **Cathedral.** Begun in 1561, the unusual, multispired facade combines several 17th-century Renaissance styles, including a touch of Gothic. An 1818 earthquake destroyed the original large towers. The present ones were designed by architect Manuel Gomez Ibarra. Inside, look over the sacristy to see the painting believed to be the work of renowned 17th-century artist Bartolomé Murillo (1617–82). Leave the cathedral and turn right out the front doors and walk along Alcalde to the:
4. **Rotunda de Los Hombres Ilustres.** Sixteen gleaming white columns without bases or capitals stand as monuments to Guadalajara's—and the state of Jalisco's—distinguished sons. To learn who they are, visitors need only to stroll

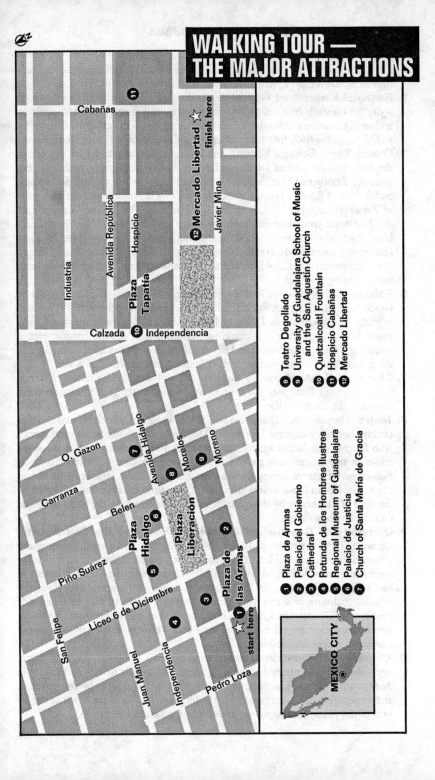

around the green and flower-filled park and read the names on the 11 nearly life-size statues of the state's heroes. There are 98 burial vaults in the park, only four of which are occupied. East of the plaza, cross Liceo to the:

5. **Regional Museum of Guadalajara.** Built in 1701 in the Churrigueresque style, this museum contains archeological pieces, including a mammoth skeleton and an 18th-century meteorite, as well as art from the 17th and 18th centuries up to the present—both folk arts and crafts and works of art by modern masters Orozco, Rivera, Quiroga, Vizcarra, and Figueroa. Rooms 6 and 7 are devoted to the history of the state of Jalisco, and others display ethnography and European painting. Another section deals with paleontology, prehistory, and archeology, and features a gigantic reconstructed skeleton of a mammoth and the Meteorite of Zacatecas found in 1792, weighing 1,715 pounds. The museum also includes the **National Institute of Anthropology and History,** which contains a large, colorful mural by J. G. Nuño showing scenes of the conquest. Frequent craft shows are held here as well. It's open Tuesday through Sunday from 10am to 4pm. Admission costs $3.45 for adults; children enter free. Outside the museum and to the right is the:

6. **Palacio de Justicia.** Built as the first convent in Guadalajara, Santa María de Gracia in 1588, it later became a Teachers College and girls school. In 1952, it was officially designated as the Palace of Justice. Inside above the stairway is a huge mural honoring the law profession in Guadalajara; it depicts historic events, including Benito Juárez with the 1857 constitution and laws of reform. Outside the palacio and directly to the right, continuing east on Hidalgo is the:

7. **Church of Santa María de Gracia,** one of Guadalajara's oldest churches, which was built along with the convent next door. Currently, it's being restored. Opposite the church is the:

8. **Teatro Degollado,** (Deh-goh-*yah*-doh) a beautiful neoclassic-style, 19th-century opera house named for Santos Degollado. Degollado was a local patriot who fought with Juárez against the French and Maximilian. Notice the seven muses in the theater's triangular facade above the columns. The theater hosts various performances during the year, including the Ballet Folklórico Sunday at noon. The **Plaza Liberación** links the cathedral and the Degollado Theater. To the right of the theater on the opposite side of the plaza from the Santa María de Gracia church is the:

9. **University of Guadalajara School of Music and the San Agustín Church.** There are continuous services in the church, and sometimes the music school is open to the public. Continuing east on the plaza, be sure to notice the spectacular fountain behind the Degollado Theater depicting Mexican history in low relief. You'll next pass the charming children's fountain, and then, the unusual sculpture of a tree with lions with nearby slabs of text by Charles V proclaiming Guadalajara's right to be recognized as a city. The plaza opens up into a huge pedestrian expanse called the **Plaza Tapatía,** framed by department stores and offices and dominated by the:

10. **Quetzalcoatl Fountain.** This towering, abstract sculpture/fountain represents the mythical plumed serpent, Quetzalcoatl, which figures so broadly in Mexican legend and ancient culture and religion. The smaller pieces represent the serpent/birds; the centerpiece is the serpents' fire. Looking down at the far end of the plaza, you'll spot the **Hospicio Cabañas** (see no. 11).

REFUELING STOP Take a short break at one of the small ice-cream shops or fast-food restaurants along the plaza, or wait and go to the small cafeteria inside the **Hospicio,** where they serve hot dogs, sandwiches, cake, soft drinks, coffee, and snacks.

11. **Hospicio Cabañas.** Formerly called the Cabañas Orphanage, and known today as the **Instituto Cultural Cabañas** (tel. 18-6003), this impressive structure was designed by the famous Mexican architect Manuel Tolsá. It housed homeless children from 1829 until 1980. Today it's a thriving cultural center offering art shows, and classes for children and adults in all the fine arts. The main building has a fine dome and the walls and ceiling are covered by murals painted in 1929 by José Clemente Orozco (1883–1949). The powerful painting in the dome, *Man of Fire,* by Orozco, is a must to see; it's said to represent the spirit of humanity projecting itself toward the infinite. Take a break and lie down on the viewing bench to see for yourself. Several other rooms hold more of Orozco's work, and there are also excellent temporary exhibits. For a free guided tour, ask for Ruben, at the front desk. He speaks English. Don't miss the contemporary art exhibit in the south wing, with the fascinating and unusual paintings by Javier Arevalo. The institute's own **Ballet Folklórico** performs here every Wednesday at 8:30pm and costs $3.75. The Instituto Cabañas is open Tuesday through Saturday from 10am to 6pm. Call extension 22 about the many cultural events happening around town. For a real change of pace, turn left out the front entrance of the Cabañas and look for a stairway that leads down to the:
12. **Mercado Libertad.** Guadalajara's gigantic, covered central market, said to be the largest in Latin America. The site has been used for a market plaza since the 1500s and the present buildings were constructed in the early 1950s. This is a great place to buy leather goods, pottery, and just about anything else you can think of.

2. MORE ATTRACTIONS

PLAZA DE LA UNIVERSIDAD

This formerly charming plaza south of the Plaza de Armas is undergoing extensive renovation and its pleasant outdoor café with umbrellas is no more. There's a huge fountain (a children's favorite) and lots of shoeshine stands and benches for weary shoppers and people just passing the time.

PLAZA DE LOS MARIACHIS

A half a block from the Libertad Market on Calzada Independencia and Javier Mina and beside the San Juan de Dios church is the Plaza de los Mariachis, actually a short street lined with restaurants and cafés. During the day, small bands of mariachis will be loafing around or sipping drinks, but at night the place is packed with them. (See also "Evening Entertainment," below.)

PLAZA & EX-CONVENTO DEL CARMEN

At the Ex-Convento del Carmen, on Juárez 4 blocks west of the historic center, offers a full range of theater, films, and musical events almost nightly. It's open daily from 9am to 10pm. Tickets are usually sold here just a short while before the performance. There are several restaurants nearby for meals and snacks before or after performances (see "Where to Dine" in Chapter 10).

Across the street, the **Plaza del Carmen,** with a bubbling fountain, roses, and shade trees is a nice place to relax. Lovers' embraces may lead to a wedding at the small **Templo del Carmen,** an old church on the plaza. There's usually a mass, wedding, or christening in progress.

PARQUE AGUA AZUL

Located near the former bus station at the south end of Calzada Independencia, this park is a perfect refuge from the bustling city. It contains plants, trees, shrubbery, statues, and fountains. The park is open daily from 10am to 6pm. Admission is 25¢.

For children there's a **Museo Infantil** (children's museum) with displays of traditional toys as well as shows. "El Chuku, Chuku," a rubber-tired minitrain, circulates through the grounds daily in the summer and the rest of the year on Saturday and Sunday from 11am to 6pm. A ride costs 45¢.

A half block from the entrance to Agua Azul Park, walking toward town from the flower market, on the same side of the street, you'll see a sign "TEJ" for **Teatro Experimental de Jalisco** marking the entrance to a modern building housing the Experimental Theater of Jalisco. There's also a Children's Theater with performances on Saturday and Sunday at 11am for a small fee.

Across the Calzada Independencia from the Experimental Theater is the **Teatro Guadalajara del IMSS,** which offers shows that sound more experimental than the Experimental Theater's (see "Evening Entertainment," below).

Across the calzada from the park entrance is the **Museo Antropología** in a small, one-story rock building. It houses a fine collection of pre-Hispanic pottery from the states of Jalisco, Nayarit, and Colima and is well worth your time. The museum is open daily from 10am to 12:45pm and 3:30 to 7:30pm. There's a small admission.

Also across the calzada (opposite Agua Azul Park) is the **Casa de la Cultura** between 16 de Septiembre and Calzada Independencia (tel. 19-3611). It offers a variety of classes in local culture by day, as well as a packed evening schedule to which the public is invited. For details see "Evening Entertainment," below.

The state-run **Casa de las Artesanías** is just past the park entrance (heading toward town) at the crossroads of Calzada Independencia and Gallo (for details see "Shopping," below).

THE ZOO & PLANETARIUM

Even those who don't like zoos will like the beautiful and spacious new Guadalajara Zoo (Jardín Zoológico), which straddles the edge of the breathtaking Huentitlán ravine at the far northeast edge of town. It's next to the Technology Center of

FROMMER'S FAVORITE
GUADALAJARA EXPERIENCES

Listening to Music Sunday afternoon and evening listen to the battle of mariachis under the portals of El Parián in Tlaquepaque. Or go to any evening gathering round the spirited mariachi bands at Mariachi Square in downtown Guadalajara, where dining tables set out in the open fill with willing listeners. In the lobby bar of the Hotel Frances, between 8pm and 3am, enjoy pianist Goyo Flores who learned his art by braille.

Visiting the Zoo Spend a half day at the new Guadalajara Zoo on the edge of the breathtaking Huentitlán ravine.

The Ballet Folklórico Attend an exhilarating performance of the Ballet Folklórico de la Universidad de Guadalajara, acclaimed as the best folkloric ballet company in all Mexico.

Walking Take a walk through the enormous Instituto Cultural Cabañas designed by Manuel Tolsá with fabulous murals by native son José Clemente Orozco. Walk through the pedestrian-only historic center, a magnificent example of urban renewal that preserves the city's history.

Museums Explore Tlaquepaque's Regional Ceramics Museum, and the National Ceramics Museum in Tonalá preserving examples of Mexico's master potters.

Glass Blowing Watch glass blowers in Tlaquepaque turn red-hot glass into fine utilitarian pieces.

The Markets Visit the Sunday and Thursday street markets in Tonalá.

Guadalajara with its planetarium and Omnimax Theater. A few hours or half a day provides a nice respite from the hectic downtown pace and affords some great people as well as animal watching. Huge, happy families with toddlers, teens, and patriarchs roam the territory, ogling at the animals.

A striking monolithic fountain of bas-relief animals in the turquoise tones of oxidized metal greets visitors at the zoo entrance. Next, a flamboyant flock of flamingos lolls in a large pond. A sightseeing train straight ahead offers a 15-minute tour of the area—a good way to get acquainted. The zoo is nicely integrated into the area's rolling topography, and all of the zoo's buildings have an attractive Aztec motif with stout round columns and zigzag painted designs. Modeled after other great zoos of the world such as those in San Diego and Berlin, this roomy zoo gives the larger animals plenty of space to roam and tries to approximate their natural habitat. Huge monkey islands with huge dead trees strung with vinelike ropes provide hours of entertainment. Most people stand mesmerized around the massive, moon-faced orangutans or the great, placid pumas and panthers. Multiple aviaries house screeching parrots and all types of colorful jungle birds. Informative signs throughout give habitat information and status of threatened or endangered species. The zoo is open daily from 9am to 6pm (tel. 37-2478).

The **planetarium,** right next door, presents programs every evening, starting at 4, 5, and 6pm with earlier shows on Saturday (tel. 37-2119 or 37-2050). Movies at the **Omnimax Theater** are at 10am and noon, and at 1, 4, 5, and 8pm.

By local bus north on Calzada Independencia, it's about a 30-minute ride. A taxi costs $4 to $5. Those going by bus, should look for the large, pale terra-cotta structure on the corner of Independencia Norte and Avenida Flores Magon, on the right-hand side of the street coming from downtown. From Independencia, it's another 5- or 6-block walk up Avenida Flores Magon to the zoo's entrance, past the huge parking lots.

3. ORGANIZED TOURS

Several times daily, **Panoramex** (tel. 10-5005, 10-5057, or 10-5109) offers bilingual tours of Guadalajara, Lake Chapala, Tequila, and Zapopan, ranging in price from $8 to $17.75. Those without a car might want to consider a tour or two, especially to the outlying regions. The office is open Monday through Friday from 9am to 7pm, or inquire in your hotel. **Viajes Copenhagen** (tel. 21-1890 or 21-1008) also organizes similar tours plus others such as golfing in Guadalajara, to the mountain resort towns, or more far-flung trips to the coast or to interior colonial villages. It's open Monday through Friday from 9am to 7pm.

THE TEQUILA PLANT

You might want to take a tour of the Tequila Sauza bottling plant, at Avenida Vallarta 3273 (tel. 15-6990 or 30-0707), on the left on the way out of town. The tours begin at 10am Monday through Friday. After the tour there's a "happy hour" where you can enjoy a variety of tequila drinks, prepared by masters of the art. You can skip the tour and come just to drink from 10am to 1pm. Both the tours and drinks are free.

By the way, this is just a bottling plant. The distillery is in the town of Tequila, off Highway 15 about 25 miles of bad road east of Guadalajara. You'll see the spiny blue agave, from which tequila is made, growing everywhere around the little town.

4. SPECIAL EVENTS

The 450th anniversary of the founding of Guadalajara will be the focal point for a week of celebration in mid-February 1992. Check with the local tourism office for details.

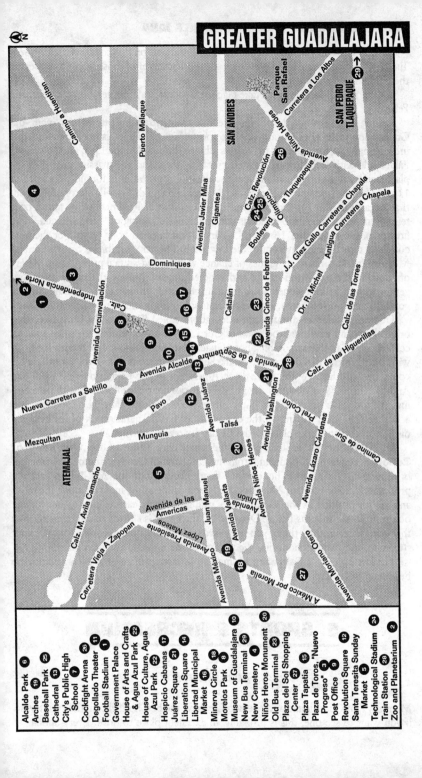

190 • WHAT TO SEE & DO IN GUADALAJARA

In the **Plaza de Armas,** the Jalisco State Band puts on free concerts usually every Tuesday, Thursday, and Sunday evening starting about 7pm. Those who want a seat in the park should arrive early.

Special month-long festivals take place in Guadalajara in September, October, and February.

During **September,** Mexicans celebrate their **independence** from Spain, but Guadalajara really goes all out. Look for poster-size calendars listing attractions that include many performing arts in theaters all over the city. On the 15th, the Governor's Palace fills with well-dressed, invited guests as they, and the massive crowd in the plaza below, await his reenactment of the traditional *grito* (shout for independence) at 11pm. The grito commemorates Father Miguel Hidalgo de Costilla's pronouncement that began the War for Independence in Mexico in 1810. There's live music on a temporary street stage, spontaneous dancing, much shouting of "Viva Mexico," and fireworks. On September 16 there's a parade that lasts an hour or so. For the next couple of days the park in front of the Degollado Theater resembles a county fair and Mexican market. There are games of chance with stuffed-animal prizes, and a variety of food, including cotton candy and candied apples. Among the many attention-getting gimmicks and games, look for a mechanized, growling, arm-flailing, stuffed gorilla wearing a sombrero. Live entertainment goes on in the park day and night.

October is another month-long celebration, called **Fiestas de Octubre,** that originally began with the procession of Our Lady of Zapopan, but has since added a celebration of all that is notable about Guadalajara and Jalisco. The month kicks off with an enormous parade, usually on the Sunday nearest the first of the month (but it could be Saturday). By the way, those Americans in the parade may be from San Antonio, Texas, Guadalajara's sister city. Festivities continue all month with performing arts, rodeos (charreadas), bullfights, art exhibits, regional dancing, a food fair, and a Day of Nations involving all the consulates of Guadalajara. Much of the ongoing displays and events take place in the Benito Juárez Auditorium.

On **October 12** around dawn, the small dark figure of the **Our Lady of Zapopan** begins her 5-hour ride from the Cathedral of Guadalajara to the Cathedral of Zapopan, a suburb. The original figure dates from the mid-1500s and the procession tradition began 200 years later. Crowds spend the night all along the route and vie for position as the Virgin passes riding in a new car donated to her for the occasion. In the months before October 12, the figure is carried to churches all over the city. During that time, you may see neighborhoods decorated with paper streamers and banners honoring the passing of the figure to the next church.

The last 2 weeks in **February** are marked by a series of cultural events before the beginning of Lent.

5. SPORTS & RECREATION

BULLFIGHTS

Many say that Guadalajara and Mexico City have the best bullfights in the country, so if you want to see one, this is probably an excellent place to do it. Every Sunday at

4:30pm (4pm in summer) there's a bullfight at the Plaza de Toros Nuevo Progreso, across from the football stadium on Calzada Independencia Norte, north of town. Tickets range from $1.50 in the sun to $65 for the best seats in the shade. Buy tickets downtown in the reception area of the Hotel Frances on Thursdays from 10am to 2pm or from 4 to 7pm. Tickets are also sold in the Restaurant Abajeno Minerva, on the Minerva Circle (corner of Vallarta and López Mateos; tel. 30-0307), or at the Plaza de Toros.

RODEOS & COCKFIGHTS

To the east of Agua Azul is **Aceves Galindo Lienzo,** or rodeo ring, where there's a Mexican rodeo (charreada) on Sunday at noon. Riding, roping and rope tricks, and a traditional grand promenade are all part of the action at the charreada. Sometimes there are evening shows, too. It's found at the corner of Dr. R. Michel and Calzada de las Palmas (tel. 19-3232).

Also nearby, cockfights are held in the **Palenque/Agua Azul,** at the corner of Washington and 16 de Septiembre (tel. 19-5993 or 19-5940), but only in the high seasons, from October to early November. For cockfights the rest of the year, visit the local "pit" at the **Plaza de Gallos, La Tapatía,** at Avenida Revolución 2120 (tel. 35-7506), on the way to Tlaquepaque (take a Tlaquepaque bus from along Calzada Independencia). Profits from the blood sport go to charity and matches are *usually* held daily. Arrive by 7pm.

6. SHOPPING

Besides the mammoth **Mercado Libertad,** described above, in which you can find almost anything, Guadalajara boasts the largest modern shopping center in Latin America. The **Plaza del Sol** megacomplex, spraws over 120,000 square yards in an area at the junction of Avenidas López Mateos and Mariano Otero, outside the center of town. Here you can buy anything from a taco to a Volkswagen; you can also cash a check, make a plane reservation, or buy a lottery ticket. There are even hotels and restaurants for weary shoppers! Take the no. 40 bus from Calzada Independencia near the Libertad Market.

There's a convenient pedestrian passageway that runs under Juárez where there are many stalls selling candied fruits, leather belts, and other goods. A better place to purchase **leather goods,** however, is down on Avenida Pedro Moreno, a street that runs parallel to Juárez, and for **shoes,** go to E. Alatorre northeast of the historic center, where 70 shoe stores are located.

One block past the entrance of Agua Azul Park in the direction of the city center (on your right at the crossroads of the calzada and Gallo), is the **Casa de las Artesanías,** Gallo 20 (tel. 19-4664). It's an enormous two-story, state-run crafts store that sells pottery, silver jewelry, dance masks, and regional clothing from around the state. The best crafts aren't necessarily found here and prices seem somewhat steep, so if you are going to the villages, such as Tonalá, you may want to postpone buying. On the right as you enter are museum displays showing crafts and regional costumes from the state of Jalisco. The craft store is open Monday through Friday from 10am to 7pm, Saturday 10am to 4pm, and Sunday from 10am to 2pm.

There's an **outdoor market** every Sunday at Santa Teresita, where you can buy clothes and anything else you have in mind, all at excellent prices; look on the map of Greater Guadalajara for an approximation of where to find it. It stretches out for blocks and blocks.

For the best shopping see Tlaquepaque and Tonalá in "Easy Excursions," below.

7. EVENING ENTERTAINMENT

MUSIC & DANCE

MAJOR PERFORMING ARTS COMPANIES

BALLET FOLKLÓRICO DE LA UNIVERSIDAD DE GUADALAJARA. Tel. 26-5455 or 25-8888, ext. 262, 264, or 266.

This wonderful dance company, acclaimed as the best folkloric ballet company in Mexico, provides the light, color, movement, and music that is pure Jalisco. Call for information. Performances are at the Degollado Theater Sunday at 10am.
Prices: $1–$6.

BALLET FOLKLÓRICO NACIONAL OF THE INSTITUTO CULTURAL CABAÑAS. Tel. 18-6003.

Performances are every Wednesday at 8:30pm at the theater of the Instituto Cultural Cabañas.
Prices: Tickets $3.

THE STATE SYMPHONY ORCHESTRA. Tel. 13-1115.

The orchestra performs regularly at the Degollado Theater. Call for the schedule.
Prices: $1–$6.

CASA DE LA CULTURA, between 16 de Septiembre and Calzada Independencia. Tel. 19-3611.

A variety of performances is offered. The Association of Composers of Jalisco offer new works on Tuesday evenings at 8pm. The state chorus group, the Coral del Estado, also performs here. On Thursday there are literary readings at 8pm, as well as experimental dance performances and Aztec music. Call for information.

EX-CONVENTO DEL CARMEN, Juárez 638. Tel. 14-7184.

Many low-cost concerts, other performances, and movies are offered here. Performances are usually on Monday and Tuesday evenings at 8 or 8:30pm. Open: Daily 9am–10pm.

GUADALAJARA: EVENING ENTERTAINMENT

MAJOR PERFORMANCE HALLS

Degollado Theater. Tel. 13-1115
Teatro Experimental. Tel. 19-3770
Casa de la Cultura. Tel. 19-3611
Ex-Convento del Carmen. Tel. 14-7184

THEATER

TEATRO EXPERIMENTAL, Calzada Independencia Sur near Parque Agua Azul. Tel. 19-3770.
Interesting experimental works are performed here and it's worth going even if you don't speak Spanish. Performances are Tuesday to Sunday from February through November, and begin around 8:30pm on weekdays and at 5 and 7pm Sunday. Call for information and prices.

TEATRO GUADALAJARA DEL IMSS, Av. 16 de Septiembre 868. Tel. 19-4121.
More conventional than the Experimental Theater, the schedule of plays is usually modern. Call for current schedule and prices.

THE CLUB & MUSIC SCENE

For rousing music, and pure Mexico/Guadalajara ambience go to the **Plaza de los Mariachis,** down by San Juan de Dios Church and the Libertad Market, junction of Calzada Independencia and Juárez/Javier Mina. Every evening the colorfully dressed mariachis of the city, in various states of inebriation, play for money (if they can get it) or for free. Enjoy a meal here, or a snack or a soft drink, or just stand around spending nothing but time. It's fun and it's free; spend at least one evening here.

Few places in Guadalajara are more enjoyable to me than **El Parián** in **Tlaquepaque** where mariachis serenade diners under the portals. See "Easy Excursions," below, for more information.

NIGHTCLUBS/CABARET

HOTEL FIESTA AMERICANA, Glorieta Minerva. Tel. 25-3434 or 25-4848.
Live jazz "English-pub style" is presented in the **Caballo Negro Bar** from 9pm until 4am. There is also a continually changing show in the **lobby bar** daily from 7pm until 1am. In another salon, **Estelaris,** there are occasional performances by nationally known artists.

Admission: Fiesta $20. Reservations necessary.

JAZZ/BLUES

RESTAURANT/BAR COPENHAGEN 77, Marcos Castellanos 140-Z. Tel. 25-2803.

This dark, cozy jazz club is by the little Parque Revolución, on your left as you walk down Juárez from downtown. There are linen tablecloths and a red rose on every table. You can come just for a drink, or for the restaurant's specialty, the delicious paella Copenhagen al vino ($9.50). The paella takes a while to prepare, but it's an enjoyable wait, while you sip a drink and listen to the jazz. Open: Daily 1pm–1:30am; live jazz trio plays Mon–Wed 3–4:30pm and 8pm–12:30am, and Thurs–Sat 9pm–1:30am.
Admission: Free.

DANCE CLUBS/DISCOS

MAXIM'S DISCO CLUB, Hotel Frances, Maestranza 35. Tel. 13-1190.

Despite the name, Maxim's is not a disco, but a dance hall with singer or a live band. There are tables around the dance floor and in the lower bar section. While you're at the Hotel Frances, check out the **lobby bar,** one of the most enjoyable in Guadalajara, due in large part to the beautiful piano playing of Goyo Flores, who learned his art by braille. Flores, who speaks a little English, takes requests and specializes in old, romantic norteamericano favorites like the theme from Casablanca ("As Time Goes By") and "Stardust"; but, he also plays lovely versions of more contemporary classics like "A Lighter Shade of Pale," and Beatles songs. (Tips are appreciated.) Open: Daily 8pm–3 or 4am; 2-for-1 drinks Mon–Wed 8–11pm.
Admission: Free.

BAR EL CAMPAÑARIO, Hotel de Mendoza, Carranza 16. Tel. 13-4646.

There is a beautiful view from this penthouse perch in the Hotel de Mendoza. Only couples or mixed-sex groups are allowed in. There is music for dancing Monday through Saturday starting at 9pm. Open: Mon–Sat 11am–1am; happy hour 6–7pm. At this writing the bar is temporarily closed, but expected to reopen soon.

MOVIES

Guadalajara is a gold mine for foreign and art films. The best-known cines de arte (art theaters) are **Cinematógrafo Sala Especial,** Avenida Vallarta 1102, at the corner of Vallarta and Argentina (tel. 25-0514), about a 10-minute walk down Juárez from downtown, and the **Sala Greta Garbo,** at Pino Suárez 183, between Juan Manuel and San Felipe (tel. 14-2275). Also check with the **Instituto Cultural Cabañas** (tel. 17-3097 or 18-6003) for its latest offerings. The **Casa de la Cultura,** near Parque Agua Azul (tel. 19-3611), shows films Saturday and Sunday usually at 4, 6, and 8pm. The **Ex-Convento del Carmen,** Juárez 638, (tel. 14-7184) shows foreign and cultural films Friday through Saturday evenings at 6 and 8pm.

For the current film showings in most of the movie houses around town, you can consult any of these daily papers: the *Informador,* the *Occidental,* and *Ocho Columnas.*

6. EASY EXCURSIONS

By car the villages below take from 30 minutes to Tlaquepaque, the nearest, to around 3 hours to the farthest, Mazamitla and Tapalpa. By public transportation it will take longer.

Tlaquepaque and Tonalá, are 7 to 10 miles southeast of Guadalajara. Lake Chapala and the village of Chapala are 26 miles south. Ajijic is 4 miles west of Chapala; San Juan Cosalá, 9.5 miles of west of Chapala; Jocotepec, 12 miles west of Chapala. Mazamitla is 170 miles south of Guadalajara. Tapalpa is 133 miles south of Guadalajara.

TLAQUEPAQUE & TONALÁ

Tlaquepaque and **Tonalá** are Guadalajara suburbs that are a special treat for shoppers. **Market days** are Sunday and Thursday in Tonalá, but on Sunday many of Tlaquepaque's stores are open only from 10:30am to 2:30pm, if open at all. To combine a trip to both villages—about 5 miles apart—Thursday is the best day. Monday through Saturday, stores in Tlaquepaque usually close between 2:30 and 4pm. It makes a nice day to wear yourself out in Tonalá, then relax at one of Tlaquepaque's pleasant outdoor restaurants for a sunset meal and wait for the mariachis to warm up at El Parián.

To reach **Tlaquepaque** (a 25-minute ride) take the A or B no. 275 bus on 16th de Septiembre/Alcalde in front of the cathedral; wait by the blue bus signs. To get off at Tlaquepaque, get off one or two stops after you see the welcoming arch on the left, then ask for directions to El Parián, Tlaquepaque's central building. To **Tonalá,** stay on the bus (another 15 minutes) and Tonalá is the last stop the bus makes before turning around.

The **Tourism Office** in Tlaquepaque is in the Presidencia Municipal (opposite El

---

IMPRESSIONS

Guadalajara is a bit too staid to go in for Acapulco-style night spots.
The gaiety is left to Ajijic.
—JAMES NORMAN, TERRY'S GUIDE TO MEXICO, 1965

It is a pretty, somnolent town [Guadalajara] with a magnificent climate and is famous for its special style of pottery as well as for a certain type of hide chair which you will recognize instantly as the kind you have sat in wherever there was a terrace.
—LEONE AND ALICE LEONE-MOATS, OFF TO MEXICO, 1935

It is earthy and noisy and very pleasant in this potters' village [Tlaquepaque].
Mexico has a good time here and so will you.
—SYDNEY CLARK, ALL THE BEST IN MEXICO, 1952

Parián), Calle Guillermo Prieto 80 (tel. 35-1503 or 35-0596); it's open Monday through Friday from 9am to 3pm, and Saturday from 9am to 1pm.

The **Tourism Office** in Tonalá is in the Casa de Cultura, at Morelos 180, around the corner from the National Ceramics Museum, upstairs on the right. Hours are Monday through Friday from 9am to 3pm and Saturday from 9am to 1pm.

TLAQUEPAQUE

This suburban village is famous for its **fashionable stores** in handsome old stone mansions fronting pedestrian-only streets and its pottery and glass factories. The village is also known for **El Parián,** a circular building dating from the 1800s in its center, where innumerable mariachis belt out rousing songs to diners in sidewalk cafés. The mariachis are especially plentiful, loud, and entertaining on weekend evenings (Sunday is best). But just about any time of day you'll hear them serenading there. The stores, especially on Calle Independencia, offer all the pottery and glass for which the village is famous, plus the best of Mexico's crafts, such as equipales furniture, fine wood sculptures, and papier-mâché.

What to See & Do

Tlaquepaque's **Regional Ceramics Museum,** Independencia 237 (tel. 35-5404), is a good place to see what traditional Jalisco pottery is all about. There are high-quality examples dating back several generations. Note the cross-hatch design known as petatillo on some of the pieces. It's one of the region's oldest traditional motifs. There's also a small display of pre-Hispanic pottery, Huichol costumes, and folk art. The museum is open from Tuesday through Saturday from 10am to 4pm, and Sunday from 10am to 1pm. (See also the National Ceramics Museum in Tonalá.)

Across the street from the museum is a **glass factory.** In a room at the rear of the patio, a dozen scurrying men and boys heat glass bottles and jars on the end of hollow steel poles. Then, blowing furiously, they'll chase across the room, narrowly missing spectators and fellow workers alike as they swing the red-hot glass within an inch of a man who sits placidly rolling an elaborate jug out of another chunk of the cooling glass. Nonchalantly, the old man will leave his own task long enough to clip off the end of the boy's vase at the exact moment at which it comes within reach of his hand. Then he drops the clippers and returns once more to his own task as the youth charges back across the room to reheat the vase in the furnace.

Shopping

Tlaquepaque has many fine shops. Below are a few special ones.

BAZAR HECHT, 158 Independencia. Tel. 57-0316. Fax 35-2241.

One of the village's longtime favorite stores, here you'll find wood objects, handmade furniture, and a few antiques. Open: Mon–Sat 10am–2:30pm and 3:30–6:30pm.

SERGIO BUSTAMANTE, 236 Independencia. Tel. 39-5519.

Sergio Bustamante's imaginative and original brass, copper, ceramic, and papier-mâché sculptures are among the most sought after in Mexico and the most copied. This is an exquisite gallery of his work. Open: Mon–Sat 10am–7pm.

CAOBA, 156 Independencia. Tel. 35-9770.

Unusual, rustic, but finely finished pottery and wood sculptures are the specialties here. Open: Mon–Sat 10am–7pm, Sun 11am–2pm.

CASA CANELA, 258 Independencia. Tel. 35-3717.

Step inside this grand mansion and discover one of the most elegant stores in Tlaquepaque. Browse through the rooms of decorative arts, among them imaginative use of Mexican and Guatemalan textiles on equipale furniture. Open: Mon–Fri 10am–2pm and 3pm–7pm, Sat 10am–3pm.

KEN EDWARDS, 70 Madero. Tel. 35-5456.

Ken Edwards was among the first artisans to produce high-fired, lead-free stoneware in Tonalá and his blue-on-blue pottery is sold all over Mexico. This showroom has a fine selection of his work not normally seen in such size or quantity elsewhere. There's a section of seconds as well. It's next door to the Restaurant With No Name. Open: Mon–Sat 10am–6:30pm. His factory is in Tonalá.

IRENE PULOS, 210-B Independencia. Tel. 57-8499.

The emphasis here is on designer clothing using hand-loomed textiles and designs from Guatemala and Mexico. There's an entire room devoted to the clothing of the Huichol of Jalisco and Nayarit. Open: Mon–Sat 10am–6pm.

TETE ARTE Y DISENO, Juárez 173. Tel. 35-7347.

Here you'll find many large architectural decorative objects mixed in with the pottery, antiques, glassware, and paintings, all in a sort of organized jumble. Open: Mon–Sat 10am–7pm.

Where to Dine

Read the fine print on menus. The 15% value-added tax, usually included in the written menu price elsewhere in Mexico, may not be included in Tlaquepaque. It may be added on when your bill is presented. Even if the fine print tells you it's included, ask—before ordering.

MARISCOS PROGRESO, Progreso 80. Tel. 57-4995.
  Specialty: SEAFOOD/MEXICAN
  $ Prices: Appetizers $1.25–$6; main courses $6–$8; ceviche $1.25–$3.25.
  Open: Daily 10am–8pm.

Formerly the Restaurant Los Corrales, this renamed restaurant has an all-new, primarily seafood menu. Its cozy tree-shaded patio, filled with leather-covered tables and chairs, makes an inviting place to take a break from your shopping. Mexican food is the specialty here. To find it, cross Juárez, one of the streets that borders El Parián, and look for this corner restaurant.

RESTAURANT WITH NO NAME (Sin Nombre), Madero 80. Tel. 35-4520
  or 35-9677.

Specialty: MEXICAN.
Prices: Appetizers $6; main courses $10–$15.
Open: Mon–Sat 8:30am–8:30pm, Sun 8:30am–6:30pm.

This all-time favorite offers excellent cuisine in a spectacular garden shaded by banana, peach, palm, and other tropical trees and guarded by strutting peacocks. A trio plays music in mid-afternoon. The menu is spoken by the bilingual waiter, not written, so ask for prices as you order. I enjoyed the excellent "No Name Chicken," cooked in onions, green peppers, and a buttery sauce, spread around a mound of rice. The quesadillas are outstanding.

Why the unusual name here? When the American-owned restaurant first opened it didn't have a liquor license, so they operated as a speakeasy, and early clients gave the place its current appellation. It's 1½ blocks from the main plaza.

LOS CAZADORES, Chamizal 606. Tel. 35-1983.
Specialty: MEXICAN.
Prices: Appetizers $4–$6; main courses $6–$18.
Open: Daily 1–6pm.

This expansive and tranquil restaurant resembles a country hacienda and is noted for good service and food in a casual atmosphere. Patrons start drifting in about 1:30pm and the dining rooms and huge shady patio are full by 3pm. The large mariachi group is one of the best I've heard, and plays without charge. *Important Note:* Waiters will bring you extra appetizers (and charge you for them). They all speak English, so make sure they know what you do and don't want. Also, alcoholic drinks can be outrageously expensive, and cocktail prices are not on the menu. Ask the price before you order! As a special treat, folk dancing is presented Friday from 2 to 3pm, and Saturday and Sunday at 4pm. It's a bit tricky to find the restaurant if you're driving, so follow these directions. Leave from El Parián via Independencia (which is one-way). At the end of this street, turn left onto Revolución, and drive back toward Guadalajara nine-tenths of a mile. At the traffic circle, go down the street to the right of the Pemex station for 2 blocks. Cazadores is on the right with a huge parking lot. Taxis charge around $3.

Special Events

The **Festival of the Immaculate Conception** is Tlaquepaque's biggest event with regional dances and parades December 8. During the **Christmas season** an almost life-size ceramic Nativity scene is set up in the central plaza. June 8 is the **Festival of St. Peter** with lively mariachis, folk dancing, and a parade.

TONALÁ

Tonalá is a pleasant, unpretentious village about 5 miles from Tlaquepaque, that many will find more authentic and easier on the wallet. The streets were paved only recently, but there aren't any pedestrian-only avenues yet. The village has been a center for pottery making since pre-Hispanic times; half of the more than 400 artists who reside here produce high- and low-temperature pottery in different colors of clay with a dozen different finishes. Other local artists also work with forged iron, cantera stone, brass and copper, marble, miniatures, papier-mâché, textiles, blown glass, and gesso.

On Thursday and Sunday **market days** vendors and temporary street stalls under flapping shade cloths fill the streets; "herb-men" sell multicolored, dried medicinal herbs from wheelbarrows; magicians entertain crowds with sleight-of-hand tricks; and craftspeople spread their colorful wares on the plaza's sidewalks. Those who love the hand-blown Mexican glass and folksy ceramics will wish they had a truck to haul the gorgeous and inexpensive handmade items. There is certainly greater variety here than Tlaquepaque—tacky and chic are often side by side.

Tonalá is the home of the **National Museum of Ceramics,** Constitución 104, between Hidalgo and Morelos (tel. 83-0494). The museum occupies a huge two-story mansion with displays of Jalisco work as well as pottery from all over the country. There's a large shop in the front on the right as you enter. The museum is open Tuesday through Friday from 10am to 5pm, and Saturday and Sunday from 10am to 3pm, admission free.

Shopping

KEN EDWARDS, Morelos 184. Tel. 83-0313.

This is the factory where the famous Ken Edwards stoneware is made. You can see the artisans at work and select pottery in the salesroom. Open: Mon–Fri 10am–2pm and 3–6:30pm.

JOSÉ BERNABE AND SONS, Hidalgo 83. Tel. 83-0040 or 83-0877.

Revered as among the best ceramic and stoneware artists in Tonalá, José Bernabe and his sons have a workshop and showroom ½ block from the Presidencia Municipal. Prices here are very expensive, but the quality is unsurpassable if a bit mass-produced looking; some pieces are museum quality and all are hand-painted by four generations of Bernabes trained in the art from boyhood. Open: Mon–Friday 10am–6:30pm, Sat–Sun 10am–2pm.

SANTIAGO DE TONALÁ, Madero 42. Tel. 83-0641 or 39-0543.

Blown glass is made at this factory ½ block off the plaza. Enter the factory by the back door to see how the work is done. There's a sales showroom as well where prices are higher than elsewhere because the glassware is commercial strength, made for heavy use in restaurants. Open: Mon–Fri 7am–3pm (factory to 7pm), Sat–Sun 7am–2pm.

ARTESANÍAS MAYORGA, Madero 43. Tel. 83-0121.

This large shop has a little bit of everything, including all kinds of crafts, from masks to colorful hanging ceramic birds. Open: Mon–Sat 10am–6pm, Sun 10am–5pm.

Where to Dine

LOS GERANIOS, Hidalgo 71. Tel. 83-0010.
   Specialty: MEXICAN.
$ Prices: Appetizers $1.25–$5; main courses $4.50–$8; plate lunches $1.50–$4.
   Open: Sun–Mon 11am–5pm.

This narrow, inviting restaurant next to El Bazar de Sermel offers a cool respite from the blazing sun. Diners can relax in the clean and comfortable white canvas chairs at white-clothed tables or in the small booths. The menu includes Mexican specialties. Start with soup, salad, or nachos, or a delicious fruit plate of fresh sliced jicama, oranges, and cucumber (*pepita*) with lime and sprinkled with chili powder. It's near the main plaza, so using that as a reference (with your back to it), walk ½ block down Hidalgo. Look for a pretty stained-glass sign with red flowers on the left.

CHAPALA

Chapala, Jalisco (pop. 32,000), 26 miles south of Guadalajara, is the district's business and administrative center as well as the oldest resort on Lake Chapala, Mexico's largest lake. Much of the town's prosperity comes from wealthy retirees who live on the outskirts and come into Chapala to change money, buy groceries, and check the stock ticker. Except on weekends when throngs of visitors fill the central village, it can be a pretty sleepy place.

Lake Chapala feeds the water needs of both Guadalajara and Mexico City more than 300 miles away, as well as providing irrigation needs for area farmers. Its depth and perimeter have been diminishing due to population growth of the cities and poorly managed upstream use of the Lerma River, a major stream which feeds the lake. Any observer can see the waters have receded several hundred yards, although rains in the summer of 1991 brought the lake edge closer to town than it had been in years. There's much controversy about whether it is dying or not and what government is or isn't doing about it. Despite the controversy, Lake Chapala is beautiful, ringed by misty forested mountains and fishing villages. It's long been popular with foreign vacationers because of its near-perfect climate, gorgeous scenery, and several charming little lakeshore towns—Chapala, Ajijic, and Jocotepec among them. Each has its own distinct ambience. There's a large expatriate community in settlements and in the villages stretching all the way from Chapala to Jocotepec. *One note:* The climate year round is so agreeable that few hotels offer air conditioning and only a few have fans; neither is necessary.

Buses to Chapala go to from Guadalajara's Old Central Camionera. The **Transportes Guadalajara-Chapala** company (tel. 57-8448) serves the route. Buses and minibuses run every half hour to Chapala, and every hour to Jocotepec. To get to Ajijic and San Juan Cosalá, walk towards the lake from the bus station and on the opposite side of the street you'll spot local buses which travel between Chapala and San Juan Cosalá. From Cosalá change buses to Jocotepec, or there are buses direct to Jocotepec from the Chapala bus station (tel. 5-2212) every 30 minutes.

Those driving will be able to enjoy the lake and its towns more fully. From Guadalajara, drive to Lake Chapala via Highway 15/80, which is being widened to four lanes. Leave Guadalajara via Avenida Gonzalez Gallo, which intersects with Calzada Independencia just before Aqua Azul Park. Going south on Independencia, turn left onto Gallo and follow it all the way out of town past the airport, where it becomes Highway 44, the main road to Chapala. The first view of the lake isn't until just outside of the town of Chapala.

The bus from Guadalajara lets you off at the central bus station on Madero, the main street, about 7 short blocks north of the lake.

The highway from Guadalajara leads directly into Chapala and becomes Madero, which leads straight to Chapala's pier, malecón (waterfront walkway and street), and

IMPRESSIONS

Chapala, which can more or less be called the Mexican Riviera, is situated on the lake of the same name and surrounded by picturesque Indian villages. It is gay with thousands and thousands of birds that migrate here from the north.
—LEONE and ALICE LEONE-MOATS, *OFF TO MEXICO*, 1935

Winging their way across the lake are countless thousands of ducks and geese. And in the shallow waters near the shore wade longlegged cranes, blue herons, white pelicans, and awkward, timid egrets with their tufts of priceless white plumes on the lower part of their backs. Furthermore, the marshy lands about the lake and the woodland that dot its shores are the home of all sorts of colorful birds that have come here to avoid the chill winds of colder climates.
—BURTON HOLMES, *MEXICO*, 1939

---

small shopping and restaurant area. The one traffic light in town (a block or so before the pier) is the turning point (right) to Ajijic, San Antonio, San Juan Cosalá, and Jocotepec. Chapala's **main plaza** is 3 blocks north of the pier and the central food **market** flanks the park's back side.

The **area code** for the whole northern lake shore (Chapala, Ajijic, San Juan Cosalá, and Jocotepec) is 376.

Libros y Revistas, at Madero 230 (tel. 5-2021), near the Chamber of Commerce and Lloyds and opposite the plaza, carries English-language newspapers, magazines, and books. It's open daily from 9am to 4pm.

Chapala's new **Chamber of Commerce,** at Madero 232, (tel. and fax 376/5-3567) has an assortment of maps and local information, and will make reservations for the Degollado Theater in Guadalajara. It's open Monday through Friday from 9am to 4pm. Zaida Reynoso, the knowledgeable office director, is there from 9am to 1pm. It's next to Banamex and upstairs over Lloyds. The **Jalisco State Information Office** is in Ajijic (see below).

Besides banks on the main street in Chapala, there's also a **money exchange** by Lloyds on Madero which is opposite the food market and main plaza.

WHERE TO STAY

Expensive

VILLA AURORA BED AND BREAKFAST, c/o Pamela Cooksey, P.O. Box 251, Mill Valley, CA 94942, Tel. 412/383-3172. Fax 415/383-6960. 6 rms (all with bath).

$ Rates (including breakfast and gratuities): $60–$80 single; $80–$100 double. Extra person $20. 3-night minimum stay.

⭐ One of the most fashionable and comfortable inns in the country, this American-owned and newly opened bed-and-breakfast was converted from a beautifully remodeled 19th-century mansion. It's 19th century on the outside, but fully 20th century on the inside. It faces the lake on the malecón in central

Chapala. And you couldn't ask for a better location, or more sumptuous accommodations. Each of the spacious rooms is different in size, and has varied pastel furnishings, beautiful new tile floors, queen-size beds, lake view, private bath with tub/shower combination, French doors open to the view, and good cross-ventilation. There's a gracious communal parlor on the second floor with a terrace facing the lake. The third-floor terrace has a hot tub for guests. Smoking is permitted outdoors only. No pets and no children under 15 are accepted. The inn is within ½ block of Chapala's pier and within walking distance of shops, restaurants, and the market. Reservations are made only in the U.S. and there's a 3-night minimum stay required.

Dining/Entertainment: Complimentary breakfast included daily; will accommodate diet restrictions if notified; complimentary afternoon snacks and self-serve beverages.

Services: With notice, owner will arrange guest pickup at the Chapala airport at an extra charge; self-operated washer and dryer free to guests.

Facilities: Lap pool.

QUINTA QUETZALCOATL, c/o Golden Ledger Bookkeeping, P.O. Box 1649, Tracy, CA 95378-1649. Tel. 209/832-8788. Fax 209/832-1204. 8 rms.

$ Rates (including daily breakfast, several meals, and four excursions): $100–$150 single or double daily. 8- or 10-night minimum; shorter stays on space-available basis.

★ The secluded, centrally located QQ, as it is dubbed, stands for *quinta* which means country inn and Quetzalcoatl, for the plumed serpent of Aztec/Toltec legend, and it's the place where D. H. Lawrence wrote *The Plumed Serpent*. It's owned by Californians Dick and Barbi Henderson, who personally attend guests. Rooms flank a large flower-, tree-, and plant-filled interior garden behind a 12-foot-high brick wall. Each room is tastefully furnished, entirely different, and intriguingly named. Lady Chatterley is one of the smaller rooms and has quaint Victorian touches with a stuffed Queen Anne chair, armoire, lace-covered table, and glass chandelier. The two-story *Castillo* (the castle) is the largest with two bedrooms, separate living and dining rooms, and an enormous tile kitchen. Henderson, an accomplished chef, prepares meals from a cozy kitchen brimming with interesting pots and jars. Summer visits, June through October, are arranged on request for eight guests minimum and require a 10-night minimum stay. During winter, December through May, there are fixed arrival and departure days and a stay of 8 nights is required. No children or pets are accepted. The QQ is a short walk from Chapala's pier, shops, restaurants, and market. Bring your own golf clubs and tennis rackets for use in area facilities. Guests must make reservations through the U.S.; no drop-in guests are accepted.

Dining/Entertainment: Meals are taken in the large dining room. The price includes daily large continental breakfast, four dinners, one afternoon taco fiesta, self-serve bar with complimentary beer and soft drinks.

Services: Afternoon airport pickup and return for guests on the QQ schedule; space-available guests may not fit this schedule, but transportation information is provided. Four optional fixed-scheduled excursions in the inn's 14-passenger van.

Facilities: Several patios and sitting areas on the shady grounds; coffee makers, hairdryers, and robes in each room.

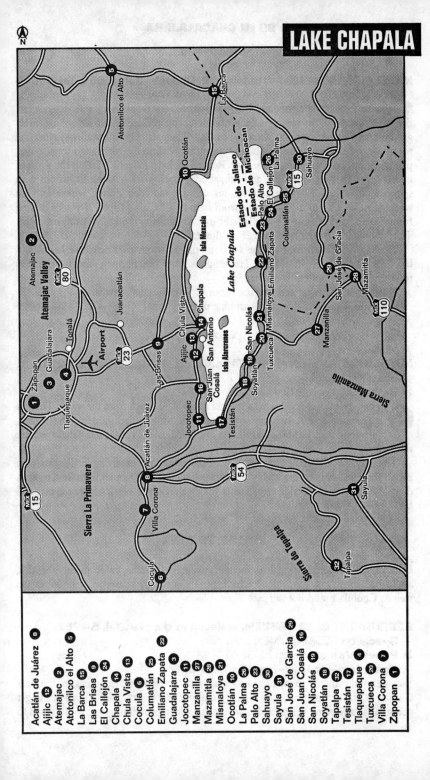

Moderate

HOTEL MONTECARLO, Av. Hidalgo 29, Chapala, Jal. 45000. Tel. 376/5-2120. Fax 376/5-2024. 46 rms (all with bath). FAN
  $ **Rates:** $45 single or double. **Parking:** Free.

Behind a high wall, the setting is delightful here, situated on a rise overlooking lovely grounds that spread down to the edge of Lake Chapala. Red-tile walkways link the room areas, restaurant, and pools, and grounds are dotted with mango trees, pines, palms, and a strolling peacock or two. Rooms all have balconies facing the gardens and come with two twin beds, and tub/shower combination in the bathroom with separate sink area. Advance reservations are a good idea during winter and on weekends. It's a 5- to 6-block walk from here to Chapala proper. If you're driving from Guadalajara, turn right at the light in Chapala which takes you toward Ajijic. The hotel is less than a mile farther on the left.

Dining/Entertainment: The spacious dining room overlooks the lawns and lake. Breakfast is served from 8 to 11am; lunch, from 1:30 to 5pm; dinner, from 7:30 to 10pm; Sunday buffet, from 2 to 5pm.

Services: Morning and evening room service; laundry service.

Facilities: 2 thermal-water swimming pools.

Budget

HOTEL NIDO, Av Madero 202, Chapala, Jal. 45900. Tel. 376/5-2116. 31 rms (all with bath).
  $ **Rates:** $16 single; $19 double.

Ⓢ The best budget hotel is in the center of town, ½ block from the water. There is a restaurant, bar, swimming pool, and a well-tended garden. The rooms, furnished with old-timey furniture, are spacious and those facing the street are the largest.

The popular restaurant attracts many of the retired people living in Chapala who eat all three meals here and highly recommend the food. It's open from 8am to 8pm daily and the comida corrida costs $6.50. It's on the right, a block before the pier and lake.

WHERE TO DINE

Lake Chapala regional specialties include caviar de Chapala, caldo michi, charales, and tortas ahogados. Viuda de Sanchez Sangrita (a tequila chaser) is made locally as well as Cholula brand hot sauce.

RESTAURANT BEER GARDEN, malecón at the pier. Tel. 5-2257.
  Specialty: REGIONAL/MEXICAN.
  $ **Prices:** Main courses $3.50–$5.50
  Open: Mon–Sat 10am–7pm, Sun 10am–8:30pm.

Facing the lake and opposite Chapala's main pier where the malecón begins, the Beer Garden is on the open patio of the long-defunct Hotel Arzapalo. Things really get going in the afternoon when strolling mariachis add a festive touch and locals begin to

CHAPALA VILLAGE

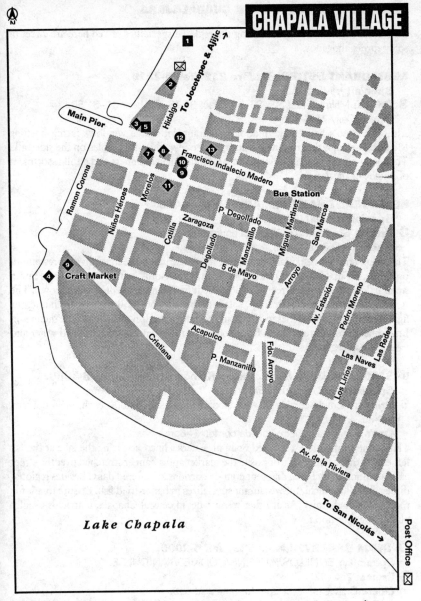

ACCOMMODATIONS:
Hotel Montecarlo 1
Nido 5
DINING:
Beer Garden 3
Beto's 6
Chemary Bar and Restaurant 13
Don Juan 4

La India Bakery 11
San Francisco 2
Super Market 7
Superior Restaurant 8
POINTS OF INTEREST:
Information 12
Central Market 9
Central Plaza 10

drift in for lunch and drinks. Among the regional specialties served here are sweet or spicy tortas ahogados.

RESTAURANT BETO'S, Madero 212. Tel. 5-2218.
Specialty: MEXICAN.
$ Prices: Main courses $3–$6; breakfast $1.75–$5; beer $1–$1.50.
Open: Daily 7am–10pm.

Although Beto's has a huge indoor restaurant with large windows facing bustling Madero, it's enjoyable to dine outdoors at the few white-iron tables on the sidewalk. The menu ranges from sandwiches to beef and chicken dinners and a full assortment of Mexican specialties.

RESTAURANT BAR CHEMARY, Madero 429.
Specialty: ASIAN/MEXICAN.
$ Prices: Breakfast $3–$5; main courses $4–$7.
Open: Daily 8am–10pm.

This small colorful restaurant, famed for its margaritas, is the most inviting restaurant on Chapala's main street. Decked out in gay tablecloths, with open windows and a small balcony facing the street, you'll notice it first thing when driving into town. The Asian specialties come with soup, salad, and main course. But there are numerous light meals from sandwiches to Mexican specialties and fish-and-chips. The menu is in English and proprietress María Rivera caters to foreign needs with purified water and treated fresh vegetables.

RESTAURANT DON JUAN, Paseo Ramón Corona 3. Tel. 5-3060.
Specialty: REGIONAL/MEXICAN.
$ Prices: Comida corrida $5–$6; tacos and quesadillas 60¢ each; main courses $4–$6.
Open: Daily 9am–6pm; comida corrida 1–6pm.

This is one of the old established open-air eateries lined up facing the lake at the far left end of the malecón. It's opposite the market and a banner stretched over the street calls attention to it. Three different comida corridas are offered daily. Besides regional dishes like caldo michi, the restaurant specializes in batter-fried fish. Be sure to ask for their home-made salsa. As at other restaurants in central Chapala, mariachis usually play in the afternoon.

LA INDIA BAKERY, Juárez 533. Tel. 5-3005.
Specialty: BOLILLOS/MUFFINS/COOKIES/PAN DULCE.
$ Prices: 25¢–$2.
Open: Daily 6am–1 or 2pm (or until sold out).

★ From this hole-in-the-wall bakery, with no visible sign to announce it, comes some of the best-tasting basic bakery products in the country. Certainly they make the best bolillos in town, but all of their cookies and pan dulce have a spark of flavor I've not tasted elsewhere. It's located directly behind the main plaza and market and next to the Casa Carocio. Get there early in the day; it sells out fast.

SAN FRANCISCO GRILL, Hidalgo 236 A.
Specialty: MEXICAN.

$ Prices: Brunch $5–$6.50; main courses $5–$8.
Open: Daily 8am–9:30pm; brunch 10am–2pm.

Although there's an entrance on Hidalgo, 1½ blocks west of Madero, you can also enter from the malecón where you see the restaurant's terrace, facing the lake, decked out with umbrella-covered tables. The service is a bit casual, but locals agree the food is great. The menu has a wide assortment of traditional favorites such as hamburgers, quesadillas, nachos, and tacos, but there are grilled steaks as well.

RESTAURANT SUPERIOR, Madero and Hidalgo. Tel. 5-2180.
Specialty: MEXICAN.
$ Prices: Main courses $2.50–$5.50; breakfast $1.25–$4.
Open: Wed–Mon 8am–10pm, Tues 8am–5pm.

$ Right in the heart of Chapala this snappy clean little restaurant, owned by the Mungia family, has been operating at the same location for 30 years. The extensive menu of Mexican specialties includes chiles rellenos, enchiladas, and tacos. The Mexican plate comes with two tacos and enchiladas, a chile relleno, rice, beans, and salsa. There are several tables outdoors and a bar upstairs which has live music weekends and overlooks Madero.

WHAT TO SEE & DO

Golf

The **Chula Vista Country Club** in Ajijic (2.5 miles west of Chapala) has a nine-hole golf course and accepts nonmembers daily from 9am to 6pm. However, beginners and children under 15 aren't allowed on the course on Saturday and Sunday. Monday through Friday a round cost is $20; Saturday and Sunday, $25. Caddies cost $3.50 for nine holes and $5 for 18. The small restaurant serves drinks and on weekends offers light snacks.

Lake Tours

Lake Chapala is dotted with several islands. Relatively nearby is the small **Isla de los Alacranes** (Scorpion Island), with a few outdoor restaurants where you can sip a drink or have a meal. Once nesting grounds for area birds, most of the trees were destroyed by rising water years ago. Fishermen net charales on the edge of the island early in the morning. Distant **Isla Mezcala** is larger and holds the ruins of a 17th-century prison fortress. Birds nest in the trees remaining on the highest part of the island, but much of the island is devoted to small plots for raising corn and chayotes (a vegetable called vegetable pear or mirliton in the U.S.). The **Cooperativo de Lanchas Guerreros Inmortales** has a small booth at the beginning of the pier in Chapala, staffed daily from around 7:30am until 5pm. Tour prices are per boat, most of which hold between eight and 10 people. A short lakeshore tour costs $10; a 30-minute ride to Isla Alacranes costs $17—long enough to enjoy a soft drink at one of the little restaurants; an hour trip to Isla Alacranes is $22—time enough to eat or watch the fishermen; a tour to both islands costs around $80 and takes around 4 hours. Weekends are best to try for a boat excursion, since without others to share the price you'll have to pay for the whole boat, and it's not worth it. Ask for **Matias**

Estrada, whose boat is the *Blanca Marcela.* He's usually around the pier mornings or call him at home (tel. 5-4326) a day in advance to arrange for an early-morning trip.

Shopping

Chapala's main street, Madero, and Hidalgo, the intersecting street leading to Ajijic, have a few shops. To find the small collection of craft stalls at the **Mercado de Artesanías,** turn left at the pier in Chapala and follow it to the end. The market is on the left. Shopping is better in Ajijic.

Horseback Riding

Horses for hire are gathered under the trees beside the Mercado de Artesanías (see above). Cost, including a guide, is $5 per hour for adults and $3.50 for children.

AJIJIC

Ajijic, another lakeside village is a quiet place inhabited by fishermen, artists, and retirees. As you reach Ajijic, the highway becomes a wide, tree-lined boulevard through a wealthy residential district called La Floresta. The La Floresta sign signals you've entered Ajijic, but the central village is about a mile farther on the left. To reach Ajijic's main street, Colón, which changes to Morelos, turn left when you see the Danny's Restaurant sign. The cobblestone streets and arts and crafts stores give the town a quaint atmosphere. The narrow streets lead past a small church and square, and end by the sunny lake. (See "Chapala," above, for bus information for Ajijic.)

The area **Tourist Information Office** is at km 6.5 on the road between Chapala and Ajijic (tel. 376/5-3135). When you see the modernistic cement sculpture on the left, turn left, then immediately right on the interior street that parallels the highway. It's on the left, next to the Casa Artesanías. Hours are Monday through Friday from 9am to 6pm and Saturday from 9am to 1pm. The telephone is that of the Casa de Artesanías and the tourist office may have its own by the time you travel.

WHERE TO STAY

Expensive

DANZA DEL SOL, Zaragoza 165, Ajijic, Jal. 45900. Tel. 376/5-2504. Fax 376/5-2474. 39 suites (all with bath). TEL
$ Rates: $49 single; $65 double.
Sequestered behind walls and spread among secluded plant-filled grounds, what you get here is not simply a room, but a massive, nicely furnished apartment complete with patio (sometimes a gigantic one), full-size living room with a fireplace, separate dining room, large complete kitchen, and from one to four spacious bedrooms, each with a separate bath. Used frequently as a small meeting hotel, you won't find a lot of tourists here, but it's one of the most comfortable places along the lake and a beautiful

discovery. Danza del Sol is a little hard to find. Head out of Ajijic toward Jocotepec and look carefully on the left for the weathered sign. Turn there and go a short distance on a beat-up road.

Facilities: Swimming pool.

HOTEL REAL DE CHAPALA, Paseo del Prado 20, Ajijic, Jal. Tel. 376/5-2416 or 5-2468, toll free 800/421-0767 in the U.S. Fax 376/5-2474. 85 suites (80 junior, 5 master; all with bath) TEL

$ Rates: $68 single; $74 double.

This hotel with towering eucalyptus and tranquil interior gardens is a good splurge choice right on the lake. The rooms could use some updating, but all are large suites with two double or one king-size bed, and large windows facing the interior garden or lake. Rooms on the lake side at the far end will be the most tranquil. A series of dining rooms with white wrought-iron furniture sprawls out on an enormous tree-shaded, flower-filled, lakeside patio with a pool. It's a most welcome and popular place to come for a drink or meal even if you aren't a guest. Tucked in La Floresta residential area, coming from Chapala, you'll see the sign for it at the large cement sculpture on the left. Turn left there and follow the signs to the hotel. It's about a 20-minute walk east from the Ajijic plaza, following 16 de Septiembre.

Dining/Entertainment: Restaurant Oscars is open from 6 to 11pm; Azulejos, open for breakfast only from 7 to 11am; and La Terraza/La Huerta on the terrace, from 12:30 to 6pm or inside from 6 to 10:30pm. Live piano music evenings at Oscar's; mariachis frequently on weekends.

Services: Laundry and room service.

Facilities: Swimming pool off the terrace and facing the lake.

Moderate

LA FLORESTA, Paseo de la Cima 4, Ajijic, Jal. 45900. Tel. 376/5-3997. 102 bungalows (all with bath).

$ Rates: $46–$65 single or double. **Parking:** Free.

In a residential neighborhood of the Ajijic's suburb of La Floresta, this hotel is a tranquil alternative with a mountain backdrop. Individually separated, each of the one- or two-bedroom units has a fully equipped kitchen and small living/dining area. All bedrooms have two single beds and bathrooms have separate sink area. If you're driving from Chapala the directional sign for the hotel will be on the right, after the Floresta subdivision sign. This is a better choice for those with cars, since the hotel is several blocks from the main boulevard, and taxis are on call, but not on-site.

Dining/Entertainment: Restaurant/bar.

Facilities: TV room, swimming pool, and Ping-Pong area.

LA NUEVA POSADA, Donato Guerra 9, Ajijic, Jal. 45900. Tel. 376/5-3395. 10 rms. FAN TEL

$ Rates (including full breakfast): $40 single; $50 double. **Parking:** Free.

⭐ This beautiful, new posada was built by the former owners of the popular Posada Ajijic, which is now a restaurant and bar under different ownership. Meticulously modeled after a gracious, traditional-style hacienda, La Nueva

Posada looks a lot more expensive than it is. French doors, marble bathrooms, a wine cellar, and a small swimming pool are some of the amenities—not to mention the elegant dining room with a glorious lake view. Pastel rose and blue decor with touches of tile and hand-painted flourishes on walls and over doorways create a rich but restful ambience. Original paintings hang in all of the color-coordinated rooms and public areas. Some rooms overlook the lake, others have intimate patios. Owned by the Eager family, the new posada is as popular as (but nothing like) their former hostelry and the hotel is often booked way ahead for holidays. The Eagers have plans to add eight more rooms. To find the hotel from the plaza, walk toward the lake on Colón, turn left on 16 de Septiembre. At Donato Guerra turn right.

Dining/Entertainment: The hotel's Restaurant La Rusa and casual bar are among the most popular meeting places in the village. There's live background music most evenings and some afternoons.

Budget

POSADA LAS CALANDRIAS, Carretera Chapala-Jocotepec poniente no. 8, (Apdo. Postal 76), Ajijic, Jal. 45920. Tel. 376/5-2819. 29 rms. TEL
$ Rates: $30 single or double 1 bedroom; $55 single or double 2 bedrooms; $300–$500 by the month.

Outside town on the main highway, this two-story brick hotel surrounds a swimming pool with bougainvillea everywhere. Guests come from all over, as the car license plates show: Rhode Island, Montana, and British Columbia. The rooms are large and comfortable and come with tile floors, fireplaces, and kitchens. There's an honor book exchange in the lobby. It's a good place to be for an extended stay, or while looking for long-term accommodations. Las Calandrias is on the main highway (left side if you're arriving from Chapala) at the west edge of Ajijic.

LA LAGUNA BED AND BRUNCH, Zaragoza 29, Ajijic, Jal. 45900. Tel. 376/5-2264. 4 rms.
$ Rates: $25–$30 single; $35–$40 double.

The rooms in this small inn are handsomely furnished with king-size beds covered in bright, loomed bedspreads. A help-yourself brunch is served in a lovely glassed-in dining room facing the back patio. To find La Laguna, from the main highway turn left on Colón and left again on the first street. It's 1½ blocks down on the left.

PAL RV PARK, Carretera Chapala-Jocotepec, San Antonio, Jal. 45900. Reservations: Madero 232, Chapala, Jal. 45900. Tel. 376/5-3764 or 5-3765. Fax 376/5-3567. 106 spaces.
$ Rates: $10 per day; $240 30 days; $190 permanent resident.

This immaculately kept park caters to visiting northerners who come for the winter. Each RV space has full hookups, a patio, and outdoor cooking grill. There's a nice recreation room for gatherings. The spotless bathrooms, separate for men and women, each have four showers and three toilets. To find the park, follow the highway from Chapala to San Antonio, which is between Chapala and Ajijic, just before the Floresta suburb, and it's easy to miss the town sign. There's a small sign to the park, but you'll also see a large Carta Blanca sign on the right. Turn right there. Make reservations by September for the winter months.

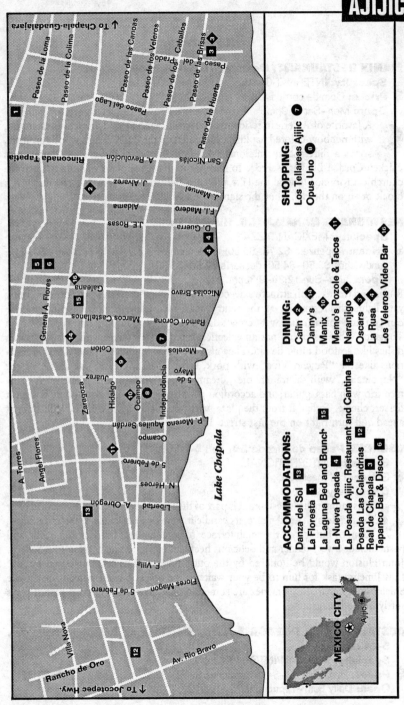

WHERE TO DINE

Moderate

MANIX RESTAURANT, Ocampo 57. Tel. 5-3449.
   Specialty: INTERNATIONAL.
$ Prices: Comida corrida $9.
   Open: Mon–Sat 1–9pm.

⭐ A favorite of American residents, this small, tranquil, and attractive restaurant, with rainbow-colored napkins to brighten up the dark, carved wood furniture, serves a different international comida daily. Seafood, beef, and sometimes chicken Cordon Bleu are served. To find Manix from the plaza walk away from the church on Morelos toward the lake and turn right on Ocampo. The restaurant is a block or so on the right, but the sign for it is hidden behind a tree.

RESTAURANT NARANJITOS, Hidalgo 10.
   Specialty: MEXICAN/PIZZA.
$ Prices: Appetizers $2.75–$5.50; main courses $5.75–$13; pizzas $4.50–$12; sandwiches $3.50–$4.50; desserts $2.50–$3.50.
   Open: Tues–Sun 12:30–9:30pm.

Rustic and trendy, with attractive decor, including yarn "drawings" and unusual fuzzy yarn lights, this restaurant off the central square has a loyal following; nowhere else can you find spinach and watercress salad or quiche on Tuesday and roast beef on Thursday. This restaurant has an eclectic, Americanized menu with some Mexican dishes like seafood mojo de ajo. They also specialize in unusual sandwich combinations like the "Pancho Villa" with pork, refried beans, cream, and sauce, or the "Napolitano," with salami, chutney, cream, lettuce, tomato, and jalapeño. A really nice trio with bass, guitar, and accordion plays at night. The lemon soufflé is a great dessert choice. To find it from the plaza, with your back to the church, walk straight ahead and turn right on the first street. It's on the left.

OSCAR'S, Paseo del Prado 20. Tel. 5-2416.
   Specialty: INTERNATIONAL.
$ Prices: Full meal $25.
   Open: Daily 6–11pm.

⭐ This intimate little restaurant is part of the Hotel Real de Chapala. Named after the Academy Award figure, its candlelit tables are set inside in the cozy dining room or outside on the small terrace. Main courses of fish, chicken, steak, and pasta include a very tender and delicious beef filet médaillon named for Tom Selleck. John Huston would be honored by the outstanding Caesar salad prepared by José Luis Jimenez (ask for him to be your waiter). The crêpes Suzette named for Brooke Shields and prepared by Jimenez are something special to remember. A pianist plays softly in the background.

RESTAURANT LA POSADA AJIJIC, Morelos and Independencia. Tel. 5-4422.
   Specialty: MEXICAN/INTERNATIONAL.
$ Prices: Breakfast $2–$4; sandwiches $2.75–$3.75; main courses $5–$7.75.
   Open: Daily 8am–10pm; lunch 2–10pm.

Formerly under the management of the owners of the Nueva Posada Ajijic, the restaurant has reopened with gracious Mexican-inspired decor and good service facing the lake. The menu covers the traditional with soups (ask about the daily specials), salads, sandwiches, and more filling Mexican specialties as well as beef, chicken and seafood dishes. The restaurant is at the end of Colón/Morelos and you enter through the back by the lake, where there's parking.

LA RUSA, Donato Guerra 9. Tel. 5-3395.
Specialty: INTERNATIONAL. **Reservations:** Suggested Dec–Apr.
$ Prices: Appetizers $4–$5; lunch $5–$7; main courses $8–$12.
Open: Mon–Sat noon–9pm, Sun 10am–8pm; Sun brunch 11am–1pm.

The mouth-watering menu here—especially the brunch specials—includes such offerings as scrambled eggs in a potato nest with sausage, broccoli rarebit, or shrimp-asparagus crêpes Newburg. And for brunch dessert: Danish kringle, granola muffins with strawberry butter, and peaches in caramel sauce. Brunch includes coffee and an alcoholic beverage such as a strawberry daiquiri or the wine of the day. The rest of the varied menu includes seafood, beef, and poultry, with changing daily specials. To reach the restaurant from the Ajijic plaza, walk toward the lake on Colón, turn left on 16 de Septiembre, and look for Donato Guerra. Turn right; the hotel/restaurant is right on the lake.

Budget

CAFIN, Carretera Chapala-Ajijic. Tel. 5-2572.
Specialty: PASTRIES/PIZZA/SANDWICHES.
$ Prices: Baked goods 25¢–$6; sandwiches and hamburgers $3.50–$4; pizza $3.75–$11.50.
Open: Mon–Sat 8am–7pm, Sun 8am–3pm.

You'll spot this cheery eatery by its green awning on the left just before Ajijic. The front part holds the bakery and booths lining one wall. There's a covered area in back beside a small lawn. Here you can purchase fresh croissants, cakes, and pies, plus sandwiches, hamburgers, and pizza. A lot of people come to enjoy the pastries with cappuccino and hot chocolate.

DANNY'S, on the highway at Colón.
Specialty: MEXICAN/AMERICAN.
$ Prices: Breakfasts $2.50–$3; Mexican dishes $2–$4; sandwiches and burgers $1.50–$4; main courses $2.50–$5.
Open: Mon–Sat 8am–4pm, Sun 8am–noon.

Those craving a hamburger or sandwich will enjoy this small, clean, and cheerful café on the main drag with a fifty-fifty American-Mexican menu. The Mexican plate with chili relleno, enchiladas, beans, and rice is a tasty choice. There are five breakfast specials that include coffee or tea, beans or home fries, juice, and toast or tortillas. Danny's is the landmark I use on the highway to turn onto Colón, the main street into Ajijic proper.

MEMO'S POZOLE & TACOS, Hidalgo 96 at 5 de Febrero.
Specialty: MEXICAN.

$ Prices: Pozole $1.50; tacos 30¢ each.
Open: Daily 6–11pm.

$ It's always a delight to discover a local favorite like Memo's. The simple specialties of pozole, tacos, enchiladas, sopes, and tostados are so good, housewives would rather buy them here than make them at home. Operated by Memo Rameño and María Robledo, the place is simple but the prices and taste are hard to top. Memo was planning to move from its location at Ocampo and Hidalgo to the address listed above.

LOS VELEROS VIDEO BAR, on the highway at Galeana.
Specialty: ITALIAN/MEXICAN.
$ Prices: Main courses $3.75–$17.
Open: Mon–Sat noon–9pm, Sun noon–10pm.

The big brick oven is always turning out one of their 14 pizzas, but the menu also includes sandwiches and other light snacks. This is a casual, comfortable place and with a choice of covered outdoor dining or inside facing the large TV screen, which is always bringing in the latest U.S. sporting event. Veleros is popular among the foreign crowd and it's a good place to meet some of the Americans and Canadians who live in the area.

WHAT TO SEE & DO

Shopping

The Casa de Artesanías (tel. 5-3135) is on the left entering Ajijic just after the La Floresta sign. When you see the cement sculpture on the left, turn left and the casa is on the left. The shop has a good selection of pottery from all over Mexico as well as locally made weavings. It's open Monday through Wednesday from 10am to 6pm, Thursday from 10am to 2pm and 4 to 6pm, Friday and Saturday from 10am to 6pm, and Sunday from 10am to 1pm.

Most of Ajijic's shops line Colón/Morelos, but don't limit your shopping to that. Wander the side streets, especially Independencia which is the street just before the waterfront. Below are only a few of the shops you'll discover.

LOS ORIGINALAES TELLARES AJIJIC, corner of Morelos and Independencia. Tel. 5-2402 or 5-4320.

Founded in 1950, this was one of the first weavers' shops in the village. Visitors can still watch men working the large pedal looms and wander through the showrooms with bolts of material and ready-made decorative goods as well as clothing from other places. Open: Mon–Fri 8am–6pm.

OPUS 1, Ocampo 30.

Here you'll find a fine line of designer clothing using Mexican colors and motifs made of handwoven cotton cloth. Open: Mon–Sat 10am–5pm.

TALLER SAÚL GUTIÉRREZ, western edge of Ajijic. Tel. 5-2074.

A studio artist whose first love is painting, Gutiérrez studied architecture, sculpture, and papier-mâché making before opening his pottery art studio. Now his line of original decorative lamps, pots, and plates is sought after by fashionable shops and snazzy hotels. The pottery is mold-made but the finished designs are hand-painted. Most of his inventory is made on request, but he usually has 20 to 30 pieces on hand for sale and a catalog of some of his most popular pieces, which can be ordered. He will ship to the States. The workshop is on the left side of the highway at the far edge of Ajijic at the Danza del Sol turn. It faces the highway. The street number 162 painted in white on the brick wall is all that designates this workshop, so you'll have to look carefully. It's best to call ahead, to make sure Gutiérrez is around.

Thermal Pools

A mile and a half west of Ajijic is the lakeside settlement of San Juan Cosalá, known for its thermal water. The Balneario San Juan Cosalá allows day use of their pools. To enter adults pay $3.50, and children $1.75. There are two huge private pools and the cost to use them is $5 per person, but only you or your group, friends, et al., are allowed in.

Rental Horses

Horses for hire are tied up on the central median of 16 de Septiembre near the Hotel Real de Chapala. Sunset rides along the lakeshore are very popular. Adults pay $5.50 per hour and children $4.

Entertainment

There's almost always a group or a crowd at the **Posada Ajijic Cantina,** Calle 16 de Septiembre 2, where a band (of sorts) plays for dancing on weekends. There's a happy hour daily from noon to 1:30pm and 5 to 6:30pm with complimentary snacks. In the evening (except Monday) drop in at **El Tapanco Bar and Disco,** on Calle 16 de Septiembre in the same block as the Posada Ajijic, on the other side of the street. They always serve drinks and sometimes have food and music. The **Nueva Posada Ajijic,** Donato Guerra 9, is a place to socialize almost anytime. Happy hour runs from noon to 1:30pm and 5 to 6pm both with complimentary snacks. For catching the latest in sports on a wide-screen TV or for just hanging out, **Los Veleros Video Bar,** on the Chapala Highway at Galeana in Ajijic, is another popular place. It's open Thursday through Tuesday, from 12:30 to 9pm and weekends it's open until 10pm.

SAN JUAN COSALÁ

Famed for its thermal waters, San Juan Cosalá is 8 miles west of Chapala and 1½ miles from Ajijic. Because of the string of establishments along the highway and dearth of signs, it's difficult to tell when you've arrived in Cosalá. The sign announcing Balneario San Juan Cosalá means you're there.

WHERE TO STAY & DINE

BALNEARIO SAN JUAN COSALÁ, Av. La Paz 420, San Juan Cosalá, Jal. **45900 (Apdo. Postal 180, Chapala, Jal. 45900). Tel. 376/3-0507** or 36/15-6728 in Guadalajara. 32 rms.

$ Rates (including breakfast): $28 single; $36 double; $46 triple. Fans $2.50 extra daily. **Parking:** Free.

The first established hotel using the area's thermal/mineral waters, it's still a popular place for day use of the huge swimming pool (with the mineral water) and for wintering northerners. Rooms are clean, freshly painted, and well-kept with decades-old veneer furniture, tile floors, and glass louvered windows. Each is furnished with two double beds and some have refrigerators. All have balconies or patios with a table and chairs facing the pool and lake. It can be a busy place on weekends with lots of good-natured noise from children enjoying the pools. The restaurant is open daily from 8am to 9pm.

VILLA BUENAVENTURA, Carretera Chapala-Jocotepec 13.5, San Juan Cosalá, Jal. 45900 (Apdo. Postal 181, Chapala, Jal. 45900). **Tel. 376/3-0050.** 6 condos, 9 villas (all with bath). TV

$ Rates: $55 1-bedroom condo for two; $80 2-bedroom condo for two; villa, add $12 to condo prices. **Parking:** Free.

Next to the Balneario San Juan Cosalá is its modern rival, with rooms spread out around a small interior shady lawn with a nice-size thermal/mineral-water pool. All of the rooms have thermal/mineral water in the tap and bath. The condominium units are in a two-story building and all have two bedrooms each with a private bath and a large shared thermal-water tub. The one- or two-bedroom villas are farther back on the property. Each has a nice fully equipped kitchen, dining room, and sitting areas in the large bedrooms. Four of the villas are large, with more stylish living room, kitchen with bar, and bubbling hot tubs in the bedrooms.

JOCOTEPEC

West of Ajijic, this small colonial-era village is becoming a center for weavers.

WHAT TO SEE & DO

Shopping

The highway through town becomes Hidalgo when it turns at the main plaza. Thursday is market day and the market is at the corner where the highway becomes Hidalgo.

Beginning on Hidalgo at the plaza you'll find several weavers' shops with locally loomed rugs and wall hangings.

WHERE TO STAY

POSADA DEL PESCADOR, Apdo. Postal 67, Jocotepec, Jal. **Tel. 376/3-0028.** 22 bungalows (all with bath). TEL

$ Rates: $20 bungalow for one; $28 bungalow for two.

This pretty motor inn is just east of Jocotepec. Its colonial-style bungalows are scattered around the swimming pool. Each apartment has a kitchenette, dining area, fireplace, bedroom, and bath. The office is frequently not staffed, but there's often someone who can help in the bungalow catercorner left from the back of the office. It's on the main highway, on the eastern edge of Jocotepec on the right if coming from Ajijic.

WHERE TO DINE

BAR JACAL, Miguel Arana Altos.
   Specialty: SNACKS/DRINKS.
$ **Prices:** Nachos $3; sandwiches $1.50–$3; beer $1.25; margarita $2.
   Open: Mon–Sat 6–11pm, Sun 10am–midnight.

To find this local watering hole, face the main plaza from the main street. On the right corner and upstairs (via a doorway without a sign) is the Bar Jacal overlooking Jocotepec's main street. It's a very casual place with equipales chairs and cloth-covered tables on an open, plant-filled balcony. The menu is mostly snack food that goes with a beer or margarita, such as queso fundido, hamburgers, burritos, and pizzas.

NEVADO DE TOLUCA, Hidalgo 158. Tel. 3-0622.
   Specialty: ICE CREAM.
$ **Prices:** Cone 90¢; one dip 50¢.
   Open: Daily 9am–8:30pm.

Good for a light treat if you're just in town shopping, this is the best ice cream in the area. Scoops are generous and two will fill up one of the huge waffle cones. There's another branch of this chain on the right side of the highway as you head back to Ajijic.

MAZAMITLA

A 3-hour drive from Guadalajara (70 miles south of Guadalajara and 45 miles south of Chapala), this mountain resort town (pop. 11,000, alt. 7,500 ft.) is a popular weekend getaway in the state of Jalisco. By bus, **Auto Transportes Mazamitla,** at Guadalajara's central bus station, has more than a dozen daily departures to Mazamitla. By car, the shortest way to get there from Guadalajara is by following the lake Highway 44 west through Chapala, Ajijic, and Jocotepec, after which it becomes Highway 15 south as it goes along the lake's southern shoreline. Just after Tuxcueca you'll see the right turn and crossroads with a sign to La Manzanilla and Mazamitla only 25 miles farther. (Most maps don't show the turnoff—trust me, it's there and the road is paved). The long way from Guadalajara is along Lake Chapala's eastern shore through La Barca and Sahuayo. Soon after the turnoff at Tuxcueca, the road climbs and winds through the mountains, the landscape becomes covered in oak and pine trees, and the climate changes from spring to winter. Bring a heavy sweater or jacket anytime of year. (Long johns and heavy socks might be called for at night in unheated hotels.) A few miles before Mazamitla is La Manzanilla, a pretty village in which you may want to take a few minutes to walk around the plaza.

Founded soon after the conquest of Mexico, Mazamitla, only 6 miles from the state of Michoacán, is architecturally more Michoacán than Jalisco. Wide wood-beamed rooflines support dark red-tiled roofs, with lots of pine balconies and window trim, all characteristic of Michoacán. It retains its colonial-era charm with the village and its cobblestone streets all branching out from the shady central plaza and church.

WHERE TO STAY

POSADA ALPINA, Portal Reforma 8, Mazamitla, Jal. Tel. 352/8-0104 or 36/41-0681 in Guadalajara. 18 rms.
$ Rates: $10 single; $20 double; triple $30.
Opposite the church and on the central plaza, this late 19th-century home has been converted into a rustically charming inn. Rooms in the front section with a large interior patio are part of the original home with polished plank floors and beamed ceilings. Those in the rear around a small patio have been added on and are smaller. Six of the rooms are large with three beds. Room no. 1 is one of these and opens onto the upper front porch which overlooks the plaza and church. Owner Guadalupe Toscano Hernandez will graciously help with directions or sightseeing suggestions.

POSADA LAS CHARRANDAS, Obregón 2, Mazamitla, Jal. Tel. 352/8-0254 or 36/14-9618 in Guadalajara. 10 rms.
$ Rates: $27 small room; $38 large room for two.
The Charrandas's natural pine exterior looks like it belongs in Switzerland and exudes the kind of quaint charm for which this village is known. The interior is brightly colored with orange walls, pine shutters and furniture, and fawn-colored tile floors. Rooms no. 5, 6, 7, and 8 have balconies with mountain views. Some rooms are a bit small, but cheery, and all come with one or two double beds. Owner Lourdes Azpeitia keeps the place spotless. There's a cozy restaurant off the lobby, open daily from 8am to 9pm.

HOTEL FIESTA MAZAMITLA, Reforma 6, Mazamitla, Jal. Tel. 352/8-0050. 24 rms (all with bath).
$ Rates: $10 single; $20 double; triple $30.
A half block off the central plaza, this new hotel, with a natural pine balcony, has rooms facing the street and interior rooms facing a small upstairs restaurant. The rooms all have tile floors, one or two double beds, and small bathrooms. Those facing the street are brighter, but may also come with a lot of street noise. The restaurant wasn't operating when I was there.

LA LLORONA COUNTRY CLUB, San Uriel 333, Col. Chapalita, Guadalajara, Jal. 45000. Tel. 36/47-5780. 10 cabañas (all with bath).
$ Rates: To be determined/expensive.
Just before you reach Mazamitla you'll see the sign on the right and highway leading to this new resort about 3 miles after you turn. The first 10 cabañas were nearing completion when I was there, and even though rates were not yet set, I would be remiss in not alerting you to this beautiful new development. The rock-walled cabañas with red-tile roofs are set widely apart, and are really small, beautiful two- and three-bedroom homes. All come with two bathrooms, sunken living room,

fireplace, spacious kitchen, dining room, and covered patio. They are the first part of a grand development, which is slated to include a hotel, golf course, tennis courts, riding club, swimming pool, and full-service country club. Whether or not anything except the cabañas are ever built may not matter. The forest setting with narrow lanes running by the cabañas makes it a secluded and beautiful getaway.

MONTE VERDE CENTRO RECREACIONAL, Calle Constitucional, Mazamitla, Jal. Tel. 36/16-1826. Fax 36/15-6812 in Guadalajara. 51 cabins (all with bath).
$ Rates: $85 small; $105 large; $105 5-night honeymoon package Sun–Thurs.

On the far edge of town, Mazamitla's original resort is spread over a mountain side surrounded by forest and gardens. Steep, paved streets wind past the Swiss-style cabins. Small cabins are those with two bedrooms, two bathrooms, kitchen/dining room, and fireplace, and sleep six to eight persons. Large cabins have three bedrooms, two living areas, kitchen, dining room, two bathrooms, and two fireplaces, and sleep eight to ten people. Most people bring their food and do their own cooking. It's the town's best-known and most popular inn and is always crowded in summer as well as all Mexican holidays and weekends. Off-times, especially weekdays, ask for a discount. To find the Monte Verde, from the main plaza go straight past the plaza (the church front will be on your right) on Reforma through town, and bear right with the main street. It's ahead on the left.

Dining: There's a small snack bar at the bottom of the resort which serves light snacks during the day. (It's an easy walk down, but a steep walk back up the hill.) The Restaurant Campestre La Carreta is across the street from the entrance to the resort and it's open for lunch and dinner.

Facilities: 3 tennis courts, volleyball, jogging path.

SIERRA PARAISO, Loma Bonita s/n, Mazamitla, Jal. Tel. 353/8-0044. 7 villas.
$ Rates: $31 double.

This, one of Mazamitla's most beautiful inns, is on three beautifully groomed and grass-filled levels edged with flowers and trees. The villas are spread about the grounds. Each one comes with a sunken living room facing a fireplace, kitchen open to the living room, wood and tile floors, and one, two, or three bedrooms. The master bedroom has a king-size bed while other bedrooms have a bunk bed and a double bed. Each villa has a furnished patio and grill for cooking outdoors. The Sierra Paraiso is straight ahead, up the hill from the Monte Verde Centro Recreacional mentioned above.

WHERE TO DINE

RESTAURANT POSADA MAZAMITLA, Hidalgo 2 at Reforma. Tel. 8-0161.
   Specialty: REGIONAL/MEXICAN.
$ Prices: Breakfast $2.50–$3.50; main courses $3–$4.
   Open: Daily 8:30am–6pm.

On one corner of the square behind a small market, you'll find this popular restaurant fashioned out of an old home with a covered interior courtyard. Main courses are usually pork and beef, but there are lighter choices of beans, quesadillas, and soup, all very inexpensive.

LA BUENA, Av. 16 de Septiembre 1. Tel. 8-0114.
   Specialty: MEXICAN.
$ **Prices:** Breakfast $3; comida corrida $3.50; tacos 3 for $1.
   Open: Daily 8am–9pm.

If you're on a budget, this two-story restaurant is a good bet. It's on the left around the left corner from the Posada Alpina and ½ block from the plaza. There's a different three-course comida corrida daily. Evenings, owner Luz María Cárdenas de Elisonto, who is also the cook, serves up tostadas, tacos, and enchiladas at very reasonable prices.

RESTAURANT CAMPESTRE LA TROJE, Galeana 53. Tel. 8-0070.
   Specialty: REGIONAL/MEXICAN.
$ **Prices:** Main courses $5–$8; appetizers $2.75–$10.
   Open: Daily 8am–7pm.

Campestre (country) restaurants are popular in this region and this one is certainly deserving of the crowds. Service is excellent and it's known for charcoal-grilled meat platters which come with rice and beans. Their specialties include chicken, beef, or shrimp fajitas (or a combination of the three), shrimp four different ways, and beef brochet. The restaurant is at the crossroads immediately outside Mazamitla on the road leading to the highway and Chapala.

WHAT TO SEE & DO

Although this picturesque resort town is largely devoted to relaxing and strolling the streets, self-guided mountain hiking is one active option. Mazamitla is among several area villages where you can buy locally made cheese and rompope, and home canned fruits temptingly displayed in glass jars. The town's patron, Saint Christopher, is honored with a large **festival** the last Sunday in July. Count on hotels being full during that festivity and for all major Mexican holidays and most weekends. If you'd like to come just for the day, and look the town over, **Viajes Copenhagen** in Guadalajara (tel. 36/21-1008) offers a day-trip with picnic lunch.

TAPALPA

Another tidy, 16th-century mountain resort town, Tapalpa (pop. 10,000, alt. 6,000 ft.) is located almost equidistant south from Guadalajara (133 miles) and north from Manzanillo (158 miles). In either direction, the trip takes about 3 hours one-way. From either Guadalajara or Manzanillo there's a turnoff from the toll road (Highway 110) to Tapalpa. Once you leave the toll road you're less than 20 miles from Tapalpa and the road begins to wind up through the mountains. If you drive from Manzanillo you'll pass the enormous, almost-dry lakebed of Sayula, which at certain times of year is a mecca for migrating birds.

The pavement gives over to cobblestones at the edge of town and the streets are lined with whitewashed, red-tile roofed buildings. Smaller and less bustling than Mazamitla, it's built around a lovely central plaza and dominated by an enormous

18th-century church dedicated to the Purísima Concepción. Arcaded buildings more than 200 years old surround the central plaza. The locally maintained **tourism office** is on Portal Morelos on the main square. Printed information is scarce there, but you can try asking questions. It's open Monday through Friday from 9:30am to 2pm and Saturday from 4:30pm to 8pm. There's a **bank** on the plaza as well. The **gas station** on the edge of town may not have unleaded gas.

WHERE TO STAY

All three hotels below are on the same side of the street facing the central plaza.

POSADA DE LA FUENTE, Matamoros 69. Tapalpa, Jal. 49340. Tel. 343/20189. 8 rms (all with bath).
$ Rates: $72 1 bedroom; $110 2 bedroom.
The front part of this hotel is a 200-year-old home built around a beautiful courtyard. High-ceilinged rooms with beamed ceilings and polished plank floors flank three sides and make up the reception area, restaurant, and gift shop. The eight cozy guest rooms, which are all new construction, are built around another courtyard in back. Designed with families in mind, the rooms with one bedroom can sleep four people. Those with two bedrooms have a master bedroom and bath downstairs and a large bedroom upstairs with four single beds. The drawback is only one small bathroom in each room. But the rooms are handsomely furnished with soft comforters, wood floors, rock and brick walls, and many Mexican decorative details.

POSADA LA HACIENDA, Matamoros 7, Tapalpa, Jal. 49340. Tel. 343/2-0193. 31 rms and bungalows.
$ Rates: $13 single; $17 double; $33 1-bedroom bungalow; $40 2-bedroom bungalow; $47 3-bedroom bungalow.
On the corner, opposite the central square, this clean hostelry is grouped around two large patios. Rooms are simply furnished with pine furniture, and tile floors. All come with kitchen and dining area. Some have balconies and fireplaces. The bungalows are more spacious rooms around the back patio.

HOTEL TAPALPA, Matamoros 35, Tapalpa, Jal. 49340. Tel. 343/2-0607. 13 rms (all with bath).
$ Rates: $11 single; $16 double.
This is a good budget choice on the central plaza. Rooms in the two-story hotel are simple and clean. Each has either one or two double beds, tile floors, and small all-tile bathrooms.

WHERE TO DINE

Roasted lamb (borrego) is the town specialty and, on weekends and holidays especially, restaurants all over town and lining the highway cook the meat over open fires.

RESTAURANT HACIENDA BUENAVISTA, Portal Morelos, upstairs. Tel. 2-0233.

Specialty: MEXICAN.
$ Prices: Main courses $2–$3.50.
Open: Thurs–Tues 8:30am–9:30pm.

From the upper floor of an old mansion you can sit inside in the large, simply furnished dining room, or out on the narrow balcony and watch what's happening on the plaza. Choose from chicken and beef main courses or for something lighter, try quesadillas or birria.

RESTAURANT TAPALPA, Matamoros 35. Tel. 2-0607.
Specialty: MEXICAN.
$ Prices: Breakfast $2; main courses $2.50–$3.75.
Open: Wed–Mon 9am–9:30pm.

Next to the Hotel Tapalpa on the main square is this clean, large lunchroom with cloth-covered tables and pine furniture. The menu offers traditional Mexican specialties such as chicken in mole sauce, carne asada, chiles rellenos, and smoked pork.

RESTAURANT TAPALPA BORREGO, Hidalgo 275. Tel. 2-0156.
Specialty: BORREGO/ROASTED LAMB.
$ Prices: Borrego dinner $5.50; borrego birria $3.50.

You'll pass this pleasant patio-centered restaurant on the right as you drive in from the main highway. But there's no sign. Metal tables and chairs under a covering line one wall of the patio. The main dish, of course, is delicious and tender borrego which comes with salsa, tortillas, and beans. The ribs have little meat, so ask for leg meat (pierna). On weekends they make borrego birria. It's about 2 blocks from the main square, walking towards the highway.

WHAT TO DO

Hiking

Like Mazamitla, self-guided walks around town and in the mountains are what most people do when they aren't relaxing. The 300-foot **Nogales waterfall,** almost 20 miles from Tapalpa, is a pleasant place to hike. You'll have to leave your car a distance from the falls and walk the rest of the way. There are modest paths to follow and the bird life may prove interesting depending on the time of year. You could see deer and fox as well. Ask directions in town for how to get there. Another local diversion, **Las Piedrotas** (the rocks), is a strange outcropping of large rocks. Ask directions to them.

Shopping

Several shops around the central plaza sell wood carvings from Michoacán—napkin holders, Christmas ornaments, etc. The gift shop of the **Hacienda de las Fuentes** has a fine selection of Mexican and Guatemalan crafts. As in Mazamitla you'll see jars of home-canned fruit, stacks of cheese, and bottles of rompope for sale. Three blocks from the main square is the **Cooperativo Ojo Zarco de Tapalpa,** Ignacio López 266 (tel. 2-0165), open daily from 9am to 6pm. Here you can buy reasonably priced, nicely designed lambswool sweaters knitted locally. Back of the showroom, men machine-card the wool and dye the yarn. Besides sweaters knitted by women, a number of men in town loom rugs and serapes. **Jesús Delgado,** Independencia 140, may have a good selection to choose from. He sells from the patio of his family home and prices are by weight per kilo.

APPENDIX

FOR YOUR INFORMATION

A. VOCABULARY
B. MENU SAVVY
C. CONVERSION TABLES

A. VOCABULARY

Traveling on or off the beaten track, you will encounter many people in service positions who do not speak English. Many Mexicans who can understand English are embarrassed to speak it. And finally most Mexicans are very patient with foreigners who try to speak their language; it helps a lot to know a few basic phrases.

Berlitz's Latin American Spanish for Travellers, available at most bookstores for $4, cannot be recommended highly enough. But for added convenience, I've included a list of certain simple phrases for expressing basic needs, followed by some menu items presented in the same order in which they'd be found on a Mexican menu.

BASIC VOCABULARY

English	Spanish	Pronunciation
Good day	Buenos días	bway-nohss *dee*-ahss
How are you?	¿Cómo esta usted?	koh-moh ess-*tah* oo-sted
Very well	Muy bien	mwee byen
Thank you	Gracias	*grah*-see-ahss
You're welcome	De nada	day *nah*-dah
Good-bye	Adios	ah-dyo*hss*
Please	Por favor	pohr *fah*-bohr
Yes	Sí	see
No	No	noh
Excuse me	Perdóneme	pehr-*doh*-ney-may
Give me	Déme	*day*-may
Where is . . . ?	¿Dónde esta . . . ?	*dohn*-day ess-*tah*
The station	la estación	la ess-tah-see-*own*
A hotel	un hotel	oon *oh*-tel
A gas station	una gasolinera	oon-nuh gah-so-lee-*nay*-rah
A restaurant	un restaurante	oon res-tow-*rahn*-tay
The toilet	el baño	el *bahn*-yoh
A good doctor	un buen médico	oon bwayn *may*-dee-co
The road to . . .	el camino a . . .	el cah-*mee*-noh ah
To the right	A la derecha	ah lah day-*ray*-chuh

English	Spanish	Pronunciation
To the left	**A la izquierda**	ah lah ees-ky-*ehr*-dah
Straight ahead	**Derecho**	day-*ray*-cho
I would like	**Quisiera**	keyh-see-*air*-ah
I want	**Quiero**	kyehr-oh
To eat	**comer**	*ko*-mayr
A room	**una habitación**	oon-nuh ha-bee tah-see-*own*
Do you have?	**¿Tiene usted?**	tyah-nay *oos*-ted
How much is it?	**¿Cuanto cuesta?**	kwahn-to kwess-tah
When?	**¿Cuando?**	*kwahn*-doh
What?	**¿Que?**	kay
There is (Is there?)	**¿Hay . . .**	eye
Yesterday	**Ayer**	*ah*-yer
Today	**Hoy**	oy
Tomorrow	**Mañana**	mahn-*yawn*-ah
Good	**Bueño**	*bway*-no
Bad	**Malo**	*mah*-lo
Better (best)	**(Lo) Mejor**	(loh) meh-*hor*
More	**Más**	mahs
Less	**Menos**	*may*-noss
No Smoking	**Se prohibe fumar**	seh pro-*hee*-beh foo-*mahr*
Postcard	**Tarjeta postal**	tahr-*hay*-ta pohs-*tahl*
Insect repellent	**Rapellante contra insectos**	rah-pey-*yahn*-te cohn-trah een-*sehk*-tos

1 **uno** (ooh-noh)
2 **dos** (dohs)
3 **tres** (trayss)
4 **cuatro** (kwah-troh)
5 **cinco** (seen-koh)
6 **seis** (sayss)
7 **siete** (syeh-tay)
8 **ocho** (oh-choh)
9 **nueve** (nway-bay)
10 **diez** (dee-ess)
11 **once** (ohn-say)
12 **doce** (doh-say)
13 **trece** (tray-say)
14 **catorce** (kah-tor-say)
15 **quince** (*keen*-say)
16 **dieciseis** (de-ess-ee-*sayss*)
17 **diecisiete** (de-ess-ee-see-*ay*-tay)
18 **dieciocho** (dee-ess-ee-*oh*-choh)
19 **diecinueve** (dee-ess-ee-*nway*-bay)
20 **veinte** (*bayn*-tay)
30 **treinta** (*trayn*-tah)
40 **cuarenta** (kwah-*ren*-tah)
50 **cincuenta** (seen-*kwen*-tah)
60 **sesenta** (say-*sen*-tah)
70 **setenta** (say-*ten*-tah)
80 **ochenta** (oh-*chen*-tah)
90 **noventa** (noh-*ben*-tah)
100 **cien** (see-*en*)
200 **doscientos** (dos-se-*en*-tos)
500 **quinientos** (keen-ee-*ehn*-tos)
1,000 **mil** (meal)

USEFUL PHRASES

Do you speak English? **¿Habla usted inglés?**

Is there anyone here who speaks English? **¿Hay alguien aquí qué hable inglés?**

I don't understand Spanish very well. **No lo entiendo muy bien el español.**

What time is it? **¿Qué hora es?**

May I see your menu? **¿Puedo ver su menu?**
The check, please. **La cuenta por favor.**
What do I owe you? **¿Cuanto lo debo?**
What did you say? **¿Mande? (colloquial expression for American "Eh?")**
I want (to see) a room **Quiero (ver) un cuarto (una habitación)**
for two persons **para dos personas**
with (without) bath. **con (sin) baño**
We are staying here only 1 night (1 week). **Nos quedaremos aqui solamente una noche (una semana).**
We are leaving tomorrow. **Partimos mañana.**
Do you accept traveler's checks? **¿Acepta usted cheques de viajero?**

BUS TERMS

Autobus Bus
Camión Bus or truck
Carril Lane
Directo Nonstop
Equipajes Baggage (claim area)
Foraneo Intercity
Guarda equipaje Luggage storage area
Llegadas Gates
Local Originates at this station
De Paso Originates elsewhere; stops if s[eats] available
Primera First (class)
Recibo de Equipajes Baggage-claim ar[ea]
Sala de Espera Waiting room
Sanitarios Toilets
Segunda Second (class)
Sin Escala Nonstop
Taquilla Ticket window

POSTAL TERMS

Aduana Customs
Apdo. Postal Post office box (abbreviation)
Buzón Mailbox
Correo Aéreo Airmail
Correos Postal service
Entrega Inmediata Special Delivery, Express
Estampilla or Timbre Stamp
Giro Postal Money order
Lista de Correos General Delivery
Oficina de Correos Post office
Paquete Parcel
Registrado Registered Mail
Seguros Insurance (insured mail)
Sello Rubber Stamp

B. MENU SAVVY

BREAKFAST (DESAYUNO)

Jugo de naranja orange juice
Café con crema coffee with cream
Pan tostada toast
Mermelada jam
Leche milk
Té tea
Huevos eggs
Huevos cocidos hard-boiled eggs
Huevos poches poached eggs
Huevos fritos fried eggs
Huevos pasados al agua soft-boiled eggs
Huevos revueltos scrambled eggs
Tocino bacon
Jamón ham

LUNCH, SUPPER & DINNER [ALMUERZO, COMIDA & CENA]

SOUP [SOPA]

Caldo broth
Caldo de pollo chicken broth
Menudo tripe soup
Sopa clara consomme
Sopa de lentejas lentil soup
Sopa de chicharos pea soup
Sopa de medula bone-marrow soup

SEAFOOD [MARISCOS]

Almejas clams
Anchoas anchovies
Arenques herring
Atun tuna
Bagre catfish
Cabrilla black sea bass
Calamares squid
Camarones shrimp
Caracoles snails
Corvina bass
Dorado dolphinfish
Gallo roosterfish
Huachinango red snapper
Jaiba crab
Jurel yellowtail
Langosta lobster
Lenguado sole
Lobina black bass
Macabi bonefish
Marlin azul blue marlin
Marlin blanco white marlin
Marlin rayado striped marlin
Mero grouper
Mojarra perch
Ostiones oysters
Pescado fish
Peto wahoo
Pez espada swordfish
Pez vela sailfish
Robalo sea bass/snook
Sabalo tarpon
Salmón salmon
Salmón ahumado smoked salmon
Sardinas sardines
Solo pike
Trucha arco iris rainbow trout

MEATS [CARNES]

Ahumado smoked
Alambre shish kebab
Albóndigas meatballs
Aves poultry
Bistec steak
Cabeza de ternera calf's head
Cabrito kid (goat)
Callos tripe
Carne meat
Carne fría cold cuts
Cerdo pork
Chiles rellenos stuffed peppers
Chicharrones pigskin cracklings
Chorizo spicy sausage
Chuleta chop
Chuleta de carnero mutton chop
Chuletas de cordero lamb chops
Chuletas de puerco pork chops
Conejo rabbit
Cordero lamb
Costillas de cerdo spareribs
Faisán pheasant
Filete de ternera filet of veal
Filete milanesa breaded veal chops
Ganso goose
Hígado liver
Jamón ham
Lengua tongue
Lomo loin
Paloma pigeon
Pato duck
Pavo turkey
Pechuga chicken breast
Perdiz partridge

Pierna leg
Pollo chicken
Res beef
Riñones kidneys
Salchichas sausages
Ternera veal
Tocino bacon
Venado venison

VEGETABLES [LEGUMBRES]

Aguacate avocado
Aceitunas olives
Arroz rice
Betabeles beets
Cebolla onions
Champinones mushrooms
Chicharos peas
Col cabbage
Coliflor cauliflower
Ejotes string beans
Elote corn (maize)
Entremeses hors d'oeuvres
Esparragos asparagus
Espinaca spinach
Frijoles beans
Hongos mushroom
Jícama potato/turnip–like vegetable
Lechuga lettuce
Lentejas lentils
Papas potatoes
Pepino cucumber
Rabanos radishes
Tomate tomato
Verduras greens, vegetables
Zanahoras carrots

SALADS [ENSALADAS]

Ensalada de apio celery salad
Ensalada de frutas fruit salad
Ensalada mixta mixed salad
Ensalada de pepinos cucumber salad
Guacamole avocado salad
Lechuga lettuce salad

FRUITS [FRUTAS]

Chavacano apricot
Ciruela prune
Coco coconut
Durazno peach
Frambuesa raspberry
Fresas con crema strawberries with cream
Fruta cocida stewed fruit
Granada pomegranate
Guanabana green pearlike fruit
Guayaba guava
Higos figs
Lima lime
Limón lemon
Mamey sweet orange fruit
Mango mango
Manzana apple
Naranja orange
Pera pear
Piña pineapple
Platano banana
Tuna prickly pear fruit
Uva grape
Zapote sweet brown fruit

DESSERTS [POSTRES]

Arroz con leche rice pudding
Brunelos de fruta fruit tart
Coctel de aguacate avocado cocktail
Coctel de frutas fruit cocktail
Compota stewed fruit
Fruta fruit
Flan custard
Galletas crackers or cookies
Helado ice cream

Nieve sherbet
Pastel cake or pastry
Queso cheese
Torta cake
Yogurt yogurt

BEVERAGES [BEBIDAS]

Agua water
Brandy brandy
Café coffee
Café con crema coffee with cream
Café de olla coffee with cinnamon and sugar
Café negro black coffee
Cerveza beer
Ginebra gin
Hielo ice
Jerez sherry
Jugo de naranja orange juice
Jugo de tomate tomato juice
Jugo de toronja grapefruit juice
Leche milk
Licores liqueurs
Manzanita apple juice
Refrescos soft drinks
Ron rum
Sidra cider
Sifón soda
Té tea
Vaso de leche glass of milk
Vino blanco white wine
Vino tinto red wine

CONDIMENTS & CUTLERY

Aceite oil
Ajo garlic
Azúcar sugar
Bolillo roll
Copa goblet
Cilantro coriander
Cuchara spoon
Cuchillo knife
Manteca lard
Mantequilla butter
Mostaza mustard
Pan bread
Pimienta pepper
Sal salt
Sopa de arroz plain rice
Taza cup
Tenedor fork
Tostada toast
Vinagre vinegar
Vaso glass

PREPARATIONS

A la parrilla grilled
Al horno baked
Asado roasted
Bien cocido well done
Cocido cooked
Cocina casera home cooking
Empanado breaded
Frito fried
Milanesa Italian breaded
Poco cocido rare
Tampiqueño long strip of thinly sliced meat
Veracruzana tomato, garlic, and onion-topped

MENU ITEMS

Achiote Small red seed of the annatto tree
Achiote preparada A prepared paste found in Yucatán markets made of ground achiote, wheat and corn flour, cumin, cinnamon, salt, onion, garlic, oregano; use mixed with juice of a sour orange or vinegar and put on broiled or charcoaled fish (tikin chick) and chicken

Agua fresca Fruit-flavored water, usually watermelon, cantaloupe, chia seed with lemon, hibiscus flour, or ground melon-seed mixture

Antojito A Mexican snack, usually masa based with a variety of toppings such as sausage, cheese, beans, onions; also refers to tostadas, sopes, and garnachas

Atole A thick, lightly sweet, warm drink made with finely ground rice or corn and flavored usually with vanilla; often found mornings and evenings at markets

Birote Similar to a bolillo, but rounder and used often as a dinner roll or for sandwiches around Lake Chapala

Birria Lamb or goat meat cooked in a tomato broth spiced with garlic, chiles, cumin, ginger, oregano, cloves, cinnamon, thyme, and garnished with onions and cilantro and fresh lime juice to taste; a specialty of Jalisco state

Borrego al pastor A specialty around Tapalpa, Jalisco, is roast lamb basted and cooked over an open wood fire

Botana A light Mexican snack—an antojito

Buñelos Round, thin, deep-fried crispy fritters dipped in sugar or dribbled with honey

Burrito A large flour tortilla stuffed with beans or sometimes potatoes and onions

Cabrito Roast kid; a northern Mexico delicacy

Cajeta Caramelized cow or goat milk often used in dessert crêpes

Caldo Michi A Lake Chapala specialty of catfish soup in a base of onions and tomatoes

Carnitas Pork that's been deep-cooked (not fried) in lard, then steamed and served with corn tortillas for tacos

Caviar de Chapala Carp eggs, usually seasoned and fried and made into tacos or soup

Ceviche Fresh raw seafood marinated in fresh lime juice and garnished with chopped tomatoes, onions, chiles, and sometimes cilantro and served with crispy, fried whole corn tortillas; in Colima sailfish is preferred and they use less lime in the preparation

Charales Dried minnows, a specialty around Lake Chapala and Lake Pátzcuaro, served with lime and sprinkle of chile pepper

Chayote Vegetable pear or mirliton, a type of spiny squash boiled and served as an accompaniment to meat dishes

Chiles rellenos Poblano peppers usually stuffed with cheese, rolled in a batter and baked; but other stuffings may include ground beef spiced with raisins

Chorizo A spicy red pork sausage, flavored with different chiles and sometimes with achiote, or cumin and other spices

Churro Tube-shaped bread fritter, dipped in sugar and sometimes filled with cajeta or chocolate

Cilantro An herb grown from the coriander seed, chopped and used in salsas and soups

Cochinita pibil Pig wrapped in banana leaves, flavored with pibil sauce and pit-baked; common in Yucatán

Corunda A triangular-shaped tamal wrapped in a corn leaf, a Michoacán specialty

Enchilada Tortilla dipped in a sauce and usually filled with chicken or white cheese and sometimes topped with tomato sauce and sour cream (enchiladas suizas—Swiss enchiladas) or covered in a green sauce (enchiladas verdes) or topped with onions, sour crcam and guacamole (enchiladas potosiños)

Epazote Leaf of the wormseed plant, used in black beans, and with cheese in quesadillas

Escabeche A lightly pickled sauce used in Yucatán chicken stew

Frijoles boda A specialty of Colima, "married beans" are refried beans (*frijoles refritos*) mixed with bacon, guajillo chile, and black pepper and sprinkled with dry cheese

Frijoles charros Beans flavored with beer, a northern Mexico specialty

Frijoles refritos Pinto beans mashed and cooked with lard

Garnachas A thickish small circle of fried masa with pinched sides, topped with pork or chicken, onions, and avocado, or sometimes chopped potatoes and tomatoes, typical as a botana in Veracruz and Yucatán

Gorditas Thickish fried corn tortillas, slit and stuffed with choice of cheese, beans, beef, chicken, with or without lettuce, tomato, and onion garnish

Guacamole Mashed avocado, plain or mixed with onions and other spices

Gusanos de maguey Maguey worms, considered a delicacy and delicious when charbroiled to a crisp and served with corn tortillas for tacos

Horchata Refreshing drink made of ground rice or melon seeds, ground almonds, and lightly sweetened

Huevos mexicanos Scrambled eggs with onions, hot peppers, and tomatoes

Huevos motuleños Eggs atop a tortilla, garnished with beans, peas, ham, sausage, and grated cheese, a Yucatecan specialty

Huevos rancheros Fried egg on top of a fried corn tortilla covered in a tomato sauce

Huitlacoche Sometimes spelled "cuitlacoche," mushroom-flavored black fungus that appears on corn in the rainy season; considered a delicacy

Machaca Shredded dried beef scrambled with eggs or as salad topping; a specialty of northern Mexico

Manchamantel Translated means "tablecloth stainer," a stew of chicken or pork with chiles, tomatoes, pineapple, bananas, and jícama

Masa Ground corn soaked in lime used as basis for tamales, corn tortillas, and soups

Menudo A stew made with cow entrails; Jalisco style is without ground masa (corn) but with a tomato base, spiced with oregano and chile arbol and often with a few leaves of yerba buena

Mixiote Lamb or chicken baked with carrots, potatoes, and sauce in parchment paper from a maguey leaf

Mole Pronounced "*moh*-lay," a sauce made with 20 ingredients including chocolate, peppers, ground tortillas, sesame seeds, cinnamon, tomatoes, onion, garlic, peanuts, pumpkin seeds, cloves, and tomatillos; developed by colonial nuns in Puebla, usually served over chicken or turkey; especially served in Puebla, state of Mexico, and Oaxaca with sauces varying from red to black and brown

Molletes A bolillo cut in half and topped with refried beans and cheese, then broiled; popular at breakfast

Pan de muerto Sweet or plain bread made around the Days of the Dead (November 1–2), in the form of mummies, dolls, or round with bone designs

Pan dulce Lightly sweetened bread in many configurations, usually served at breakfast or bought at any bakery

Papadzules Tortillas are stuffed with hard-boiled eggs and seeds (cucumber or sunflower) in a tomato sauce

Pavo relleno negro Stuffed turkey, Yucatán style, filled with chopped pork and beef, cooked in a rich, dark sauce

Pibil Pit-baked pork or chicken in a sauce of tomato, onion, mild red pepper, cilantro, and vinegar

Pipian Sauce made with ground pumpkin seeds, nuts, and mild peppers

Poc-chuc Slices of pork with onion marinated in a tangy sour orange sauce and charcoal-broiled; a Yucatecan specialty

Pozole A soup made with hominy and pork or chicken, in either a tomato based broth Jalisco-style, or a white broth Nayarit-style, or green chile sauce Guerrero-style, and topped with choice of chopped white onion, lettuce or cabbage, radishes, oregano, red pepper, and cilantro

Pulque Drink made of fermented sap of the maguey plant; best in state of Hidalgo and around Mexico City

Quesadilla Flour tortilla stuffed with melted white cheese and lightly fried or warmed

Queso relleno "Stuffed cheese" is a mild yellow cheese stuffed with minced meat and spices, a Yucatecan specialty

Rompope Delicious Mexican eggnog, invented in Puebla, made with eggs, vanilla, sugar, and rum

Salsa mexicana Sauce of fresh chopped tomatoes, white onions, and cilantro with a bit of oil; on tables all over Mexico

Salsa verde A cooked sauce using the green tomatillo and puréed with mildly hot peppers, onions, garlic, and cilantro; on tables countrywide

Sopa de calabaza Soup made of chopped squash or pumpkin blossoms

Sopa de lima A tangy soup made with chicken broth and accented with fresh lime; popular in Yucatán

Sopa seca Not a soup at all, but a seasoned rice which translated means "dry soup"

Sopa Tarascan A rib sticking pinto bean–based soup, flavored with onions, garlic, tomatoes, chiles, and chicken broth and garnished with sour cream, white cheese, avocado chunks, and fried tortilla strips; a specialty of Michoacán state

Sopa Tlalpeña A hearty soup made with chunks of chicken, chopped carrots, zucchini, corn, onions, garlic, and cilantro

Sopa tortilla A traditional chicken broth–based soup, seasoned with chiles, tomatoes, onion, and garlic, bobbing with crisp fried strips of corn tortillas

Sope Pronounced "*soh*-pay," a botana similar to a garnacha, except spread with refried beans and topped with crumbled cheese and onions

Tacos al pastor Thin slices of flavored pork roasted on a revolving cylinder dripping with onion slices and juice of fresh pineapple slice

Tamal Incorrectly called tamale (*tamal* singular, *tamales* plural), meat or sweet filling rolled with fresh masa then wrapped in a corn husk, a corn or banana leaf and steamed; many varieties and sizes throughout the country

Tepache Drink made of fermented pineapple peelings and brown sugar

Tikin xic Also seen on menus as "tikin chick," charbroiled fish brushed with achiote sauce

Tinga A stew made with pork tenderloin, sausage, onions, garlic, tomatoes, chiles, and potatoes; popular on menus in Puebla and Hidalgo states

Torta Sandwich, usually on bolillo bread, usually with sliced avocado, onions, tomatoes, with a choice of meat and often cheese

Torta ahogados A specialty of Lake Chapala is made with scooped out roll, filled with beans and beef strips, and seasoned with either a tomato or chile sauce

Tostadas Crispy fried corn tortillas topped with meat, onions, lettuce tomatoes, cheese, avocados, and sometimes sour cream

Venado Venison (deer) served perhaps as pipian de venado, steamed in banana leaves and served with a sauce of ground squash seeds

Xtabentun Pronounced "*shtah*-ben-toon," a Yucatán liquor made of fermented honey, and flavored with anise; it comes seco (dry) or crema (sweet)

Zacahuil Pork leg tamal, packed in thick masa, wrapped in banana leaves and pit baked; sometimes pot-made with tomato and masa; specialty of mid- to upper Veracruz

C. CONVERSION TABLES

METRIC MEASURES

Length

1 millimeter	=	0.04 inches (or less than 1/16 in)
1 centimeter	=	0.39 inches (or just under ½ in)
1 meter	=	1.09 inches (or about 39 inches)
1 kilometer	=	0.62 miles (or about ⅔ of a mile)

To convert kilometers to miles, multiply the number of kilometers by .62 (for example, 25 km × .62 = 15.5mi).

To convert miles to kilometers, multiply the number of miles by 1.61 (for example, 50 mi × 1.61 = 80.5 km).

Capacity

1 liter = 33.92 fluid ounces or 1.06 quarts or 0.26 gallons.

To convert liters to gallons, multiply the number of liters by 0.26 (for example, 50 liters × .26 = 13 gallons).

To convert gallons to liters, multiply the number of gallons by 3.79 (for example, 10 gal × 3.79 = 37.9 liters).

Weight

1 gram	=	0.04 ounces (or about a paperclip's weight)
1 kilogram	=	2.2 pounds

To convert kilograms to pounds, multiply the number of kilograms by 2.2 (for example, 75kg × 2.2 = 165 pounds).

To convert pounds to kilograms, multiply the number of pounds by 0.45 (for example, 90 lb × .45 = 40.5 kg).

Temperature

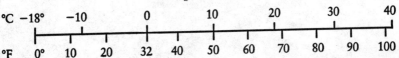

To convert degrees C to degrees F, multiply degrees °C by 9, divide by 5, and add 32 (for example 9/5 × 20°C + 32 = 68°F).
To convert degrees F to degrees C, subtract 32 from degrees F, then multiply by 5, and divide by 9 (for example, 85°F − 32 × 5/9 = 29°C).

CLOTHING SIZE EQUIVALENTS

You'll want to try on clothing you intend to buy, but here are some equivalents in case you're buying gifts for friends. Note that women's blouse sizes are the same in the U.S. and Mexico.

Women's				Men's					
Dress		Shoes		Collar		Jacket		Shoes	
U.S.	Mex.	U.S.	Mex.	U.S.	Mex.	U.S.	Mex.	U.S.	Mex.
6	36	5	35	14	36	38	48	8	41
8	38	5.5	35.5	14.5	37	40	50	8.5	41.5
10	40	6	36	15	38	42	52	9	42
12	42	6.5	36.5	15.5	39	44	54	9.5	42.5
14	44	7	37	16	40	46	56	10	43
16	46	7.5	37.5	16.5	41	48	58	10.5	43.5
18	48	8	38	17	42	50	60	11	44
20	50	8.5	38.5	17.5	43	52	62	11.5	44.5
22	52	9	39	18	44	54	64	12	45

INDEX

GENERAL INFORMATION

AAA discounts and services, 54, 62, 66
Abbreviations of Mexican words, 63
Accommodations: see ACCOMMODATIONS *index*
Adventure/wilderness travel, 47–8
Airfares, 51
Airlines, 50–1, 54–5, 71–3, 118, 119, 155–6
　charters, 51
　regional flights around country, 54–5
Airport taxes, 55
Air travel:
　to and from Guadalajara, 155–7
　to and from Manzanillo, 118–19
　to and from Puerto Vallarta, 71–3
Ajijic, 208–15
　accommodations, 208–10
　dining, 212–14
　shopping, 214–15
　sights and attractions, 214–15
Alternate/adventure travel, 47–8
Altitude sickness, 41
American Express:
　Guadalajara, 162
　Manzanillo, 123
　Puerto Vallarta, 77
Art galleries, Puerto Vallarta, 107–8
Attractions: see SIGHTS & ATTRACTIONS *index*
Automobile organizations, 54, 62, 66

Bar scene:
　Guadalajara, 192–4
　Manzanillo, 140
　Puerto Vallarta, 108–9
Baskets, shopping for, 48
Beaches:
　Manzanillo, 139
　Puerto Vallarta, 102–3, 106
　San Blas, 113
Birding, Manzanillo, 139
Boat trips:
　from Barra de Navidad, 143
　from Puerto Vallarta, 102
Botaneros, 131
Bribes, 34–5
Bugs and bites, 41
Bullfights:
　Guadalajara, 190–1
　Puerto Vallarta, 103
Business hours, 63
Bus travel:
　to and from Chapala, 200
　to and within Guadalajara, 156, 157
　within Manzanillo, 122–3
　to Mexico, 51
　within Mexico, 57–8
　within Puerto Vallarta, 77

Cameras and film, 63
Camping, general information about, 62
Cantera stone, shopping for, 48
Careyes, 147–50
Carnaval, 37
Car rentals in Mexico, 58–60
　Guadalajara, 161
Cars and driving, 51–4
　accidents, 62

auto insurance, Mexican, 52–3
breakdowns, 61
car papers, 52
crossing the border, 53–4
driving around Mexico, 58–62, 72, 157
parking, 62
Charter flights, 51
Chapala, 200–8
　accommodations, 201–4
　dining, 204–7
　lake tours, 207–8
　sights and attractions, 207–8
　tourist information, 201
Cigarettes, buying, 63
Cockfights, Guadalajara, 191
Colima, 151–3
Comala, 153–4
Crafts and folk art, Puerto Vallarta, 107
Credit cards, 32–3
Cruises to Mexico, 54
Currency exchange, 31–2
Customs, 31, 63
Cuyutlán, 151

Dentists, 63
Día di Guadalupe, 39, 106
Disabled travelers, tips for, 44
Discos, Puerto Vallarta, 109–10
Diseases prevalent in Mexico, 41–2
Diving, Puerto Vallarta, 103
Doctors, 63
Drug laws, 63–4
Drugstores, 64

Ecology-oriented adventure travel, 47–8
Electricity, 64
Embassies and consulates, 64–5
Emergencies, 65
Entertainment and nightlife: *see specific city names*
Entry requirements, 30–1
Equipale furniture, shopping for, 48
Etiquette, 65

Families, tips for, 46–7
Family stays for students, 47
Fast Facts: Mexico, 62–70
Ferries from Baja California, 62, 72
Fishing:
　Barra de Navidad, 143
　Manzanillo, 139
　Puerto Vallarta, 103–4, 106

Gasoline, 60
Glass, shopping for, 48
Golf:
　Ajijic, 207
　Chapala, 207
　Manzanillo, 139
　Puerto Vallarta, 104
Guadalajara:
　accommodations: see ACCOMMODATIONS *index*
　arriving, 155–7
　bullfights, 190–1
　bus service to and around, 57, 156, 157–8, 160–1
　city layout, 158–60

Guadalajara: *(cont'd)*
  cockfights, 191
  colectivos, 161
  dance clubs and discos, 194
  departing, 157-8
  excursions from, 195-223
  fast facts, 162-4
  getting around, 160-2
  getting there, 155-7
  horse-drawn carriages, 161-2
  layout, 158-60
  neighborhoods, 158-60
  nightlife, 192-4
  organized tours, 188
  orientation, 155-60
  restaurants: *see* RESTAURANTS *index*
  rodeos, 191
  shopping, 191-2
  sights and attractions: *see* SIGHTS & ATTRACTIONS *index*
  special events, 188-90
  sports and recreation, 190-1
  suggested itineraries, 181-2
  taxis, 161
  theater, 193
  tourist information, 163
  walking tour, 182-5
  what things cost in, 34
Guides, Mexican tourist, 65
Guitars, shopping for, 49

Hammocks, shopping for, 49
Health preparations before trip, 40-2
Hiking:
  Mazamitla, 220
  Tapalpa, 222
Hitchhiking, 62, 65
Holidays, 36, 65
Holy Week celebrations, 37
Homestays, 47
Horse-drawn carriages in Guadalajara, 161-2
Hotels: *see* ACCOMMODATIONS *index*
Huaraches, shopping for, 49
Huipils, shopping for, 49
Hunting, Puerto Vallarta, 104

Information sources, 29-30
Insurance, travel and health, 43

Jocotepec, 216-17

Lacquer goods, shopping for, 49
La Manzanilla Beach, 102
Languages spoken, 65
Las Alamandas, 150-1
Las Animas Beach, 102
Las Brisas, 122, 125, 134
Leather goods, shopping for, 49
Legal Aid, 66

Mail and mail service, 66
Manzanillo:
  accommodations: *see* ACCOMMODATIONS *index*
  arriving, 118-19
  beaches, 139
  birding, 139
  city layout, 119-22
  excursions from, 140-54
  fast facts, 123
  favorite experiences, 138
  fishing, 139
  getting around, 123
  getting there, 118-21
  golf, 139
  layout, 119-22
  neighborhoods, 188-22
  nightlife, 140
  orientation, 118-22
  restaurants: *see* RESTAURANTS *index*
  shopping, 139
  sights and attractions: *see* SIGHTS & ATTRACTIONS *index*
  sports and recreation, 139
  suggested itineraries, 137-8
  tennis, 139
  tourist information, 123
  tours, 138
  what things cost in, 33-4
Masks, shopping for, 49
Mazamitla, 217-20
Melaque, 143-6
Mexico City, train service to and from, 56

Newspapers and magazines, 66
Nightlife:
  Barra de Navidad, 146
  Guadalajara, 192-4
  Manzanillo, 140
  Puerto Vallarta, 108-11

Onyx, shopping for, 49

Pacific Coast region of Mexico:
  art and architecture, 16-19
  boat trips, 102
  books about, 25-6
  bribes, 34-5
  calendar of events, 37-40
  cuisine, 24-5
  dining customs, 23-4
  disabled, tips for the, 44
  entry requirements, 30-1
  families, tips for, 46-7
  famous people, 11-15
  films about, 27
  geography and ecology, 4-5
  getting around, 54-62
  getting there and departing, 50-4
  health preparations before trip, 40-2
  history, 5-11
  holidays, 36
  information sources, 29-30
  insurance, 43
  introduction to, 1-4
  literature, 18-19
  map of, 3
  money, 31-3
  packing tips, 43-4
  performing arts, 21-2
  recordings of, 28
  religion, myth and folklore, 19-21
  scams, 35-6
  seniors, tips for, 44-5
  single travelers, tips for, 45-6
  sports and recreation, 22-3
  what's special about, 2
  when to go, 36
  women, tips for, 46
  see also specific destinations
Package tours, 54
Packing tips, 43-4
Playa Yelapa, 106, 111
Police, Mexican, 66
Puerto Vallarta:
  accommodations: *see* ACCOMMODATIONS *index*
  air travel to and from, 71-3
  arriving, 71-2
  bars, 108-9
  beaches, 102-3, 106
  bullfights, 103
  bus travel around, 76
  city layout, 73
  climate, 77
  cruises at sunset, 102, 106
  discos, 109-10
  diving, 103
  driving to, 72
  excursions from, 111-17
  fast facts, 77
  ferry service, 72

INDEX • 237

Puerto Vallarta: (cont'd)
  fiestas, 110–11
  fishing, 103, 106
  getting around, 76–7
  getting there, 71–6
  golf, 104
  hunting, 104
  information, 77
  laundry, 77
  layout, 73
  neighborhoods, 73–6
  nightlife, 108–11
  organized tours, 102
  restaurants: see RESTAURANTS index
  shopping, 107–8
  sights and attractions: see SIGHTS & ATTRACTIONS index
  special events, 106
  sports and recreation, 102–6
  stroll through town, 104–6
  suggested itineraries, 101–2
  taxis, 77
  tennis, 104
  tips on hotels, 79
  tips on restaurants, 93
  tourist information, 77
  what's special about, 72
  what things cost in, 33

Quimixto Falls, 102

Radio and TV, 66
Rebozos, shopping for, 49
Reconfirming air flights, 555
Recreational vehicles, touring with, 62
Restaurants: see RESTAURANTS index
Rest rooms in Mexico, 66–7
Rodeos, Guadalajara, 191

Safety, 67
Salahua, 122, 125–8
San Blas, 111–16
  accommodations, 114–15
  beaches and watersports, 113
  jungle cruise, 113–14
  nightlife, 116
  restaurants, 115–16
  sights and attractions, 112–14
San Juan Cosalá, 215–16
Santiago, 122, 128–30, 134–5
Scams, 35–6
Seasons and booking, 67
Senior citizens, tips for, 44–5
Serapes, shopping for, 49
Ship travel to Mexico, 54
Shopping in Mexico, 48–50
  Ajijic, 214–15
  Chapala, 206

  Guadalajara, 191–2
  Manzanillo, 139
  Puerto Vallarta, 106–8
  Tapalpa, 222–3
  Tlaquepaque, 196–7
  Tonalá, 199
Sights and attractions: see SIGHTS & ATTRACTIONS index
Sightseeing, 67
Silver, shopping for, 49–50
Single travelers, tips for, 45–6
Snorkeling, Puerto Vallarta, 102
Spanish lessons/family stays, 47
Sports: see specific destinations
Stones, shopping for, 50
Students, tips for, educational/study travel, 47

Tapalpa, 220–3
  accommodations, 221
  dining, 221–2
  hiking, 222
  shopping, 222–3
Taxes, local, 67
Tecuan, 147
Telephones/telex/fax, 67–9
Tennis:
  Manzanillo, 139
  Puerto Vallarta, 104
Textiles, shopping for, 50
Thermal pools, San Juan Cosalá, 215
Time, 69
Tipping, 69
Tlaquepaque, 195–8
  dining, 197–8
  shopping, 196–7
Tonalá, 198–200
Tortoise shell, shopping for, 50
Tourist information, 29–30, 69
Tours, organized:
  Guadalajara, 188
  Lake Chapala, 207–8
  Manzanillo, 138
  package, 54
  Puerto Vallarta, 102
Train travel, 51
  around Mexico, 55–7
  Guadalajara hub, 56, 156, 157
  to and from Manzanillo, 118
  Mexico City hub, 56
Traveler's checks, 32
"Turista," 40–1

Villa and condo rentals, 69–70
Vocabulary, Mexican, 224–33

Water, information about, 70
Whale watching, Puerto Vallarta, 104
Wilderness travel, 47–8
Women, tips for, 46

SIGHTS & ATTRACTIONS

PUERTO VALLARTA

Burton (Richard) and Taylor (Elizabeth) houses, 106
Cathedral, 104
Gringo Gulch,* 106
House and Garden Tour,* 106
Lepe (Manuel) mural, 104
Libertad shops, 104

Municipal building, 104
Museo de Cuale, 106
Public market, 106
Sunset cruise,* 106
Yelapa Beach, 106, 111

NOTE: An asterisk (*) indicates an Author's Favorite

238 • INDEX

PLAYA YELAPA, 106, 111

SAN BLAS
Birdwatching, 114
Borrego Beach, 113

EXCURSION AREAS

Jungle cruise, 113–14
La Contadura, 112–13
Las Islitas Beach, 113
Matanchan Bay, 113
Playa Los Cococs, 113

MANZANILLO

La Audiencia Beach, 139
Playa Azul, 139
Playa Las Brisas, 139

Playa Miramar, 139
Sunset cruise, 138–9

EXCURSION AREAS

BARRA DE NAVIDAD
Boat ride, 143
Lagoon tour, 143

CAREYES, 149

COLIMA
Museo de Historia de Colima, 153
Museum of Popular Culture María Teresa Pomar, 153
Museum of Western Culture, 153

GUADALAJARA

Ballet Folklórico, 185
Casa de la Cultura, 186
Casa de las Artesanías, 186
Cathedral, 182
Church of Santa María de Gracia, 184
Hospicio Cabañas, 185
Instituto Cultural Cabañas, 185
Mercado Libertad, 185
Museo Infantil, 186
Museo Antropología, 186
National Institute of Anthropology and History, 184
Omnimax Theater, 187, 188
Palacio del Gobierno, 182
Palacio de Justicia, 184

Parque Agua Azul, 186
Planetarium, 186, 188
Plaza de Armas, 182
Plaza de la Universidad, 185
Plaza del Carmen, 186
Plaza de los Mariachis, 185
Plaza Liberación, 184
Quetzalcoatl Fountain, 184
Regional Museum of Guadalajara, 184
Rotunda de los Hombres Illustres, 182–4
Teatro Degollado, 184
Teatro del Carmen, 186
Zoo, 186–8

EXCURSION AREAS

AJIJIC
Sunset horseback rides, 215
Thermal pools nearby, 215

CHAPALA
Horseback riding, 208
Lake tours, 207–8

MAZAMITLA
Self-guided mountain hiking, 220

SAN JUAN COSALÁ
Thermal pools, 215–16

TAPALPA
Las Piedrotas, 222
Nogales Waterfall, 222

TLAQUEPAQUE
El Parián, 196
Glass factory, 196
Regional Ceramics Museum, 196

TONALÁ
Market days, 198–9
National Museum of Ceramics, 199

ACCOMMODATIONS

PUERTO VALLARTA

HOTEL ZONE
Fiesta Americana Plaza Vallarta Tennis & Beach Resort (VE), 83–4
Fiesta Americana Puerto Vallarta (VE), 83
Krystal Vallarta (E), 84–5
Omni Puerto Vallarta Hotel and Grand Spa (E), 85
Plaza Las Gloria Puerto Vallarta (E), 85–6

MARINA VALLARTA
Marriott CasaMagna (VE), 78–9
Melia Puerto Vallarta (E), 79–82
Quinta Real (VE), 82
Velas Vallarta Grand Suite Resort (VE), 82–3

KEY TO ABBREVIATIONS: B = Budget; E = Expensive; M = Moderate; VE = Very Expensive; * = an Author's favorite; $ = Super-special Value

NORTH OF THE RIO CUALE
Buenaventura, Hotel (M), 86
Chez Elena Inn (B), 86
Encino, Hotel (B$), 86

SOUTH OF THE RIO CUALE
Casa Corazón (M), 88
Casa Panoramica (E), 87-8
Casa Pilitas (VE), 87
Fontana del Mar (M), 88
Marsol, Hotel (B), 89

LAS BRISAS/SAN BLAS
Flamingo Hotel (B), 115
Las Brisas Resort, Hotel (M*), 114
Los Cocos Trailer Park, 115
Mission San Blas Hotel (B), 115

Molino de Agua, Hotel (M), 88
Playa Los Arcos (M*), 88-9
Posada de Roger, Hotel (B$), 89
Posada Río Cuale (B), 89

SOUTH TO MISMALOYA
Camino Real (E), 90-1
Graza Blanca (VE), 89-90
Hyatt Coral Grand (E), 91
La Jolla de Mismaloya (E), 91-2

EXCURSION AREAS

Suites San Blas (M), 114

PLAYA YELAPA
Lagunitas, Hotel (B), 111

MANZANILLO

DOWNTOWN
Colonial, Hotel (B), 124
Emperador, Hotel (B), 124

LAS BRISAS
Club Vacacional Las Brisas (M), 125
La Posada, Hotel (M), 125

SALAHUA
Condominios Arco Iris (M), 125-6

SANTIAGO PENINSULA
Las Hadas (VE), 128-9
Marlyn, Hotel (M), 130
Playa de Santiago, Hotel (M), 130
Plaza Las Glorias, Hotel (VE), 129
Sierra Manzanillo, Hotel (VE), 129

EXCURSION AREAS

BARRA DE NAVIDAD
Cabo Blanco, Hotel (B), 140-2
Delphin, Hotel (B*$), 142
Sands, Hotel (B), 142
Tropical, Hotel (B), 142

CAREYES
Club Med Playa Blanca (VE), 149-50
Costa Careyes, Hotel (VE), 148-9

COLIMA
America, Hotel (M), 152
Ceballos, Hotel (B), 152

LAS ALAMANDAS
Las Alamandas (VE), 150

MELAQUE
Bungalows Villamar (B), 145
Club Nautico Melaque (M*), 144
Coco Club Melaque (E), 144
Legazpi, Hotel de (B$), 144-5
Posada Pablo de Tarso (M), 145

TECUAN
El Tecuan, Hotel (M*$), 147

TENACATITA
Fiesta Americana Los Angelos Locos Tenacatita (E), 146-7

GUADALAJARA

Aranzazu, Hotel (M), 168-9
Canada, Hotel (B), 173
Carlton Hotel (E), 165
Don Quijote Plaza, Hotel(B), 170-2
El Parador (B), 173
El Tapatío Gran Spa & Resort (E), 168
Fiesta Americana (E), 165-6
Frances, Hotel (M), 169

Holiday Inn Crowne Plaza (E), 166-7
Hyatt Regency (E), 167
Mendoza, Hotel de (M), 169
Posada Regis (B), 172
Quinta Real (E*), 167-8
Río Caliente Spa (M*), 169-70
San Francisco Plaza, Hotel (B*), 172-3
Suites Bernini (B), 170

EXCURSION AREAS

AJAJIC
Danza del Sol (E), 208-9
La Floresta (M), 209
La Laguna Bed and Brunch (B), 210
La Nueva Posada (M), 209-10
Pal RV Park (B), 210
Posada Las Calandrias (B), 210
Real de Chapala, Hotel (E), 209

CHAPALA
Montecarlo, Hotel (M), 204
Nido, Hotel (B), 204

Quinta Quetzalcoatl (E*), 202
Villa Aurora Bed and Breakfast (E*), 201-2

JOCOTEPEC
Posada del Pescador (B), 216-17

MAZAMITLA
Fiesta Mazamitla (B), 218
La Llorona Country Club (E), 218-19
Monte Verde Centro Recreacional (E), 219
Posada Alpina (B), 218

Posada Las Charrandas (B), 218
Sierra Paraíso (B), 219

SAN JUAN COSALA
Balneario San Juan Cosalá (M$), 215–16
Villa Buenaventura (M), 216

TAPALPA
Posada de la Fuente (M), 221
Posada la Hacienda (B), 221
Tapalpa, Hotel (B), 221

RESTAURANTS

PUERTO VALLARTA

AMERICAN
Pancake House (Casa de Hotcakes) (B), 98
Tutti Frutti (M), 96

BREAKFAST
Fonda La China Poblana (M), 87
Pancake House (Casa de Hotcakes) (B), 98

CONTINENTAL/ECLECTIC
Archie's Wok (M), 96
Bogart's (E), 93

FRENCH
Patachu Pastelería (B), 98

HEALTH/VEGETARIAN
Tutti Frutti (B), 96

ICE CREAM
Helados Bing (B), 94–6

INDONESIAN/MEXICAN
Chez Elena (M), 94

INTERNATIONAL
El Set (E), 100
Le Kliff (E), 99–100

ITALIAN
Pietro Pastas & Pizzas (B), 96
Pizza Joe (M), 97

JAPANESE
Mikado Restaurant (E), 92–3

JUNGLE RESTAURANTS
Chico's Paradise (E), 99

Chino's Paraíso (E), 99
El Edén (E), 99
El Set (E), 100
Le Kliff (E), 99–100
Restaurant Primitivo (M*), 100

MEXICAN
Aquarena, Restaurant/Bar (M), 97
Brazz (M), 94
Chez Elena (M), 94
El Dorado (M*), 97
El Ostión Feliz (M), 94
Fonda La China Poblana (M$*), 97
La Casa del Almendro (M), 93–4
Puerto Nuevo (M), 98
Restaurant Juanita (B), 96

ORIENTAL
Archie's Wok (M), 96

SANDWICHES
Tommy's Tortas (B*), 98

SEAFOOD
Aquarena, Restaurant/Bar (M), 97
Chico's Paradise (E), 99
Chino's Paraíso (E), 99
El Edén (E), 99
El Ostión Feliz (M), 94
Le Kliff (E), 99–100
Puerto Nuevo (M), 98
Restaurant Primitivo (M*), 100

EXCURSION AREAS

LAS BRISAS/SAN BLAS
El Delfín (M; Mexican), 115

McDonald's (B; Mexican), 116
Tony's La Isla (M*$; Mexican), 115–16

MANZANILLO

AMERICAN
Juanito's (M), 135–6
Teto's Cantina Grill (M), 134

BOTANEROS [DRINKS/SNACKS]
Bar Social (B), 131
El Ultimo Tren (B), 131–2

CHINESE
Ly Chee (M), 130
Uncle Chen (M), 208

GRILLED SPECIALTIES
Carlos 'n' Charlie's (E), 132

HAMBURGERS
Juanito's (M), 135–6

ICE CREAM
Helados Bing (B), 131

INTERNATIONAL
Legazpi (VE), 134–5

KEY TO ABBREVIATIONS: B = Budget; E = Expensive; M = Moderate; VE = Very Expensive; * = an Author's favorite; $ = Super-special Value

Manolo's (E), 132
Osteria Bugatti (E), 132-4
Willy's (E), 134

MEXICAN
Cafetería/Nevería Chantilly (B), 130-1
Juanito's (M), 135-6
La Perlita Restaurant (B), 131
Teto's Cantina Grill (M), 134

SEAFOOD
L'Récife Restaurant & Bar (E), 135
Oasis (E), 135
Willy's (E), 134

STEAKS
L'Récife Restaurant & Bar (E), 135

EXCURSION AREAS

BARRA DE NAVIDAD
Panchos (M*; seafood), 142-3
Veleros (M*$; seafood/beef), 143

COLIMA
Las Palmas (B; Mexican), 152

Los Naranjos (M; Mexican), 152

MELAQUE
El Buen Gusto (B$; Mexican), 146
Fonda Los Portales (M; seafood), 145-6

GUADALAJARA

BEEF
Las Banderillas (M*), 176-7

CREPES/MEXICAN
Sandy's Restaurant (M), 178

FRENCH/CREOLE
La Vianda (E), 176

FRENCH PASTRIES
Acropolis Cafe & Restaurant (M), 176

INTERNATIONAL
El Mesón del Chef (E), 174
La Copa de Leche (E), 174
Restaurant La Rinconada (M), 178-9
Rose Cafe (E), 174-6

MEXICAN
Acropolis Cafe & Restaurant (M), 176
Cafe Madrid (M*), 177

Cafe Restaurant Agora (B), 179-80
Don Quijote Restaurant (M), 177
El Farol (M), 177
Las Baderillas (M*), 176-7
Los Itactes Fonda (B*), 80
Restaurant La Rinconada (M), 178-9
Tamales Sinaloenses (B$), 180

SEAFOOD
Restaurant/Bar Mi Tierra (M), 178

TAMALES
El Farol (M), 177
Tamales Sinaloenses (B$), 180

VEGETARIAN
Acuarius (B*), 179
El Aguacate Loco (B$*), 179
Las Margaritas (M), 177-8

EXCURSION AREAS

AJAJIC
Cafin (B; pastries/pizza/sandwiches), 213
Danny's (B$; Mexican/American), 213
La Rusa (M*; international), 213
Los Veleros Video Bar (B; Italian/Mexican), 214
Manix Restaurant (M*; international), 212
Memo's Pozole & Tacos (B$; Mexican), 213-14
Oscar's (M*; international), 212
Restaurant La Posada Ajijic (M; Mexican/international), 212-13
Restaurant Naranjitos (M; Mexican/pizza), 212

CHAPALA
La India Bakery (B*; bolilloas/muffins), 206
Restaurant Bar Chemany (M; Asian/Mexican), 206
Restaurant Beer Garden (B; regional/Mexican), 204-6
Restaurant Beto's (B; Mexican), 206
Restaurant Don Juan (M; Mexican), 206
Restaurant Superior (B; Mexican), 207
San Francisco Grill (M; Mexican), 206-7

JOCOTEPEC
Bar Jacal (B; snacks/drinks), 217
Nevado de Toluca (B*; ice cream), 217

MAZAMITLA
La Buena (B; Mexican), 220
Restaurant Campestre La Troje (M; Mexican/regional), 220

TAPALPA
Restaurant Hacienda Buenavista (B; Mexican), 222
Restaurant Tapalpa (B; Mexican), 222
Restaurant Tapalpa Borrgeo (B; borrego), 222

TLAQUEPAQUE
Los Cazadores (M*; Mexican), 198
Mariscos Progreso (M; seafood/Mexican), 197
Restaurant With No Name (M*; Mexican), 197-8

NOW, SAVE MONEY ON ALL YOUR TRAVELS!
Join Frommer's™ Dollarwise® Travel Club

Saving money while traveling is never easy, which is why the **Dollarwise Travel Club** was formed 32 years ago to provide cost-cutting travel strategies, up-to-date travel information, and a sense of community for value-conscious travelers from all over the world.

In keeping with the money-saving concept, the annual membership fee is low—$25 for U.S. residents and $35 for residents of Canada, Mexico, and other countries—and is immediately exceeded by the value of your benefits, which include:

1. Any TWO books listed on the following pages;
2. Plus any ONE Frommer's City Guide;
3. A subscription to our quarterly newspaper, *The Dollarwise Traveler;*
4. A membership card that entitles you to purchase through the Club all Frommer's publications for 33% to 40% off their retail price.

The eight-page ***Dollarwise Traveler*** tells you about the latest developments in good-value travel worldwide and includes the following columns: **Hospitality Exchange** (for those offering and seeking hospitality in cities all over the world); and **Share-a-Trip** (for those looking for travel companions to share costs).

Aside from the various Frommer's Guides, the Gault Millau Guides, and the Real Guides you can also choose from our Special Editions, which include such titles as **Caribbean Hideaways** (the 100 most romantic places to stay in the Islands); and **Marilyn Wood's Wonderful Weekends** (a selection of the best mini-vacations within a 200-mile radius of New York City).

To join this Club, send the appropriate membership fee with your name and address to: Frommer's Dollarwise Travel Club, 15 Columbus Circle, New York, NY 10023. Remember to specify which single city guide and which two other guides you wish to receive in your initial package of member's benefits. Or tear out the pages, check off your choices, and send them to us with your membership fee.

FROMMER BOOKS
PRENTICE HALL TRAVEL
15 COLUMBUS CIRCLE
NEW YORK, NY 10023

Date_____

Friends: Please send me the books checked below.

FROMMER'S™ COMPREHENSIVE GUIDES
(Guides listing facilities from budget to deluxe, with emphasis on the medium-priced)

☐ Alaska	$14.95	☐ Italy	$19.00
☐ Australia	$14.95	☐ Japan & Hong Kong	$17.00
☐ Austria & Hungary	$14.95	☐ Morocco	$18.00
☐ Belgium, Holland & Luxembourg	$14.95	☐ Nepal	$18.00
☐ Bermuda & The Bahamas	$17.00	☐ New England	$17.00
☐ Brazil	$14.95	☐ New Mexico	$13.95
☐ California	$18.00	☐ New York State	$19.00
☐ Canada	$16.00	☐ Northwest	$16.95
☐ Caribbean	$17.00	☐ Puerta Vallarta (avail. Feb. '92)	$14.00
☐ Carolinas & Georgia	$17.00	☐ Portugal, Madeira & the Azores	$14.95
☐ Colorado (avail. Jan '92)	$14.00	☐ Scandinavia	$18.95
☐ Cruises (incl. Alaska, Carib, Mex, Hawaii, Panama, Canada & US)	$16.00	☐ Scotland (avail. Feb. '92)	$17.00
		☐ South Pacific	$20.00
☐ Delaware, Maryland, Pennsylvania & the New Jersey Shore (avail. Jan. '92)	$19.00	☐ Southeast Asia	$14.95
		☐ Switzerland & Liechtenstein	$19.00
☐ Egypt	$14.95	☐ Thailand	$20.00
☐ England	$17.00	☐ Virginia (avail. Feb. '92)	$14.00
☐ Florida	$17.00	☐ Virgin Islands	$13.00
☐ France	$15.95	☐ USA	$16.95
☐ Germany	$18.00		

FROMMER'S CITY GUIDES
(Pocket-size guides to sightseeing and tourist accommodations and facilities in all price ranges)

☐ Amsterdam/Holland	$8.95	☐ Minneapolis/St. Paul	$8.95
☐ Athens	$8.95	☐ Montréal/Québec City	$8.95
☐ Atlanta	$8.95	☐ New Orleans	$8.95
☐ Atlantic City/Cape May	$8.95	☐ New York	$12.00
☐ Bangkok	$12.00	☐ Orlando	$12.00
☐ Barcelona	$12.00	☐ Paris	$8.95
☐ Belgium	$7.95	☐ Philadelphia	$11.00
☐ Berlin	$10.00	☐ Rio	$8.95
☐ Boston	$8.95	☐ Rome	$8.95
☐ Cancún/Cozumel/Yucatán	$8.95	☐ Salt Lake City	$8.95
☐ Chicago	$9.95	☐ San Diego	$8.95
☐ Denver/Boulder/Colorado Springs	$8.95	☐ San Francisco	$12.00
☐ Dublin/Ireland	$10.00	☐ Santa Fe/Taos/Albuquerque	$10.95
☐ Hawaii	$12.00	☐ Seattle/Portland	$12.00
☐ Hong Kong	$7.95	☐ St. Louis/Kansas City	$9.95
☐ Las Vegas	$8.95	☐ Sydney	$8.95
☐ Lisbon/Madrid/Costa del Sol	$8.95	☐ Tampa/St. Petersburg	$8.95
☐ London	$12.00	☐ Tokyo	$8.95
☐ Los Angeles	$8.95	☐ Toronto	$8.95
☐ Mexico City/Acapulco	$8.95	☐ Vancouver/Victoria	$7.95
☐ Miami	$8.95	☐ Washington, D.C.	$12.00

FROMMER'S $-A-DAY® GUIDES
(Guides to low-cost tourist accommodations and facilities)

☐ Australia on $40 a Day	$13.95	☐ Israel on $40 a Day	$13.95
☐ Costa Rica, Guatemala & Belize on $35 a Day	$15.95	☐ Mexico on $45 a Day	$18.00
		☐ New York on $65 a Day	$15.00
☐ Eastern Europe on $25 a Day	$16.95	☐ New Zealand on $45 a Day	$16.00
☐ England on $50 a Day	$17.00	☐ Scotland & Wales on $40 a Day	$18.00
☐ Europe on $45 a Day	$19.00	☐ South America on $40 a Day	$15.95
☐ Greece on $35 a Day	$14.95	☐ Spain on $50 a Day	$15.95
☐ Hawaii on $70 a Day	$18.00	☐ Turkey on $40 a Day	$22.00
☐ India on $40 a Day	$20.00	☐ Washington, D.C., on $45 a Day	$17.00
☐ Ireland on $40 a Day	$17.00		

FROMMER'S CITY $-A-DAY GUIDES

☐ Berlin on $40 a Day	$12.00	☐ Madrid on $50 a Day (avail. Jan '92)	$13.00
☐ Copenhagen on $50 a Day	$12.00	☐ Paris on $45 a Day	$12.00
☐ London on $45 a Day	$12.00	☐ Stockholm on $50 a Day (avail. Dec. '91)	$13.00

FROMMER'S FAMILY GUIDES

☐ California with Kids	$16.95	☐ San Francisco with Kids	$17.00
☐ Los Angeles with Kids	$17.00	☐ Washington, D.C., with Kids (avail. Jan '92)	$17.00
☐ New York City with Kids (avail. Jan '92)	$18.00		

SPECIAL EDITIONS

☐ Beat the High Cost of Travel	$6.95	☐ Marilyn Wood's Wonderful Weekends (CT, DE, MA, NH, NJ, NY, PA, RI, VT)	$11.95
☐ Bed & Breakfast—N. America	$14.95	☐ Motorist's Phrase Book (Fr/Ger/Sp)	$4.95
☐ Caribbean Hideaways	$16.00	☐ The New World of Travel (annual by Arthur Frommer for savvy travelers)	$16.95
☐ Honeymoon Destinations (US, Mex & Carib)	$14.95		

(TURN PAGE FOR ADDITONAL BOOKS AND ORDER FORM)

0891492

☐ Paris Rendez-Vous $10.95	☐ Travel Diary and Record Book. $5.95
☐ Swap and Go (Home Exchanging). $10.95	☐ Where to Stay USA (from $3 to $30 a night). $13.95

FROMMER'S TOURING GUIDES
(Color illustrated guides that include walking tours, cultural and historic sites, and practical information)

☐ Amsterdam. $10.95	☐ New York $10.95
☐ Australia $12.95	☐ Paris $8.95
☐ Brazil $10.95	☐ Rome. $10.95
☐ Egypt. $8.95	☐ Scotland. $9.95
☐ Florence. $8.95	☐ Thailand. $12.95
☐ Hong Kong. $10.95	☐ Turkey $10.95
☐ London $12.95	☐ Venice $8.95

GAULT MILLAU
(The only guides that distinguish the truly superlative from the merely overrated)

☐ The Best of Chicago $15.95	☐ The Best of Los Angeles $16.95
☐ The Best of Florida $17.00	☐ The Best of New England $15.95
☐ The Best of France $16.95	☐ The Best of New Orleans. $16.95
☐ The Best of Germany $18.00	☐ The Best of New York $16.95
☐ The Best of Hawaii $16.95	☐ The Best of Paris $16.95
☐ The Best of Hong Kong $16.95	☐ The Best of San Francisco $16.95
☐ The Best of Italy. $16.95	☐ The Best of Thailand. $17.95
☐ The Best of London $16.95	☐ The Best of Toronto $17.00
	☐ The Best of Washington, D.C. $16.95

THE REAL GUIDES
(Opinionated, politically aware guides for youthful budget-minded travelers)

☐ Amsterdam $9.95	☐ Mexico. $11.95
☐ Berlin. $11.95	☐ Morocco $12.95
☐ Brazil $13.95	☐ New York $9.95
☐ California & the West Coast $11.95	☐ Paris $9.95
☐ Czechoslovakia $13.95	☐ Peru. $12.95
☐ France $12.95	☐ Poland $13.95
☐ Germany $13.95	☐ Portugal $10.95
☐ Greece. $13.95	☐ San Francisco $11.95
☐ Guatemala $13.95	☐ Scandinavia $14.95
☐ Hong Kong $11.95	☐ Spain. $12.95
☐ Hungary $12.95	☐ Turkey $12.95
☐ Ireland $12.95	☐ Venice $11.95
☐ Italy. $13.95	☐ Women Travel $12.95
☐ Kenya. $12.95	☐ Yugoslavia $12.95

ORDER NOW!

In U.S. include $2 shipping UPS for 1st book; $1 ea. add'l book. Outside U.S. $3 and $1, respectively.

Allow four to six weeks for delivery in U.S., longer outside U.S. We discourage rush order service, but orders arriving with shipping fees plus a $15 surcharge will be handled as rush orders.

Enclosed is my check or money order for $_____

NAME_____

ADDRESS_____

CITY_____ STATE _____ ZIP _____